9/2367237

THE CORNFIELD

THE CORNFIELD

Antietam's Bloody Turning Point

David A. Welker

CASEMATE

Philadelphia & Oxford

Published in the United States of America and Great Britain in 2020 by
CASEMATE PUBLISHERS
1950 Lawrence Road, Havertown, PA 19083, USA
and
The Old Music Hall, 106–108 Cowley Road, Oxford OX4 1JE, UK

Copyright 2020 © David A. Welker

Hardback Edition: ISBN 978-1-61200-832-5
Digital Edition: ISBN 978-1-61200-833-2

A CIP record for this book is available from the British Library

Printed and bound in the United States of America

Typeset in India for Casemate Publishing Services. www.casematepublishingservices.com

For a complete list of Casemate titles, please contact:

CASEMATE PUBLISHERS (US)
Telephone (610) 853-9131
Fax (610) 853-9146
Email: casemate@casematepublishers.com
www.casematepublishers.com

CASEMATE PUBLISHERS (UK)
Telephone (01865) 241249
Email: casemate-uk@casematepublishers.co.uk
www.casematepublishers.co.uk

Front cover image: Antietam battle reenactment. (Rear Rank Productions)

For Marilyn Welker—my guide, my inspiration, my mother

"Whoever stood in front of the corn field at Antietam needs no praise."

—Major Rufus Dawes (1862), p. 93.

Contents

Acknowledgments

Any work such as this is never the result of just one person's efforts, even if only one name is printed on the cover. While it is impossible to name all those who contributed their support, expertise, and knowledge to creating this volume, I want to note a few individuals who were particularly instrumental in making this book a reality. Jeffrey Fortais—my friend, brother-in-law, and fellow historian—created the unsurpassed maps that grace this work and provided his own detailed, thorough cartographic research that informed my research. Without his contribution, it would be impossible for most readers to comprehend the often-complex movements that occurred in the Cornfield and elsewhere at Antietam. His ability to transform my simple sketches and vague ideas into such clear, concise maps is unique, and I could not have written this book without him. Ted Alexander, Antietam National Battlefield's former chief historian, reviewed an early draft of my book and offered invaluable advice and insight. The rangers and volunteer staff of Antietam National Battlefield contributed both by maintaining a national treasure—making it possible to walk the battleground of September 17, 1862—and by always happily answering odd, highly detailed questions—they are a model of true public service. I received tremendous assistance from the staffs of the National Archives, the Library of Congress, the US Army's Heritage and Education Center (formerly the Military History Institute), and the various universities, libraries, and historical societies listed in the notes and bibliographic entries at the end of this volume. Their unique knowledge and stewardship of America's irreplaceable documents makes it possible to dig deep into the battle—they are all a national treasure in their own right. The living historians of the 3rd US Regular Infantry helped me better understand nineteenth-century military tactics and life, and they routinely served as a sounding board to test my ideas and theories about military movements and tactics employed in the Cornfield. My cousin, Robert W. Austin, who served in the 105th New York and survived wounding in the Cornfield, inspired me throughout this volume's creation and reminds me daily what it is to be an American. Lastly, and most importantly, this book would not be possible without the love and support of my wife, Margaret, and my children Rebecca and Thomas. Their patience with my spending too many days and evenings in front of the keyboard and their willingness to support my writing habits, whether wandering with me over obscure parts of Antietam Battlefield or enduring yet another visit to the Archives or Library of Congress, is the love that makes such a book—and anything in life—possible.

List of Maps

The ford near the Upper Bridge, where most troops engaged in and around the Cornfield crossed Antietam Creek. (Battles and Leaders)

A *c.* 1890 view of the northern fence and end of the Cornfield, along with the southern end of the East Woods, looking eastward. This view offers some idea of the undulating terrain and how Ricketts' and Doubleday's attacking Union brigades—who would move over the horizon on the right—could disappear from view before reaching Jackson's Confederate salient. ("Rare Images of Antietam," Another Software Miracle, LLC)

A 1906 view of the D. R. Miller farm, looking south. The house is on the left of the photo, with the springhouse in the center and the Millers' barn on the right. The Hagerstown Pike bisects the picture. Gibbon's Brigade was the first to advance over this ground, moving southward. (Antietam National Battlefield)

Austin Stearns' sketch of himself in the Cornfield after being wounded during the advance of Hartsuff's Brigade. (Associated University Press, used with permission)

Private Austin Stearns of the 13th Massachusetts. Though wounded in the Cornfield, he would endure many more battles—including Fredericksburg, Gettysburg, Cold Harbor, and Petersburg—before being discharged in August 1864 and returning home to Boston. (Associated University Press)

Edwin Forbes' sketch, "the Fight in the Cornfield." Though likely depicting no specific moment, it nonetheless captures the intensity and confusion of the combat in Miller's Cornfield. (Library of Congress)

A postwar drawing of Union troops attacking though the Cornfield. Though somewhat fanciful, it nonetheless shows how widely planted were nineteenth-century corn plants—the width of one man—and the presence of hillocks in which they stood—all of which channeled Hooker's attacks directly south rather than at the Dunker Church. (Battles and Leaders)

A post-war drawing depicting the 27th Indiana—on the left—from Gordon's Brigade and Gibbon's 3rd Wisconsin advancing through the grassy field to strike Colquitt's Confederate brigade at the northern end of the Cornfield. Note the north-south orientation of the rows of corn, which channeled the Union attacks until the corn had been trampled. (*The Twenty-Seventh Indiana Volunteer Infantry in the War of the Rebellion*)

A 1904 picture of the portion of the East Woods through which the 10th Maine drove Confederate skirmishers. The column in the center marks the general area where General Mansfield was mortally wounded. (J. B. Lyon Company, Printers, 1904)

Confederate dead on the western side of the Hagerstown Pike, photographed by Gardner after the battle. Both spans of the post and rail fence remain standing, even after the intense combat that swirled around it. (Library of Congress)

Famous Alexander Gardner image of the Dunker Church taken on September 19, 1862. The battle-scarred church, the nominal objective of Hooker's opening attack, is framed by the dense West Woods. The limber chest and Confederate dead may belong to S. D. Lee's artillery that was posted here during much of the battle. (Library of Congress)

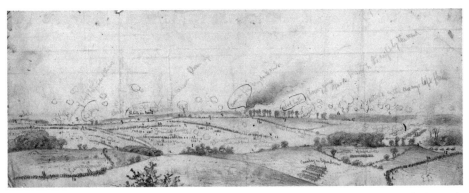

Edwin Forbes' sketch of the battle of Antietam, made at 10:30 a.m. on September 17, which reveals the limited view General McClellan had of the battle as it unfolded. Though Forbes' vantage point for this work is considerably higher than McClellan's at his Pry House headquarters (depicted at number 1, in the center), he still is unable to see fighting in the Cornfield, East Woods, or West Woods because of terrain obstructions and smoke from the burning Mumma farm buildings. He can, however, see French's and Richardson's troops attacking the Sunken Road, as well as the Dunker Church (number 5). (Library of Congress)

The position held by Greene's Division before advancing to the south of the Dunker Church. Greene made effective use of the "military crest" of this otherwise modest swell in the ground to protect his command from Confederate fire, enabling it to hold on here for an extended period. (J. B. Lyon Company, Printers, 1904)

The ground over which Greene's Division charged—moving from right to left—to reach the Dunker Church, which is just off the left of the photo. The West Woods is in the left background and the limber chest and casualties on the horizon may be those depicted in Gardner's famous photo of the Dunker Church. (Library of Congress)

The Middle Bridge, looking west toward Sharpsburg and the battlefield, taken by Alexander Garner. This is the bridge seized by the US Regulars on September 16 which was to be the venue for staging McClellan's planned final, main attack by the Regulars – which never occurred. (Library of Congress)

The Middle Bridge, looking southeast, taken by Gardner in 1862. The US Regulars and Union artillery held the significant high ground behind the bridge. This dominating terrain reflects in part why the three bridges were so significant to both Lee and McClellan's plans for the coming battle. (Library of Congress)

Prologue

It was just after 6:00 in the morning. Back home in New York and Pennsylvania, the men's families were just rising for the day's work on the farm, to open the shop for business, or for breakfast before school. Their day ahead might be filled with the routine hum of daily life in 1862, but these men had entered a surreal existence where even simple acts carried an odd and ominous significance. They clambered over Miller's sturdy rail fence, each front-rank man picking his own row. Sliding into the thick corn seemed to sweep away the fatal landscape they'd just escaped. For a few moments, at least, no more shells burst around them and even the sound of their own Union batteries was nearly absorbed by the full, green leaves that washed their sweaty faces in passing. As if diving into a green sea of plants, it swallowed them whole, and they could neither see out nor be seen beyond this fragile, temporary state of existence. For a few minutes, at least, they were lost in this cornfield. Yet on they pressed, each soldier maintaining his dress with the man on either side, listening for commands from the voices of their now-familiar officers. The loose Maryland dirt pulling at their boots and the stalks grabbing at equipment slung over their shoulders, trying to steal a bayonet from its scabbard here and wrest a tin cup away from its owner there. Regardless who won each of these tiny struggles, on they pressed to the southern end of the field where, as they all by now knew, the enemy waited.

CHAPTER I

Planting the Seed of a Campaign

Tuesday, September 2, 1862 dawned bright and clear on the rolling hills of western Maryland. David Miller was likely up early that morning, working as usual around his small but prosperous farm. Known to all by his initials, D. R. could consider himself lucky in comparison to most of his neighbors because not only had his wealthy father, 1812 war veteran Colonel John Miller, originally financed the farm but he provided a safety net few other farmers enjoyed. This boost and hard work had been providing David and Margaret Miller and their children a solid living for many years.

The Millers' farm sat about one half mile north of the quiet hamlet of Sharpsburg, Maryland, straddling the Hagerstown Pike that ran north out of town. Across the Pike, the first sight greeting D. R. each morning as he walked from the house was his sizable barn, with its attached, single-story extension. The acres he owned on the eastern side of the road that year had held the straw and hay to sustain his livestock through the winter, but by September, these were gathered in huge stacks across the road from his house. On the eastern side of the Hagerstown Pike stood the Millers' small but comfortable two-story, whitewashed house, behind which sat a separate kitchen reflecting the home's early 1800s origin—replaced now by a modern in-house kitchen—and a small building first created as a blacksmith's shop by a previous owner. Along the road was a springhouse that provided the family's water, located about halfway between the barn and the house. Behind the main house and two outbuildings stood an orchard from which Margaret Miller could put some treats on the table throughout the year. The nearby garden was planted in pumpkins, potatoes, and beans, although by September, much of its bounty was already canned for the coming winter. The bulk of D. R.'s land, though, lay on the eastern side of the road behind the farmstead. The northernmost field was plowed in an effort to turn the remains of its already harvested crops into fertilizer by the time of spring planting. The next field to the south, directly behind the house, was a 20-acre plot then covered in grass and probably a pasture for the cattle to graze in. Another pasture, this one nearly 40 acres, stood on the southern end of Miller's land and sloped down gently to border the Smoketown Road and the Mumma family's farm. Skirting the farm to the north, east, and west were woodlots that D. R. owned completely or in part, which offered his animals shelter and provided the farm a plentiful source of wood for fence rails and to serve the Millers' home. In nearly the center of D. R.'s property stood a 24-acre field, situated partly on a small hill and this year planted with corn.[1]

Surveying his cornfield, D. R. might have felt a mix of satisfaction and dread. By September this crop was green and tall, bearing many thousands of nearly ripe ears that awaited harvest, before being stored in the corn crib that doubled as a wagon shed. Harvesting crops was a backbreaking task so difficult that its completion was celebrated in many farming communities with a social gathering, often held more out of relief than in thanks for a generous bounty. Some young men so hated this chore that they fled to join the Union or Confederate armies just to avoid this annual burden. Seeing the morning sun glisten off the rainwater on the tall, waving cornstalks this clear September morning could only have reminded D. R. that a long, difficult job lay before him in the coming weeks. David Miller had no way to know that in two weeks' time his rich, ripe cornfield would become the most dangerous place to be on earth.[2]

***

That Tuesday morning, Robert E. Lee woke in his new headquarters on the Little River Turnpike near Chantilly, Virginia, and was instantly greeted by pain. Both wrists still throbbed with a constant, sharp ache from having been thrown to the ground by his horse Traveller nearly three days ago. The injury—severely sprained wrists, the surgeon said—wasn't unbearably painful, but Lee remained unable to manage a horse and had arrived in an ambulance. He was here because Jackson's Command reached just this far the previous day in an effort to cut off John Pope's Union army from its capital. Jackson had become bogged down in a fight near Ox Hill that had ended at dark after a violent rainstorm. Sunrise on September 2 revealed that the Yankees had slipped away and were once again between the Army of Northern Virginia and Washington. Even so, Lee's plan might be revised and resurrected, but he needed information about the position and state of the enemy before anything further could be decided. In response, Lee directed Major General "Jeb" Stuart's cavalry to probe the new Union position around Fairfax Court House.

As morning wore on Lee received two unsettling pieces of news. The first being that Union Major General Philip Kearny had been killed the previous day in the battle the men were calling Ox Hill. Lee had known Kearny from the Mexican War and after directing that Kearny's boots, sword, and other personal effects which had found new owners be turned in—they were eventually shipped to Kearny's widow—directed his aide Major Walter Taylor to escort Kearny's body through the lines under a flag of truce. The second piece of news Lee received was more unsettling and of greater immediate consequence. Stuart's cavalrymen reported the Yankees had retreated beyond Fairfax Court House and were moving into the Washington defenses. Lee well knew that attacking these strong fortifications would be too costly and that besieging the city was beyond the means of his tired and hungry army. His effort to "bag" Pope's army had failed.[3]

Lee, however, knew his next step even before learning this news. That afternoon Lee boarded his ambulance and journeyed the half-mile or so to Jackson's headquarters in the Stuart family house, "Linden Lee." There, Lee informed Stonewall that the time had come to implement the invasion of the North that Jackson had advocated for months. Jackson's original plan, spawned during his incredible Shenandoah Valley Campaign that spring, proposed marching on Pennsylvania with his independent command. Lee and Davis had liked the plan but not the timing; reaching Richmond in early June, when McClellan's army was banging on the doors of the Confederate capital itself, Jackson's Command was needed instead at Richmond. The plan remained on the Confederate table, however, awaiting the right time to put it in action.

With the Federal army falling back to Washington, leaving open the path to Maryland and Pennsylvania, Jackson could only be pleased that his plan was being adopted. Although Lee listened to "General Jackson, who advised him to go into the Valley and cross the Potomac at or above Harpers Ferry, cleaning out the enemy forces at Winchester…," the situation on the ground was different now, and Lee had broader objectives than those Jackson outlined months earlier. Lee instead "ordered Jackson to take command in advance and cross in Loudon County and move toward Frederick, Maryland, destroying the [Chesapeake and Ohio] canal." September 2, 1862 would be recorded as the start of Lee's Maryland Campaign.[4]

The following day, while his men rested, Lee turned his attention to Richmond. Earning President Davis's approval for the Maryland invasion was critical, even though Lee already had his conditional support. "The present seems to be the most propitious time since the commencement of the war for the Confederate army to enter Maryland," wrote Lee, "If it is ever desired to give material aid to Maryland and afford her an opportunity of throwing off the oppression to which she is now subject, this would seem the most favorable time." His plans revealed, Lee next explained the risky move's timing. "The two grand armies of the United States that have been operating in Virginia, though now united, are much weakened and demoralized." Lee must have hoped this would convince Davis of the wisdom of his Maryland plan for advancing Confederate strategic objectives and persuade him that nothing useful would be gained by attacking or besieging Washington.[5]

Richmond's goal for the war remained, as it had from the beginning, simply securing Southern independence. In the war's early days, achieving this goal had been pinned on winning one, decisive battle. When the Union army arose from the ashes of defeat at First Manassas, Southern strategists quickly adopted a new approach. This new strategy, like the very goal of the Confederacy itself, drew inspiration from American rebels a generation before seeking independence from Britain. Like Washington and his compatriots, for whom French entry altered the war and ensured success, President Davis sought help from a major European power, chiefly Britain or France. Their diplomatic recognition, it was hoped, would set the stage for military support, particularly breaking the Union naval blockade and, with it, the Northern public's will to fight. If troops from either or both powers joined Confederate armies in the field or independently opened a second front against the Union, the tables of manpower and resources would be turned, and Lincoln would have little choice but to accept Southern independence, through a negotiated peace or military defeat of the North.

Initially, Richmond used the South's main leverage over the Europeans—cheap cotton, the staple of each nation's textile industry—to prod Britain and France toward breaking the Union naval blockade. When that failed because London deemed the blockade lawful, Richmond backed away from economic blackmail to more closely following the American Revolution's example, seeking diplomatic recognition as a first step to intervention. Richmond also believed recognition would spur Northern peace advocates—deridingly referred to as "Copperheads" throughout the North—to press for peace, resulting in Southern independence. "Our recognition would be the signal for the immediate organization of a large and influential party in the Northern States favorable to putting an end to the war," noted Confederate Secretary of State Judah P. Benjamin. Because Richmond assumed other European nations would follow a British or French lead, it expected to negotiate treaties with other nations as well, increasing prospects for foreign military aid. General Lee, knowing a long war favored the North's manpower, supply, and financial advantages, had long supported such European intervention and he eagerly welcomed the Confederate diplomatic second front.[6]

Although support existed in both Britain and France for these efforts, it was viewed there mostly as a means to suit European objectives. British and French politicians welcomed America's sectional divide, hoping that breaking the United States into two or more parts would preclude the emerging nation from competing with Europe's global strategic and economic dominance and *The Times* of London in August 1862 crowed that the United States's breakup would represent the "riddance of a nightmare." In London, this view was partly driven by a sentimental, inaccurate view of the South as the true heir to British nobility in North America. Although slavery was highly unpopular among all British classes, the "peculiar institution" didn't cloud popular support for the Confederacy, and British disdain for stereotypes of the North's tight-fisted, heartlessly capitalistic Yankees portrayed in English newspapers and popular fiction only aided the South. The same could be said for the view of most Frenchmen in explaining their support for the Confederacy.[7]

However, turning this political support into troops on the battlefield, or even just formal diplomatic recognition, was proving more difficult than Southern officials expected. British politicians had made it clear to Confederate Envoy to Britain James Mason that recognition required proving the South's staying power on the battlefield; a requirement Paris echoed. The importance of military victory was known to the Yankees, too, and the *New York Times* wrote in February, "If our armies now advancing shall generally be stopped or beaten back, France, England, and Spain will make haste to recognize Jeff's Confederacy as an independent power." The South, indeed, had done its best to fulfill that requirement, but Union victories at Forts Henry and Donelson undid the progress of Manassas and other Southern wins. Mason wrote to Richmond that the news of these defeats "had an unfortunate effect on the minds of our friends here." Although prospects for formal recognition seemed dim, news of twin Southern victories turned these hopes on a dime.[8]

The results of Jackson's Valley Campaign and Lee's victory in the Seven Days fight—Europe viewed McClellan's "change of base" as a decisive Union failure—reopened prospects for British and French recognition. At the same time, a Confederate cotton embargo was beginning to hurt British and French economies, throwing thousands out of work for lack of raw materials. In response, local press renewed pressure for London and Paris to intervene and end the war. Napoleon III even told Confederate Envoy to Paris John Slidell that "accounts of the defeat of the Federal armies before Richmond [prove that] re-establishment of the Union [is] impossible." Three days later, the French leader sent a telegram directing his foreign minister, then visiting London, to ask the English if they believed the time had come to intervene in the American war.[9]

A member of the British Parliament responded to this renewed support for the South by introducing a motion on July 18, 1862 for the British government to join France in offering mediation to end the war. Just when the motion seemed sure of approval, Prime Minister Palmerston implored Parliament to let the Cabinet instead decide when, though not if, to mediate. The prime minister's short speech did the trick and the motion was withdrawn. Palmerston made it clear that what would trigger intervention was tangible proof the Confederacy was a truly viable military partner; one or two more military victories was what he needed. Disappointed the motion had failed, James Mason remained optimistic Richmond could expect "intervention in some form." This news persuaded Richmond it stood poised to finally obtain the European intervention it so desperately needed to secure independence. Just as the American victory at Saratoga had persuaded Paris to join the war in support of colonial independence, what the South needed now was one more great military victory.[10]

***

President Lincoln and his cabinet fully understood the South's strategy for securing independence and were doing their best to counter it. Like Lee, the president understood that a long war enabled the North's advantages—particularly in manpower and manufacturing—to outlast and overwhelm the South, and Lincoln's administration had early on developed a two-pronged war strategy: establish a naval blockade to starve the Confederacy's economy and war machine, while simultaneously launching a series of land campaigns to break the South's ability and will to fight. This sea-land strategy depended heavily on maintaining the Union's advantages in economic and military power, and although the South itself could do little to alter this state, British or French entry to the war might undo Washington's efforts almost overnight. The United States's Minister to Britain, Charles Francis Adams, had led a diplomatic campaign for months opposing his Confederate counterpart, James Mason's, work but Adams could do little more than filter the news of war's developments; he could not change the facts arriving from North America, which since June 1862 had only undermined his efforts. Adams repeatedly warned Washington that the issue of British—and, therefore, European—intervention turned on the outcome of the land war. Until the Confederate army was crushed, any relief from this threat was temporary.[11]

Lincoln realized that leaving the nation's fate solely in the hands of his less-than-dependable generals, McClellan and Pope, risked disaster and so some other means must be found to forestall European intervention. Soon it became clear that these means had been available all long, waiting only to be discovered. "I cannot imagine that any European power would dare to recognize and aid the Southern Confederacy if it became clear that the Confederacy stands for slavery and the Union for freedom," Lincoln commented in January 1862. This one simple, obvious statement summarizes what became the Union's new approach to denying Richmond's means for turning the strategic tables. Once the North's war aim became a quest for freedom, Europeans would have little alternative but to leave the North alone to continue the war for however long, in whatever way it saw fit. President Lincoln now had a practical reason to advance emancipation of America's slaves.[12]

Ending slavery had two other equally practical benefits for the Union. First, it would exacerbate the Confederacy's manpower shortages. The South depended heavily upon slaves to free soldiers from mundane but important manual labor duties—digging trenches, driving wagons, etc.—to serve as armed combatants. Offering slaves working for the Confederate army new incentives to flee would deny the enemy their services, thinning Southern ranks by diverting soldiers to perform these tasks. Ending slavery also would free the Union army to fight an aggressive, no-holds-barred style of war. So long as the war's objective was to preserve the Union in its pre-war state, Washington could not afford to destroy the South's economy and strike at civilian targets, fearing doing so would complicate reintegration. Freeing the slaves sent a message that events had progressed beyond the point of restoring the Union as it was and that the war was taking a more aggressive turn; a change Washington was driving.

President Lincoln had long personally opposed slavery but understood the Constitution prohibited imposing his views on the entire nation. "If slavery is not wrong, nothing is wrong," Lincoln famously wrote to a friend, but then added "I have never understood that the Presidency conferred upon me an unrestricted right to act officially upon this judgment and feeling." Lincoln's need for support from Congressional Democrats and leaders in border states—where slavery remained economically and socially important—early on had worked to protect the institution. By early 1862, however, Lincoln's personal inclinations had aligned with the nation's vital interests.[13]

In March 1862, Lincoln fired the first shot of this political battle by urging Congress to support a joint resolution offering special aid to "any state which may adopt gradual abolishment of slavery." Aimed not at Europe but instead at stopping Maryland, Kentucky, and Missouri's flirtations with joining the Confederacy, the resolution also sought to deny Southern territorial expansion. The measure was vigorously opposed by border state congressmen, however, who met with Lincoln on March 10 to express their displeasure. The meeting ended amicably, though coolly, demonstrating that Lincoln still faced considerable obstacles to emancipating the slaves, even if doing so was now vital to saving the Union.[14]

By late spring and summer 1862, the rising threat of European intervention increased the strategic need—and political will—for emancipation, prompting the president to act. Lincoln reconvened the border state congressmen on July 12 to offer one last chance to willingly accept emancipation. Lincoln summarized the situation bluntly, stating if they did not make "a decision to emancipate gradually … the institution in your states will be extinguished by mere friction and abrasion," but this meeting ended much as had the March gathering. Faced with looming threats of foreign intervention and his failure to persuade border state leaders, Lincoln apparently decided that night that the time had come to announce general emancipation, grounded in his Executive powers to seize enemy property—the slaves themselves—being used to wage war on the United States.[15]

Lincoln shared his plan to announce general emancipation with Secretary of State William H. Seward and Navy Secretary Gideon Welles on July 13, while riding to the funeral of Secretary of War Stanton's infant son. Lincoln described it to Welles as "a military necessity, absolutely essential to the preservation of the Union … We wanted the Army to strike more vigorous blows. The Administration must set an example, and strike at the heart of the rebellion," commented the president. Regardless, if Lincoln was informing his secretaries or testing the waters, the die was cast—slavery would be legally abolished in the United States.[16]

In a July 22 meeting, Lincoln informed his Cabinet of the decision. Only Postmaster-General Blair, a former Democrat and the most conservative of Lincoln's inner circle, opposed the move. Secretary of State Seward expressed full support but cautioned he would withdraw this if the Emancipation Proclamation was publicly announced in the coming weeks. Only two weeks before, the Army of the Potomac had narrowly escaped defeat at Malvern Hill and now lay immobile, backed to the James River and with little prospect of advancing on Richmond. In Europe, these developments played poorly; despite support for emancipation prospects, European press decried the recent drive to this end as the last gasp of a defeated government. "[U]ntil you can give it to the country supported by military success," counseled Seward, it would seem "as the last measure of an exhausted government, a cry for help … our last shriek, on the retreat." Seward's advice "struck me with great force," noted the president, and he changed course. The Emancipation Proclamation would remain in Lincoln's drawer until the Union had a military victory to back up this shrewd political and social move.[17]

***

If Lincoln was frustrated about repeated Union military failures, Major General George B. McClellan shared the president's concern but for a very different reason because the past few weeks had been trying for the Army of the Potomac's young commander. General McClellan arose in his house on Washington's H Street on September 2 secure in the knowledge of Pope's defeat and that as his professional rival's troops came into the Washington defenses, they automatically fell under his command. None of this prepared him for the visitors interrupting his breakfast. President Lincoln and commander of the Union Army Major General Henry W. Halleck, after being ushered in, "expressed the opinion that the troubles now impending could be overcome better by me than anyone else. Pope is ordered to fall back upon Washn & as he reenters everything is to come under my command again! A terrible & thankless task—yet I will do my best with God's blessing to perform it." In the face of another major defeat, not twenty miles from the capital, Lincoln had little choice. For better or worse, George McClellan once again commanded the Union's main army in the east.[18]

Few men possessed more solid military credentials than Major General George B. McClellan. Despite recent setbacks on the Peninsula and challenges dealing with official Washington, McClellan's combination of energy, unequalled recent field service, Old army experience, personal intelligence, mastery of military strategy and art, support both high and low throughout the army, and bearing and gentlemanly pedigree made him the obvious candidate for the job. Had observers been able to look behind George McClellan's professional accomplishments and public façade to understand his character and innate personally traits, however, many in McClellan's legion of supporters might have reconsidered the wisdom of restoring his to command.

George Brinton McClellan was born December 3, 1826 in Philadelphia, the third child of Dr. George McClellan and Elizabeth Steinmetz Brinton McClellan.

His mother provided young George an excellent classical education; four years in one of Philadelphia's best private schools, a year with a private tutor—with whom he spoke only French and Latin—and at 11 years of age entry to a preparatory program at the University of Pennsylvania. That unique experience well-prepared George to enter West Point on July 1, 1846; a day the 15-year old McClellan became the youngest boy in the class, showing such academic promise that examiners waived the 16-year age restriction, and passed the principal exam 30 other hopeful plebes failed. McClellan thrived in West Point's first-year academic program, consisting of military drill and two classroom subjects—French language and mathematics—at which he already excelled. Graduating in 1846 ranked second overall, George's impressive academic abilities and class standing enabled his joining the elite Corps of Engineers, and barely after leaving the academy, McClellan's military training was tested in the war with Mexico.

McClellan departed for Mexico on September 26, 1846 as part of an engineer company of which he soon became second in command. Serving on General Winfield Scott's staff as an engineer, McClellan participated in the Veracruz and Mexico City Campaigns, as well as the battles of Cerro Gordo, Contreras, Churubusco, and Chapultepec. McClellan also met some of the army's most promising young officers, including Captains Robert E. Lee and Joseph Johnston and Lieutenants P. G. T. Beauregard, Isaac I. Stevens, and George G. Meade. Sometime during this service in Mexico, George contracted malaria; although recovering, McClellan battled the lingering illness the rest of his life, including during the Civil War.

McClellan's Mexico experience proved tremendously valuable and influential. The young lieutenant learned how an army operated in the field, chiefly by personally observing the actions of General Scott, whom McClellan credited as "the General under whom I first learned the art of war." McClellan recorded these lessons in an 1848 memorandum that highlighted the importance of careful planning to determining military success—reflected in the outcome of the fight for Puebla—and the value of turning movements and siege tactics, which he deemed the reason behind American success at Veracruz and Cerro Gordo. McClellan's Mexican experience also provided some lessons in army and national politics. On October 31, 1847, he wrote a US senator complaining about volunteer Generals Pillow and Patterson's failings and about an officer's commission in the Mounted Rifles undeservedly given to mountain man Kit Carson. McClellan's voice was influential in ultimately barring Carson's commission, and despite meddling in matters beyond his station and rank, McClellan suffered no rebuke from his superior officers. Although not the only young officer to draw such conclusions from the Mexico war, few other officers would have the opportunity to apply these lessons with such devastating effect during the Civil War.[19]

Transitioning from the thrill of war to routine peacetime service tested George's dedication to this still-new career, just as it challenged other young officers.

McClellan returned to West Point in 1848 and for the next three years served on the academy's staff, teaching mathematics and practical engineering. Compared to Mexico, this was dull stuff and George repeatedly sought new and more interesting posts. Referring to this return to West Point as "an infernally monotonous life" it nonetheless enabled McClellan's study of military art in greater depth and he joined the "Napoleon Club," an unofficial post-graduate seminar open only to officers and faculty and run by Dennis Hart Mahan, America's leading voice on military art and tactics. The club's discussions and cutting-edge ideas bolstered the lieutenant's knowledge of military history and deepened the well of his thinking about military issues, providing examples for applying classroom learning to real battle situations during wartime.[20]

McClellan next served in a variety of positions which, although lacking the thrills of Mexico, proved more enjoyable and interesting than West Point. These included aiding in building Fort Delaware, serving as second in command on an expedition to uncover the sources of the Red River in Arkansas, surveying the Texas coast, leading efforts to uncover rail routes through the Cascade Mountains in Washington territory, and secretly surveying anchorages for the Navy in the Dominican Republic. George McClellan emerged from these years both having met the woman he would marry—Mary Ellen Marcy, daughter of his Red River expedition commander—and gaining Secretary of War Jefferson Davis's attention. Davis became McClellan's benefactor for the remainder of his pre-Civil War army career, securing his promotion to captain, arranging a posting to the newly formed 1st US Cavalry—despite McClellan's complete lack of cavalry experience—and appointing him to the prestigious Delafield Commission, which journeyed to view the Crimean War and gather lessons for the US Army.[21]

Captain McClellan and his much older companions on this Commission—Major Richard Delafield and Major Alfred Mordecai—visited London, Paris, St. Petersburg and other important European cities, as well as witnessing the scene of the siege at Sevastopol and touring fortifications in Crimea. Returning home in spring 1856, McClellan settled in Philadelphia to write his portion of a report of the group's findings and how they might be applied to the American military situation. The report McClellan produced as a Congressional document in 1857 contained a detailed critique of the Sevastopol siege operations and an extensive "order of battle" study of the engaged European powers. The report highlighted the European armies' training, supply, and transport functions and their role in supporting forces in the field, all areas McClellan knew only too well were shortfalls of the US Army then. McClellan concluded his time in Philadelphia by preparing a manual of cavalry tactics based on his Crimea observations and a pattern for a new saddle. Both were later adopted and continued in use long after George McClellan left military service. Young Captain McClellan seemed poised to rise quickly through the ranks of the peacetime army.[22]

In November 1856, however, George McClellan abruptly notified Washington of his intention to resign from the army the following January. Though he never recorded what motivated this surprising move, it was certainly a carefully considered decision. One reason may have been Secretary Davis's recent rejection of his post-Delafield Commission plan to create a "Cavalry Board," modeled on the army's powerful Ordnance Board. Davis opposed the idea outright—McClellan's sharp reaction ended their close professional relationship—and left what remained of the matter in the hands of senior cavalry officers, William J. Hardee and Edwin Vose Sumner. At the same time, his impending assignment to join the 1st US Cavalry on the remote frontier—a tough post which sharply contrasted to his recent series of interesting and varied assignments—probably played a key role in the move, too. Joining the 1st US Cavalry also meant serving under Colonel Sumner, the very man Davis expected to quash McClellan's Cavalry Board proposal. On top of that, throughout the ranks of young officers, Sumner was known as a difficult commander under whom the only means of survival was to quickly understand that the junior officer "is utterly ignorant, professionally —& that his colonel is not."[23]

Resigning his commission soon proved a shrewd move because in January 1857—the month it took effect—McClellan accepted a position with the Illinois Central Railroad, a job offering financial rewards beyond anything the army could offer. McClellan quickly proved an able administrator and business negotiator, becoming a rising star in the railroading world. Within a year, he was named that railroad's vice president, after serving as chairman of a committee that guided the financially strapped line through the American economic Panic of 1857. In August 1860, McClellan continued his climb through the business world by becoming the Ohio and Mississippi Railroad's superintendent, along with the promise of being named president of the line's eastern portion and the highest paid railroad man in the nation. His ability to set goals and work tirelessly to carry a plan through to success were key to McClellan's rapid success in the business world. It quickly became clear to George, however, that the business world would never prove as interesting or personally engaging as had been military service.[24]

Marrying Mary Ellen ("Nelly") Marcy on May 22, 1860 similarly was a seminal event in McClellan's life, although their courtship presented George new and difficult challenges. First meeting in April 1854 in Washington, George immediately fell wildly in love with the beautiful, dark-haired daughter of his former commander. Barely a month later, George wrote Mary Ellen's parents (Captain Marcy was then stationed in Texas) asking permission to propose marriage. Their approval secure, he proposed in June, barely two months after their first meeting. This was perhaps the rashest thing George McClellan had ever done and it ended badly; Mary Ellen rejected his proposal but pledged to remain friends. Crushed, George responded by assessing the situation, learning from his error, and thoroughly planning his next move. He concluded it was "a very great blunder & doing a very foolish thing in the way of pushing too far & too quickly..." but having learned, McClellan began methodically pursuing Mary Ellen. Her parents' support secure, George regularly wrote Mary Ellen, building a groundwork of contact. He similarly built friendships with Mary Ellen's sisters, slowly enlisting their support. McClellan remained determined and methodical, even in the face of a potentially serious setback. Shortly after spurning George's proposal, Mary Ellen met Lieutenant Ambrose Powell Hill and, in the spring of 1856, accepted Hill's proposal. Nelly's parents immediately and forcefully objected; not only was Hill an infantry officer with little promise, but Nelly's mother soon learned he struggled with bouts of illness caused almost certainly by a venereal disease. McClellan's methodical approach never wavered throughout this crisis; when Mary Ellen wrote asking George's guidance, he calmly advised her "to govern yourself by the dictates of your good sense & true woman's feeling." Mary Ellen soon broke off the engagement with Hill. A few months later, Mrs. Marcy quietly suggested Nelly rethink her feelings about George McClellan. In October 1859, the Marcy family—including Mary Ellen—stayed at McClellan's Chicago home en route to a new posting in Minnesota. McClellan accompanied the family on their remaining journey and—after five years of methodical, reasoned effort—George again proposed, this time successfully. He had won perhaps the most hard-fought battle of his young life and had learned much from the experience.[25]

The outbreak of Civil War offered McClellan a return to the career he so missed, as well as advancement opportunities he could scarcely have dreamed of before. Senior command offers—of the New York and Pennsylvania volunteers, among others—began arriving at McClellan's office and he ultimately selected Ohio Governor Dennison's request to command that state's forces. Beginning his Civil War service in the Western Theater ensured McClellan's rise to the top echelons of command in two important ways. Most critically, it removed him from participation and association with the Union's disastrous first battle of Manassas. At the same time, it allowed the new general time to prepare his own military operations without the intense official and public pressure for quick action and success endured by his Eastern Theater counterparts. When McClellan finally opened his first significant battle of the war—at Rich Mountain in western Virginia on July 11, 1861—it foreshadowed his future as a military commander.[26]

McClellan had laid thorough groundwork preparing for and planning this action, noting he "had provided against & foreseen every contingency..." McClellan planned to turn the Confederate position at Rich Mountain, using Brigadier General William S. Rosecrans's Brigade, after which McClellan would lead the main attack to finish off the Rebels. The fight, however, went awry almost at once when heavy rain, torturous terrain, and inexperienced troops delayed the flanking move; worse, Rosecrans failed to keep McClellan apprised of his progress as expected. The 3rd Ohio's John Beatty noted that when McClellan and his staff appeared to inspect Rosecrans's fight, he "sat there with indecision stamped on every line of his countenance." The battle hadn't unfolded as planned and McClellan was immobilized by this state of chaos. Any move now fell beyond his prepared plan and was fraught with indeterminate risk, so McClellan chose the safe course and did nothing beyond reacting to Confederate moves. Once again, however, fate smiled on George McClellan. Rosecrans's attack, sloppy as McClellan might have viewed it, was successful and the fight's result ultimately led Confederate Colonel John Pegram to surrender 600 men to McClellan. Union victory at Rich Mountain also drove Brigadier General Robert S. Garnett and the remaining Confederate forces from the region. McClellan had had little to do with driving the Rich Mountain fight to victory—save being in overall command—but quickly claimed the full credit. "Our success is complete & secession killed in this country," McClellan telegraphed Washington following the surrender. Despite the message's hyperbole, forces under McClellan had in fact secured the strategically important western portion of Virginia for the Union.[27]

The Rich Mountain victory further accelerated McClellan's rise when news of it reached the Northern public just after the rout at Manassas. Union military and political leaders needed to replace failed Brigadier General Irvin McDowell and George McClellan would be that man. On July 22, George McClellan received word that, at 35 years of age, he would command the Union's eastern forces. Suggesting Washington had chosen wisely, he methodically and tirelessly worked to build the ragged Manassas force and the thousands of new, untrained troops flooding the capital in the weeks following into a solid fighting force; McClellan personally named it "The Army of the Potomac" on August 20. Once finally in the field, only a small portion of the army's 85,000 men were required to sweep the Rebels from Washington's vicinity, eliminating the threat of Confederates shelling the city from Arlington heights and driving General Joseph Johnston's Rebel army into strong fortifications at Centreville, Virginia, to await a Union assault. Union newspapers and politicians clamored for a quick, direct assault on these positions, but General McClellan rejected this rash and risky approach, determining instead to launch his own carefully prepared—if bold—advance. Like General Scott had in the Mexican War, McClellan would put his army on boats and land them on the enemy's flank; at once making moot Confederate defensives at Centreville and setting in motion a grand flanking maneuver that, if successful, might take the enemy's capital at Richmond and potentially end the war. On April 2, 1862, General McClellan joined his army at Fort Monroe for the start of his campaign on the Virginia peninsula.[28]

The Peninsula Campaign proved a test of the young General Commanding's abilities, while similarly testing the Union's resolve and military skill. Despite extensive preparation, McClellan's carefully thought-out plans went awry almost at once. One attraction of the peninsula as an avenue of approach to Richmond had been that the Union Navy could secure the army's advancing flanks by sailing up the York and James Rivers. The Confederate ironclad CSS *Virginia*, however, posed an almost overwhelming threat to the Navy's mostly wooden fleet, leaving the army to secure its own flanks as it advanced. McClellan's response to this unexpected setback was to stick largely unchanged to his plan, just without any Navy support. When on April 5 scouts reported Major General John Magruder—commanding Confederate forces at Yorktown—had erected defenses across the peninsula's width, McClellan knew the flanking maneuver couldn't work. He immediately planned to besiege the Confederates at Yorktown; extending 30 days, it ended when Johnston—commanding the forces defending Richmond—pulled Confederate troops back to Williamsburg. The May 5 battle of Williamsburg ended with Confederates falling back toward Richmond yet again, but McClellan took no part in directly leading the fight at Williamsburg. For the next three weeks, General McClellan held the Union army at bay, largely to ensure the final push on Richmond would be thoroughly coordinated and used the greatest possible number of men. Washington's patience with Little Mac—and McClellan's corresponding tolerance for perceived meddling by politicians—was strained to the breaking point. His glacial drive on Richmond was, in fact, positioning to strike the enemy capital but no one in Washington seemed to appreciate, or even understand, the general's methods. Actions at Hanover Court House and Fair Oaks—both, like Williamsburg, were fought without McClellan taking an active tactical role, although he missed Fair Oaks ill with recurring malaria, his "Mexican disease"—brought the Army of the Potomac to Richmond's outskirts, but no closer. And just as McClellan was laying the final groundwork to besiege Richmond—his originally planned climax—Confederate forces refused to follow the Union playbook and struck first, initially at Oak Grove on June 25, opening what would become known as the Seven Days Battle. A week of desperate fighting, adding names like Gaines's Mill and Mechanicsville to America's history lexicon, ended on July 1, when George McClellan surrendered the initiative. Believing he faced an overwhelming Southern attack, McClellan retreated to Harrison's Landing. McClellan had steered the Union army literally to the gates of Richmond—so close men could see church spires and hear the steeple bells ringing—but seemed incapable of getting them any closer.[29]

In the wake of this failed campaign, McClellan's star began being eclipsed in Washington by the newest luminary in the Union firmament, Major General John Pope. Bit by bit, Washington leaders and press placed faith in Pope's newly christened Army of Virginia, replacing McClellan and the Army of the Potomac as the force able to find and destroy Lee's enemy host. Pope seemed to justify this support by taking the war to a new level by attacking civilian support for the Southern war effort, something McClellan had assiduously avoided doing. On August 14, the first Army of the Potomac units boarded ships for the long journey back to northern Virginia, fully aware this meant their—and McClellan's—efforts on the peninsula had failed. When fighting began late on August 29 near the Manassas battlefield of barely a year before, McClellan's forces sent to aid Pope were stripped from his command and placed under Pope, a move infuriating the young general. McClellan perceived Pope's rise and his corresponding decline as further indication that radicals in Washington, who sought to destroy the South in order to free the slaves and remake the post-war Union in their preferred image, were gaining control of the war's policy course. Similarly, McClellan viewed Pope's defeat at the second battle of Manassas as vindication for the personal slights and insults to his military skill McClellan had suffered over the preceding weeks. McClellan himself had even indirectly aided defeat by failing to encourage his friends in senior posts—like William Franklin—from moving aggressively to aid Pope. Although his behavior wasn't meant to be overtly treasonous, it revealed that George McClellan could be petty and selfish.[30]

George McClellan's behavior at Rich Mountain, as the senior commander during the Peninsula Campaign, and during the August days running through the Second Manassas battle had begun revealing the man behind a carefully manicured façade. His friends and family probably knew this man very well but others—including President Lincoln—only now were seeing him with increasing transparency. It was this man—not the hero of Rich Mountain or the dashing "Little Mac" of his self-cultivated image—who was about to lead the army north into Maryland, who would be apparent on September 17. For while George McClellan's approach to decision making was like that of anyone else, a combination of natural inclination and learned behavior, the character traits of this one man would soon directly affect the course of a great battle and, ultimately, a nation's future.

Perhaps General McClellan's most significant character trait was a natural deliberateness, reinforced and exacerbated by a learned belief that reason, not emotion or intuition, should guide all decision making. This natural deliberateness was honed and influenced by the example of his father, whose own life had been a testament to this approach. Along with hard work, reason-based decision making had been a key factor propelling the McClellan family to Philadelphia society's top echelons, despite the perpetually meager finances Dr. McClellan shared with other medical men of the time. Dr. McClellan's belief in the importance of reason drove his politics, too, resulting in strong support for the Whig Party, which held as one of its central features the importance of employing reason over emotion on the national political stage. George later recalled that in the household of his youth "traditions and associations … were all on the side of the old Whig Party." Even as a young man, George strongly accepted the Whig ideal of "statesmanship that looked for men of reason, moderate temperament, and refinement who could forge compromises that preserved social order and stability." In the Whig Party, young McClellan found a perfect fraternity through which to turn his natural deliberateness and sense of reason into national service.[31]

Dr. McClellan also passed his son a stubbornness that certainly was genetic but made more pronounced and fixed by their shared belief that because reason guided their actions any conclusion they reached was inherently correct. Adopting greater responsibilities, particularly during the Civil War, this personal confidence grew and mutated into a form of hubris which General McClellan increasingly ascribed to God's will being carried out through his person and actions. Reflecting this, McClellan wrote General Burnside that "When I see the hand of God guarding one so weak as myself, I can almost think of myself a chosen instrument to carry out his schemes." Making similar comments in letters to Mary Ellen, McClellan's belief that he was God's chosen instrument only grew deeper as an ever-widening chorus questioned his actions and decisions, prompting him to hold ever more tenaciously to his chosen, deliberate course.[32]

This stubborn deliberateness in decision making is something quite different, however, from the excessive caution historians have long ascribed to the general and blamed for Antietam's outcome. Those who exhibit excessive caution in life are rarely driven to do great things, more often preferring to hide in mediocrity or in the comfort of the familiar. An overly cautious person might pursue a military career because it offers structure and sameness, but they hardly would leave that comfort for the uncertainty of civilian life when faced with an obstacle; maintaining order, even at a cost, would likely win out over the uncertainty of change. George McClellan never sought out the familiar or commonplace, rather he was always drawn to big—often risky—actions. Leaving home at age 15—after a generally sheltered existence—to attend West Point was a risk, as was leaving the army for the uncertainty of a railroad business career. Bucking Washington's conventional wisdom in planning the Peninsula Campaign as he did—putting his army on ships for a risky flanking maneuver with uncertain landing conditions and unknown enemy positions, rather than just marching safely over known territory to Centreville's well-scouted Confederate position—was full of risk. No, George McClellan wasn't overly cautious; he understood that doing great things entailed risk and that that risk was best managed and mitigated by deliberate, thorough planning.

What determined General McClellan's approach to planning and executing battles, though, was something even more intrinsic to the general's nature than learned reason and deliberate calculation. For those men he led, whose very lives weighed in these decisions, what mattered most were two fixed traits of George McClellan's mind, both of which played a central role in his actions at Antietam.

The first trait was George McClellan's inability to create original or innovative ideas, even though he was tremendously smart and a quick study. Historian Ethan Rafuse observed that the workings of McClellan's mind were "derivative and deductive, rather than innovative and analytical, and preferred to work within existing paradigms, rather than think creatively." In other words, George McClellan mind was "hardwired" in a way that allowed him to quickly absorb information but prevented him from using that information to create or innovate. It is this that probably explains both why George was an excellent student—in his youth and at West Point—but one who seldom did more than achieve his marks when tested on knowledge of classroom material. As his West Point classmate and academic rival Charles Stewart observed of McClellan, "He was well educated and, when he chose to be, brilliant." Stewart's observation is apt, even if it blames his intellectual shortfall on laziness.[33]

McClellan repeatedly demonstrated this limitation throughout his early life and military career, although it rarely held him back personally or professionally. George excelled as a student and a young officer in the Mexican War and in other assignments probably because he was working within the confines of a classroom or as a subordinate officer, reacting to the direction of superiors. When faced with having to innovate or create—writing original thought or making command decisions outside of established models—he repeatedly fell short, however. The 1857 reports McClellan prepared after his Delafield Commission experience observing the Crimean War—which earned accolades from the War Department—were little more than recitations of standard European writing and thoughts on the war. A chapter in the published version of these reports is long on description and what passes for analysis is merely opinion, not reasoned argument that creates new thoughts and ideas. Even McClellan's observations offering lessons for the US Army—the importance of an elite, standing officer corps and the utility of thoughtful use of artillery and engineers in battles—were already conventional wisdom within the army and War Department; McClellan was merely telling leaders what he knew they wanted to hear. Similarly, McClellan's highly touted cavalry tactics manual was not an original work based on his observations in the Crimea, but rather a translation of a Russian manual that copied Russian Army thinking on the use of light cavalry. So much was this a copy of the Russian work that McClellan in many places simply replaced "Cossacks" with "Indians." His proposal to create a cavalry school at Jefferson Barracks in Missouri simply copied the long-established French cavalry school at Saumur. Even the famous "McClellan saddle"—still in use today—was in fact a copy of a Prussian Saddle of Hungarian design.[34]

The advent of the Civil War and McClellan's rise to senior command only made more evident his inability to innovate, even when fate and social connections intervened to protect, or even accelerate, his career. McClellan's inability to think innovatively or independent of external models probably helps explain in part his love of military history. The campaigns and battles he studied provided a professional framework, tried-and-true models for his own military actions. Planning the attack at Rich Mountain, General McClellan didn't evaluate the challenging topography and seek ways to use this to his advantage, rather he turned to a model from the Mexican War and made it fit the situation he faced. On July 5, 1861, McClellan informed General Scott in Washington of his intention to "if possible repeat the maneuver of Cerro Gordo," adding "no prospect of a brilliant victory shall induce me to depart from my intention of gaining success by maneuvering rather than by fighting." Similarly, McClellan's campaign on the Virginia peninsula—sometimes portrayed as a masterstroke of military innovation and planning—was really little more than a copy of Scott's plans for the 1846 Veracruz expedition. Just as Scott had the Navy land his troops south of the city before supporting his advance from the sea while the Army maneuvered to besiege Veracruz, McClellan envisioned using Navy ships to land troops at the peninsula's southern tip before supporting from the flanking rivers the Army's advance to besiege the Rebel capital. Even McClellan's "active siege" of Richmond—using artillery to press Lee's army and the city into surrender, rather than launching a costly direct assault or a drawn-out siege—mirrored Scott's siege of Veracruz. The fact that McClellan played almost no personal role in executing specific battles fought during the Peninsula Campaign—which would be attacked both by his contemporaries and historians—may have been his way of acknowledging this shortcoming, leaving command of active troops in battle to his most capable subordinates. In fact, the only tactical action McClellan successfully oversaw on the peninsula was his army's infamous retreat. Military historian John Keegan wrote that "Retreat in the face of the enemy was a technical problem; echoing the classic masters, McClellan called it 'one of the most difficult undertakings in war'. Since, however, it could be done by the rule book—the rules laid down that a general should fight a firm delaying action while clearing the routes to his rear, evacuating the army's train of transport, and then falling back behind strong rearguards—and adherence to the rules calmed, we may surmise, the anxieties to which McClellan's mind was prey whenever he had to grapple with the uncertainties of pressing forward into ground controlled by the enemy, he solved the problem very efficiently."[35]

That's not to say General McClellan was unable to plan a battle. McClellan was as capable as any of his West Point contemporaries of evaluating the conditions on a potential field of battle—its terrain, the state of his and the opposing army, the objective of the fight, etc.—and in devising a plan accounting for these factors to reach a tactical or strategic goal. He had, after all, successfully completed West Point's military training program and well knew the various models that might be employed. His mastery of military history and participation in the Napoleon Club at West Point exposed him to the thinking of Dennis Hart Mahan—the most innovative American military mind of his day—so in many respects George McClellan was better prepared for such a task than many other generals. Selecting a model to apply in planning a battle George McClellan could do. Like other generals, McClellan knew how he was expected to manage a battle, seeing developments in the action and putting troops in to reinforce success or forestall failure. This, too, he could do.

What General McClellan could not do was see in the events and occurrences of battle anything more than met his eye. Successful attacks and retreats were perceived as little more than advances or setbacks to his carefully prepared and thoughtful plan, not as opportunities to be seized upon and used in innovative ways to achieve success. Failed enemy attacks would not reveal to General McClellan anything more than proof that his plan was working and his men fighting well, he could not see that they might offer unexpected signs of weakness on another part of the line that could be struck quickly as an alternative path to success. McClellan's style of command at Rich Mountain amounted to little more than managing the battle and reacting to events, not taking initiative and steering them in any path necessary to reach victory. His willingness throughout the Peninsula Campaign to let trusted subordinates plan and execute all the actions of their respective corps might reflect an army commander performing his very senior role, but McClellan's detached approach could also indicate that the general knew he was incapable of leading his army in the complex, swirling nature of unfolding battle. The complexity and speed with which Civil War battles progressed certainly denied enough time for McClellan's mind's deliberate approach to decision making to work effectively, and in any case, General McClellan simply lacked the ability to innovate under fire in order to skillfully wrest a battle's course toward a successful conclusion.

The second trait of George McClellan's mind that had such a devastating effect at Antietam was his innate linear thinking. Psychologists and other scholars of human thinking approaches describe linear thinking as "the inability to understand the interdependence or web of relationships that exist in a complex world." Another scholar put this same idea into layman's terms, writing "Linear thinkers look at traveling from point A to point B, and see a straight line between the two points. They will deviate from that line only if it is absolutely unavoidable." George McClellan's personal history was a testament to the impact of his linear thinking. His excellence in school—particularly language study and mathematics—was aided by nineteenth-century educational practices which emphasized following a learning sequence in which each building-block step led to another and another, in turn, until the material was mastered. He approached courting Mary Ellen, too, in a linear fashion, following a logical progression of steps to build family and personal affinity to win her heart—convince her parents, gain her sisters' support, carefully wooing her after his rejected first proposal—with the final goal of making her his wife. Even his military career and his decision to leave the army reflected McClellan's linear approach. Each assignment sought positioned him for advancement and he resigned only after encountering insurmountable obstacles, serving under Colonel Sumner or overcoming the peacetime army's glacial promotion pace. McClellan's linear approach dictated that battles, too, should occur in the same logical manner, each step of the plan unfolding just as intended.[36]

Nowhere is McClellan's linear thinking and approach more clearly reflected than in his August 4, 1863 report of the actions and movements during the Peninsula Campaign. After opening by summarizing his plan to drive on Richmond, McClellan quickly turns to blame Lincoln and Washington for ruining his campaign by unexpectedly removing troops from his army. "I may confess to having been shocked by this order, which … reduced my force by more than one-third after its task had been assigned, its operations planned, its fighting begun. To me the blow was most discouraging. It frustrated all my plans for impending operations. It fell when I was too deeply committed to withdraw. It left me incapable of continuing operations which had been begun. It compelled the adoption of another, a different, and a less effective plan of campaign. It made rapid and brilliant operations impossible. It was a fatal error." In other words, General McClellan's response to Washington's unexpected change wasn't to devise the best campaign possible with the resources he had at hand, but rather to push on with a lesser, flawed version of his original plan. Another general might have seen in this change opportunity to move more quickly or used the smaller force—which in any case still greatly outnumbered Confederate defenders—to strike rapidly and unexpectedly toward Richmond. To George McClellan's linear mind, however, such change was no opportunity, only an immovable obstacle.[37]

So it was that President Lincoln on September 2 had unknowingly placed the fate of the Union and its army in the hands of a man severely limited as a military field commander by his own nature. A man possessed of a great intellect who was deliberate and calculating, but who was unable to innovate or to think and act outside of his preselected linear approach. The time was soon coming when George McClellan would once again face the prospect of planning and leading a battle. The question on which General McClellan's professional fate turned, along with the fate of the entire Union, was: Would luck or the enemy's lack of skill once again intervene to save General McClellan from himself?

CHAPTER 2

The Road to Antietam: September 4–15, 1862

Early on September 4 Lee ordered his army once more in motion. Although few in the ranks knew where they were headed, nearly everyone knew they were moving north. Lee's men, 70,000 by a generous count, were now at least partly rested after the nearly two weeks of constant marching and fighting that had led them to within a dozen miles of the enemy's capital in Washington. Even so, most of Lee's regiments lacked enough to eat. Supply wagons had brought forward what food was available, but many still had little more than what was already in their haversacks. Nonetheless, when the orders came to "Fall in!" Lee's men responded like the battle-tested veterans they were.

Lee had laid the groundwork for this momentous advance the previous day by sending part of his force northward. On September 3—the day he wrote President Davis asking approval—Lee ordered Jackson's Command out of its Ox Hill position toward Leesburg, Virginia. The decision to act without waiting for final approval may have been politically bold but was a militarily necessity. Not only would doing so preserve the initiative Lee retained after the second Manassas victory, but it cleared the road northward, allowing his remaining force to move quickly and unopposed toward its objective. Lee was at the same time conducting a reconnaissance-in-force to detect the presence and extent of any Union force that might resist his northward move.[1]

Led by McLaws's and D. H. Hill's Divisions, Lee's advance force made camp east of Leesburg around midnight. Behind them moved the rest of Jackson's and Longstreet's Commands at such a slow pace that they only reached Dranesville by nightfall. Nonetheless, the following day, Lee's force was poised to cross the Potomac River and, best of all, had so far encountered no Federal resistance.[2]

Men in D. H. Hill's Division were the first to cross the Potomac into Maryland; to establish a Confederate hold on the river's crossing points and search out the location and strength of any Union presence on the opposite shore. Lee's men stepped into the Potomac River at Point of Rocks and Monocacy Aqueduct, where the river was both narrow and shallow, and although most men celebrated upon reaching the

9/2367237

opposite shore, they were by then already some 100 or more yards inside Maryland; Virginia's border ended at the western bank due to a colonial-era charter creating the two colonies in the seventeenth century. On September 5, Jackson's Command crossed the Potomac at White's Ford and pressed on toward Frederick, Maryland; the army's first main objective. Reaching Frederick the next day, Major General James Longstreet's Command was just then crossing at White's Ford and moving to unite with Jackson.

Nonetheless, General Lee had much to worry about. For one thing, his army remained without sufficient food and forage, shortages which only grew worse with time. Lee also had to deal with the war going on among his top echelons. Division commander Brigadier General John Bell Hood rode into Maryland at the rear of his command. Major General Ambrose Powell Hill, too, rode behind his division as it entered enemy territory, having been placed under arrest by General Jackson. These incidents probably resulted from the dangerous mix of too many stressful days on the march and in battle, with naturally volatile tempers and egos. Both conflicts would be resolved in the coming days by necessity borne of war. Hill, three days after his arrest, and Hood, on the eve of battle at Antietam, would be restored to full command of their respective divisions. Whatever the cause, Lee knew as he moved deeper into Maryland that these problems only hurt his army's ability to carry out this most risky of operations.[3]

Arriving at prosperous Frederick, Maryland offered an answer to Lee's food and forage problem. The men quickly took their own initiative to find food, although most apparently followed orders directing that they pay for taken goods. September 8 marked the fourth day the Army of Northern Virginia spent unmolested on Northern soil and the second day in Lee's nearby new headquarters at Monocacy Junction. So confident of their ability to remain unhindered in Maryland was the Confederate high command that Lee's cavalry commander, Major General James Ewell Brown (Jeb) Stuart, spent the day chiefly attending to details of a grand ball planned for that evening.[4]

General Lee spent September 8 busy with more substantive issues, writing President Davis a letter suggesting Richmond offer Lincoln an opportunity to recognize Confederate independence and end the war. Although Davis had already reached this conclusion and written as much to Lee and Western Theater military leaders the previous day, Lee had yet to receive the message. Lee that day also issued a circular to the people of Maryland explaining the Confederacy's reason for being here and—in a calculated and strikingly conciliatory note—suggesting they could now determine their fate without fear—and that the Confederacy would welcome them with open arms. Privately, Lee had offered that Maryland was unlikely to leave the Union, even voluntarily, but it was critical to demonstrate to other northern governors—particularly Pennsylvania's Governor Curtin—that his army was comprised of civilized gentlemen who could be trusted to keep their word in any negotiations. Both documents reflect Lee's desire to tie his actions in the field to Richmond's diplomatic and political maneuvering on the wider stage of events.[5]

If Lee didn't believe Maryland would join the Confederacy, the campaign nonetheless served to advance other Confederate strategic objectives. Moving into Maryland and remaining unmolested might create fear of a wider invasion among the Northern public and with influential Northern governors, possibly creating advocates to pressure the Lincoln administration to accept Richmond's impending peace offer. Being in Maryland also would eventually draw Union forces away from the Shenandoah Valley, permitting farmers in the Confederacy's "breadbasket" to harvest their crops unmolested.[6]

For any of that to happen, though, the Army of Northern Virginia had to remain in Maryland for an extended period—and staying in Maryland meant facing the Union Army in battle, possibly soon. In fact, Lee wanted—the Confederacy needed—a major battle in Maryland or Pennsylvania to demonstrate its military worth to Europe. To prepare for this, Lee wrote President Davis that he intended to leave Frederick and move the whole army to Hagerstown, Maryland or Chambersburg, Pennsylvania, opening a new line of communication to Richmond through the Shenandoah Valley. If the Federals refused to engage his force, it could remain at the end of this supply line for an extended period, perhaps even through the winter.[7]

Before moving away from Frederick, however, Lee needed to dislodge Federals from Martinsburg and Harpers Ferry in order to open the new line of communication through the valley via Harpers Ferry, replacing the current, longer route through Leesburg and Frederick. Walker's Division, just arrived from Virginia, was a vital part of this effort and Brigadier General John G. Walker recalled on September 9 being told of plans for his own division and possibly the next moves of Lee's nascent campaign as well.[8]

Walker claimed General Lee shared with him both the army's ultimate objective and his strategic thinking behind the campaign. "In ten days from now, if the military situation is then what I confidently expect it to be after the capture of Harpers Ferry, I shall concentrate the army at Hagerstown, effectually destroy the Baltimore and Ohio [rail] road, and march to this point." Reportedly pointing at Harrisburg, the Pennsylvania capital, on a map before him, Lee continued "That is the objective point of the campaign. You remember, no doubt, the long bridge of the Pennsylvania railroad over the Susquehanna, a few miles west of Harrisburg. Well, I wish effectually to destroy that bridge, which will disable the Pennsylvania railroad for a long time. With the Baltimore and Ohio in our possession, and the Pennsylvania railroad broken up, there will remain to the enemy but one route of communication with the West, and that very circuitous, by way of the [Great] Lakes. After that I can turn my attention to Philadelphia, Baltimore, or Washington, as may seem best for our interests." Although some historians doubt Walker's account, Lee may well have intended to eventually enter Pennsylvania—he had told President Davis so on the 8th—and strike the railroad bridge there. This much, though, is certain: Lee planned to first eliminate the Federal threat in the nearby lower Shenandoah Valley, establish a new line of communication through the valley, then reunite his army before moving to the Hagerstown area.[9]

An important uncertainty facing Lee, as he weighed these moves, remained locating and determining the enemy's intentions. If McClellan moved quickly to intercept him, then Lee and his army had much to do in preparing for the expected major battle. If McClellan delayed returning to the field or moved slowly into Maryland, it offered Lee additional time to attain the three initial goals outlined to Walker, even if it meant facing a more effective, reorganized, and rejuvenated Federal enemy. Regardless, since entering Maryland four days ago Lee had received no indication McClellan and his army were moving north. On September 8, Lee wrote President Davis, "As far as I can learn, the enemy are not moving in this direction, but continue to concentrate around Washington." Although this assessment was based on all the intelligence available to Lee, it simply could not have been more wrong.[10]

***

For days now, George McClellan had been doing his best to shatter Lee's careful planning. A key first step was placing his new cavalry division under Brigadier General Alfred Pleasonton's command, unifying his important mounted forces, which mirrored somewhat the organization of Lee's already renowned cavalry arm. Pleasanton's cavalry force took to the field in search of the Rebels almost the instant it was created.

McClellan meanwhile rebuilt his army to meet whatever Pleasonton's cavalry found. He merged the Army of Virginia into his own Army of the Potomac— redesignating Pope's I, II, and III Corps as the Army of the Potomac's XI, XII, and I Corps, respectively—though many of the name changes wouldn't be official until September 12. On the 6th, McClellan issued Special Order 3, distributing 37 newly arrived infantry regiments more or less evenly among the army's seven corps, adding 10,000 men to his ranks. McClellan evened the strength of his existing corps by shifting and reordering entire divisions so most—excepting the V and XII Corps—had three full divisions. Under this effort, a third division under Brigadier General William H. French was assigned to Major General Edwin V. Sumner's II Corps and Major General Darius Couch's First Division of the IV Corps was temporarily moved to Major General William Franklin's VI Corps. Brigadier General Jacob Cox's recently arrived Kanawha Division was assigned as the IX Corps's Third Division, finally filling out this new corps comprised of units previously serving in the eastern Carolinas. The IX Corps's finishing touch was the eventual arrival of its commander, Major General Ambrose Burnside.[11]

Sometime prior to September 10, McClellan formed his army into three wings—comprised of two corps each—and directed three of his most senior corps commanders to each assume their command. Burnside would lead the left wing, consisting of Major General Joseph Hooker's I Corps and the IX Corps, under the acting command of Major General Jesse Reno; General Sumner would command the center wing, his own II Corps and the XII Corps; while Franklin would head the right wing comprised of the VI and Couch's Division of the IV Corps. Major General Fitz John Porter's V Corps would serve as the army's reserve, once pried loose from the Washington defenses. In many respects, this new formation well-suited the army's then-primary objective, finding Lee's army. McClellan was seeking an unlocated enemy and this structure allowed covering a wide area, in effect sweeping the Maryland countryside as it advanced. Having an experienced or trusted commander leading these wings also ensured that if one was found and forced into battle by the ever-aggressive Lee, he could hold his own until the entire army unified.[12]

This important change in the army's senior command structure came, however, without any attendant written order, even if orders drafted (beginning on September 10) suggest the three commanders were already acting in their new capacity. Perhaps it was a simple oversight by McClellan amidst the tremendous press of business. Maybe McClellan intended the wings and their elevated commanders to be temporary and so avoided issuing written orders to speed and ease abolishing them when necessary. It would not be until September 14, in an unnumbered special order, that McClellan formally elevated Burnside and Sumner to wing command; curiously, William Franklin was left out of the order. Implemented at least four days after the wing formations began functioning, the order also recognized that the left and right wings had in fact swapped their respective positions in his advancing line. Nonetheless, the oddly timed special order suggests something was amiss among the Union's senior command. If so, it would not be the last time in this campaign that fragile senior egos would drive McClellan's actions and affect the course of Union military actions.[13]

On September 7, McClellan led his reorganized, expanded army from the Washington defenses to the vicinity of Rockville, Maryland, where he established his first field headquarters of this new campaign. Though the army had moved only 12 miles or fewer, it was still in the field, which McClellan probably hoped would show Washington—and his critics there—that this time the Army of the Potomac's chief was acting aggressively. Nonetheless, until Pleasonton's cavalry found the enemy and offered a clue to his intentions, McClellan had to both guard Washington from attack—from Maryland and from Virginia—and be ready to quickly intercept any advance on Baltimore, Harrisburg, or Philadelphia. For two days, the Army of the Potomac would remain anchored to its capital.[14]

McClellan finally received word from cavalry scouts on September 9 that Lee's army was near Frederick, providing the key intelligence he needed to act. He could now move deliberately to Frederick and engage Lee's army in battle or perhaps threaten it enough to force it back into Virginia and off Northern soil. At 11:55 on September 10, McClellan informed army head General Henry Halleck, "I have ordered a general advance to-morrow. Send me up all the troops you can spare."[15]

McClellan's closing plea for more men suggests that beneath the image of a new, proactive general, lurked the deliberate military manager of the Peninsula Campaign. McClellan took to the field an army that on paper numbered nearly 90,000 men, but the reality, as McClellan knew, was that just under 75,000 of these men actually fired a weapon; the remainder were teamsters, cooks, orderlies, and other support troops. McClellan might draw on the Harpers Ferry garrison for 12,000 more men if Halleck and the situation allowed. Staying behind to guard Washington—Halleck remained worried by a few reports of Confederates remaining in Virginia, despite other intelligence to the contrary—was Major General Franz Sigel's XI Corps and Heintzelman's command. These troops numbered an additional 25,800 men which might be sent to McClellan if the situation changed. Even after Halleck ordered Porter's V Corps to join McClellan in the field, the Army of the Potomac's commander still wanted more men.[16]

Uncertainty about the exact size of Lee's army was another factor certainly driving McClellan's plea for more troops. As intelligence dribbled in, McClellan quickly adopted the belief that Lee had no fewer than 100,000 men in Maryland. These numbers were reported by Allan Pinkerton—founder of the detective agency—and supported by other sources and reports similarly indicating a large enemy force. That McClellan so quickly accepted these as accurate—at 9:30 on the 9th he wired Halleck that he doubted the figure, but by evening had confidently adopted an even larger number—suggests he was predisposed to believe Lee outnumbered him and waited only for information from the right, trusted source to confirm his fears. Added to this predisposed view, facing a numerically superior foe gave McClellan a useful tool with which to pry from Halleck's grasp the thousands of troops guarding Washington and Harpers Ferry. On the evening of September 9, McClellan warned Halleck that "From such information as can be obtained, Jackson and Longstreet have about 110,000 men of all arms near Frederick..." Having laid this groundwork, McClellan daily from September 10 to 13 sent Halleck a request for more troops. This unholy combination—a predisposed belief of being outnumbered and the utility of that view as a bureaucratic weapon—quickly wove its way into McClellan's plans and actions. Regardless if it was willful self-deception, an intelligence failure, or a combination of the two, McClellan's view that Lee had as many or more troops in Maryland as he possessed would color nearly all of his plans for the coming fight.[17]

Early on September 10, the Army of the Potomac began moving northeast toward Frederick. Franklin's left wing advanced with its left pinned roughly on the Potomac River. Sumner's center wing covered the most direct route from Washington, holding the army's flanks together and keeping open their communications. Burnside's right wing drove with its right guiding roughly along the Baltimore and Ohio Railroad's route. The entire army moved deliberately, despite McClellan's awareness by now that much of Lee's force was at Frederick. Even so, by midday on the 13th, the Army of the Potomac was encamped on Frederick's outskirts.[18]

***

On September 9, General Lee, in his headquarters at the Best farm, drafted orders providing the army's objectives after leaving Frederick. Designated Special Orders No. 191, it outlined only the coming campaign's first step, securing a line of communication along which would flow food, ammunition, and other supplies of the army's life blood. Leaving Frederick on the 10th—Lee was now aware McClellan's army was coming his way—Jackson's Command would lead the way, moving through Sharpsburg before crossing back into Virginia to take the Baltimore and Ohio Railroad, capture the small Union garrison at Martinsburg, and move on Harpers Ferry. There, Jackson's men would sweep up any of the 10,000-man Union garrison seeking to escape capture. Longstreet's Command would move shortly after Jackson's departure, crossing the Cotoctin and South Mountain ranges until reaching Boonsboro, halting there to guard the army's supply wagon train and await Jackson's return. Major General Lafayette McLaws would take his own and Major General Richard H. Anderson's divisions, follow Longstreet to Middletown before turning toward Maryland Heights, from which McLaws's force would aid in capturing Harpers Ferry and the surrounding, strategically important area. Walker's Division would complete destroying the Chesapeake and Ohio Canal's aqueduct—having told Walker this during their earlier meeting, written orders called it "the object in which he is now engaged"—before reentering Virginia and possessing Loudon Heights, after which it would join in capturing and securing Harpers Ferry. D. H. Hill's Division would be the army's rear guard, protecting the slow-moving wagon train until safely in Longstreet's care. Stuart's cavalry would detach squadrons as needed to support each larger unit and sweep up the inevitable stragglers left in the army's wake. With Harpers Ferry securely in Confederate hands and the wagon train over the mountain passes, Lee's army would reunite at Boonsboro or Hagerstown. In short, Lee was again—as he had before Second Manassas—dividing his army in the face of a much larger enemy. The largest portion would capture Harpers Ferry, while the remaining third guarded supplies and the rear, awaiting reunification. Lee expected to accomplish these moves by Friday September 12—as noted in the orders—after which the next campaign element could be planned.[19]

Lee's forces wasted little time moving from Frederick on September 10 toward their new respective objectives. In fact, the only impediment slowing the move was a traffic jam resulting from the entire army marching west through town on the same road, the Hagerstown Pike. During this move, one Confederate soldier committed perhaps the most egregious error of the war when he dropped a copy—probably meant for General D. H. Hill—of Lee's highly detailed Special Orders No. 191, wrapped around three cigars. Found by men of the 27th Indiana, the papers were quickly passed to General McClellan, who became excited almost beyond words at his luck. As he commented to Brigadier General John Gibbon—in full view of local citizens—only moments later, "Here is a paper with which, if I cannot whip Bobbie Lee, I will be willing to go home." McClellan continued, "We will pitch into his center, and if you people will only do two good, hard days' marching I will put Lee in a position he will find hard to get out of."[20]

***

McClellan quickly set to work taking advantage of this intelligence windfall. He first prudently directed Pleasonton's Cavalry into Cotoctin Valley to confirm the Special Order's movements. He next moved to hit the divided portions of Lee's army in turn, first Longstreet's thinned command and then Jackson's isolated force. Key to success of this plan was Franklin's left wing, which would drive quickly through South Mountain's southern-most pass, Crampton's Gap, before pressing on to Maryland Heights and Harpers Ferry. There, Franklin would hold McLaws's men—the only large Confederate force north of the Potomac River that might aide Longstreet—in check. Meanwhile, Burnside's right wing would push through the remaining passes—Turner's Gap and Fox's Gap—to strike Longstreet's Command near Boonsboro.[21]

At 6:20 on the evening of September 13, McClellan sent General Franklin a dispatch apprising him of Lee's movements outlined in the Special Orders—making Franklin one of only three men with whom McClellan shared the specifics—and explaining in detail his vital role and the timing and routes he was to take. McClellan directed Franklin to "move at daybreak in the morning … If you find this pass held by the enemy in large force, make all your dispositions for the attack and commence it about half an hour after you hear severe firing at the pass on the Hagerstown pike, where the main body will attack. Having gained the pass, your duty will be first to cut off, destroy, or capture McLaws's command and relieve Colonel Miles." McClellan then explained the importance of Franklin's role. "My general idea is to put the enemy in two and beat him in detail. I believe I have sufficiently explained my intentions … [Y]ou are fully authorized to change any part of the details of this order as circumstances may change, provided the purpose is carried out; that purpose being to attack the enemy in detail and beat him … I cannot too strongly impress upon you the absolute necessity of informing me every hour during the day of your movements, and frequently during the night. Force your colonels to prevent straggling, and bring every available man into action." Having the key role in McClellan's campaign, it remained to be seen if William Franklin would rise to the occasion.[22]

McClellan moved early on the 14th, intending to press his army over South Mountain and attack Longstreet's isolated command, which Lee's Special Order indicated would be waiting near Boonsboro. When Pleasonton's cavalry reported finding greater-than-expected Confederate resistance before Turner's Gap—D. H. Hill's rear guard—McClellan brushed aside this intelligence and hewed to his plan, advancing into the three main passes. Soon, however, it became all too clear that the situation on the ground had changed from that suggested by Lee's Special Order.[23]

At 9:00 that morning skirmishing began before Turner's Gap, opening the battle of South Mountain. Burnside arrived around 11:30, General Reno in tow, and quickly prepared his attack. With Turner's and Fox's Gaps in his immediate front and a third one, Crampton's Gap, two miles south, Burnside's plan combined a frontal assault with—if needed—a turning maneuver. Burnside knew the geographic reality of this position was that once the Confederate hold on any one of these passes was breached, the entire position would be compromised. Lee would have to retreat.[24]

Intense fighting in Turner's Gap, the northernmost pass, yielded little for the Union. Although a stubborn attack by Gibbon's Black Hat Brigade eventually earned them a new nickname—the Iron Brigade—it did little to change the Union's fortunes there. Stiff resistance by Confederate defenders bought the South time, though little more; by sundown fighting at Turner's Gap simply ceased.[25]

Just to the south, General Reno directed his IX Corps in a broad assault, eventually using all four divisions to force a passage through Fox's Gap. Intense fighting by D. H. Hill's Confederate defenders ended the battle here too with another stalemate, though one costing the life of Confederate Brigadier General Samuel Garland, Jr. and, for the Union, that of General Reno.[26]

Union success at South Mountain now depended on William Franklin, who at midday sought to make good on McClellan's directive—and lead the first true attack of his military career. Franklin's 12,000-man VI Corps faced five Confederate regiments holding Crampton's Gap, a thin force he might have brushed aside with the sheer weight of his own numbers. However, the scattered but constant fire his advance received from Confederates behind a low stone wall proved too much for Franklin. At 3:20, he apprised McClellan that "The force of the enemy is too great for us to take the pass to-night, I am afraid. [S]hall … attack again in the morning." Franklin had abandoned the attack after it had barely begun.[27]

Franklin's senior officers were unwilling to give up so quickly, however, and at 4:00 launched an attack of their own. Torbert's New Jersey Brigade rushed forward of Major General Henry W. Slocum's advancing division and quickly broke through the very center of the Confederate defensive position. Colonel Thomas Munford's Confederates broke and ran for the summit and an effort by Brigadier General Howell Cobb's Georgia Brigade to stem the tide failed. The Union took Crampton's Gap and won the battle of South Mountain, but no thanks to General Franklin.[28]

Worse than Franklin's absence during the battle was his decision to hold the corps in place that night. At 1:00 in the morning on the 15th, McClellan directed Franklin to march his VI Corps into Pleasant Valley, securing the Union's left flank, before moving to reinforce Harpers Ferry. Franklin then was to bring the 10,000 men there to Boonsboro, at which point, McClellan probably planned to strike Longstreet's nearby command. It wasn't until 7:00. on September 15, however, that Franklin bothered to ride to the top of Crampton's Gap and peer down into Pleasant Valley. There he saw a line of Confederate troops stretching across the valley floor and heard sounds of battle from the direction of Harpers Ferry. What he observed was McLaws's thin line meant to uncover and slow any Union efforts to reach the besieged Harpers Ferry Federal Garrison, then in the process of falling to Jackson. At 8:50, Franklin sent McClellan a dispatch apprising him of the situation and explaining that he would do … nothing.[29]

Franklin had dithered while Harpers Ferry fell and the tone of his 11:00 message suggests Franklin knew he'd failed. "The enemy is in large force in my front … It will, of course, not answer to pursue the enemy under these circumstances. I have not the force to justify an attack…," he offered. This "strong force" consisted of but 2,725 men and five artillery batteries—facing his own 12,000-man VI Corps. Whether to avoid overreaching and undoing "his" success at South Mountain or from fear of moving alone against an unknown enemy, William Franklin had failed and it played a role in Harpers Ferry's fall and in denying McClellan its 10,000 troops. This failure now hung like an albatross around General Franklin's professional neck.[30]

Troubles facing General Lee from September 11 to 15, though, were far greater because Lee had misjudged the Federal reaction to his entering Maryland. Only after learning on the 13th that the bulk of the Union army was already in Maryland did Lee realize that initiative and control of the campaign had slipped from his grasp. That McClellan had a copy of Lee's immediate plans and knew the army was widely divided, only made Lee's prospects bleaker than he knew. Lee's stand at South Mountain by D. H. Hill's Division was a bold effort to buy time and save the campaign. By late on the 14th, however, Lee must have wondered if what he had bought was worth its price. Contesting the three South Mountain passes cost Lee nearly 3,000 men from an army so small that Lee obsessed about stragglers thinning its ranks on the march north. On top of that, the Federals now possessed the three passes and were poised to sweep off the mountain and toward his divided army early the next day. Compounding Lee's woes, Jackson, McLaws, and Walker were stalled outside Harpers Ferry—his operational timetable was shot to pieces. Following a meeting in Boonsboro that night with Longstreet, D. H. Hill, and Hood, Lee dictated two dispatches, one ordering Jackson to abandon his position at Harpers Ferry and return to Virginia, and a second directing McLaws to cross the Potomac and prepare to receive the remainder of the army as it retired through Sharpsburg to Virginia. Lee opened his message to McLaws bluntly, "The day has gone against us," and on the evening of September 14 nothing could have been truer.[31]

***

Before dawn on the 15th, following a night nearly devoid of sleep, General Lee stepped from his ambulance transport in Keedysville; a hamlet also known as Centerville, Maryland. After reviewing the ground, he abandoned plans to stand here while uniting his army, in favor of better ground to the west at Sharpsburg. Arriving there at around 8:00, Lee strode atop "Cemetery Hill" just east of town to better assess this new ground. Looking through his spyglass to the east—the direction from which the Union army would come—Lee could see rolling terrain sloping gently down to the western edge of Antietam Creek. To his left and right—running from north to south—was a nearly four-mile-long ridge that, although not as commanding as the rise on which Lee now stood, clearly offered good fields of fire for his infantry and artillery. To the west of Sharpsburg were more rolling hills over which ran the Shepherdstown Road, while to the south lay the road to Harpers Ferry. Standing like a picket line between his intended position and the Union enemy lay Antietam Creek. Because in the vicinity of Sharpsburg this obstacle was wide, deep in places, and lined by steep banks, it could be crossed nearby only at several predetermined points—three bridges and two related fords. McClellan would have to cross his artillery and wagons—if not much of his infantry, too—at these points, which created "choke points" that allowed Lee to maximize his limited fire- and manpower. If a fight came, the Sharpsburg ridge was the place for Lee's army to stand.[32]

Lee posted the troops already at Sharpsburg into defensive positions holding the Boonsboro Pike, which ran like a dagger through the center of his position. General Longstreet joined Lee on Cemetery Hill at 9:30, well ahead of his command's arrival, deploying his troops as they appeared. By 10:00, Brigadier General David R. Jones and three of his brigades formed Lee's right on the heights south of town. Early in the afternoon, they were joined by Hood's Division, Toombs's Brigade, Cutt's Battalion of 32 guns, and four batteries of the Washington Artillery, posting immediately south of the pike. Guarding the Lower Bridge, they were to prevent Federals from crossing and seizing the Harpers Ferry Road, one of the army's two routes back to Virginia and the most direct route McLaws's and Jackson's reinforcements could take from Harpers Ferry. On the left of Lee's line, D. H. Hill's Division posted in a farm road worn into a natural trench with erosion and use. This important position gave Lee some hold on the wide, sloping valley laying east of the heights on which his army deployed. Law's, Wofford's, Evans's, and G.T. Anderson's Brigades arrived about 11:00, allowing Lee to strengthen and extend both ends of his line. By mid-day, Longstreet had personally posted artillery overlooking the Antietam, extending Southern control to its banks, while token infantry stood picket on the span soon to be known as the Middle Bridge. By early afternoon, Lee's available force was prepared to stand at Sharpsburg for either a holding action before retreat or for a decisive battle.[33]

Although Lee anticipated a defensive stand, he nonetheless kept open the door to regaining the offensive, an objective almost certainly behind two important decisions affecting the coming battle. In particular, deploying on the Sharpsburg ridge offered maneuver room if and when the opportunity came to attack, even though doing so required sacrificing potentially the best defensive terrain Lee could have here. Posting his troops along the Antietam's western bank—particularly concentrated on the bridge and ford-based choke points—would have better aided a defense but greatly restricted Lee's opportunities to regain the offensive through maneuver. Perhaps the greatest risk in holding the Sharpsburg ridge was that it required surrendering the initiative—Lee needed McClellan to cross the creek and attack first before somehow wresting back control of the fight mid-battle. Confederate forces had done so in both Manassas battles, and if they could do it again, the creek would become McClellan's worst nightmare, potentially trapping Union men and artillery across the creek to face destruction or capture. A desire for the offensive probably also explains why Lee avoided directing his men to dig defensive works. Historians have long argued Lee should have entrenched, agreeing with Scott Hartwig who most recently noted, "it was an error." Lee, however, probably wanted nothing to impede moving quickly to aggressively attacking, which fighting behind works would certainly do. West Point, after all, taught budding officers that because men behind entrenchments would resist leaving this protection to attack, attaining the offense required avoiding building works in the first place. So desirous was Lee to somehow gain the offensive in any coming fight that he placed trust in the skill and fighting ability of his men over the advantage of offensive-deterring entrenchments.[34]

About noon, a courier arrived at Lee's Cemetery Hill headquarters bearing news that changed Lee's plans in an instant. Sent by Stonewall Jackson, he advised that "Through God's blessing, Harpers Ferry and its garrison are to be surrendered." Lee simply responded, "This is indeed good news! Let it be announced to the troops." Jackson had that very day captured the critical Harpers Ferry crossing and was ready to join Lee at Sharpsburg as directed. Although he'd done so nearly three days later than Lee wanted, this was probably the best news Lee had received since leaving Frederick. In one stroke, it breathed new life into both Lee's Maryland Campaign and the Confederacy's prospects for independence.[35]

***

George McClellan began the 15th in his headquarters at Bolivar, flush with awareness that the previous day's battle had been perhaps the greatest Union victory of the war to date. Despite missing an opportunity to build on the South Mountain victory by immediately advancing, McClellan's corps were nonetheless now primed to renew the drive. Franklin's VI Corps held the army's left flank beyond Crampton's Gap. Hooker's I Corps and Major General Israel Richardson's II Corps division, after clearing Turner's Gap the previous evening, held the right flank. Burnside and his IX Corps remained in Fox's Gap as a reserve to move north to Boonsboro or south to Pleasant Valley as the situation required during the planned pursuit of Lee. Sumner held the center with his remaining two II Corps divisions and the newly arrived XII Corps, commanded by Major General Joseph K. F. Mansfield. More encouraging, Brigadier General George Sykes's Regular Division was already up and ordered to reinforce Burnside and the Union reserve, indicating Porter's V Corps had arrived. Completing its appearance, Morell's Division was marching from Frederick and Humphreys's Division was nearing that town.[36]

Perhaps best of all, a message from Hooker early that morning indicated the Confederates had abandoned Boonsboro and were running for the Potomac. Franklin's dispatch confirmed the good news, adding that McLaws was leaving Pleasant Valley. The only hitch in this run of good news came from the signal station at Monument Hill, reporting the enemy had stopped and was forming lines behind Antietam Creek. This development could mean Lee intended to recross the Potomac and sought to prevent Union attacks on his scattered and retreating army—or, Lee might be preparing to stand and fight. Only pressing the Confederate position would reveal the truth. McClellan ordered Hooker to drive on Boonsboro and, sending the entire army over the mountain, began a "reconnaissance in force."[37]

Hartsuff's I Corps Brigade was first to move off the mountain, at dawn on the 15th. With skirmishers out in front feeling the way, Hartsuff's men found only dead and wounded from the previous day's battle, so they pressed on toward Boonsboro. There, Hartsuff's men were replaced in the Union vanguard by Richardson's Division, which was soon joined by Pleasonton's cavalry. Turning southwest onto the road to Sharpsburg, Richardson's men encountered nothing to block their progress until reaching the eastern bank of Antietam Creek. There, they found the enemy drawn up in line of battle along the opposite bank, holding the only bridge in view. Orders governing the advance prohibited engaging the enemy until the bulk of Hooker's I Corps arrived but was silent on Richardson poking his opponent from a distance, so the aggressive Richardson "borrowed" a section of Alfred Pleasonton's artillery—Tidball's Battery A of the 2nd US—and opened fire. These shells arcing over the Antietam's warm, summertime flow marked the first scattered shots in what would soon enough grow into a major battle.[38]

McClellan followed his cautiously advancing army, arriving in Boonsboro at 1:25 in the afternoon, and established his headquarters. Then his day turned sour. Hooker's messenger arrived cautioning that the Rebel line across Antietam Creek was formidable. This bad news was made worse later in the afternoon with word that Harpers Ferry had fallen. Not only had the Union lost the river crossing and supplies there but, most importantly, Miles's reinforcements. Worse, Jackson was free to move from his known position of the past few days. McClellan now faced another critical intelligence gap that complicated his decision about what to do next.[39]

Shortly after hearing the news of Harpers Ferry, McClellan moved his head-quarters to Keedysville. Tarrying only briefly, he rode with General Sumner to observe the army's location and condition as it neared the new Antietam position. Riding west along the Sharpsburg–Boonsboro Pike, McClellan was disturbed to find the I and II Corps not deployed or moving into position but rather clogging the road in a huge, immovable mass. Pressing on, often to the sound of ringing cheers, McClellan and Sumner soon found General Hooker and an explanation for the massive traffic jam. Hooker had discovered Richardson's artillery engaged against "as nearly as I could estimate, about 30,000 men,"—a number too high by several thousand—and "[f]ully conscious of my weakness in numbers and morale," explained Hooker, "I did not feel strong enough to attack him in front, even after the arrival of the First Corps…" Uncertain what to do, Hooker stopped and posted Sykes's newly arrived V Corps division on Richardson's left in a line of battle.[40]

Hooker also reported he'd sent his engineer, Major D. C. Houston, upstream looking for other crossings; the major had found a bridge and, immediately to its south, two fords suitable for infantry use. This and Hooker's own reconnaissance revealed the Rebels were gradually pulling back from the Antietam crossings. Important as this information was, it left unanswered just why Lee was yielding the crossings. Regardless, watching the opposing Confederate force gradually disappear, Hooker at 5:00 or so decided that it was "too late to make the detour, in order to come up with the enemy, without a night march through a country of which we were profoundly ignorant." Hooker and his corps would remain camped that night along the Antietam and see what tomorrow might bring.[41]

Arriving on the banks of Antietam Creek late on the 15th, McClellan, Porter, and their respective staffs climbed the same hill used earlier by Hooker—and General Lee—which offered a good view of the enemy's position and terrain beyond the creek. Looking west across the hills and vales, McClellan could see some undetermined number of Rebel infantry and artillery deployed for battle. One or more of these guns soon opened fire on the large group of blue-clad men, forcing away all but McClellan and Porter. When he finally descended the hill to safety, McClellan apparently had gathered much, though not all, the information necessary to plan his next move. Though he still didn't know Lee's intentions or how much of the Army of Northern Virginia remained, McClellan knew the Rebel position was too strong to strike in a simple frontal assault. If the Army of the Potomac was to attack, something more sophisticated—and complex—was needed.[42]

McClellan began deploying his army during the remaining half hour of daylight, which would greatly affect his actions in the coming days. He directed Hooker's I Corps to move upstream to the two crossings reported earlier; once there, he should conduct a reconnaissance in force to find and measure the strength of Lee's position. McClellan posted his artillery along the high eastern bank of Antietam Creek; a point from which they might support Hooker and the I Corps or hold off a Confederate attack. Sumner's II Corps was posted astride the Boonsboro Pike, with Richardson's Division in advance on the very banks of the creek along the right side of the road, holding the Middle Bridge's eastern end. Burnside and the IX Corps were ordered left of the pike, posting on Sykes's Division's left, widening the Union position. Well to the rear was the XII Corps, in reserve. The bulk of Union forces remained on the pike or nearby, awaiting orders to move. That these deployments were largely defensive—holding the eastern bank of the Antietam—suggests McClellan remained undecided about what to do next at nightfall on September 15.[43]

At the same time, Hooker's men were settling in for the night on the eastern bank of Antietam Creek, Confederate soldiers barely a mile away were trying to clear civilians from the farms and buildings in front of their growing defensive line. The Southern men knew the morning would probably bring a Union advance and had too often seen what happened to buildings and their inhabitants standing between the two armies. It apparently took little persuading for 60-year-old Samuel Mumma to gather up his wife and eight children, moving hastily to a church four miles away. That Union shells were already falling near his house, in search of the Confederate host assembling nearby, probably was prodding enough. The Mummas would have to be content with escaping the coming battle with their lives; when two of the older boys returned home the following day, they discovered Southern troops had ransacked their house and snatched up everything of any value.[44]

***

As night fell over the hills around Sharpsburg on September 15, there were many things the opposing commanders didn't know. Lee had taken a defensive stance, for now, but was uncertain if McClellan would attack and where that advance might come. McClellan knew a major enemy force was deployed on the ridge around Sharpsburg but remained uncertain if this was the entire Rebel army and of Lee's intentions to remain or to retreat. For the men in the ranks, it had been a busy day of marching that left only uncertainty about what was coming next. George Beidelman of the 71st Pennsylvania expressed these sentiments, writing in his diary that night; "There are many rumors about the rebels, which a person don't know whether to believe or not…" For now, the prevailing sense in both armies, from Generals McClellan and Lee to their lowliest private, was uncertainty.[45]

CHAPTER 3

Emerging from the Fog: September 16

September 16 brought an unexpected new obstacle to both Lee's and McClellan's plans in the form of simple ground fog. The humidity in the Potomac River valley had risen so much overnight that even before the first rays of light appeared to prove it, no one could see anything farther away than a few dozen yards.[1]

Even before knowing of this obstacle, General McClellan had worked to fill key intelligence gaps about Lee's army. Sometime during the night, McClellan ordered Colonel Thomas Devin and his 6th New York Cavalry across the Middle Bridge to determine if the Rebels still held the span and, if so, exactly with what size force and where it was positioned. General Sumner, too, wanted intelligence of the position before him and independently ordered Lieutenant Colonel Nelson Miles and four companies of the recently combined 61st/64th New York across the bridge sometime after 2:00 in the morning. Despite a brief friendly fire incident between the two probes at roughly 8:00, Devin crossed a second time and reached the Newcomer farm before encountering opposition. Discovering Confederates had abandoned their new position, Devin's intelligence most importantly showed Lee planned to stand at Sharpsburg rather than immediately retreating to Virginia.[2]

***

Confederate troops, too, were preparing for what lay ahead. At midnight Longstreet—overseeing these early deployments for Lee—moved Hood's Infantry Division from near Sharpsburg to the left. Colonel Stephen D. Lee's Artillery Battalion, too, was ordered left, moving from the Boonsboro Pike's left edge to a broad plateau in front of a small, white church. Belonging to a group known as the Dunkards or Dunkers—formally the German Baptist Brethren; a sect of Anabaptists who practiced total-immersion baptism—the church sat on land donated by Samuel Mumma, whose farm lay within view of the small building. Reaching the church, Lee's Battalion turned right and deployed for battle facing their guns northeast. Once in place and the horses secured, Lee's artillerymen grabbed what little sleep this night might offer. Here, Lee's artillery could broadly support his overall position's left flank, by now joining three of D. H. Hill's Brigades—Ripley's, Anderson's, and Garland's—posted in a sunken farm road. Neither Lee could know then just how great an impact these few guns would have in the coming hours.[3]

Robert E. Lee emerged from the Jacob Grove house in Sharpsburg well before sunrise. Receiving Jackson's message that his command had departed Harpers Ferry and would arrive by dawn, Lee mounted his horse, Traveller, for the first time since spraining his wrists on August 31. Lee's wrists still hurt, though, and a staff officer helped him mount before leading Lee to Cemetery Hill. Arriving just after first light, Lee quickly discovered the same fog that bedeviled George McClellan only a cannon-shot away. Dismounting, Lee wandered the hillside searching in vain for a view of the Union line, before pacing anxiously among the Washington Artillery's guns. Like George McClellan, Lee could do little more than wait.[4]

Lee used the fog-imposed delay to prepare his position, however, making three key moves. The first ordered Stuart's Cavalry to probe the Maryland side of the Potomac, probably to detect any effort to turn his left flank under cover of the fog. Reflecting its importance, Stuart personally led the 3rd, 4th, and 5th Virginia Cavalry Regiments out shortly after receiving the orders. Lee's second order cleared away the army's remaining cumbersome, vulnerable wagon train—bearing supplies, ammunition, food, and such—sending it across the river to join Longstreet's and D. H. Hill's trains at Shepherdstown. Lastly, Lee directed Lieutenant Colonel E. Porter Alexander to forward ammunition from Harpers Ferry to Sharpsburg, ensuring this most valuable commodity would be ready for the coming battle.[5]

Although Jackson's Command and Walker's Division were on their way to Sharpsburg, Lee still worried about Lafayette McLaws's Division, unlocated since departing for Sharpsburg. "All will be well if McLaws gets out of Pleasant Valley," Lee commented to one of Longstreet's staff officers on Cemetery Hill early that morning.[6]

Around 8:00 Stonewall Jackson appeared and joined Lee on Cemetery Hill. His top leadership team now on the field, Lee shared his intention to stay and fight, offering details of Jackson's role and locations for deploying his troops. Lee recalled Jackson "emphatically concurred with me" and soon departed to deploy his men. If McClellan would cooperate by giving him a little more time, Lee's army might just be fully ready for battle.[7]

***

McClellan spent the foggy morning at his Keedysville headquarters, drafting his only written correspondence of September 16. The first two, crafted at roughly 7:00 addressed the two most important people in his life not then on the field, his wife and General Halleck. Assuring Mary Ellen all was well, he advised Halleck and Washington he would "attack as soon as situation of the enemy is developed."

Forty-five minutes later, McClellan wrote his only dispatch of the day bearing tactical guidance, to William Franklin. "[T]he rebels on this side of the river are rapidly recrossing to the Virginia side by our pontoon bridge at Harpers Ferry. I think the enemy has abandoned the position in front of us, but the fog is so dense that I have not yet been enabled to determine. If the enemy is in force here, I shall attack him this morning."[8]

These last two messages reveal that by 8:00 General McClellan believed the Confederates were retreating but intended to attack if Lee remained when the fog lifted. A general in McClellan's place might have seen opportunity in this fog-driven delay to prepare for battle or perhaps to steal a march on his foe, as Lee's orders to Stuart suggest he feared. McClellan alternatively might have hoped to find Lee's army gone when the fog lifted, creating a bloodless, costless victory in Maryland. George McClellan, however, apparently was unable to see in the fog-driven delay anything but what met his eye—an obstacle to his preconceived intention to attack. Beyond the correspondences, McClellan's only action that morning was sending his aide Colonel Ruggles at 8:45 to urge Sumner "to hurry up Banks's Corps" in joining Hooker's force, completing previously planned deployments for his assault. McClellan's limited mindset had cost the Union a missed opportunity, perhaps the first of the day. It would not be the last.

Other Federal officers, however, were active during the fog-driven lull. Major Jonathan Letterman, the Army of the Potomac's Medical Director, busily prepared area buildings to serve as field hospitals for the thousands of wounded any battle would create. A Union Signal Corps station was created on Elk Ridge, a prominence just behind the Federal line, affording McClellan a means of relaying orders to far-flung parts of the field and of receiving updated tactical intelligence from the front. At the Middle Bridge, Brigadier General George Sykes at 7:00 deployed his Second Division of the V Corps—US Regulars—to ensure Union control of the critical span, while the Army of the Potomac's new artillery chief Brigadier General Henry Hunt followed McClellan's order from the previous night, deploying four batteries on the high bluff overlooking the Middle Bridge.[9]

As the fog lifted around 9:00, both armies began stirring. Confederate skirmishers nearest the Middle Bridge, now aware of the Union artillery before them, began shifting. Uncertain what this movement meant, two of Hunt's newly deployed batteries unleashed the fury of their ten guns, driving off the skirmishers before turning on a larger infantry force—probably Brigadier General Nathan "Shanks" Evans's two brigades—which "drove them in confusion into a ravine." Soon, the Washington Artillery's Colonel James B. Walton on his own initiative ordered Captain Squires's battery and those of Bachman and Riley to open in response. For nearly 45 minutes, the two artillery lines dueled as the sun rose in the sky. Eventually, the weight of Union firepower convinced General Longstreet to end the mismatched fight by ordering his batteries away, ending what General D. H. Hill described as "the most melancholy farce of the war." Nonetheless, the Union now decisively owned the tactically important Middle Bridge.[10]

Union batteries soon opened a general bombardment, raining fire down on Sharpsburg itself. For nearly half an hour, Yankee guns tore at the town's modest buildings, bringing Sharpsburg to life as if someone had stepped on an anthill. People raced from their homes, loading any available conveyance to get themselves and their belongings away from the two armies. Young William Houser recalled a shell blasting apart a fence as his family raced past out of town. The Grice family shoved some food and clothes into a case and, sitting as many of the children as possible on their horse, set off to join their neighbors in nearby Killiansburg Cave. D. R. and Margaret Miller had taken their family to D. R.'s father's home, west of the two armies and beyond Hauser Ridge. Amidst the shelling, the Millers realized the family parrot had been left behind in its cage. Returning home, D. R. dashed to his porch where the cage still hung from the porch roof by a leather strap. Barely had he arrived before a shell fragment severed the cord, sending the cage crashing to the ground and killing poor Polly. His mission having failed, D. R. raced away, before the cost of this effort grew greater than the life of a bird. The bombardment probably convinced Lee to move his headquarters from the shell-damaged Grove house to a tent pitched in a wooded lot three-quarters of a mile farther west of town on the Shepherdstown Road, beyond most Union guns' range.[11]

By 10:00, George McClellan knew roughly the new disposition of Lee's expanding force and that Lee meant to fight. This intelligence must have reinforced McClellan's determination to attack, as he'd promised Washington, but one major problem remained—the Union controlled only two of the three bridges needed to support an advance. Addressing this, around noon, McClellan ordered Burnside's IX Corps forward to secure approaches to the Lower "Rohrbach" Bridge and by 3:00 they were deploying.[12]

***

Initially, opposing Burnside was the small brigade of Brigadier General Robert Toombs, who immediately grasped that the key to controlling the bridge was the small elevated strip of woods overlooking its western approach. When Hood's Division moved left after midnight, Toombs advanced the 20th and 2nd Georgia Infantry into positions on the bluff to the left and right, respectively, of the bridge's entrance. Together they fielded only 400 or so muskets, but the position's topography would magnify their presence. Although Munford's Brigade appeared midday on the 16th, it was to guard the Antietam's three fords on the Confederate far right. Toombs's Georgians were the only force Lee employed to contest Union control of a bridge over the Antietam.[13]

Lee early that afternoon wrote President Davis updating him about the army's recent movements, progress, and challenges. Lee admitted he had miscalculated both the enemy's rapid pursuit and the need to have earlier reinforced his South Mountain defenders, as well as admitting the battle there had failed to stop McClellan's advance. Closing with good news, the surrender of Harpers Ferry and its war booty, Lee left Davis with a blandly factual summery of the moment; "The enemy have made no attack up to this afternoon but are in force in our front." Before Davis could read the message, either retreat or a great battle would change the closing statement's accuracy.[14]

***

During that same time, General McClellan rode along the Antietam's eastern bank, "reconnoitering the new position taken by the enemy, examining the ground, finding fords, clearing the approaches…" Historians have complained that this was an inappropriate task for the Army of the Potomac's commander at this critical moment—mundane duties better left to cavalry or aides—which demonstrates McClellan's micromanagement and lack of strategic leadership. Perhaps so, but McClellan obtained during this ride important first-hand tactical intelligence that probably fine-tuned his plan to attack Lee's army.[15]

As finally conceived, McClellan's attack would begin by striking the Confederate left. His attacking corps would cross at the Union's by now securely held Upper Bridge and the nearby fords, moving through a series of fields and woodlots before striking Lee's line on the Sharpsburg ridge north of town. Once the Rebel position was been broken, Union attackers and their reinforcements would turn southward toward Sharpsburg and the Confederate center, driving retreating Rebs as they went. Hitting Lee's left first offered several advantages including that the rolling, generally open ground there offered considerable maneuvering space and that striking there would cut the Hagerstown Road, which Lee might use to move north/left out of McClellan's grasp. Two important challenges existed here, however. First, breaking Lee's left required a challenging, potentially costly direct assault on some part of the line because no one wearing Union blue that day had any solid idea where the actual end of the Southern left really was; without better intelligence, a maneuver-based turning of the Confederate left was out of the question. Secondly, because this position was well in advance of the main Union line and largely isolated, the general commanding this opening attack must be capable of independent action. Addressing this last challenge, McClellan chose Major General Joseph Hooker—whose aggressive, skillful command of fighting on the Peninsula and at South Mountain had gained the General Commanding's attention—to plan and lead his opening attack.

Once the assault on Lee's left was underway, a similar attack would strike the Confederate right on the ridge south of Sharpsburg. Though the initial objective here was to tie up a significant portion of Lee's army, preventing these troops from reinforcing other parts of the Southern line, this was hardly a diversionary assault. The attack's objective was reaching the Harpers Ferry Road, at once breaking Lee's right flank and—most importantly—cutting off any retreat south along that road. The geographic isolation of the Lower Bridge position, like on the opposite flank, required a general capable of managing a largely independent command. Major General Ambrose Burnside, who had planned and executed successful operations on the North Carolina coast and much of the South Mountain fight was chosen to command this portion of the battle.

Facing two simultaneous attacks on his flanks, Lee would be forced to weaken his center by sending available troops to forestall those assaults. At that moment, McClellan would launch his main attack against Lee's weakened center just north of the town. Two of the army's most capable corps—the solid V and VI Corps, led respectively by two of McClellan's most loyal friends, Fitz John Porter and William Franklin—would spearhead this effort. That Porter's Corps contained Sykes's Division of US Regulars—in McClellan's West Point-centric view, the steadiest and most skilled single division in the army—further argued for its participation. Pleasonton's Cavalry Division would add its weight, too, launching a Napoleon-style cavalry charge on weak points in the Southern defense. Union artillery already massed on the eastern bank of the Antietam would support this grand assault. The three Federal assaults would unite just west of Sharpsburg, cutting off the retreat of all but the swiftest of Lee's once-formidable army. Lee would face surrender of the bulk of his army or risk its destruction at the hands of the Union juggernaut.[16]

Aiding McClellan's prospects was the considerable manpower advantage he possessed. In truth, determining the actual numbers engaged at Antietam with great accuracy remains nearly impossible, even today, because neither army compiled detailed, accurate "returns"—an accounting of those present for duty—on the eve of battle. Ezra Carman's late-nineteenth century study lists the Army of the Potomac's engaged strength as 55,956 men and the Army of Northern Virginia's as 37,351. Scott Hartwig's 2012 study lists McClellan's force as 72,727 and Lee's army as 38,095. Regardless of the exact numbers, McClellan's force was considerably larger than Lee's on September 17.[17]

More important than the actual numbers, however, was McClellan's and Lee's perception of the size of his opponent's force and accounting for these differences in a battle plan. Although Lee never recorded the number of men he believed McClellan possessed, he noted in his report that it was "much exceeding the number of our own." Since leaving Virginia, Lee had used initiative and maneuver to minimize this Union advantage and preparing for battle, Lee now shifted to choosing the battle's terrain and creating interior lines to compensate—to the extent possible—for McClellan's numerical superiority.[18]

Historians have long suggested McClellan believed Lee's force greatly outnumbered his own, drawing on a combination of the general's reports and post-war statements, but if this was so then his plan to "divide and conquer" was doomed from the start. For example, McClellan's 1863 report to Secretary Stanton, provided to Congress, lists his force on the eve of battle at 87,164 and Lee's total as 97,445. Reinforcing the origin of this figure for Lee's forces, the Bureau of Military Information's civilian analyst John C. Babcock in late 1862, as part of an analytic exercise, arrived at 97,175 for Lee's army by using the same War Department reports from before the battle that had been available to McClellan. McClellan repeated these ratios testifying before Congress in March 1863, citing his own force as 94,000 and Lee's total as 100,000 men. These numbers are deceptive, however, because McClellan limits his own troops in these counts to those "present and fit for duty" or "in action" but includes all Confederates in uniform—including support troops—in Lee's totals. Although the politically shrewd general's inconsistent counting scheme might have fooled some in Washington, McClellan certainly understood the difference and knew his battle plan should consider only Lee's available combatants, those firing weapons and their officers. Given these numbers, counting distinctions, and McClellan's known battle plan, in all likelihood he probably believed Lee's force outnumbered his own but only by a small margin. If this is so, McClellan might have considered Hooker's and Burnside's flanking attacks would be costly, but manageable; Lee could throw most of his army into resisting these flanking assaults but possess only thin resistance when the battle-hardened V Corps and shock-troop cavalry struck the Confederate center. Outnumbered he might be, but by a margin George McClellan probably figured he could handle through reasoned, skillful planning and effective execution.[19]

During McClellan's early afternoon ride, events at the Army of the Potomac's headquarters ground to a halt. Albert Richardson, *New York Tribune* correspondent, recorded that General Sumner rested idly under a tree while General Hooker lay on the ground nearby, napping. These two corps commanders must have been anxious for word of their next move but were experienced enough to know that a wise soldier grabbed rest whenever it was offered. McClellan's return around 2:00 in the afternoon, ended their break.[20]

Hooker was the first to have McClellan's attention. "I received my instructions from the major-general commanding the Army of the Potomac to cross the river with the First Corps and attack the enemy on his left flank, Meade's and Ricketts's Divisions crossing the bridge near Keedysville and Doubleday's Division at the ford just below it." Hooker later told a Congressional committee that McClellan also shared with him the Union's overall battle plan. "When I had left with my corps to make the attack I had been assured that simultaneous with my attack, there should be an attack upon the rebel army in the centre and on the left the next morning." Sumner and his two corps would remain in the center for now and the general might as well have resumed his nap. Hooker, on the other hand, rode off to prepare his corps. Although the army was in motion, McClellan had shared his battle plan with Hooker alone—even that had lacked detail—and on the eve of battle his remaining five corps commanders apparently were completely ignorant of the army's plans and intentions.[21]

McClellan had considerable justification in assigning Major General Joseph Hooker this critical role. Graduating in the middle of West Point's Class of 1837, Hooker served with distinction in the Mexican War and demonstrated aggressive, skillful leadership during the war to 1862. Although Hooker had a flair for self-promotion in the press and a willingness to bad mouth superiors, McClellan apparently had not seen this side of him. So confident was McClellan of Hooker's abilities that on September 12 he'd written Mary Ellen that his only concern before the coming battle was for the steadiness of McDowell's old troops, the I Corps; nonetheless, he assured her "Hooker will however soon bring them out of the kinks & will make them fight if anyone can." This was Hooker's greatest opportunity to shine of the war so far; a fact not lost on the ambitious officer. What General Hooker almost certainly didn't realize, riding then to join his corps, was that McClellan's distant role and linear approach to battle meant he alone then held in his hands the Union's fortunes at Antietam.[22]

Leaving headquarters, Hooker rode north along the eastern ridge of Antietam Creek to his I Corps command. Passing through the bulk of his corps' three divisions, Hooker found the men lounging in the late summer heat, cooking their dinners—the army's term for lunch—or performing various camp duties. Just how temporary those camps really were, only General Hooker knew at that moment. Hooker quickly passed word to his division commanders—Brigadier General Abner Doubleday, commanding the First Division; Brigadier General James B. Ricketts, commanding Hooker's Second Division; and Brigadier General George G. Meade, commanding the Third Division—to have their commands ready to move to the right within the hour. Unlike McClellan, Hooker told his subordinates where they were going and why—after crossing the Antietam, they would seek the Confederate left flank. With these orders issued, the once-calm, restful field camp came alive as men reflexively packed their gear, quickly fell into ranks, and waited to move.[23]

Once assured his corps was underway, Hooker returned to McClellan's new forward headquarters at the Pry House. Hooker explained "I rode to the headquarters of the commanding general for any further orders he might have to give me..." Hooker also took an opportunity to request support for his attack on the Confederate left. "I was informed that I was at liberty to call for re-enforcements if I should need them, and that on their arrival they would be placed under my command." This was a double stroke of good fortune for "Fighting Joe;" he secured the promise of reinforcements and would, in fact, command two full army corps in battle. For the ever-ambitious Hooker, this opportunity meant he stood above his peers and—if successful—his name would rise on the list of potential army commanders if Washington eventually replaced the politically-volatile McClellan.[24]

Beginning their move about 3:00p.m., within an hour Hooker's first troops were crossing to Antietam Creek's western side. First across were three companies of the 3rd Pennsylvania Cavalry, escorting the massive infantry column, acting as scouts, and searching for indications of the location of Lee's left flank. Behind them Meade's and Ricketts's Infantry Divisions crossed the Upper Bridge, while Doubleday's men crossed at a ford south of the span that had been cut the day before by Union pioneers. Once across, each of Hooker's ten brigades reformed their lines and his 9,423 men marched slowly northward along the Keedysville–Hagerstown Road.[25]

After crossing, several men noticed the remains of cattle lying where presumably a group of Rebels had left them the day before. Being battle-tested veterans, they knew such opportunity might not come again soon. "[S]ome of our boys had detached strips of fat from the intestines of the animals which they applied to their guns to prevent rust," wrote Private Bob Patterson of the 19th Indiana's Company E. "I had unconsciously raised the hammer of my gun and was applying the grease about the tube as the regiment halted, when I rested the muzzle of my gun against my left shoulder, and in drawing the string of fat through the (trigger) guard, the gun was discharged and the ball passed through the rim of my hat." Though Patterson was deafened by the accident, he was otherwise unhurt and rejoined the ranks. By the close of the next day, Private Patterson could say with honesty that despite being in some of the thickest fighting on September 17, he'd come closer to killing himself than would any Rebel in the coming fight. It was a boast not all of his comrades would be able to make.[26]

Once all three divisions were across, Hooker deployed his force into three parallel divisions. Doubleday's Division formed the left column, with Ricketts's column in the center and Meade's men on the right. Though Hooker never explained his thinking in choosing this formation, it ensured maximum control and cohesion as Hooker's corps advanced into the unknown.[27]

Barely after moving again, General McClellan and two riders—staffer David Strother and a civilian who joined en route—unexpectedly appeared. Hooker recalled "we had not proceeded over a half mile before the commanding general with his staff joined me, apparently to see how we were progressing." Hooker again asked for reinforcements and emphasized how important the corresponding attack on Lee's right flank was to his own success. Apparently convinced Hooker was progressing satisfactorily, McClellan and his entourage departed for headquarters.[28]

McClellan responded quickly to Hooker's request. At 5:50p.m., staffer Colonel Ruggles wrote Sumner that "General McClellan desires you to move Mansfield's corps across the fords and bridge over the Antietam and to take such positions as may be designated by General Hooker. General McClellan desires that all the artillery, ammunition, and everything appertaining to the corps be gotten over without fail to-night, ready for action in the morning. He also desires you to have the other corps of your command ready to march one hour before daylight to-morrow morning."

Receipt of this order prompted Sumner to ride to headquarters, apparently to enjoin McClellan to send both corps forward under his authority. Sumner might have believed doing so ensured the greatest mass of troops and unity of command in battle but conveniently it also reinforced his standing as a wing commander. Regardless, Sumner's pleas fell on deaf ears. His wing command was divided and the XII Corps sent to Hooker's support, while the II Corps remained in reserve.[29]

Sometime after McClellan departed, Hooker set in motion a "reconnaissance-in-force" to find the Confederate left flank. The 3rd Pennsylvania Cavalry probed across country almost directly west of the two crossing points, exploiting their speed and maneuverability. At the same time, Hooker ordered Meade's Division out of the roadway to follow the cavalry, providing infantry support in the event the Pennsylvanians found the enemy in force. While the bulk of Hooker's Corps resumed its advance via the Williamsport Road, Meade's reconnaissance set off.[30]

*****

Unfortunately for Hooker, the Union crossing was detected almost immediately. Cavalrymen from Brigadier General Fitzhugh Lee's Brigade, watching the Upper Bridge and Pry Ford, first noticed the Union advance and instantly notified General Stuart who quickly warned General Lee, then meeting with Longstreet and Jackson in the Jacob Grove house in Sharpsburg. Lee now knew McClellan's opening move and responded at once to check it. General Longstreet ordered Hood—with the only Southern force then near the Upper Bridge—to advance toward the crossing, while Jackson moved his entire Command to deploy on Hood's left. Soon another message arrived warning Lee of Union movements threatening the Lower Bridge. Lee's response to this new intelligence reflected his usual measured reaction; the threat to his left was immediate and real, so his initial response would come here. Countering the less-imminent, potential threat on his opposite flank, Lee directed Brigadier General Alexander R. Lawton's Division to the left. For the first time at Antietam, Lee used his possession of "interior lines" in responding to Union advances. Lee possessed this advantage because his line's ends turned backward from the center, like the inside of a bowl, allowing him to move reinforcing troops more directly and quickly from one point to another. It was a tool he would use frequently and well throughout the next two days.[31]

Word of Lee's response reached Generals Stuart and Hood in their field headquarters at the Dunker Church. Most of Hood's men were then deployed on the Hagerstown Pike, resting and cooking what food they had. Deployed in advance of Hood's position was Fitzhugh Lee's Cavalry Brigade, spread across a wide arc beyond the East Woods from the Hagerstown Pike to the southern edge of the Smoketown Road. Supporting this position on the right were two artillery pieces from Major John Pelham's Battery of Stuart's Horse Artillery, hidden behind bushes in the woods on the Samuel Poffenberger farm. Cavalry was incapable of stopping a major Union advance, though, and the two generals could do little to prepare until they knew from where and in what strength the Union advance emerged. Stuart ordered Fitzhugh Lee's Brigade to prepare to support General Hood's infantry, sending the 9th Virginia Cavalry into the woodlot northwest of the Samuel Poffenberger farm for this purpose. Hood then ordered forward some of his infantry in skirmish order—meant to cover a wide portion of the field with a limited number of troops—to create a defense without committing his force to any one point on the field. One company of the 2nd Mississippi and another company from the 6th North Carolina moved north on the Hagerstown Pike to D. R. Miller's farm. Another company, of the 4th Texas, marched west through Miller's cornfield to the gap between the North and East Woods. On the 4th Texas's right, running through the eastern end of the East Woods bordering the Morrison farm, was a battalion from Colonel Alfred H. Colquitt's Brigade. Two howitzers from Rhett's Battery of South Carolina Artillery and a section of Parker's Battery, posted in the Miller fields between the Hagerstown Pike and the Smoketown Road, backed up Hood's force. Farther left, Hood posted Lane's and another Confederate battery on the ridge south of the Miller cornfield; a position providing an excellent field of fire for holding off any Union breakthrough into the Miller farm fields. Once in place, Hood's and Stuart's widely dispersed force was ready to meet the enemy. For better or worse, they would not have long to wait.[32]

***

The three-company squadron of Owen's 3rd Pennsylvania Cavalry, commanded by Captain Edward S. Jones, leading Hooker's reconnaissance, moved cautiously westward. Well to their rear advanced four companies of the 13th Pennsylvania Reserves (also known as the 1st Rifles), which had originally covered Meade's Division, but which now supported the cavalrymen. Cavalry Companies C and I struck from the road, pressing westward up the steep bank into the more gently rolling fields and woodlots. Company C led the advance, with Company I riding behind and slightly to their right in support. This position kept Company I in view of Company H, commanded by Lieutenant William E. Miller. Fanning out over nearly a full mile of front, Owen's men pressed on. Companies C and I rode over the Smith farm without incident and through a wood to the west, which divided that property from the Michael Miller farm. The only sign of the enemy so far had been a few scattered Rebels who had run away at their approach without firing a shot. Crossing through the woods, Company C rode on until their left reached Miller's farm lane, which ran westward to the house before taking a sharp left turn to the southwest toward the Morrison farm. Guiding left on the farm lane, past the Samuel Poffenberger farm on their right, the Yankee horsemen headed toward the Morrison farm. Barely after passing the Morrison house, however, the war once again found them.[33]

Confederate riflemen—probably Colquitt's skirmishers, concealed in the East Woods—opened on the horsemen as soon as they appeared. Company C's troopers, however, held their ground. Sergeant Thompson Miller, commanding Company C's second platoon, ordered his best marksman, John McCoubrie, to dismount and return fire. Instantly, he and three other privates raced to the fence bordering the eastern edge of the East Woods and opened fire on those targets they could find. Although Sergeant Miller's action perhaps allowed his men to feel useful, it effectively glued the company to this spot. Company I's Captain James Walsh raced forward to undo this error. "Who ordered these men to dismount? This is no place for the men to be off their horses!" Walsh shouted. Miller shot back that he didn't like being a defenseless target but nonetheless, ordered the four back onto their mounts.[34]

***

As Company C resumed advancing, Lieutenant Willard Warren and Sergeant Miller decided to see just what they were up against. Riding swiftly into the southeast edge of the East Woods, the two discovered two Rebel cannon posted in the open field beyond the woods, revealing just how dangerous was their exposed position on the Morrison farm fields. Rejoining their platoons, the two cavalrymen might have considered that what they needed now was infantry. Fortunately, help was already on its way.[35]

Hooker apparently first learned his command was under fire while riding across the Hoffman farm and wasted little time expanding the fight, ordering forward Brigadier General Truman Seymour's Brigade. The 13th Pennsylvania Reserves (commonly called the "Bucktails" for the deer tails these Western Pennsylvanians wore on their caps) deployed on the right of Seymour's line, while the 3rd Pennsylvania Reserves formed on the left. The 13th Reserves was a good choice for this task because the men carried model 1859 Sharps infantry rifles; a breech-loading gun capable of firing roughly five aimed shots a minute rather than the two rounds of a conventional rifled musket. Deploying skirmishers, Seymour's Brigade started forward to support Owen's cavalrymen.[36]

***

Confederates too were reinforcing the fight. Hood's Division came forward from the Hagerstown Pike, buying time for Jackson's Command to complete deploying on Lee's left. Dressing their lines, Hood's veteran column pressed east until reaching the western edge of the East Woods. Deploying there in a battle line, Colonel William T. Wofford's Brigade (it remained Hood's Brigade in the records) held the left of

Hood's Division in the open fields astride the Smoketown Road. On their right was Colonel Evander M. Law's Brigade. Out in front of Law's position, behind the East Woods, was a section of Rhett's Battery from S. D. Lee's artillery.[37]

Well to their rear, the rest of Jackson's Command moved into position about sunset. It filed north, "leaving Sharpsburg to the right," before posting along the ridge north of the Dunker Church. Facing his troops northward on the flanks of the Hagerstown Pike, on high ground west of the road, provided Jackson control of both roads the enemy might use to strike the Confederate left—the Hagerstown Pike itself and the smaller Smoketown Road, that cut in from the northeast—as well as of the open, rolling fields in front of his position. Jackson's Division—commanded by Brigadier General John R. Jones—held the left flank of this position, Jones's Brigade and Grigsby's Stonewall Brigade in the first line; side by side, with Jones's left on a fenced wood line and Grigsby's right on the Hagerstown Pike. Jackson's Division's second line was comprised of Starke's Brigade and Taliaferro's Brigade, similarly side by side with their right on the Hagerstown Pike but hidden under the cover of a woodlot's fenced edge. Out in front of the entire position on a small knoll was Poague's Battery of three guns, two ten-pound Parrot guns and one Napoleon. Ewell's Division deployed behind and on the left flank of Jackson's line. Early's Brigade moved to the far left of Jackson's second line, posting its left on the Poffenberger farm buildings and its right on the left of Starke's Brigade. Behind this strong division-plus sized formation was Hays's Brigade, and in their rear—around the Dunker Church—Lawton's and Trimble's Brigades. Stuart's cavalry held the two or so miles between Jackson's left and the banks of the Potomac River.

Well in front of Jackson's deploying Command, Hood's men readied for battle. Arriving at the eastern fence of Miller's cornfield, Colonel Wofford sent several companies of his 4th Texas forward in skirmish order through the East Woods and into the plowed field beyond, supported by the 5th Texas. Peering through the brush and around tree trunks, the Texans first glimpsed the enemy marching right at them across the plowed field.[38]

***

Colonel Hugh McNeil pressed his 13th Pennsylvania Reserves forward, moving southwest beyond the Hoffman farm. Poor health had forced McNeil in 1857 to leave a promising legal career in New York to pursue a banking career back home in Pennsylvania. Physical troubles couldn't prevent his enlisting as a private to serve the Union, though, nor from rising quickly to become the regiment's colonel. Now he led them cautiously forward through a small strip of woods and into the plowed fields beyond, just west of the Samuel Poffenberger farm buildings, until they reached the Smoketown Road. Deploying his regiment astride the road, McNeil pressed on. Now nearly a mile from its starting point on the Williamsport Road, the 13th Reserves's skirmishers trampled Sam Poffenberger's once neatly plowed fields underfoot. Barely had they crushed a quarter of the field's furrows, when the enemy appeared.[39]

Suddenly, a handful of Rebel cavalry charged from the East Woods, right through McNeil's stunned skirmishers. A scattered volley from the 13th Reserves main body halted the charge, though, sending the cavalry racing for the woods and safety. Starting forward once more, McNeil's command now attracted Rebel infantry and dismounted cavalry fire, again halting them. In an open field, the 13th had only scattered haystacks as protection; then artillery began raining solid and spherical case shot on them from beyond the woods. The Bucktails were trapped in a battlefield purgatory; almost completely exposed and unable to retreat or easily advance, they faced an enemy partly hidden by the woods. McNeil could only reunite his regiment, seeking to better concentrate the rapid firepower of their Sharps infantry rifles.[40]

After a long 15 minutes, the rest of Seymour's Brigade appeared to reinforce McNeil. Directing the 13th Reserves toward the East Woods's fence and its Texas defenders, McNeil cried "Forward, my Bucktails, forward!" and it had the desired effect. 75 yards or so from the woods, however, a Rebel ball slammed into his chest, ending the war and life itself for Colonel Hugh McNeil.[41]

The 13th Reserves, though, kept on as if nothing had happened. Breaking down the remains of a worm fence, they pressed into the woods itself. The Bucktails had seen such action before—on Virginia's peninsula—and as Company F's Captain Dennis McGee recalled, "[h]ere our boys were at home." Guiding around thick trunks and over massive rocks imbedded in the ground, they shoved the 5th Texas out of the woods until the Pennsylvanians could see the white Dunker Church and the tall corn in D. R. Miller's field. Barely could they comprehend what they'd just won when a four-gun Confederate battery opened on them from the grassy field beyond, firing grape and canister. Reforming along the western edge of the Miller cornfield, the 5th Texas joined in pouring Southern fire into the Bucktails's now-ragged line.[42]

"Numerous irregularities of ground & rock sheltered their sharpshooters," reported General Seymour, and "sheltered by these advantages the Rebels kept up a strong & accurate fire" which stalled the Bucktails's advance until the rest of Seymour's Brigade surged into the East Woods, securing it for the Union. The 6th Pennsylvania Reserves shifted from the Bucktails's right and rear, dressing on the 13th's left. Behind them in the woods deployed the 1st Pennsylvania Reserves, adding depth to the new front. Holding Seymour's left, the 5th Pennsylvania Reserves posted in the plowed field, "refusing the left" by angling its left end back to prevent the enemy from easily turning the brigade's exposed flank. Next, Seymour ordered forward Cooper's Battery B of the 1st Pennsylvania Artillery, which had followed the Bucktails down the Smoketown Road; unlimbering west of the road, in the northwest corner of Sam Poffenberger's farmyard, it returned Lane's Georgia Battery's fire.[43]

Having secured the woods, the 6th Reserves, on Seymour's right flank, pressed forward from the woods into D. R. Miller's corn. In so doing, they unknowingly became the first Union troops to enter "the Cornfield." Almost at once, the 6th's veterans discovered a stronger-than-expected Rebel presence—Wofford's Brigade, which had pushed forward to the edge of Miller's field and the East Woods to check the Union advance. Overwhelmed, the 6th Reserves fell back into the woods, stalling Seymour's attack in its tracks.[44]

George Meade had monitored Seymour's advance with intense interest for the last half hour. His original plan envisioned using Seymour to hold back the Rebel cavalry threat on his division's left, while the remaining two brigades—Colonel Albert Magilton's Second Brigade and Lieutenant Colonel Robert Anderson's Third Brigade—marched west to take a ridge on which ran the Hagerstown Pike. Seymour's ongoing firefight meant taking this high ground now would expose the left flank of his two-brigade force. Upon reaching Joseph Poffenberger's barn, Meade's scouts spied Rebel infantry in a woodlot to their south, soon known as the West Woods, indicating the force facing Seymour had reinforcements. Abandoning taking the ridge to support Seymour's fight was the sensible thing to do, although Meade at that moment could have no idea just how hard—and how costly in human lives—it would be for McClellan's army to once again get this close to the ridge.[45]

Meade turned his column south toward the firing; the 3rd Pennsylvania Reserves advancing as skirmishers with the 4th Reserves deployed in a battle line behind. Meade's remaining brigades marched "closed in mass," a formation offering security and flexibility while moving. Reaching the northern edge of the North Woods, Meade's column drove the Rebs away with barely firing a shot. On they swept into the woods, until nearly at its southern edge. Scanning the ground beyond, a grassy field lay before them and beyond that, a ridgeline along which ran a cornfield. In a few hours that cornfield would trouble them greatly but for now their attention focused on a Confederate battery—probably Lane's Battery and a single gun from Blackshear's Battery, commanded by Sergeant Major Robert Falligant—on the field's edge, which was pouring fire into Seymour's right flank. Something had to be done.[46]

Major John Nyce watched horrorstruck at what was happening to his fellow Pennsylvanians in the East Woods. Realizing the Confederate battery lacked infantry to protect it, Nyce ordering his 4th Reserves to "Fix, bayonets!" ahead of an impromptu attack. Colonel Magilton, however, quickly cancelled the attack because the 4th Reserves was Meade's only unit already deployed for battle. Instead, Meade called forward Battery C of the 5th US Artillery, which thundered through the North Woods and into the grassy field beyond. Captain Dunbar Ransom deployed his battery a few rods beyond the southern edge of the North Woods and at right angles to Cooper's Battery to the left, opening fire with case shot on the Confederate guns so troubling Seymour.[47]

Ransom's and Cooper's united artillery fire did the trick and the Confederate battery retreated to the Dunker Church ridge. Now Ransom's Battery and Seymour's Infantry turned on Wofford's exposed Southern infantrymen. Colonel Wofford was so angered that this battery had drawn fire, only to run away and expose his men, that he later reported "I feel it due to truth to state that the enemy were informed of our position by the firing of a half dozen shots from a little battery of ours on the left of the brigade, which hastily beat a retreat as soon as their guns opened upon us."[48]

Shortly, though, Wofford received help from Poague's Battery, atop the ridge on the western side of the Hagerstown Pike. Concentrating fire on Ransom's Battery, the Union guns responded by ignoring Wofford's infantry to counter the Rebel artillery. Joined at Hooker's direction by Simpson's four Napoleons of the 1st Pennsylvania Artillery's Battery A, firing from a slight ridge to the northeast of the East Woods, the three batteries dueled it out until General Meade pulled Ransom's guns back behind the safety of the North Woods, joining the division's infantry on the Joseph Poffenberger farm. Poague's Battery had indeed deflected the threat facing Wofford's exposed infantry, but other Confederates weren't so lucky. Union shells found easy targets among Jackson's men filing into the West Woods in the gathering dark, such as Lieutenant A. M. Gordon of the 9th Louisiana who was killed when a shell tore off both of his legs.[49]

Darkness quickly ended the 16th's fighting. Measured by what lay ahead, the day's human cost had been light but not for those bearing the burden. Perhaps the most significant Confederate loss was Colonel Liddle of the 11th Mississippi, killed while supporting Wofford's Brigade. On the Union side, the fight cost the Bucktails their colonel and 110 officers and men. The 5th Pennsylvania Reserves lost Lieutenant Hardman P. Petrikin after dark when a volley from the 4th Alabama of Trimble's Brigade left him in agony, close to the enemy's pickets. Hearing someone walking nearby who might help him, Petrikin called into the darkness "I am an officer of distinction, an officer of rank, for God's sake come over and send my dying words to my family!" The 4th Alabama's Captain William Robbins was disappointed to find only a lieutenant behind the cry. By any measure, fighting of the 16th was little more than a skirmish, but it nonetheless set the ground and terms for the coming battle.[50]

***

During the night, Jackson's troops continued filling out the left of General Lee's defensive arc. General Lawton led his division—formerly Ewell's Division, renamed for its new commander—from the high ground opposite the Lower Bridge, where no fighting threatened, to form in Jackson's second line near the Dunker Church. General Jackson personally moved Early's Brigade into position holding his second line's left flank, deployed refusing the left. At about the same time, the last of Stuart's cavalry moved into position between the West Wood and the Potomac River. During the dark of night, Fitzhugh Lee's Brigade of Virginians deployed atop Nicodemus Heights, after which Fitz Lee tied his horse to a small tree and lay down to grab what rest he could. Shortly, General Jackson too reached the same spot and joined Lee in sleep, leaning against the base of another nearby tree.[51]

Having slept less than an hour, Jackson was suddenly prodded back to consciousness by John Bell Hood, who likely begged for forgiveness before explaining that the desperate state of his men required this interruption. Save for a half-ration of beef over the last three days, Hood explained, his exhausted men had eaten nothing but green field corn pulled from nearby farms. They'd been on the front line nearly all day and so unable to cook what little they did have to eat. He'd asked General Lee for relief, Hood explained, but Lee lacked replacements and, in any case, only General Jackson might make such a decision about his own Command. Jackson listened quietly and offered to send Lawton's and Trimble's Brigades to replace him, on the condition that Hood promise to support Lawton if called upon. Hood quickly agreed and, with a salute, returned to his division satisfied. By 10:00 Hood's exhausted division fell back from the East Woods and Miller's cornfield to a clearing 200 or so yards beyond the Dunker Church, prompting Hood to ride toward Sharpsburg in search of supply wagons and rations.[52]

As Lawton's Division moved forward through the dark replacing Hood's troops, Lawton's former brigade posted on the left facing north toward the North Woods. Trimble's Brigade, commanded by Colonel James A. Walker, moved into the center of the Confederacy's forward-most line, nearly where Law's Brigade had been. To their immediate rear, Ripley's Brigade, from D. H. Hill's Division, formed to back up Trimble's Brigade. With these three brigades well out front of the main line, Jackson could rest assured the Yankees wouldn't surprise him in the night. It was a much smaller formation, however, that would have the greatest impact on the coming fight.[53]

In front of Trimble's Brigade, two companies of the 31st Georgia—commanded by Lieutenant W. H. Harrison—deployed in skirmish formation moved cautiously eastward through D. R. Miller's fallow field. Reaching the corn, the Georgians pressed into the field another 50 feet before stopping; this put most of their line in the thick corn but the right-most third found itself in the southern tip of the East Woods. With the Yankees of Seymour's Brigade within shouting distance, the Georgians quietly grabbed for the Confederacy a foothold in the East Woods. By morning, this seemingly mundane act would prove to be worth a dozen daring charges.[54]

General Lee, too, must have spent an unpleasant night in his headquarters because his situation was grim. Lee's army faced a numerically superior enemy; his troops were tired, hungry, and had limited ammunition at hand; his rush to consolidate the army at Sharpsburg had winnowed his ranks through straggling, decreasing by nearly half his force available to fight in the morning; he had a river at his back that offered only two crossings to safety and using his one land-based escape route would require exposing his army's flank to the enemy; the enemy's artillery could shell positions deep into his rear with impunity; and he'd surrendered the tactical initiative to McClellan. Reflecting Lee's concerns, at 4:30a.m. Lee directed Brigadier General Nelson Pendleton, his Artillery Reserve chief, that "I desire you to keep some artillery guarding each of the fords at Williamsport, Falling Waters, and Shepherdstown, and have some infantry with it if possible." Ignoring that Pendleton had already been given these orders on the 14th and was unlikely to have infantry to spare, protecting the hard-won communication line and double-ensuring his army's escape routes had been prepared indicates just how heavily the decision to remain and fight weighed on Lee's mind that night. The only bright spots in this dim picture were that his army grew stronger each passing hour as new units arrived, he held interior lines for the coming fight and—most importantly—his Maryland Campaign was still alive.[55]

***

Sometime after dark, General Hooker rode onto the field where Meade's men had fought during the late afternoon. He led the remaining two I Corps divisions over roughly the same route Meade had used. As Doubleday's men moved onto the Joseph Poffenberger farm, they rejoined Brigadier General Marsena R. Patrick's Brigade, already deployed along the Hagerstown Pike. Sent forward to aid Meade's fight, Patrick's men hadn't been engaged but nonetheless suffered a few casualties from Confederate artillery. Doubleday posted Lieutenant Colonel John William Hofmann's Brigade along the road to Patrick's left, perpendicular to the road in order to connect with Meade's right at the North Woods. The rest of Doubleday's men went into bivouac on Joseph Poffenberger's farm fields, immediately north of the North Woods. Hooker's remaining division, under Ricketts, moved into the Samuel Poffenberger woods on both sides of the Smoketown Road, grabbing what sleep they could amidst the trees and rocks. Deployed as pickets behind the infantry and providing security were two squadrons of the 3rd Pennsylvania Cavalry, which remained on this duty throughout the coming battle. Ordered to remain clothed, wearing their accoutrements, and with weapons loaded signaled—if the men needed any such message—that this would be a tense, fitful night. Still, Hooker now had his entire I Corps on the field and ready to resume their drive the next morning.[56]

Hooker established his headquarters that night in Joseph Poffenberger's barn (although confusing it with D. R. Miller's barn in his report). A drizzling rain started falling about 9:00 as Hooker rode to the East Woods's eastern edge to check on Seymour's Brigade and probably to determine if the scattered firing there posed a significant threat. Hooker was surprised to find that "the lines of pickets of the two armies were so near each other as to be able to hear each other walk" but comforted that "Seymour's officers and men [were] keenly alive to their proximity to our enemy and seemed to realize the responsible character of their services for the night. Indeed, their conduct inspired me with the fullest confidence…"[57]

Hooker spent the remaining night in his headquarters and, like his nearby foe Jackson, probably got but little sleep. Unlike Lee and Jackson, Hooker's situation was risky but promising. His force held an advanced position within rife shot of the enemy, anchored on two woodlots. The Union advance had driven the enemy before it with only token resistance and no significant reinforcements had appeared to confront him. Restarting the attack at dawn, his men need advance only a few hundred yards before striking the line they sought to break. Hooker also enjoyed the only real element of surprise left about the morning's battle, determining exactly when and where to attack Jackson's line.[58]

Although General McClellan too probably spent a fitful night, events of the 16th had certainly followed his ordered plan. The day's movement and fighting ensured the battle's critical first phase—threatening and breaking Lee's left flank—was poised to succeed. Hooker had proven himself the aggressive, capable officer McClellan thought him, and the I Corps would awake within easy striking distance of the Confederate left. A message from General Hooker, sent very late that night, promised to renew the attack early the next morning, and McClellan was only too willing to send Hooker the additional reinforcements he wanted, although this would wait until early morning. September 16 had probably gone about as well as George McClellan could have expected, and maybe even better than he'd hoped.[59]

Historians have long been highly critical of McClellan's performance on the 16th, often seeing it as little more than a series of blunders and mistakes. These voices—from participant analysts like Ezra Carman to a host of modern historians—chiefly complain that by moving his army across the Antietam so late in the day, McClellan left too little daylight in which to attack and worse, alerted Lee of his intentions and provided his enemy nearly eight hours to prepare a defense. Ezra Carman nicely summarized this view when he wrote "[McClellan, through Hooker's actions] had given Lee complete and reliable information as to [his] intentions on the morrow." These critics, however, miss the point.[60]

Certainly, McClellan knew such a large, three-pronged assault by nearly his entire army couldn't be carried to conclusion in the few remaining hours on September 16. McClellan's comments to Hooker that day that "there should be an attack upon the rebel army in the centre and on the left the next morning" reflect as much. McClellan must also have expected the Union crossing would be detected before nightfall, given how far forward he pushed Hooker's corps late that day. Why then did he not wait until morning to send Hooker forward?[61]

Although we cannot discount the entire move was a tremendous blunder—McClellan never explained his decision—more likely, McClellan probably actually wanted Lee to know about and react to the attack on his left. Such awareness and time to respond would compel Lee to move troops to resist the Union assault, weakening other portions of his line, particularly at McClellan's still-unrevealed main objective in the Confederate center. Letting Lee so prepare would certainly make the opening attack more difficult and costlier, but Hooker's men only needed to reach the Dunker Church ridge, not defeat the entire Confederate army and McClellan had already offered Hooker reinforcements, with potentially more to come. It was a risk but, like all of McClellan's plan at Antietam, a calculated one. If, indeed, telegraphing his intentions and objectives to Lee was McClellan's intention, then by dark on September 16, he was more successful then he could have hoped.[62]

One important change in McClellan's leadership style after September 16 was his shift from detail-oriented micromanagement to a detached, deferential approach to the coming battle's maneuvering and engagements. He'd spent part of the day deploying individual batteries but having crafted his plan and launched the battle, George McClellan now largely stepped out of the machine he'd set in motion, leaving it to his subordinates—Hooker, initially, later Mansfield, Sumner, Burnside, and Porter—to make the plan work. The implication of this shift was that the Union plan would either hold together by its preconceived, deliberate, step-by-step application or it would not hang together at all. There would be almost no careful adjustment of actions and movements by its architect, as Lee would do throughout the day on the opposite side of the field. Instead, all would depend on the skill and energy of Joe Hooker and his I and XII Corps officers to implement McClellan's plan just as intended. Now, only time and many lives would tell if this approach would work.

CHAPTER 4

America's Bloodiest Day Dawns: Midnight to Sunrise

The night that brought into being the single bloodiest day in American history was hardly one anyone would choose as their last on earth. Drizzling precipitation started around 9:00 on the 16th, building into a solid rain by midnight. General Hooker called the night "dark and drizzly," a view many men shared. Despite the weather and the pall of impending battle, many soldiers slept unusually well. Newly minted Corporal Austin Stearns of the 13th Massachusetts's Company K recalled "I was tired, and sitting down soon lay down, falling asleep immediately; the last thing I remember was some horses of a neighboring battery stamping and their shoes striking fire on the rocks. The skirmishers were busy all night, so twas said, but I did not hear them, and as there was no alarm given I slept soundly till morning…" The 124th Pennsylvania's Sergeant Charles Broomhall—like others in his regiment, this would be his first battle—wrote "We lay down about 11 o'clock for the night along with thousands of others who were unconsciously taking their last earthy repose. Sorrowful to contemplate it." A veteran in the 35th New York from Patrick's Brigade complained matter-of-factly "throwing out pickets we lay there until morning, not resting, however, on account of the alarms during the night."[1]

***

Across the Hagerstown Pike, Confederate troops too spent a restless night of anticipation. One soldier of Hood's 4th Texas recalled "Here we lay down on the ground and let the shells fly over us, looking like balls of fire in the heavens. I don't know how long this lasted, for I went to sleep…" The 5th Virginia's Major Hazel Williams wrote of the artillery firing that night "The display was grand, and comparatively harmless, except to the stragglers in the far rear." Colonel Grigsby's orderly Ezra Stickley was less troubled by Yankee artillery than by an annoying discovery. Walking the line to ensure the Stonewall Brigade's men put fresh caps on their muskets, Stickley suddenly realized his right buckskin glove of a brand-new pair was missing, never to be found again.[2]

***

The men of Mansfield's XII Corps were kept awake by marching. Sometime late on September 16, General Sumner reluctantly complied with McClellan's order advancing the remaining corps of his wing across the Antietam to join and support Hooker's I Corps. By 11:30, the first of Mansfield's regiments were moving toward the Upper Bridge crossing. The 27th Indiana's Edmond Brown recalled "The awakening was not by the usual method of squeaking fife and rattling drum. On the contrary, officers went to the low tents of the men and, stooping down, called in subdued tones. All fires or lights were prohibited, and orders were stringent against noises of any kind. Packing up quickly, the column moved stealthily in murky darkness. No conversation, except whispers, being permitted, there was nothing to do, but each to follow his file leaders and meditate upon the situation." Plodding through the rain along the Williamsport Road for nearly a mile, they turned left and marched westward through fields and woodlots for a short distance. Finally, around 2:30, on September 17, the XII Corps stopped and went into bivouac on the plowed fields between the Line and Hoffman farms to the north and northeast, and the Samuel Poffenberger farm to the southwest. As 20-year-old Abiel Edwards of the 29th Maine recalled they "halted us on a ploughed feild close to where our Pickets were fighting all night. [W]e had the privilage of sleeping the remainder of the night on the ploughed ground…" Nearby, corps commander Major General Joseph K. F. Mansfield spread his blankets in a corner of one of the Line farm's fields, joining his men in grabbing a few hours of fitful sleep. Some, like those 10th Maine men cautioned by Mansfield to lower their voices to a whisper, remained awake throughout the night, talking and smoking, fueled by nerves and anxiety for what dawn would bring. Though a short night, most men in the XII Corps—like their experienced counterparts in the nearby I Corps—grabbed what rest and sleep they could.[3]

Few awaiting the coming battle that morning probably knew the significance of September 17 in their shared history. That day in 1787 the Constitutional Convention in Philadelphia had completed signing the young nation's new constitution. Adoption of this historic pact between very different states had staved off internecine conflict, transforming a loose collection of shared interests into a unified nation that had, if imperfectly, grown together, waged war together, and protected and advanced the experiment in democracy launched by Washington, Franklin, Madison, and the other Founding Fathers. On September 17, only a few hundred miles away and 75 years earlier, bonds had been formed between the states. Now, the resolve of a new generation to either preserve or to end those bonds was about to tested in the fields around Sharpsburg.

By 3:00, George McClellan had on his right flank a force both large and experienced enough to spearhead his opening attack on the Confederate left. The 8,372 men of the XII Corps nearly doubled Hooker's force, to 17,815 men under arms. They would face Stonewall Jackson's roughly 14,320 men (later swelled by 2,961 when McLaws's Division arrived). Although McClellan certainly was unaware of Hooker's slight manpower advantage, his selection of the XII Corps as Hooker's reinforcements reflect yet another indication of careful preparation. Although the XII Corps was comprised mostly of inexperienced men in newly formed regiments—only Brigadier General George S. Greene's Division included significant numbers of veteran troops—the battle-tested I Corps would spearhead the assault, leading the new men by steady example. Moving quietly in the sound-muffling rain, the XII Corps arrived largely unnoticed by the enemy, giving the Union an element of surprise even if an unintended one.[4]

At the same time, McClellan's command structure remained far from seamless on the eve of battle. Although his corps had been operating as independent entities for nearly a week, McClellan hadn't formally abolished the two-corps wings created when leaving Washington. These large, independent commands had been useful sweeping through Maryland in search of Lee's army but had grown increasingly cumbersome, unnecessarily tying McClellan's hands when planning the coming battle, and McClellan had begun gradually undoing the wings. On the 15th, McClellan had "temporarily suspended" Burnside's wing and directed Hooker (and presumably his I Corps) to report to army headquarters; now placing Hooker's I Corps on the opposite end of the Union line from its nominal wing commander was a strong signal to Burnside that the wings—and his own elevated position—no longer existed in practice. Ordering the XII Corps to the right sent the same message to General Sumner. However, McClellan failed to issue a clear, written order abolishing the wing commands and worse, he periodically acted as if the two-corps wings still existed. McClellan's order directing the XII Corps forward went not to corps commander Mansfield but rather to General Sumner, its wing commander. Equally confusing, by placing Hooker in de facto command of two full corps on the Union right, McClellan had created a new "wing command" of sorts. Retaining Sumner and his II Corps on the eastern bank of the Antietam made clear who now commanded the XII Corps, but who was in command when Sumner appeared at the front, as he would later in the day? McClellan could ill-afford this avoidable confusion on the eve of battle.[5]

General Hooker had promised McClellan yesterday that "the battle would be renewed at the earliest dawn," but making good on this promise required creating a workable attack plan for his two corps. First, though, Hooker needed intelligence about the field, the location of his own troops, and those of the enemy. Leaving his headquarters in the thick of night, apparently with George Meade in tow, Hooker intended to personally gather this information and lay the attack's final groundwork. Reaching the edge of the North Woods, the two generals surveyed the ground—what they could see of it—and discussed the situation.[6]

Whatever Joe Hooker learned from Meade, this darkness-shrouded reconnaissance probably did more harm than good to his planning. The ride gave Hooker updated tactical intelligence about his corps' position, but darkness prevented obtaining an accurate picture of the terrain on which his impending attack would occur. Hooker later admitted he was preparing to fight on "country of which we were profoundly ignorant." What lay before him in the dark was a broad, open series of fields bounded on three sides by woods, which offered considerable space for maneuver in division-sized units. However, unable to see the actual ground and assuming the terrain here was similar to the series of small woodlots and fields he'd passed through the day before, Hooker decided that "[t]he cleared space between the forests necessitated a change in my front from a division to a brigade." Ignorance of the terrain prompted Hooker to limit the overall mass of his coming assault, diminishing the manpower and firepower weight of his main attacking unit from a roughly 8,000-man division to a 2,500-man brigade.[7]

Hooker compounded this error by ignoring intelligence that should have been obvious from his ride. Throughout the night, skirmishers of Seymour's Brigade continued trading a scattered fire with counterparts from Lawton's and Trimble's Brigades on the edge of the East Woods, which Hooker later cited as the reason for surveying his lines in the dark. Although what Hooker learned of the enemy before him remains uncertain, the presence of a broad front of Confederate skirmishers alone should have tipped him to the presence of another, nearer, large body of infantry. Hooker in turn should have sought to learn the size and location of this force, particularly determining if it would affect the attack plan he was then crafting. Hooker, however, apparently ignored this significant intelligence. Regardless what they learned on this reconnaissance, Hooker and Meade returned to the I Corps headquarters in the damp darkness to set in motion the battle of Antietam's opening attack.[8]

Before daybreak, General Doubleday, peering through his binoculars, could see silhouetted against the lightening sky outlines of Rebel batteries on Nicodemus Heights readying for action. What must have more horrified the general was that his still-sleeping division—scattered, slumbering on a hill south of the Sam Poffenberger farm and well within the guns' range—was clearly their intended target. Instantly, Doubleday was on his horse, racing to warn his men. Riding the lines of Gibbon's and Phelps's Brigades, he called indiscriminately for the men to rise up and move back. Suddenly, cries of nearly every officer in the division roused the men, who surged as an amorphous blob back toward the safety of Poffenberger's nearby barn. Atop the hill, the Danville and the Staunton Artillery trained their four guns—each battery had only two—on the blue mass below, as soon too did the Alleghany Battery. But it was the Staunton Artillery—commanded by Lieutenant A. W. Garber—that probably first opened on the Yankees below.[9]

The first round exploded harmlessly above Gibbon's men, adding forcefully to the officers' warning message. Nearing Poffenberger's barn, two more shells came through the dark, the last of these crashing to earth amidst one of Sam Poffenberger's threshing machines and sending jagged shards of metal flying wildly through

Gibbon's Brigade. When the smoke cleared, three men of the 6th Wisconsin were dead. Like that shell, they were a first this day—the first of thousands of Union casualties to fall before Rebel artillery. Eleven more of Gibbon's men were soon killed or wounded in this opening Confederate barrage. Because these guns were beyond the range of Doubleday's infantry, his only hope for silencing them was to get his own artillery into action, and shortly, Doubleday deployed his guns on the slope between the North Woods and the Hagerstown Pike, before they began lobbing shells though the dim morning light. Simpson's 1st Pennsylvania, Battery A quickly added its fire from north of the Joseph Poffenberger barn. It took Union gunners a bit longer to find their targets, though, and the first shells flew beyond the crest of Nicodemus Heights, completely missing their mark. These rounds instead found Lieutenant Colonel John T. Thornton, resting with his 3rd Virginia Cavalry behind the hill. Killed before he knew he was under fire; Colonel Thornton became the first Confederate victim of the day's Union artillery fire.[10]

***

In response, artillery all over the field opened fire. Joining Stuart's guns, S. D. Lee's six batteries near the Dunker Church fired at Yankees in the two woods in their front. Joined by fresh batteries brought in late the previous day, Lee now possessed a formidable line of firepower. Holding his right flank on the Mumma farm lane was the Ashland Artillery (Woolfolk's Battery) of two Parrott guns, to their left was Brooks's Artillery (Rhett's Battery, commanded by Lieutenant William Elliot) with two Parrot guns, Parker's Battery and its two ordnance rifles, and a bit farther to their left was the Bedford Artillery (Jordan's Battery) with a three-inch ordnance rifle, a Parrott gun, and a 12-pound howitzer. The Confederate artillery line continued on across the Hagerstown Pike with Patterson's Battery B of the Sumter Artillery and its six howitzers. Farther left, in the field before the West Woods, was Brockenbrough's Baltimore Battery of two ordnance rifles and one howitzer. Well in front of Lee's main Southern artillery line was Poague's Rockbridge Artillery with two Parrott guns and a Napoleon (guessing the Yankees would soon come to him, Poague swapped his long-range Parrot guns for two short-range howitzers, pulled from Raine's nearby battery). All told, the Confederate artillery line before the Dunker Church comprised 21 guns. Facing them on the western side of the Antietam was a Union artillery force that—for now—was nearly equal in size. Doubleday's entire artillery component—four batteries, comprised of 18 Napoleons and three three-inch ordnance rifles—all fired at Confederates on the I Corps's right. Soon, even more Union shells began raining onto the field, as if dropping from heaven. The dozens of batteries lining the eastern bank of the Antietam had opened without any apparent reason other than to join the growing bombardment.[11]

Doubleday's batteries covered the Nicodemus farm with shells meant for Southern troops posted around it, but unknowingly flushed from the Nicodemus's stone-walled house a group of women and children. To cavalryman William Blackford they seemed "like a flock of birds…, hair streaming in the wind and children of all ages stretched out behind. Every time one would fall, the rest thought it was the result of cannon shot and ran the faster." Seeing they'd only increased their danger by leaving the house, Blackford raced to their aid; gathering them, he escorted the women and children safely to the rear. Blackford later recorded, with satisfaction, that the Union gunners ceased firing long enough for the innocent victims to move to safety.[12]

D. R. Miller's farm was empty now, save for a single large bull which had refused being driven to safety the night before. The randomly exploding artillery rounds apparently changed the animal's mind and it bolted from the barn, "smashed through the barnyard gate, and with flaming eyes and waving tail charged along through the entire length of the cornfield…" according to Alexander Davis, one of the Nicodemus farm hands.[13]

Other Union artillery fire wasn't random at all. The lightening sky outlined wig-wagging flags of the Confederate signal station in the steeple of Sharpsburg's Lutheran church, drawing Union shells like moths to a flame. As shelling resumed, the seemingly deserted town sprang to life once again and the remaining civilians raced for cover. "[The] cannon shot from the enemy literally rak[e] the streets and batter houses," wrote one Confederate in town at dawn that morning. Women and children were "running, crying, and screaming so loud that their combined voices could be heard above the roaring battle… It was sad to see so many people deserting their homes … Narrow-souled men were seen nailing up their cellars and smoke house doors to prevent starved soldiers from taking advantage of their absence and helping themselves to something to eat … I saw middle aged women running through the streets literally dragging their children after them; the little fellows had to take such tremendous strides that it seemed to me they hit the ground but seldom. Then came a dozen young ladies, each with a stuffed sack under each arm, some of which in their haste they had forgotten to tie, and as they ran the unmentionables were scattered behind them." One young girl ran crazily through the streets with no seeming objective, screaming madly at the approach of each new round. At the same moment, an older black man was seen running through the streets wearing a kettle as a makeshift helmet.[14]

Not every Sharpsburg resident fled the carnage, though. Henry Kyd Douglas recalled young Savilla Miller calmly standing on her family's front porch early in the day amidst the barrage. "It gave one an odd sensation to witness it," he recalled, and tried persuading her to seek shelter. "I will remain here as long as our army is between me and the Yankees. Won't you have a glass of water?" Stunned, Douglas accepted the water and watched as "a shell with a shriek in its flight came over the hill … [but] over the face of the heroic girl only a feint shadow passed." Savilla remained on her porch until well past noon, apparently buoyed by patriotic secessionist fervor. A group of Confederates found an old couple sitting on their back porch, calmly watching the carnage unfold before them. When the soldiers advised they leave, "the old man replied that they had no place to go, that this had been their home all their lives ... and they would rather die here than leave it; he had not done the Rebels any harm ... that they should not come and drive him out of his house; no they would not go; they intended to stay. 'Do we not?' he added, appealing to his aged spouse, who only answered with an emphatic nod." Another Sharpsburg resident, Henry Hebb, remained to sightsee, taking shelter in the door frame of a building on the town square. When a 12-pound solid shot tore through the spot, moments after he slipped farther into the building, Hebb decided he'd had enough and fled the shelling tearing his hometown apart.[15]

**

Potentially the most important immediate result of the Union shelling was a single round that killed no one. Brigadier General John R. Jones recalled "[i]t was during this almost unprecedented iron storm that a shell exploded a little above my head, and so stunned and injured me that I was rendered unfit for duty, and retired from the field, turning over command to Brigadier General William E. Starke..." Command of Jackson's Division—fully half of Jackson's two-division force holding Lee's left flank—had changed in an instant, testing the strength and flexibility of Jackson's command structure and Starke's own skills. This much William Starke knew as he accepted command; what he could not know was the effect this "promotion" would have on his very life.[16]

Virginian William Starke had suddenly found himself in command but was more than prepared for this moment. Leaving behind a successful New Orleans cotton brokerage, Starke was commissioned a colonel and aide to General Robert S. Garnett, until Garnett's death at Corrick's Ford on July 13, 1861. Starke then assumed command of the 60th Virginia Infantry, which he led though the regiment's baptism at the Seven Days Battle. At Mechanicsville, Colonel Starke suffered a severe wound but was so determined to resume his duty that three days later he was back with his regiment, leading them at Frayser's Farm (or Glendale). Recognizing his skill and dedication, William was promoted to brigadier general on August 6, 1862, and assigned command of the second Louisiana Brigade in Jackson's Division. Barely three weeks later, Starke was commanding a division, replacing General William Taliaferro upon his wounding at Second Manassas. Those men of General Jones's Division aware of the sudden change might well have been confident—if not perhaps relieved—at having Brigadier General William Starke as their new division commander.[17]

This artillery was wreaking havoc, but mostly to the town and the nerves of infantrymen who would soon march through this fire. Harnessing the massive barrage's full power would have aided both Union and Confederate prospects, but from a tactical standpoint, it was so disconnected from Lee's or McClellan's immediate plans that this initial artillery fire was little more than a deadly sideshow; a warm-up before the day's main event—the Union infantry assault.[18]

Hooker probably planned this attack sometime overnight. His I Corps would drive across the open fields between the east and west woodlots, striking for the small, white Dunker Church as their objective. Reaching the church would put Hooker's corps at once within Lee's line and atop the ridge commanding the rest of Lee's position north of Sharpsburg. Once there, they could turn south toward Sharpsburg and roll up what remained of Lee's line. Hooker certainly had to consider and adjust for Lee's use of reinforcements to resist his attack, at least until Burnside's corresponding attack on the Confederate right could begin and take some pressure from his front. Hooker by that time almost certainly had already decided the role his corps' three divisions would each play. Doubleday's Division, on the right, would drive nearly due south along the Hagerstown Pike toward the church, while Ricketts's Division, on the left, would strike diagonally across the open field for the same objective. Meade's Division, in the center, would form the reserve, ready to reinforce success or hold off disaster if the attack failed. It was a classic West Point-taught attack, sending two divisions forward to maximize the corps' attacking power and holding one division in reserve.

Hooker's plan was as well-suited to potentially achieving his objective as it was fatally flawed. In its favor, Hooker's plan could be easily understood by his senior officers and maximized his attacking force's striking power by giving both divisions the same objective. The small but bright-white Dunker Church was a clearly understood, shared objective that every I Corps officer and man could easily see from nearly any point on the field, diminishing some of the "fog of war" confusion that would inevitably appear. Further reducing confusion and streamlining communication, Hooker directed the attacking units to advance independently, requiring no coordination beyond their immediate division chain of command. Hooker also ensured the two attacking divisions would launch their assaults simultaneously, creating independent coordination of their actions. Even an element of surprise was built into the attack, improving its prospects. Though Lee would know—and already knew—an attack was coming against his left, he could not know exactly where Union troops would strike until they were nearly upon it. By the time Lee or Jackson realized the objective was the high ground around the Dunker Church, it would be too late to do much more than dig in and fight.

Nonetheless, Hooker's faulty understanding of the situation facing his attacking force sowed the seeds of looming failure. Hooker apparently remained convinced the ground allowed maneuver by brigades alone—not entire divisions—and both

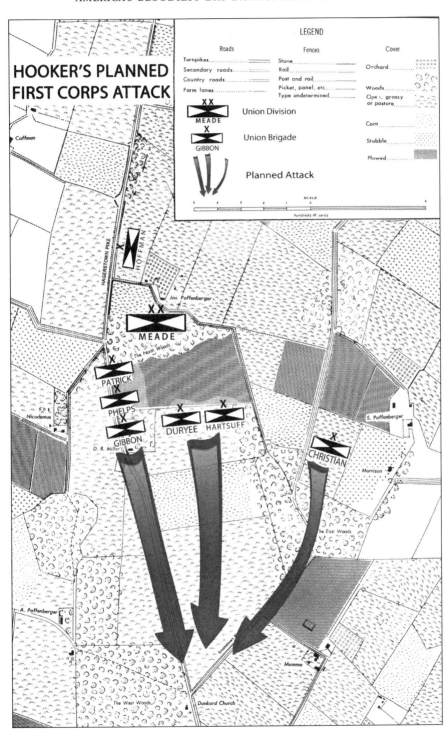

Doubleday's and Ricketts's reports clearly state Hooker ordered them to maintain no larger than a two-brigade front. This ensured McClellan's opening assault would consist of no more than four brigades, throwing away the numerical superiority and mass the Union host enjoyed in the fields around Sharpsburg. By striking at the Dunker Church position, near the center of Jackson's actual line, Hooker played into Lee's advantage afforded by interior lines, greatly increasing the weight of Confederate opposition his attackers would face to simply reach the church. Worse, Hooker had no idea that in the dark the previous night, Jackson had deployed three brigades in advance of, and perpendicular to, the main Southern line, facing exactly north—the direction from which Hooker's attacking brigades would come. Hooker's attackers were unknowingly walking into the center of a Rebel vice.

Once Hooker informed his three division commanders of their respective roles, they in turn chose the brigades leading the assault. Spearheading General Doubleday's assault, on the right, would be Brigadier General John Gibbon's Brigade. Thirty-five-year-old Gibbon graduated in the same West Point Class of 1847 as now-Confederate General A. P. Hill and Union Major General Ambrose Burnside. He'd fought in Mexico and against the Seminole Indians in Florida, as well as spending five years at West Point as an artillery instructor. His early Civil War service included a stint as Irvin McDowell's artillery chief, and he'd received his general's star the previous May 2nd. It was his command of this brigade—a Midwestern unit, comprised of the 2nd, 6th, and 7th Wisconsin regiments and the 19th Indiana—that had cemented his reputation as a fighting general. The brigade earned the sobriquet the "Black Hat Brigade" because, unlike other volunteer units, Gibbon dressed his men in the Regular Army style—knee-length frock coats and broad-brimmed, tall back hats—and insisted on Regular Army discipline, too. They'd demonstrated their skill when facing down the Stonewall Brigade at the Brawner Farm, opening fighting at the second battle of Manassas. On South Mountain, they earned a new nickname, based not on their attire but rather on their fighting skill in confronting Colquitt's entrenched Georgians at Turner's Gap—the Iron Brigade.[19]

On the field's opposite end, Brigadier General James B. Ricketts chose the brigade under Brigadier General George L. Hartsuff to lead his attack. A New Yorker, Hartsuff graduated 19th in West Point's Class of 1852 and had commanded detachments fighting Indians in Florida before the war. Starting the Civil War as a second lieutenant in the 2nd US Artillery, his exemplary service in the Department of the Ohio, Western Virginia, the Mountain Department, and the Shenandoah Department sent him soaring through the ranks. Of Ricketts's three brigade commanders, Hartsuff was the natural choice to guide his attack.[20]

Supporting Hartsuff were Ricketts's remaining two brigades, commanded by Brigadier General Abram Duryee and Colonel William H. Christian, both hailing from New York. Abram Duryee was born April 29, 1815 and became a highly successful importer of goods to New York City. First joining the 27th New York

State Militia as a private in 1833, by 1849 Duryee had risen to become its colonel and held the post for the next 14 years. With the outbreak of civil war, Duryee used his considerable military leadership skills and personal connections to raise the 5th New York; a regiment that soon became "Duryee's Zouaves" and was distinguished on any battlefield by the men's bright red, fanciful North African-style uniforms. It was their fighting skill on Chinn Ridge at the second battle of Manassas, not their fancy dress, which earned Duryee's command its reputation as one of the toughest, hardest-fighting units in the Union army. Duryee's leadership and military skills quickly elevated him to brigade command in Ricketts's Division and to promotion to brigadier general on February 7, 1962.[21]

William Henry Christian, too, started in the ranks, though he didn't enjoy the same civilian success as had Abram Duryee. Joining the 7th New York Volunteer Infantry as a private during the Mexican War, Christian rose by war's end in 1848 to be a first sergeant. At the outbreak of the Civil War, Christian was tapped to serve as colonel of the new 26th New York in May 1861. On August 30, 1862—filling a sudden command vacancy created during fighting at Second Manassas—he assumed a brigade command in the Army of Virginia's III Corps, which became Hooker's I Corps in the Army of the Potomac. While Duryee gained experience as a brigade commander for over a year, William Christian had been in his post for barely two weeks. It was this difference in command experience—as well as something intangible which hadn't yet revealed itself in the predawn hours of September 17—that would starkly separate these men with otherwise so much in common.[22]

Growing daylight and perhaps the widening artillery duel caused the long-running infantry skirmishing to boil over into a general firefight. Seymour's Brigade countered annoying fire from skirmishers of Lawton's Brigade—two 31st Georgia companies commanded by Lieutenant Harrison—by pushing from the East Woods into the western end of the cornfield before them, capturing Lieutenant Harrison as an added prize. Without a commander and having learned how treacherous command and control was going to be in this fight, the Georgians were recalled and joined Lawton's and Trimble's Brigades, waiting silently along the southern border of the corn. The 13th Pennsylvania Reserves pushed into a void as far as the Smoketown Road, where they discovered a large body of troops. Opening a "fire, at will" upon the weak flank of Trimble's Brigade, the rest of Seymour's Brigade moved up to aid the 13th. At the same time, the 5th Pennsylvania Reserves pressed around the rear of the 13th Reserves—clearing Confederates completely out of the East Woods—and continued forward until they crossed the Smoketown Road. Posting their right on the 13th's left they, too, opened fire on the flank of Trimble's Brigade. Colonel Walker's five regiments of Trimble's Brigade got the worst of this fire, unlike the wooded Yankee position, they had been in the open field for hours with no cover at all but the darkness to hide them. That, too, was now gone.[23]

***

Stephen D. Lee could see Trimble's Brigade's plight and resolved to do something about it. Two guns of Jordan's Battery soon raced forward, but barely had they unlimbered in the rear of Trimble's Brigade when they discovered the Union had batteries on this side of the creek, too. Hooker had closely watched Seymour's action and quickly ordered General Ricketts—soon to be attacking from that direction anyway—to support Seymour's fight. Pushing forward Ricketts's entire division, Hooker directed artillery to deploy on the ridge immediately in front of—south of—the North Woods. In response, Captain Ezra W. Matthews's 1st Pennsylvania Light Artillery, Battery F, moved forward from its bivouac in Samuel Poffenberger's woods to the clearing between the North and East Woods. Before deploying there, however, Captain Matthews found a better position and ordered his men forward once more. When finally unlimbering their guns, Battery F found itself in a very exposed position; the ridge just south of the North Woods. Shortly, though, Matthews's guns poured a deadly accurate fire onto the beleaguered men of Trimble's Brigade. Within minutes, Captain James Thompson's 1st Pennsylvania Light Artillery, Battery C, moved from the North Woods to join Matthews's men, deploying on their right before opening on S. D. Lee's batteries. Before barely five rounds were fired, though, Thompson realized Confederate guns in the rear of Trimble's Brigade by the East Woods—Jordan's Battery—were dropping shells with increasing accuracy on their position, so Thompson turned his fire on Jordan's guns. Nonetheless, Trimble's Brigade's situation remained desperate and making matters even worse, Thompson's fire drove away their only help, the two guns of Jordan's Battery.[24]

The minutes in that exposed position must have seemed like hours to Walker's men. Finally, Union fire slackened a bit; men in Trimble's Brigade could see the Yankee regiment on the right—the 13th Pennsylvania Reserves, running low on ammunition—pulling back. Even better, the 5th Pennsylvania Reserves, too, ceased firing and formed into a column before marching for the rear. Walker's men could not have known it but confusion—the "fog of war"—had bought them a brief break. The 5th Reserves's Colonel Fisher, from an obscured position across the field, assumed the 13th Reserves's had been driven away by superior Confederate fire then underway farther to his right. To avoid exposing his own flank, Fisher moved his command to the rear, too, intending to reform near Samuel Poffenberger's spring. Walker's respite proved only too temporary, however, when the 2nd Pennsylvania Reserves flooded into the gap, opening an even greater fire than before. Worse, Union batteries firing from the other side of the Antietam soon gained the range of Trimble's Brigade. Taking heavy musketry from their front and with shells raining in from positions they couldn't even see, much less respond to, things seemingly couldn't get much worse for Colonel Walker and his men.[25]

Although Jackson's artillery was his position's backbone in the early hours of September 17, artillery alone would never stop a concerted Union infantry attack.

With the Yankees enjoying superior numbers, Southern infantry would have to put itself in order—soon. Even with recent adjustments, Jackson's line was weak and poorly deployed. Lawton's Brigade held the center of the grassy field, commanding a wide and long field of fire before him, but both flanks were vulnerable. On Lawton's right, a 120-yard gap remained between his command and Trimble's Brigade; on the left, a nearly 200-yard gap existed between Lawton's left and the right flank of the Stonewall Brigade, which faced north on the west side of the Hagerstown Pike. Given this, General Lawton certainly understood his ability to hold this spot grew more tenuous by the minute.

Needing to do something, Lawton sent a verbal order advancing Brigadier General Harry T. Hays's Brigade out of the woods north of the Dunker Church and onto the field. At the same time, he sent a message warning General Hood to ready his division to advance and support Lawton's men. Lawton apparently wanted Hays to plug the 120-yard gap on Lawton's Brigade's right; however, confusion over Lawton's order instead sent Hays to "a point in our lines yet unoccupied." Hays marched his men uncertainly forward and sent a staffer to sort out where they were supposed to be. After three moves, General Lawton finally settled things by posting Hays behind Lawton's Brigade, commanded in Lawton's stead by Colonel Marcellus Douglass.[26]

Despite Marcellus Douglass's brief military career, few in Lee's ranks were more able in command or more devoted to the Confederate cause. After attending Georgia's 1861 succession convention, Douglass formed the Randolph Volunteers, serving as their captain, even after merging into the 13th Georgia that June as its Company E. Barely three weeks later, Marcellus became the 13th's second-in-command and promoted to lieutenant colonel. In this role, he served in western Virginia's Kanawha Valley and later on the Georgia coast, after the regiment was recalled home. When the 13th's commander died, Douglass instantly assumed command and was promoted to colonel on February 1, 1862. He ably led the 13th Georgia through terrific combat at Gaines's Mill and Malvern Hill. Assigned to Lawton's Brigade in Ewell's Division during Lee's 1862 Virginia Campaign, Colonel Douglass assumed brigade command when Lawton replaced the wounded Ewell; a role he slipped into easily and naturally. Marcellus Douglass stood once again with his men as they faced another battle, this time on D. R. Miller's farm fields.[27]

The sun first appeared at 5:53, quickly burning off the misty ground fog blanketing the terrain once again. Although it was a comfortable 65 degrees at dawn, the temperature would reach nearly 75, making the day only a little warmer than normal for this time of year. What was occurring on the fields around Sharpsburg, however, was anything but normal. Everyone within miles of the town already knew that; what they didn't yet know was just how unusual this day would become.[28]

CHAPTER 5

The Cornfield: Ricketts's Division Opens the Ball

Hooker's attacking I Corps brigades were moving even as sunlight first poked through the clouds. Charles Davis, of the 13th Massachusetts in Hartsuff's Brigade, recalled, "It was a gray, misty morning, and like the girl who was called to be Queen of the May, we were called early." Corporal Austin Sterns, Davis's compatriot in the 13th Massachusetts, added "each army was astir early and preparing for the deadly struggle that the lowest private knew was to take place, without building any fire to cook our coffee or anything else, but simply eating our dry hard bread. We were prepared for what was to come."[1]

Although the previous night, General Hooker had missed Jackson's two brigades south of Miller's cornfield, by dawn, sunlight revealed their presence. In response, Hooker—or perhaps Ricketts, acting in his stead—altered the plan slightly. Hartsuff's and Duryee's Brigades would still advance through the open field but now strike Lawton's line frontally; Christian's Brigade would move along the eastern edge of the East Woods until reaching the Smoketown Road, then turn west to hit Lawton's line in flank. Once reunited, Ricketts's Division would head for the church. This new approach skillfully employed the maneuver of a pincer attack and the increased mass of two brigades carrying out a frontal assault to clear away Lawton's men. Regardless who ordered this change, it failed to consider only one variable—human frailty.[2]

Almost immediately, the human weakness in Hooker's plan appeared. All seemed well as Hartsuff's and Duryee's Brigades reached Joseph Poffenberger's farm's fields, where they faced left and prepared to move south toward Lawton's waiting Confederates. Deploying his brigade in a battle front—the 12th, 11th, 13th Massachusetts, and 33rd New York, formed from right to left—Hartsuff halted, possibly to wait for Duryee's Brigade to appear on his right. General Hartsuff used this time to reconnoiter the ground over which he would be attacking, but once into D. R. Miller's plowed field, a single round fired by a Southern sharpshooter found him. Though the wound would not prove mortal, it stripped away Ricketts's most capable and experienced brigade commander at just the moment Hooker's attack was getting underway.[3]

General Duryee, however, was almost certainly ignorant of Hartsuff's wounding and started his brigade forward, as ordered. Duryee led his command south through the North Woods, passing through Magilton's men lying among the trees for relief from the relentless Confederate shelling and, when in Miller's plowed field, deployed the brigade in a column of divisions, each of his four regiments in its own battle line. At the same time, it aligned on the right of Hartsuff's now-immobile brigade and stopped there for nearly five minutes. Like Hartsuff's and Magilton's men, Duryee's Brigade instantly became a Confederate artillery target. "[T]he enemy shell and round shot flying around us like hail, killing and wounding some of our poor fellows" explained the 107th Pennsylvania's Captain James MacThomson. Fourteen-year-old John Delaney, also serving in the 107th, recalled "the rain of shot and shell from the vicinity of the Dunker Church was fearful." Then, they were moving forward. Perhaps General Duryee moved them to limit damage from the Rebel artillery fire or maybe confusion was already setting in. Regardless, without waiting for Hartsuff's Brigade to join them, Duryee pressed his men onward, deeper into D. R. Miller's grassy field.[4]

Alone, Duryee's men marched through Miller's open field as Rebel artillery rained shells down on them, tearing holes in their lines and ripping apart the lives of those fathers and sons, husbands and brothers whose bodies made those lines. These men, however, were veterans who'd experienced such horrors before, so they tried as best they could to ignore the sound of the shells, simply "dressing down" to fill the gaps those shells created. Onward they pressed, into a swale so deep it swallowed the North Woods from view of those few who might have looked to the rear. Once at the swale's base they were briefly hidden from view of Confederate artillery on the Dunker Church ridge, though not from guns on Nicodemus Heights which continued pounding away. Rising from the swale to crest a slight ridge, they once again became targets for S.D. Lee's gunners by the church.[5]

Confederate artillery made the most of this situation, but the Union had an answer. Thompson's Battery—advancing with Duryee's men—deployed behind the infantry. Soon Matthew's Battery too came thundering across the field, advancing "Forward on the right, into line, gallop!" Matthews quickly unlimbered his four ordnance rifles nearly in line with Thompson's guns and, as battery members recalled, barely 10 feet from the western edge of the East Woods. As Duryee's men started forward once more, a detachment from the 105th New York remained behind as infantry support for Thompson's Battery. Short of men, Thomson quickly pressed some 105th infantrymen into service as ersatz gunners. The lot of this detachment was unpleasant, being sitting ducks for Confederate shells, but it unknowingly spared them what awaited their comrades who marched rapidly away. If Duryee's infantrymen welcomed moving away from the static artillery target, that ended abruptly as they reached a rail fence and, beyond it, a field tall with corn. They had found D. R. Miller's cornfield.[6]

A bad situation facing General Duryee suddenly worsened with the prospect of marching his brigade through a cornfield, which by its very nature challenged maintaining good order. First, the corn's height in this particular field—"the corn stalks were from seven to eight feet high, and while we were in the cornfield, we could neither see nor be seen," described the 6th Wisconsin's Rufus Dawes—meant that once barely ten paces in, Duryee and his officers would effectively command only their immediate vicinity. Moreover, the thick, ready-to-harvest corn and the field's ground forced Duryee to send the brigade straight down the plant rows; there simply was no other option. Nineteenth-century farming techniques required corn to be planted in a checkerboard pattern that created long rows of plants roughly two feet apart—the width of a man's shoulders—to allow a horse-drawn plow through to clear choking weeds. This weeding process created roughly six-inch high mounds around each stalk, which aligned into ridges that worked to channel movement along the planted rows. Moving diagonally across a cornfield was possible but posed a serious challenge to preserving the linear formations Duryee required for his brigade to be organized and effective in battle. Perhaps Duryee's only luck here sprang from one set of rows running north to south, generally the direction he wanted to go. In the tension of the moment, however, Duryee likely instantly knew his course.

The five minutes here amidst constant shelling must have seemed like an eternity. Shouting orders, Duryee shifted his formation from a column of divisions into a line of battle. Once completed, the 107th Pennsylvania held Duryee's right flank, with the 97th, 104th, and 105th New York to their left. Every man awaited the order to advance, not least because doing so would put them under the admittedly limited cover the corn provided from shelling. The order that came, however, was not "forward," but instead for all 1,100 men to lie down.[7]

While his men hugged the ground, Thompson's and Matthew's batteries lobbed several rounds into the center of the corn. This certainly was intended to flush out any Rebs lurking there unseen—skirmishers or more—ahead of their advance. As shells screamed overhead to begin the process of wrecking D. R. Miller's cornfield, Duryee ordered "Rise up!" and to a man, they were on their feet in seconds. Each man knew the next order would be "Forward, march!"[8]

***

Lawton's men watched for signs of the Yankees they all knew were in there somewhere. Yankee shells dropped into the corn had their desired effect, driving the 31st Georgia's skirmishers to seek safety in Lawton's main line. "What's the matter? What are you running for?" called Lawton's men to the scrambling Georgians. "You'll soon see!" they replied. Those who stood could already see the tops of the "striped banner" and the regimental flags bouncing roughly in their direction but knew little else of exactly where the enemy was. On the right of the tense Confederate line, men of

Trimble's Brigade remained locked in a firefight with the Pennsylvanians holding the southern end of the East Woods, too distracted to pay attention to other threats. Those focused solely on the still-unseen foe waited, watching "their" row because Colonel Douglass directed each man to pick a row and fire down it when the enemy showed his face. In the brigade's rear Douglass paced, reminding everyone to fire low and make every shot count. Nearer and nearer they came, until suddenly...[9]

For the first time in several minutes, Duryee's men could see through the sea of green into the brown and gray fields beyond. They'd covered 245 yards; though taking only minutes to do, it might have seemed to have taken hours. The 105th New York's John Whiteside recalled "As we advanced through this field the enemy artillery opened on us, and did us severe damage. Here Rufus Barnhart of our Co. was struck or shot with a solid shot and his head blown from his body. But on we went paying no attention to those who fell in our ranks, no more than if nothing had happened." Even before reaching the fence at the cornfield's southern end, Minie balls made their inevitable appearance. Tearing like an unwanted hailstorm, they ripped through plant and flesh alike. While the corn stood and simply absorbed the assault, Duryee's men continued advancing to resist this fate. Reaching the field's end, they finally opened fire on the Rebs.[10]

The 107th Pennsylvania, holding Duryee's right, emerged to see Lawton's men some 230 yards in front of them, scrambling for cover behind the low remains of a dismantled fence. Without orders, the Pennsylvanians dressed their lines and opened fire. On the opposite end of the Union line, the 105th and 104th New York found the enemy in their front not focused on them, but rather on Federals in the East Woods to their left. The enemy line here angled back a bit, they discovered, offering room for maneuver and the two New York regiments pressed into the opening beyond the corn. Up and over the fence they went, forward nearly 150 yards into the clearing, trying all the while to remain connected to the 97th New York in the center of Duryee's line. They halted nearly 40 yards from the corn, opening a withering fire on the Rebs in their front. As firing intensified into one continuous roll of musketry, Duryee's regiments, apparently without specific orders, instantly lay down as a simple survival technique.[11]

Colonel Walker watched his men of Trimble's Brigade stop the Yankee advance and focus their fire on the men in their front, hoping to drive them back into the corn or kill them where they stood. Walker's situation was little better than that of his Union counterpart, Abram Duryee, only a few dozen yards away. His right flank rested in a plowed field north of the Mumma house and units there were taking casualties fast. Something had to change, or his command could be swept away by a single blue wave. Observing two federal regiments appear to pull back from the western edge of the East Woods—the 2nd Reserves moving to align with the 105th New York and the 13th Reserves adjusting to that move—Colonel Walker made a snap decision, probably a move of simple survival, for his small brigade. Walker directed his skirmishers forward into the East Woods seeking a safer, more secure position there, while also pushing the 100 men of his 12th Georgia northward across the Smoketown Road to close a regiment-sized gap between his brigade's left and the right of Lawton's Brigade. Wheeling left, the Georgians found a low rock ledge, running parallel to the road, upon which to anchor their position. Colonel Walker's move hadn't closed the gap but unknowingly had put his men into just the right position at the right time.[12]

The tiny 12th Georgia found their rock ledge an unexpected gift, a strong defensive position placing them directly on the enemy's flank. Within seconds, the Georgians began pouring an enfilading fire into Duryee's left flank, the men of the 105th New York, which could do little against this low-profile target but stand and take it. Seeing their effect, Walker ordered the 21st Georgia and 21st North Carolina to join the 12th at the rock ledge. Soon, all three regiments were tearing apart Duryee's left flank.[13]

***

The 105th and 104th New York had barely reached the new position in the open field beyond the corn when they were staggered by Southern fire, which also forestalled Seymour's 2nd Pennsylvania Reserves from extending its right beyond the East Woods to connect with the 105th New York's left. The right of Lawton's line and Walker's three regiments of Trimble's Brigade at the rock ledge poured in a withering infantry fire which, joined by S. D. Lee's artillery from the Dunker Church ridge, simply overwhelmed the New Yorkers. Falling back into the relative safety of the corn, they raced to join the rest of their brigade. Bodies of dozens of their dead and wounded comrades and commanders, including the 105th New York's Lieutenant Colonel Howard Carroll, marked their just-failed advance. They couldn't know it then, but these dead and wounded New Yorkers represented the high-water mark of the I Corps effort to reach the Dunker Church.[14]

***

Walker knew this opportunity to dislodge the Yankees might not soon come again. Walker also could for the first time see that Hays's Brigade was on the field to his left and advancing on the retreating enemy. Racing forward, Walker ordered his brigade on. Though slow to respond—probably loath to give up that rock ledge—soon the whole of Trimble's Brigade pressed forward. As they advanced, Walker glanced backward and observed a considerable portion of the stout 12th Georgia remaining glued to their rock ledge. Instantly, he ran to rouse these men to their duty but reaching the 12th's position Walker realized these men weren't shirkers, they were dead. A final tally of the 12th's butcher's bill revealed 59 of its 100 men had died or were mortally wounded behind that rock ledge, including its commander, Captain James C. Rogers.[15]

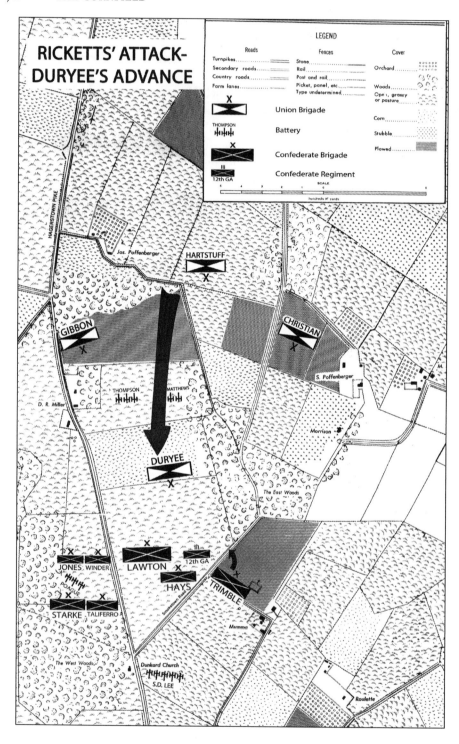

RICKETTS' ATTACK— DURYEE'S ADVANCE

LEGEND

Roads	Fences	Cover
Turnpikes..........	Stone..........	Orchard..........
Secondary roads......	Rail..........	
Country roads........	Post and rail..........	Woods..........
Farm lanes..........	Picket, panel, etc..........	Open, grassy or pasture..........
	Type undetermined..........	Corn..........

Union Brigade

THOMPSON
Battery

Confederate Brigade

12th GA
Confederate Regiment

SCALE
hundreds of yards

Upon rejoining his advancing brigade, Colonel Walker encountered a completely different situation than he'd left only moments before. Hays's Brigade hadn't been moving to the attack, as he assumed, but rather was aligning with Lawton's right flank, as ordered. Retreating Yankees hadn't broken and run but only fallen back to their original position, from which they reopened fire. Worse, Federals in the East Woods now poured fire into his right flank, returning the 12th Georgia's "favor." It was a situation they couldn't stand for long and moments later his brigade—whether under orders or spontaneously—fell back to their original post on the Mumma farm fields, along the rock ledge.[16]

The situation on the left, facing Lawton's Brigade, was little brighter. The 107th Pennsylvania and 97th New York were engaged in a costly frontal firefight with Lawton's Brigade's left-most regiments; the 26th, 38th, and 61st Georgia. Seeing opportunity, the 26th Georgia marched at the "left oblique" to a patch of high ground near the Hagerstown Pike, hoping to find a way around the right end of Duryee's line, and once there reformed and fired into Duryee's right. Barely after gaining this advantage, the Pennsylvanians instantly robbed them of it. "Refusing the right"—bending the right half of the 107th back from the main line a few paces—removed their once-exposed flank from the Georgians's fire, who were now themselves exposed and, even worse, were disconnected from the rest of Douglass's main line. When the 26th Georgia had moved, their comrades in the 38th Georgia raced forward in hopes of reaching a rock ledge in their front. The 38th instantly discovered, however, that the ledge was simply too close to the main Union line and the enemy's still-withering fire stalled the 38th's effort almost as it began.[17]

The fighting was so desperate and close that Colonel Douglass, commanding Lawton's Brigade, had been wounded numerous times. Still he paced the line, closing up gaps and exhorting his men to fight. Finally, a Yankee ball—reportedly the eighth to pierce his body—felled him, robbing the brigade of its daring commander. Making matters worse for the Confederates, General Lawton too was wounded and forced from the field; though he would recover many weeks later, for now, the South's senior commander of this position was taken away in the midst of battle. Lawton's final order of the day proved critical for the South's prospects that morning, however. Calling over an aide, Lawton ordered him to find Brigadier General John Bell Hood, inform Hood he was wounded, and that now was the time for Hood to bring up his men.[18]

***

Duryee's line was holding on, but just barely and at a tremendous human cost. Second Lieutenant Louis Dallarmi, who had served 19 years in the army of his native Bavaria—after emigrating to America, he'd recruited the 97th New York's German-speaking Company H and was so skilled that a comrade noted "his superior military attainments would have given him a higher rank, had his acquaintance with the English language justified"—had his promising military career cut short while leading Company H into battle. Private Charles Hayden of the 97th's Company K lost his left thumb and finger to a Rebel ball but kept fighting until another round found his chest. Amazingly, Hayden collapsed and remained on this spot until soldiers of another Union regiment helped him find the field hospital in Smoketown later in the day. Lieutenant Rush Cady recorded the fate of other Company K men, writing "[Storrs] Sherman was squatting down in the act of priming, when hit by a solid shot, which nearly severed both legs at the knees, & took of [off] his right hand at the wrist, the same shot killing Dick Handley instantly, going completely through his body. Sherman's blood, flesh & pieces of bones flew all over & in the faces of the boys who were next to him. He asked for a drink of water, & then begged Alek to cut his throat, he was in such agony." The 107th Pennsylvania's Edwin Pearce wrote his aunt that "a ball passed threw my coat and shirt making 2 holes in each but I thank the Lord it was no worse." Pearce closed his letter by asking if his Uncle Otto could arrange a transfer to the Navy.[19]

Duryee's men were fighting well, but how long could they keep this up? The 105th New York's John Whiteside recorded that "we were severely cut up, perfectly slautered. But our General was determined to hold that point at all hazards until reinforced...." The general could clearly see fresh Confederate brigades to his right— Grigsby's Stonewall Brigade, and others—that could instantly be upon his flank. New gaps appearing in his ranks were no longer being filled; what his thinning line needed—now—were reinforcements—but where were they? He'd passed Hartsuff's Brigade when moving forward; why had it not appeared as expected? Where was Christian's Brigade? It had the farthest to march and could be forgiven for being last on the field, but why was there no sign of it? Duryee's command had been here for nearly 30 minutes, fighting almost alone, and when final counts were made at nightfall, nearly a third of his brigade would prove to have been lost in this spot. To withdraw signaled failure and dishonor but to remain much longer begged for the death of his brigade. Duryee chose retreat.[20]

The men about-faced and left the field in generally good order, walking rapidly back through the cornfield which, too, had suffered from this fight. The corn offered Duryee's weary men little of the protection it had afforded earlier. The southern end had been crushed by movements and fighting, while the rows of corn farther north now regularly opened into wide gaps; the deadly work of artillery shells that had felled men and plants alike. Here and there, the flight of Minie balls had clearly cut down corn plants, their existence ended just as surely as the lives of too many New Yorkers and Pennsylvanians. Just as this experience had transformed Duryee's men, so too had it changed this place. No longer was it a common Maryland cornfield; forever after it would be "the Cornfield." And like so many of the men and units around Sharpsburg this day, D. R. Miller's Cornfield was slowing being killed.

Amidst this death and carnage, though, men still cared enough to preserve their honor. Rising from the kneeling position in which he'd been fighting to join the retreat, John Delaney noticed the 107th Pennsylvania's flags laying under a pile of dead men from Company C. Although his instinct was to remain and recover his regiment's colors, John could see the Confederates advancing directly at their retreating line and knowing he'd need help called out to the only two men he could see—his company commander Captain Henry Sheafer and tentmate James Kennedy. Hearing Delaney's plea, the two instantly returned to their former position and "in an instant we pulled them out and with our hearts in our mouths dashed away." Ignoring shouted Confederate orders to drop the flags, the three sprinted away to restore their colors and join the regiment in falling back.[21]

Moving beyond the corn, Duryee finally found the reinforcements he'd so longed for just minutes ago. Letting Hartsuff's fresh ranks pass though his own, Duryee ordered his surviving men to deploy along the field's northern edge as Hartsuff's Brigade slipped deeper into the Cornfield, covering the same ground they'd just yielded. Now out of the Cornfield's firestorm, perhaps Duryee wondered what had kept Hartsuff from advancing for nearly half an hour.[22]

When stretcher-bearers removed wounded General Hartsuff from the field, they carried away both the brigade's experienced commander and its sense of purpose and direction. Apparently, the general had failed to pass along to his second-in-command, Colonel Richard Coulter of the 11th Pennsylvania—or anyone else—even the most basic details of Ricketts's orders. Deployed for battle just as General Hartsuff had left it, confusion kept the brigade glued in place for nearly half an hour—the very half hour Duryee's men were fighting Lawton's and Trimble's Brigades across the Cornfield. Still, once Captain William Candler from Hooker's staff rode up with orders to advance, Colonel Coulter set Hartsuff's Brigade in motion at once.[23]

Ricketts's remaining brigade, Christian's, suffered similar paralysis but for a very different reason. Moving into position between the North and East Woods before dawn, Christian's men had endured the same terrific Rebel artillery fire as the rest of Ricketts's Division. Private John Vautier of the 88th Pennsylvania's Company I recalled "the hideous noise made by these projectiles as they screamed through the air was indescribable; it appeared to the blue masses in that advancing host as if all the devils infernal had been incarcerated and assembled on this horrible field, with the power to make the most terrible noises ever heard. At any rate, the appalling sound was enough to terrify the heart of the bravest and cause the blood to chill in ones veins." Perhaps the man in Christian's Brigade most horrified by Confederate shelling that morning, however, was Colonel Christian himself.[24]

William Christian had assumed command of the Second Brigade from Brigadier General Zealous Tower upon Tower's wounding at Second Manassas, barely two weeks before. This fight, however, would be Christian's first test commanding the brigade in battle because the colonel had missed the Second Manassas fighting claiming "sunstroke" made him ill and unable to command. Ready or not, Colonel Christian now had orders to advance his brigade as part of Ricketts's main attack. Even before issuing his first order, though, something seemed wrong. He'd moved his brigade from the relative safety of the North Woods only with General Ricketts's prodding, through a staff officer, and once again safely under cover of woods, he appeared reluctant to leave. So, while Duryee's men fought in the Cornfield for half an hour, Christian held his command—and himself—safe in the East Woods.[25]

***

Watching Duryee's worn Yankee brigade falling back the way they'd come, Major J. H. Lowe—replacing Colonel Douglass commanding Lawton's Brigade—apparently realized the opportunity before him and ordered his brigade forward. Up they rose and pressed swiftly into the corn. In the excitement, Private Martin Van Buren Hawes, an 18-year-old serving in the 31st Georgia, seized the colors and found himself leading the regiment forward. The brigade advanced, moving up the slope through the wounded Cornfield and, in doing so, Lawton's Brigade retook the Cornfield for the first time that day. In just 35 minutes, it had changed hands three times.[26]

The Southerners's hurried advance stretched order to the breaking point, but every inch of ground gained unopposed was a gift they couldn't ignore, so on they pressed. Nearing the field's northern end would certainly reveal more Yankees, but how many? Their answer soon appeared when Matthews's and Thompson's Batteries shifted from blindly lobbing shells into the corn to firing canister rounds at this clear, advancing enemy. Now it was the Southern boys' turn to see if they could withstand murderous blasts of artillery fire, coming from only dozens of yards away.[27]

The hasty advance of Lawton's Brigade unwisely exposed its right flank, but soon help arrived in the form of Hays's Brigade. It apparently took little urging to get the five "Louisiana Tigers" regiments—the 5th, 6th, 7th, 8th, and 14th—moving forward. The 6th Louisiana's Lieutenant Ring told his wife "We lay in that position with a fire from three Yankee batteries and one from a battery of our own answering, firing over our head, besides a fire of Infantry on the Brigade in front of us. I thought, darling, that I had heard at Malvern Hill heavy cannonading, but I was mistaken." Advancing offered relief from this fire, which had been claiming casualties and about which Hays's men could do nothing. Rising up, they quickly dressed their lines and headed toward Lawton's Brigade's advanced position. The isolated advance proved costly, though. Nearing the East Woods, Colonel Strong of the 6th was killed atop his white horse—which also fell—and officer and mount passed from this world as a pair. Before even reaching Lawton's right, the 6th lost all 12 company-grade officers—five killed outright—and the first of its color sergeants. Other regiments in Hays's Brigade suffered similarly. Although Hays's men opened fire immediately upon reaching Lawton's flank, its appearance did little more than shore up Lawton's static line. The Confederate counterattack had stalled.[28]

What stopped Lawton's Brigade at the Cornfield's northern edge wasn't Union artillery, but rather the appearance of fresh infantry threatening each of its vulnerable flanks. The left of Lawton's Brigade suddenly came upon fresh and unbloodied Yankees who were clearly not the command they'd recently driven into the corn. What they'd found was Hooker's other attack—the Iron Brigade's 2nd and 6th Wisconsin of Doubleday's Division—and advancing farther risked offering their unprotected flank to the Yankees. The right of Lawton's attack met an even more direct threat that literally stopped them in their tracks. They found Hartsuff's Brigade.[29]

***

Colonel Coulter had led Hartsuff's Brigade forward through the northern end of the East Woods, but upon entering the thick woods, units struggled to maintain order as men broke ranks to move around trees and climb over the piles of rock and fallen logs littering the lot. Midway in, Coulter ordered a "right oblique" march—turning the advance slightly right in order to clear the ranks of Seymour's Brigade—until nearly beyond the trees. Stopping briefly, certainly to dress their lines, Coulter pressed once more forward. The brigade's 1,000 or so men cleared the East Woods at an angle, emerging into the deadly open of the grassy field as if water pouring from it one file at a time. Coulter now had room for maneuver and immediately set the brigade on a collision course with the enemy.[30]

Marching through the grassy field, at first only the deadly effect of nearly unseen Confederate artillery was evident. Reaching the ridge just north of the Cornfield, Coulter could for the first time see what awaited his men. A strong line of Rebels moved gradually north through the center of the Cornfield beyond. The 12th Massachusetts's George Kendall recalled "The Cornfield … seemed alive with men. I could see the corn wave as if swept by the wind." At that moment, it must have occurred to Coulter that moving his brigade forward quickly might just turn the exposed right flank of that enemy line.[31]

In the center of Hartsuff's line, Corporal Stearns of the 13th Massachusetts vividly recalled this advance. "[W]e were quickly in line and advanced out of the friendly shelter of the woods into an open field; the stubble had but just been turned in. Directly in our front and but a short half mile away was the rebel line of battle awaiting to receive us. The ridge behind their line was crowned by their batteries and I remember one planted near a stone church that opened fire on us as soon as we showed ourselves. The first shots went over our heads, the second came nearer, but on we went, and were soon up to the fence that separated the fields. I remember of looking back when a shell came screeching past and seeing it strike in the midst of the brigade following us; we were quickly over the fence and advancing through a mow[n] field. The next field was a large cornfield and we were soon going through the corn. Our batteries, as well as the rebs, kept up a continuous shelling, making music for our advance."[32]

This shelling was tearing huge gaps in Coulter's line and soon took a very personal toll on Austin Stearns. "While going through the corn I was struck by a piece of shell on my right side that tore my blouse and shirt, and scratched my side a little, just drawing blood; it completely knocked the wind out of me, and I doubled up like a jack knife and sank down on a corn hill. Sergeant Fay seeing me drop asked me 'if I was hit?' and Cap't. Hovey coming repeating the question, as soon as I could regain my wind I told them 'I was not hurt much[,] only lost my wind.' The Cap't. told me 'to sit there till I would be able to follow on,' and [they] went on with the line. I had not sat there a half a moment when just behind me, where the ledge cropped out of the ground, a shell struck not a rod away and went into a thousand pieces, causing me to evacuate that place rather suddenly." Escaping the shelling put Austin back into the line to face a different, but no less deadly threat—Rebel infantry.[33]

Hartsuff's Brigade was within a few dozen yards of Lawton's Brigade's right flank and things were going so smoothly that Coulter recalled one of the two companies of skirmishers he'd pulled from the 12th Massachusetts, putting them back in the main line. So swift was their progress that Thompson's Battery limbered up its guns to advance in the brigade's wake. Suddenly, as if from nowhere, over the rise and through the shattered corn came Hays's Brigade at the double-quick.[34]

Seeing the enemy advancing with speed and determination, Coulter decided to secure a better position than standing in this open field. The right of his line would have to make do being in the open, but his left flank might be secured if he moved quickly. Coulter instantly directed his two left-most regiments to "Right wheel, March!" and the 83rd New York and 13th Massachusetts swung to their right, moving like a barn door hinged on the right. Once completed—in fewer than three minutes, one veteran recalled—the New Yorkers faced almost directly west, aligned with the western edge of the East Woods. Now the 83rd held a strong, terrain-anchored position from which they could fire on the enemy's flank. The 13th Massachusetts boys weren't quite so lucky, though. Although their left was with the 83rd in the woods, most of the regiment remained in the open, alongside the 11th Pennsylvania and the 12th Massachusetts. Regardless, here they would stand to face Hays's Rebel brigade.[35]

"The skirmishers had all disappeared," recalled Austin Stearns of that moment, "we boys thought we were to go for them with the bayonet, and we fixed the same. Neither side, with the exception of the skirmishers and batteries had fired, but now it was time for the infantry to take their turn, and we were getting uncomfortably near." George Kendall in the 12th's Company A observed that "Never did I see more rebs to fire at then that moment presented themselves." Hays's Brigade reached a point where it could go no farther on momentum alone. Having passed beyond Lawton's right flank, Yankees were now on their right and blocking their path in

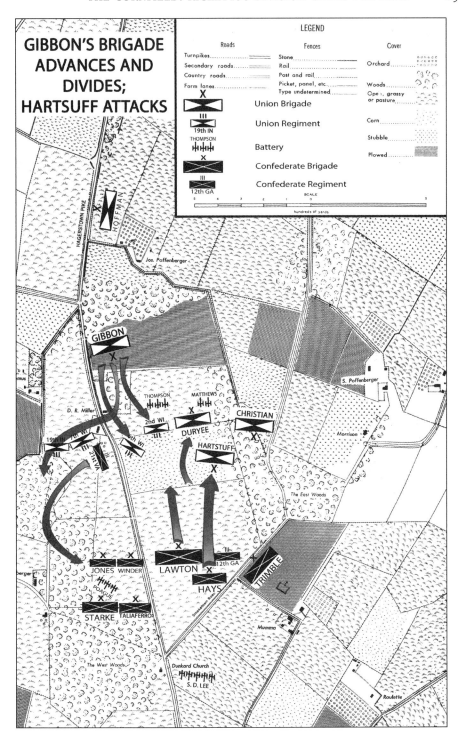

GIBBON'S BRIGADE
ADVANCES AND
DIVIDES;
HARTSUFF ATTACKS

LEGEND

Roads	Fences	Cover
Turnpikes	Stone	Orchard
Secondary roads	Rail	
Country roads	Post and rail	Woods
Farm lanes	Picket, panel, etc.	Open, grassy or pasture
	Type undetermined	

X Union Brigade

III 19th IN Union Regiment

THOMPSON Battery

X Confederate Brigade

III 12th GA Confederate Regiment

Corn

Stubble

Plowed

SCALE

hundreds of yards

front. Halting the men, General Hays ordered his brigade to open fire. "The rebs fired first but we being so near, many of the balls went over our heads, but still many took effect," Corporal Sterns wrote. Now the men of Hartsuff's Brigade had their turn, commencing one of the deadliest firefights of this most deadly day. It was 6:40.[36]

"We halted and commenced firing immediately. Men now commenced to drop on all sides," Austin Stearns recalled. "I remember now, as I was loading my gun, of looking up the line and seeing a man of Co. D who I was quite intimate with throw up his hands and fall to the ground; one little struggle more and then all was quiet. Being intensely engaged in loading and firing, I had not noticed in particular all that was going on around me; I knew that many were hit and had left the ranks, but how many I did not know, when Cap't. Hovey gave the order to 'close up to the right.' Looking to the right, and left as well, I saw that there was quite a space between me and my right hand man; at my left stood Henry Gassett, and repeating to him the Cap't. order, [I] stepped to execute the same. Just then Henry said 'Jim, I'm hit,' and throwing his gun down, ran to the rear perhaps a rod and fell. I went to him as quick as I could and … putting my right arm around his waist and having him put his left arm around my neck, we started for a piece of woods that was a few rods away." For Austin Stearns, the battle of Antietam was over.[37]

For his comrades in Hartsuff's Brigade, though, the battle in the Cornfield raged on. Musket fire from Rebs in their front was bad enough, but S. D. Lee's artillery on the Dunker Church ridge continued, unexpectedly ripping holes in their lines. The intense fire claimed the 12th Massachusetts's commander, Major Burbank, and at one point the 12th's entire color guard was swept away by a single shell, dragging the colors to the ground. The fighting was so terrific, the Bay Staters ignored their fallen flag for some time, preferring instead to close up gaps and continue firing. Colonel Coulter watched his line grow thinner by the minute and knew they couldn't stay here much longer. Not wanting to yield this hard-won ground, Coulter looked to the rear for the reinforcements he so desperately needed. In the East Woods nearby, the colonel observed a body of troops standing stock-still, presumably awaiting orders to move. Getting this force to help his brigade would require his personal intervention, so Coulter raced there on foot. Leaving his command amidst such a fight was risky but doing nothing to secure reinforcements might mean soon having no command at all.[38]

Barely 150 yards away in the East Woods, Christian's Brigade was being sucked into a situation few of its men would ever fully understand. Some of the officers knew they were to move down the Smoketown Road in support of Hartsuff and Duryee's attacks in the fields on the opposite side of the East Woods. While the battle raged and as Hartsuff's men passed on their right, Colonel Christian decided to run the men through the manual of arms. While moving unnecessarily from "Right shoulder, shift!" to "Support, arms!" and back, Confederate batteries on Nicodemus Heights and the Dunker Church ridge poured a continual stream of missiles into the woods, sending huge, sharp splinters flying through the air and felling entire trees.

Perhaps to avoid these missiles, Christian suddenly ordered the brigade to move but soon it was clear to the men they were going nowhere fast. "First it would be 'Forward, guide center,' then 'By the right flank,' and then 'Forward, guide center,' again, … and then we would oblique to the left, and so on," complained Private John Vautier of Christian's 88th Pennsylvania. What they were doing wasn't clear, but they all knew something was horribly wrong.[39]

As Christian's Brigade returned to the wooded swale from which it had begun these maneuvers, up dashed a messenger, perhaps sent by General Ricketts, ordering the brigade forward to support Hartsuff's heavily engaged brigade in the Cornfield. Christian, however, stood glued to the spot as if he'd grown roots and become part of the forest. Perhaps knowing this order meant he could no longer continue the elaborate charade of the past half hour, William Christian snapped. He simply turned and led his horse away, muttering something later recorded as "he'd always had a great fear of shelling." Had he been German or Irish, the men's prejudice would have told them he was drunk, but they'd seen him now acting stranger than any drunken man and had no immediate explanation. Later explaining that his sunstroke—presumably from Second Manassas—had again overtaken him, two days later this once-gallant soldier would resign in disgrace. Few of the men ever knew that William Christian spent much of his remaining years in various sanatoriums and homes, battling what today might be diagnosed as a form of mental illness. What mattered right then, during this terrible fight, however, was that Colonel Christian abandoned his brigade and the men of Coulter's command to their own fates.[40]

As Christian fled, he left in his wake a nearly complete leadership vacuum. His subordinate officers must have been stunned; the brigade's commander had simply left without saying why, where he was going, or when he'd return. They had no idea what had just happened and so, as men often do when faced with confusion and disorder, they did nothing and waited for the situation to sort itself out.

Not every officer in Christian's Brigade was willing to sit by, though. Colonel Peter Lyle of the 90th Pennsylvania, leading his regiment in rejoining the brigade from detached duty, encountered Hartsuff's replacement, Colonel Coulter. Coulter begged "For God's sake, come and help us out, our ammunition is exhausted!" As Coulter raced back toward the corn, showing where the help was needed, Lyle knew he had to act. "We received no orders what to do and the balance of the brigade was at a standstill in the hollow of the woods," recalled Major Alfred Sellers, "without waiting for any command from anyone, for certain reasons, Colonel Lyle marched the 90th out of the East Woods into a pasture or rock ledge field. Coulter's plea was irresistible; there were no orders from higher authority." Confederate artillery fire ripping through the woods now focused on the 90th alone, but on they pressed. Cresting the ridge north of the Cornfield brought Hartsuff's thinning line into view, giving them new purpose. Identifying a hole, Lyle aimed his regiment for the widening gap between the 11th Pennsylvania and the 13th Massachusetts. Marching through this gap, the 90th halted and opened fire. Despite their exposed position, the Pennsylvanians now stood as a wall between Hartsuff's men and the Rebels. With help arrived, Colonel Coulter returned his command to the safety of the East Woods. Fortunately for the 90th Pennsylvania, the Rebs fell back from their front and faced left to move off the field. It seemed the 90th Pennsylvania had come into the fight at just the right time.[41]

The rest of Christian's Brigade—which the 90th Pennsylvania's Major Sellers noted was "at a standstill in the hollow of the woods"—finally moved toward the fight. General Seymour, seeing fresh regiments standing only yards away from his thinning, weary lines, decided they were just what he needed to shore up the Union hold on the East Woods and ordered Christian's men due south through the heart of the woods. At the same time, Seymour retired his Pennsylvania Reserves, providing the first break for these men since twilight the previous day. Upon reaching the southern end of the woodlot, Christian's men halted and formed a battle line facing south to await whatever came next. Shortly, a body of the enemy appeared on the right of Trimble's Brigade and immediately opened fire. This was Ripley's Brigade, ordered by General D. H. Hill to leave its position in the sunken road and go to the front. As Ripley's line moved into position, the weary men of Trimble's Brigade fell back, quite willingly trading places with these fresh troops with full cartridge boxes. As Trimble's Brigade retired, it left behind the 21st Georgia. Having been detached at the battle's opening to deploy on the rock ledge, the 21st's officers failed to receive the orders to fall back. So, while the rest of the brigade moved to the rear and well-deserved rest, the Georgians continued holding on against Christian's Brigade, formed in the woods. Unlike the rest of their brigade, the 21st Georgia still had a critical role play in this fight.[42]

Hartsuff's 12th Massachusetts eventually recovered its fallen colors, but only after wresting them from amidst a pile of fallen color-bearers. Dan Warren, of the 13th Massachusetts, later told Austin Sterns what had happened to the regiment after his departure. "The line fell back and the rebs advanced until our line was reinforced, when they in turn drove the rebs back." Describing the fight's intensity, Warren added that "[He] counted thirty three dead rebs in the length of four fence rails." Their brigade comrade in the 12th, George Kendall, noted "We literally wiped out the rebs in our front, from a beautiful line of battle they became squads behind stumps, etc." but, he added, "[a]nd we suffered likewise. We 'closed upon the colors' till there were not enough for a decent company." As Hartsuff's Brigade emerged from the Cornfield fight with Hays's Confederates, it carried away some of the highest casualty rates of the entire war. The 12th Massachusetts suffered 76 percent casualties—the highest for any Union regiment at Antietam—and the 11th Pennsylvania lost 53 percent of its men.[43]

***

The 6th Louisiana's Lieutenant George Ring offered his wife nearly the same account of Hays's Brigade's experience from the opposite side of the field. "We advanced some three hundred and fifty yards and then commenced firing upon the enemy who were in front of a wood about two hundred yards off, protected by a battery. We stood there about a half an hour and found ourselves cut all to pieces." The Louisianans lost their commander, Colonel Strong, and five of their 12 officers. Ring added of the combat's intensity "I was struck with a ball on the knee joint while I was kneeling by Col. Strong's body, securing his valuables. I got another ball on my arm and two on my sword in my hand, so you can see I have cause to thank God that he has protected me in this great battle." Hay's Brigade had held on as long as possible but soon found its position literally melting away. When Confederate reinforcements appeared, the brigade fell back to its original position near the Smoketown Road, where it reformed to hold off any Yankee counterattack.[44]

Hays's men would face no such counterattack, however. It probably didn't occur to these Southerners at that moment, though, that their gallant charge and considerable loss had accomplished little more than uncovering the strong Union position in the East Woods. Perhaps their only consolation was that the Federals in the Cornfield and the East Woods had sacrificed just as much for roughly the same small gain. Worse for the Union, half of Hooker's opening attack was stalled and two of Ricketts's brigades were spent, while its third—Christian's—had become little more than a guard force in the East Woods. In fact, the only thing obvious to everyone on the field that still-early morning was that this fight was far from over.

CHAPTER 6

The Cornfield: Doubleday's Attack

If General Abner Doubleday weighed his division's role in Hooker's attack that morning, he might have considered he'd drawn the short straw. Although both assaults faced Confederate artillery shelling, his command would suffer enemy infantry fire almost at once because it would march across the front of the Confederate left flank to reach its objective at the Dunker Church. That the enemy was close to his right flank was about all Doubleday probably knew of the position he was attacking; much of the terrain and the exact location of the enemy's flank remained a mystery that only time, and probably many lives, would reveal.

As first light poked through the haze, Doubleday's four brigades were already moving to their tasks. Hofmann's Brigade had drawn the lightest duty, remaining in the Union rear to guard artillery and the staging area on the Joseph Poffenberger farm. Once deployed facing west along the Hagerstown Pike, it also guarded against any turning movement Lee might throw at the Union right. Phelps's and Patrick's Brigades would advance in that order as reinforcement for Gibbon's Iron Brigade, which had drawn the toughest role, leading Doubleday's attack. Rising from their sleep on the ground north of the Poffenberger orchard before dawn, the Iron Brigade's mid-westerners readied themselves for yet another hard fight.[1]

***

Only a quarter mile or so south, General Starke readied Jackson's Division—still named after its famous first commander—for whatever the Yankees would soon throw at it. Starke's first line consisted of Grigsby's Stonewall Brigade, facing north with its right anchored on the Hagerstown Pike, and Jones's Brigade—now headed by Captain J. E. Penn—to Grigsby's immediate left. Directly in front of Grigsby's position and similarly facing north was Poague's Rockbridge Artillery, crewing the three howitzers it had swapped for the previous night. Starke's second line was about 100 yards to the rear, along the north-facing section of the West Woods. Here, Taliaferro's Brigade—led by Colonel E. Warren—held the right of the line, while to its left was Starke's Brigade, the last of the division's four brigades to receive a new commander—the 9th Louisiana's Jesse Williams. Between the two lines was Brockenbrough's Battery; facing northeast, it had already opened fire on Yankees in the East Woods. Deployed well in front of Jackson's Division was a line of skirmishers running from D. R. Miller's place on the right of the Hagerstown Pike to beyond the Nicodemus home on the left. With woods holding the left flank of his position and the road his right, General Starke probably considered this as strong a position as he could have hoped for at the moment.[2]

***

Gibbon's men had barely recovered from being roused by General Doubleday's warning of Confederate shelling when they were forming to advance. "After much shaking and kicking and hurrying [the men] were aroused and stood up in their places in the lines," recalled Major Rufus Dawes of Gibbon's 6th Wisconsin. After marching only a few yards, Confederate artillery showed itself. "[W]hiz-z-z! bang! burst a shell over our heads; then another; then a percussion shell struck in the very center of the moving mass of men," Dawes wrote of the moment. "It tore off Captain David K. Noyes's foot, and cut off both arms of a man in his company." The horror of seeing their comrades so suddenly and hideously wounded instantly brought home what this day had in store for Gibbon's men. The brigade now moved forward with a purpose—and without complaint.[3]

Gibbon's Brigade swept past the scattered ranks of Magilton's Brigade and the North Woods's trees, deployed in a "column of divisions"—in which each regiment formed a column of companies, rather than their usual broad battle line—which eased passing by such scattered obstacles. This was a moving formation, however, not a fighting one, and everyone knew they'd soon be shifting again. Though Gibbon's men were unable to see it, well to their left Ricketts's Division was beginning its own odyssey. It was just 6:00 in the morning when Gibbon's men first stepped from the North Woods into the grassy field beyond.[4]

"In front of the woods was an open field; beyond this was a house, surrounded by peach and apple trees, a garden, and outhouses," Major Dawes recalled upon first seeing D. R. Miller's farmstead. Once clear of the woods, Gibbon pulled two companies of the 6th Wisconsin from the brigade's right to deploy across its front as skirmishers. As the skirmishers moved into their staggered position, the rest of the brigade deployed in a two-rank-deep battle line, then Gibbon continued his advance. General Hooker inserted himself, too, directing Gibbon to advance his brigade at the right oblique—marching gradually to the right—until they found the Hagerstown Pike, then it was forward once more toward the Dunker Church. Some in Gibbon's left-most regiment, the 2nd Wisconsin, could at that moment see Duryee's Brigade well to their left and front reaching the fence line of the Cornfield.[5]

Gibbon's men encountered their first enemy infantry when Rebels hiding among trees in Miller's orchard suddenly opened on them. It was clear that there were relatively few of these men, though, so Captain John A. Kellogg—commanding Company I, one of two skirmish companies—decided that rushing the position would overwhelm the Rebs with simple numbers. Ordering the skirmishers to "At the double-quick, Charge!" the scattered line surged rapidly forward, each man struggling to run and maintain his position in the line. Kellogg had been correct; the Rebels fled without contesting the orchard, leaving the skirmishers waiting for the rest of the brigade to catch up. No sooner had the formation closed up when the Iron Brigade met a new obstacle—Mrs. Miller's garden.

Two days earlier the Miller garden had been a simple plot bearing the fading remains of the fruits and vegetables not stored in jars for the coming winter. Now, however, the garden and its surrounding wooden picket fence became an immovable obstacle that stopped the left half of the 6th Wisconsin in its tracks, once again making them a stationary target for Confederate shells. Worse, the regiment's right half continued forward past the garden, while the rest of the brigade swept around the house to the left—the 6th Wisconsin's five left-hand companies risked being disconnected from their command. Seeing disaster forming before his eyes, Major Dawes ordered the front rank to pull down the garden fence. However, several tries failed to budge the sturdy fence, which now performed the picket duty its Confederate defenders had been unable to. Thinking quickly, Dawes surrendered to the fence and ordered his companies to fall out, pass through the open gate, and reform on the opposite side. Captain Edwin A. Brown was standing amid the brambles, waving his sword, shouting "Company E, on the right, by file, into line!" when a Rebel ball drove into his open mouth, suddenly and painfully silencing him forever. Nonetheless, Brown's effort had paid off and the 6th Wisconsin soon reformed south of the garden and rejoined the regiment. With the 6th's return, Gibbon's reunited Iron Brigade resumed its drive toward the Dunker Church.[6]

Seeing the Rebs ceding the 75-yard-wide patch of open ground between the Miller house and the Cornfield, General Gibbon quickly pushed his brigade forward into the gap. Reaching the end of Miller's Cornfield, Gibbon and the Iron Brigade faced the same challenges that had bedeviled General Duryee. Rather than lobbing shells to clear the unknown in the corn, Gibbon sent forward his 6th Wisconsin as skirmishers to flush out any Rebels there. While the skirmishers advanced, Gibbon's command again attracted the unwanted attention of S. D. Lee's guns on the Dunker Church ridge and Poague's artillery, to its front and right.[7]

General Hooker, watching Gibbon's advance from near the North Woods, must have had the same thought. As the Iron Brigade passed the Millers's yard, Hooker ordered forward Colonel Walter Phelps's Brigade—the 22nd, 24th, 30th, and 84th (14th Brooklyn) New York regiments, along with the 2nd US Sharpshooters—as reinforcements. Joining Phelps was Reynolds's 1st New York Light Artillery, Battery

L, which left its post north of the Poffenberger house and raced down the road toward the front. Phelps's command possessed two of the army's most distinctively dressed regiments; the 84th New York (14th Brooklyn) wore the baggy Zouave uniforms modeled on French North African troops and were distinguished by their red stockings, while the 2nd US Sharpshooters wore uniforms identical to the rest of the army save that they were solid green as camouflage. Twenty minutes later, Hooker sent Patrick's Brigade—the 21st, 23rd, 35th, and 80th New York (20th NYSM)—to join Phelps and Gibbon. As Gibbon's 6th Wisconsin probed the corn and Reynolds's artillerymen tried their best to silence the Rebel batteries, these roughly 1,250 men joined their First Division comrades crowding the small grassy strip of land between the Miller house and the corn. For now, these reinforcements mainly provided Confederate gunners more targets to kill. Gibbon needed to find the enemy and get his attack underway again, fast, or he'd soon have nothing at all to advance.[8]

Ahead in the Cornfield, the 6th Wisconsin pressed toward wherever the enemy might be. Unlike Duryee's swiftly advancing brigade across the field, the Badger State men under Major Dawes on the left plowed slowly though the tall sea of green enveloping them, harassed periodically by the 21st Virginia's retreating skirmishers. On the right, the 6th's remaining companies followed their regimental commander, Colonel Bragg, through the Hagerstown Pike's open roadbed and the grassy fields to the righthand, west side of the road. It quickly became clear the 6th's two wings were moving at very different speeds; the obstacle the corn and enemy skirmishers presented to Dawes's half of the regiment wasn't shared by Bragg's men in the open fields and road. As the gap widened, the 6th split into two sections moving increasingly apart. The thick corn and the undulating ground further prevented Dawes and Bragg from knowing what was occurring with the other's command. Worse, Bragg had no intention of slowing his men so on they pressed, dragging the left of the regiment like a heavy fishing net pulled through rough seas. Nonetheless, the 6th headed toward the southern end of the Cornfield, where it could align on Duryee's position to their left. Suddenly, however, everything changed.[9]

Approaching the southern end of the Cornfield put the 6th Wisconsin atop a rise, nearly level with the Hagerstown Pike. They arrived here nearly unopposed but, in an instant, a solid enemy volley brought the Wisconsin men back to a horrible reality. This fire came not from the corn in their front but from the woods on their right. Bragg halted his companies, now crowded together on the western edge of the road, knowing instantly they couldn't remain here long. The fire was tearing them apart and Colonel Bragg could finally see what stood between him and the church—the two Confederate brigades of Jones and Grigsby. As the enemy rose from their hiding place and readied another full volley, Bragg snapped into action and ordered his men back to the protection of the post and rail fence at the Cornfield's western edge. The men scattered, racing for the fence, upon which they instantly realigned and regained order. Doing so, however, reoriented Bragg's companies facing not forward and south toward the church, but instead west to the West Woods. Despite the confusion, Bragg's wing quickly opened fire on the enemy now before them.[10]

No longer being dragged forward by the companies on their right, Major Dawes stopped his command in the corn, ordering it to the ground. Although lowering their profile, this again made them sitting ducks for nearby Rebel batteries and infantry. "The bullets' began to clip through the corn," recalled Dawes, "and spin through the soft furrows—thick, almost, as hail. Shells burst around us, the fragments tearing up the ground, and canister whistled through the corn above us. Lieutenant Bode of company "F" was instantly killed, and Lieutenant John Ticknor was badly wounded." In the midst of this deadly hail, Dawes was called to the right by Colonel Bragg. Dawes raced through the corn to find he'd been given command of the regiment by his now badly wounded superior, who quickly went to the rear. Dawes now led the divided wings of the 6th Wisconsin, which faced two very different directions. Barely could Dawes consider his very limited options when the "Ragged Ass" 2nd Wisconsin—so named for their tattered sky-blue trousers—swept up on the left. Instantly ordering his regiment up, the major barked "Forward, Guide Center, March!" and eight of his companies joined the 2nd's advance. The remaining two—Companies G and K, commanded now by Captain Kellogg—remained pinned to the fence by "murderous" fire. Although to Dawes the 2nd Wisconsin's help had appeared unasked for, it had hardly arrived without purpose.[11]

General Gibbon only ten minutes earlier had surveyed the situation before him with dismay. His probing force, the 6th Wisconsin, was bogged down in an increasingly desperate firefight against a much larger force. Although his attack was barely underway, something had to be done to get it moving again. Within moments, Gibbon ordered the 19th Indiana and 7th Wisconsin across the Hagerstown Pike, heading southwestward toward the left flank of the two enemy brigades. Next, he directed the 2nd Wisconsin forward on the left to help the beleaguered 6th. Gibbon next called forward a two-gun section from Campbell's Battery, commanded by Lieutenant James Stewart, deploying it in the center to support the two infantry forces. Gibbon's adaptation had the right of his brigade striking the left flank of these two defending Southern brigades—Jones and Grigsby—while the left half hit them in front and on the right. If this pincer movement worked, Gibbon's Brigade would soon reunite and resume driving to the Dunker Church.[12]

Stewart's two guns raced up the Hagerstown Pike at a run. Reaching their objective, Stewart led them right of the road and into D. R. Miller's barnyard, still flush with haystacks. Posting both guns facing south and directing them to open fire immediately, Stewart sent his caissons back toward the barn and safety from the increasingly deadly Rebel gunfire.[13]

At almost the same moment, the right wing of Gibbon's pincer—the 19th Indiana and 7th Wisconsin—moved across the Hagerstown Pike and between the Miller's house and barn. Reaching the northern end of the West Woods, they halted because

Confederate skirmishers blocked their path. The 19th Indiana's Lieutenant Colonel Bachman had Captain W. Dudley deploy his Company B as skirmishers to clear this threat. Simply advancing had driven the Rebel skirmishers into the woods, and the Indiana boys pressed on after them. Stepping into the woods, Company B unknowingly became the first Union troops to enter Antietam's West Woods.[14]

***

To the 21st Virginia's Captain Page, these Union skirmishers presented a serious threat. Abandoning their rock-ledge breastwork, adopted after falling back from the Miller house, the Virginians raced for the safety of the woods. Finding reinforcements there, sent forward by the 42nd Virginia's Captain Penn who now commanded Jones's Brigade, Page rallied his men on his former regiment. Penn had orders to keep the Yankees away from the position's left flank, a tough task given that only 271 men were at his disposal. Barely had Penn's advanced command deployed when the 19th Indiana skirmishers again opened fire. Penn's force offered its own volleys and for a time the two sides were locked in a slugfest. Despite the trees and ground cover, Southerners fell in growing numbers, including Captain Penn. Eventually, the larger and fresher 19th Indiana overwhelmed the rapidly diminishing Virginia line, working around its flanks. Unable to stem this tide, the 21st Virginia and Penn's reinforcements raced for the safety of Jones's Brigade's main line behind them. Captain Page might have been relieved to rejoin the brigade's position; if so, it probably was dashed when the captain learned he now commanded Jones's Brigade.[15]

***

With the skirmishers gone and the woods clear, the 19th Indiana and 7th Wisconsin renewed their attack. The Indiana boys pressed deeper into the woods, keeping their right on the 7th Wisconsin, which guided its southward movement on the woods' eastern edge. Seeing Confederates to their left—and probably fearing they were too far from the other half of their brigade in the Cornfield—the 19th and 7th executed a "left wheel" movement that would eventually reunite them with the 2nd and 6th Wisconsin across the road. Although well executed, time and the fighting's flow would prove it had been for naught.[16]

Watching this from within the Cornfield, General Doubleday ordered Patrick's Brigade onward to support the 19th Indiana and 7th Wisconsin in taking the northern end of the West Woods. Doing so reflected Doubleday's common-sense leadership style here, working to support tactical decisions made by Gibbon, who was effectively commanding the forward-most elements of Doubleday's Division in this battle. Contributing in his own way at that moment, too, was Abner Doubleday's African American servant. As the general recalled "Temple was a very religious negro

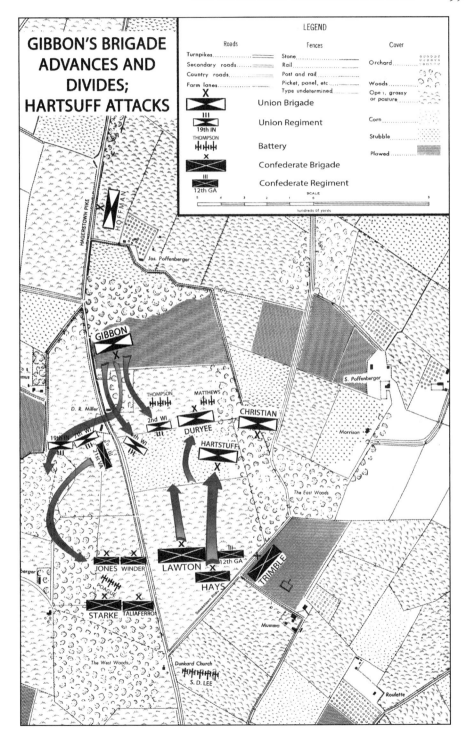

GIBBON'S BRIGADE ADVANCES AND DIVIDES; HARTSUFF ATTACKS

and while the battle of Antietam was raging, he knelt down in the bloody cornfield for which the two armies were contending and prayed for a long time in a loud voice for the success of the Union cause. This supplication made in the midst of the flying bullets was a remarkable one…"[17]

***

Gibbon's pincer attack was putting ever-growing pressure on nearby Confederate defenders in Jones's and Grigsby's Stonewall Brigades. Their right had for some minutes been threatened by Yankees from the Cornfield across the road and now two Union regiments had entered the woods in their front and were moving to threaten their left flank. Worse, two fresh enemy brigades had appeared from the North Woods, adding more power to the Union attack. Once the skirmishers of Jones's Brigade became engaged, Captain Raine's howitzers and William Poague's single 12-pounder Napoleon—which all morning had stood before the Southern line, shelling advancing Yankees—moved to the rear of Jones's and Grigsby's infantry. It was a common-sense move but one that signaled the Confederate left was on the verge of collapse.[18]

As the two Wisconsin regiments pressed south along the road, Grigsby grew increasingly concerned. The Stonewall Brigade's 450 men were an even match for Gibbon's advancing 2nd and 6th Wisconsin, which together totaled 486 men, but the retiring skirmishers from Jones's small brigade suggested his left was in trouble. Worse, Grigsby could see the fire from across the turnpike winnowing his ranks and so Grigsby sent staffer Lieutenant J. M. Garnett to find General Starke, warning him the Stonewall Brigade simply couldn't hold on much longer. Grigsby knew it was now a race against time.[19]

Though doing all he could to hold on, the situation was rapidly spinning beyond Grigsby's control. Soon the 5th Virginia's Major Williams pleaded with Grigsby to be allowed to retire his regiment to safety at the wood line. Though sympathetic of the major's plight, Arnold Grigsby was desperately trying to balance the survival of his command and his career, hoping that soon Lieutenant Garnett would return with Starke's approval to move. Regardless, the major had had enough; orders or no, Williams directed the 5th Virginia to "About face, Forward March!" Barely had the 5th stepped away when, one by one, the rest of the Stonewall Brigade joined them. Nearby, Lieutenant Garnett found General Starke, who was watching the broken remains of Grigsby's Stonewall Brigade streaming to the rear and safety, now joined by Jones's regiments. Colonel Grigsby's command—and with it the Confederate left flank—was disintegrating.[20]

***

Across the Hagerstown Pike in the corn, the 2nd and 6th Wisconsin continued driving toward the unknown. The presence of Rebel skirmishers meant there was more infantry ahead, but where? Just as mysterious was the situation beyond their own small bubble of reality inside the corn. They couldn't know that Duryee's Brigade had already found the Rebs and been repulsed, nor were they aware that the losses they'd already suffered had been of almost no help at all to Duryee's men. All that, however, was about to change.[21]

Forging through the thick corn, the Wisconsin boys continued down the gentle slope until they could see the field's end. At its immediate edge was a worm fence and beyond that, what? Only upon reaching the fence and halting was it apparent they'd found the Rebs. These were the left-most regiments of Lawton's Brigade, the 26th, 38th, and 61st Georgia. At first, the Georgians seemed simply to stand there, some of them still rising from the ground while others readied muskets to fire. Almost at once, the opposing ranks, blue and gray, opened fire on each other over the barely 200 yards separating them.[22]

The Iron Brigade's two regiments had no idea at that moment, caught up with the fury of battle, what they'd done or what it meant to Duryee's boys only a few hundred yards away on the eastern edge of the field. The 2nd and 6th Wisconsin's unexpected appearance in the corn had halted the drive of nearly a third of Lawton's troops, counterattacking in the wake of Duryee's retreating brigade. The presence and firepower of these two Wisconsin regiments also helped Hartsuff's advancing brigade; stopping the left half of Lawton's counterattack had robbed this drive of momentum and denied him the mass of the superior Confederate numbers then at his disposal—both Hays's and Trimble's Brigades were nearby—to turn Hartsuff's right, unprotected flank hanging in the corn. With this help, Hartsuff's Brigade and the 90th Pennsylvania stopped what was left of Lawton's counterattack from reaching deeper into the Cornfield.[23]

***

Eventually, Lawton's Georgians, running low on men and ammunition, began falling back. If Federals in Gibbon's two regiments or Phelps's Brigade—advancing immediately behind Gibbon—took any relief from this retreat, it was short-lived. Almost on cue, fresh Confederate infantry appeared from the depths of the West Woods, heading right for Gibbon's exposed right flank. General Starke had sent these troops—Taliaferro's Brigade, on the right, and his own brigade—forward at the double-quick to stem the rising Yankee flood after seeing Grigsby's and Jones's Brigades racing rearward. Starke knew pushing these brigades into the same weak position just yielded by Grigsby and Jones only invited defeat; they needed to be advancing with a viable target to strike. At that moment, the only vulnerable Union target available was across the Hagerstown Pike, where a strong blue line was foolishly offering its unprotected flank. Starke's brigades were on a collision course with Gibbon's 2nd and 6th Wisconsin and Phelps's Brigade.[24]

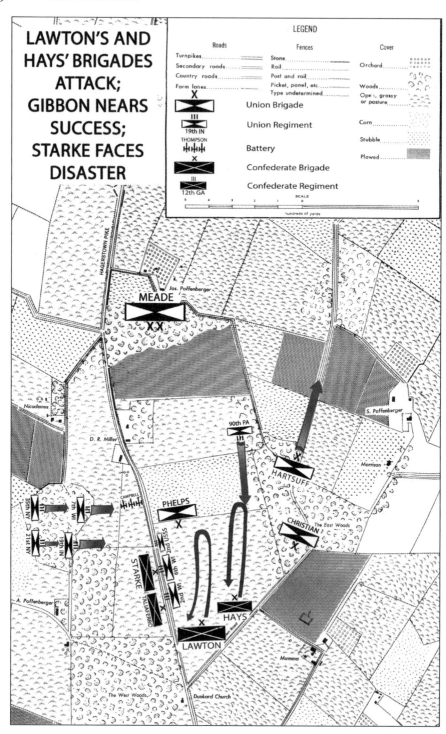

LAWTON'S AND HAYS' BRIGADES ATTACK; GIBBON NEARS SUCCESS; STARKE FACES DISASTER

LEGEND

Roads	Fences	Cover
Turnpikes	Stone	Orchard
Secondary roads	Rail	
Country roads	Post and rail	Woods
Farm lanes	Picket, panel, etc.	Open, grassy or pasture
	Type undetermined	Corn

Union Brigade

Union Regiment
19th IN

Battery
THOMPSON

Confederate Brigade

Confederate Regiment
12th GA

Stubble

Plowed

SCALE

hundreds of yards

HAGERSTOWN PIKE

Jos. Poffenberger

MEADE

Nicodemus

D. R. Miller

S. Poffenberger

90th PA

HARTSUFF

Morrison

CAMPBELL

34th NY

7th IN

PHELPS

CHRISTIAN

The East Woods

21st NY

19th IN

6th IN

2nd IN

STARKE

A. Poffenberger

TALIAFERRO

HAYS

LAWTON

Mumma

The West Woods

Dunkard Church

General Starke, sword held aloft, led his two brigades forward to exactly where he wanted them. They began drawing Federal fire immediately after leaving the woods, musketry pouring upon them from their front and left flank—the work of the 19th Indiana and 7th Wisconsin, which had just cleared the woods 100 yards to Starke's north—along with shells from Lieutenant Stewart's two guns. This fire was more effective than any Federal could have hoped; it felled General Starke, midway between the woods and his objective along the Hagerstown Pike. The general was carried to the rear and medical aid, but it was for naught; within the hour, like so many of his men, General William Starke was dead.[25]

Even so, Starke's two brigades continued wheeling right into position. Pivoting on the far right of Taliaferro's line, they swung like a door slamming shut the gaping hole in Jackson's left flank. Reaching the Hagerstown Pike, they stopped, the men finding spots along the post and rail fence and opening fire. Their immediate target was the 2nd US Sharpshooters, deployed along the Pike's eastern fence line by Colonel Phelps in order to prevent his brigade's right from being turned. Soon, though, Starke's and Taliaferro's men saw the Wisconsin boys—just south of the Cornfield's edge—offer their exposed flank and they shifted to this new target with a will. Without orders, the 6th and 2nd Wisconsin retreated into cover of the remaining corn, reforming and dressing their line. Then they instantly moved again toward the Sharpshooters's left, sweeping through the worm fence protecting the southern end of the Cornfield.

***

"Men I cannot say fell," wrote Major Dawes, "they were knocked out of the ranks by the dozens. But we jumped over the fence, and pushed on, loading, firing, and shouting as we advanced. There was, on the part of the men, great hysterical excitement, eagerness to go forward, and a reckless disregard of life, of everything but victory." The two Wisconsin units' movement mirrored what Starke's two brigades had executed only moments before. Pivoting on the 2nd US Sharpshooters's left, the two Yankee regiments executed their own right-wheel movement. When completed, the identical commands brought these lines into a close and deadly standoff, only 30 yards apart across the Hagerstown Pike.[26]

"Now is the pinch," recalled Major Dawes, "Men and officers of New York and Wisconsin are fused together into a common mass, in the frantic struggle to shoot fast. Every body tears cartridges, loads, passes guns, or shoots. Men are falling in their places or running back into the corn. The soldier who is shooting is furious with energy. The soldier who is shot looks around for help with an imploring agony of death on his face."

Such huge gaps were appearing in both lines that before long one of the two immovable forces would simply disintegrate into nothingness and loss. The appearance of Phelps's remaining men did little more than buy the Union line time. Still, reinforcements were a luxury the Confederates didn't enjoy; they had to do something if they were to survive this situation any longer. Almost as if in slow motion, first one and then another man began crossing the fence over, under, through; any way possible—until so many men were moving it seemed to be part of a plan. If only they could turn the Yankees' exposed flank—as their desperate movement suggested—the killing would stop. For a moment, it seemed to be working. The 6th Wisconsin and the 14th Brooklyn of Phelps's Brigade fell back into the corn. But the 2nd US Sharpshooters plugged the gap, creating an anchor upon which the 6th and 14th clung to restore their line. The Sharpshooters's breech-loading Sharps infantry rifles' greater fire rate only aided their hold on the spot. The Confederates had been so close to victory, but it was no use; the unending Union fire turned that section of roadway into a dead zone, which no one could enter and survive. Although this standoff seemed to those taking part in it to last for hours, the watches in their pockets would count off only ten minutes.[27]

So intense was the firing that some men failed to even notice their fresh wounds. Corporal Sherman of the 6th Wisconsin's Company D had repeatedly fired at a Confederate color-bearer, hoping to bring down his waving banner. Finally, seeing it fall, Sherman yelled out "felled it," but in doing so he failed to notice a Rebel ball that had struck his arm, paralyzing it. Private Thomas Barcus, too, fired at the Confederates so intently he only realized he'd been shot upon finding his legs wouldn't bend to permit him to join the advance. The round had cut his flexor tendon, rendering his legs stiff and unresponsive, but nonplussed by this horror Private Barcus simply called out "Here is where you get your stiff legs!"[28]

Perhaps the most touching personal story playing out on the Hagerstown Pike that morning was that of Captain Werner von Bachelle, commander of the 6th Wisconsin's Company F. Von Bachelle had served in the French Army before coming to America and his previous military experience, commanding bearing, and natural leadership skills impressed all who met him, particularly those in his command. Captain von Bachelle had no family save one—a Newfoundland dog who was his constant companion in camp and on the field. Sharing in his master's military life, the dog had learned to perform "military salutes" and other tricks which entertained Company F. Even in the midst of Antietam's Cornfield, von Bachelle and his dog were together, leading Company F into the fight across the Hagerstown Pike. When Werner was killed in the firefight, his canine companion refused to join the rest of the 6th in falling back, remaining instead with his fallen master. Two days later, returning to the spot to retrieve their captain's body, the men of Company F found a terrible sight. Von Bachelle and his beloved dog lay together in death and so would the two casualties of Antietam's Cornfield remain together for all eternity.[29]

Gibbon could see his men were on the verge of success but needed immediate help to turn the tide of this fight for good. Looking right, Gibbon saw just what he needed and ordered Lieutenant Stewart's artillery section forward again, this time 150 yards closer to the enemy to a rise in the ground providing a clear and commanding field of fire on Starke's left flank. Stewart objected that doing so placed his two guns in a vulnerable position but acceded to Gibbon's orders. After moving their heavy guns along the road's western edge, Stewart's men immediately opened fire. Despite being so near the enemy, Stewart couldn't use his devastating canister rounds and instead "ordered the guns to be loaded with spherical case, [with] 1¼ and 1½ seconds [timed fuses], because the ground was undulating and not suitable for canister." Soon the 80th New York from Patrick's Brigade double-quicked into view and formed on Stewart's left and right-rear as infantry support; perhaps easing Stewart's fears a bit, Major Hardenburgh led the 80th New York's left-most companies farther forward along the Pike, pushing the Rebs from the battery's front and back into the Cornfield. Gibbon's risky moves paid off almost at once for barely had the two guns of the 4th US fired two or three rounds each, when Starke's line almost literally melted away.[30]

***

Breaking to the rear amidst Starke's crumbling line, the 1st Louisiana's color-bearer was struck, dropping his precious flag across the fence rails and into the roadway. Seeing their colors drop into the pike's dusty no-man's land, nearby men on both sides were instantly drawn to but one goal—securing that flag. Some 2nd US Sharpshooters scrambled to seize it but Louis C. Parmelee, adjutant to the 2nd's Colonel Post, was first over the fence. The 1st Louisiana's men were just as determined to regain their colors and fired a scattered volley to clear the Yankee usurpers. This swept away Adjutant Parmelee but in the confusion another sharpshooter grabbed the prize and sprinted to the rear. The 1st Louisiana had lost its battle flag.[31]

As Starke's Louisianans fled, the 2nd Sharpshooters followed. Rather than climbing the fence in headlong pursuit, the sharpshooters remained in the road and worked their way left to turn the enemy's right flank. With a strong pivot point for his right flank now secure in the roadbed, Phelps ordered the rest of his brigade forward to the fence. Gibbon's 2nd and 6th Wisconsin joined the advance, too, on Phelps's left. The target of Phelps's leftward shift, Taliaferro's Brigade, had barely been holding on at the fence; with Starke's Brigade crumbling on its left and Yankees threatening its flank, it instinctively joined Starke's retreating men.[32]

Advancing to the fence had cost the two brigades dearly. Starke's Brigade lost its namesake commander and his replacement, Colonel Jesse M. Williams, too. Leroy A. Stafford was now the 9th Louisiana's fourth commander of the day and six other officers of the brigade lay near the Hagerstown Pike. A final tally revealed some

274 of Starke's 650 men—almost half the brigade—had been killed or wounded. Taliaferro's Brigade similarly lost two commanding officers and 171 of its nearly 500 men. All of this had happened in a single half hour.[33]

***

General Hooker finally had reason to believe his attack could succeed. Doubleday's attacking brigades under Gibbon and Phelps had pushed back four Confederate brigades and were now about 500 yards from their original objective; the Dunker Church. The Confederate left had been uncovered and was being driven in toward the Confederate center, thanks to Gibbon's 19th Indiana and 7th Wisconsin, and Patrick's advancing brigade. More promising, the two wings of Hooker's attacking force—which so far had fought separate actions, linked only by Gibbon's and Doubleday's decisive and effective leadership—were on the verge of joining for a final drive to the church. Artillery to support this push was already in place in the form of Campbell's Battery in the center of this evolving line. The situation on Hooker's left was less promising but nonetheless positive. Although only the now independent 90th Pennsylvania and Christian's Brigade remained of Ricketts's attack, they held the eastern Cornfield and the East Woods respectively.

Although Hooker's attack was slightly more than an hour old, much remained to be done. It had not broken Lee's line and two of Hooker's three I Corps divisions had been expended just getting to this point; only Meade's Division remained intact and fresh for the coming push to the church. Certainly, determined Confederate resistance and skillful use of interior lines had been central to preventing his success. At the same time, Hooker's decision limiting his attacking divisions to maneuvering and fighting in units no larger than brigades continued weighing down his unfolding plan. Although Hooker had taken an active role in guiding the evolving battle, his role had done little to address this fatal error.

Hooker wasn't the only Union officer falling short that morning, though. Ricketts's attack had faltered because of his command shortcomings, particularly failing to adjust to unexpected developments. Ricketts should have insisted his brigade commanders clarify before battle their respective command chains to avoid the confusion created upon Hartsuff's wounding. Although Ricketts couldn't have predicted the troubles plaguing Christian's Brigade, he should have intervened when its odd movements demonstrated that something was wrong. Gibbon's attack had fared somewhat better, largely because Gibbon remained more actively engaged in his attack's progress, making adjustments while underway.

So far, Hooker's men had walked obligingly into a situation of Stonewall Jackson's creation. Jackson had chosen the ground and, inadvertently, the objectives for which Hooker's men would fight. Jackson's position south of the Cornfield had forced Hooker and his officers to fight not for their objective at the church, but rather for one of several intermediate objectives Jackson had placed in their path. Nearly two thirds of Hooker's attacking corps had been spent securing the most significant of those unexpected intermediate objectives, D. R. Miller's Cornfield. Despite Jackson's tactical foresight and the skillful leadership of his division and brigade commanders, nothing could change the facts of that moment. Tough fighting had bought the Union hold of those critical intermediate objectives—the Cornfield, the northern end of the West Woods, and the entire East Woods—and the I Corps was poised to finish the work it had started.

Having set all this in motion the night before, General McClellan remained in his headquarters watching smoke rise above the trees and listening to the sound of distant battle. He certainly awaited news of this opening attack, not least because Hooker's success was the trigger for launching his unfolding plan's next phase. Nonetheless, McClellan was certainly secure in believing he was where he ought to be and doing what an army commander should be doing at such a moment. If McClellan was encouraged by what little he could observe of the unfolding fight, he apparently had no idea just how much in the balance his entire battle plan was at that moment.

CHAPTER 7

The Cornfield: Hood's Division Counterstrikes

The hour-old battle's fate indeed hung in the balance. Despite gaining little ground at a high cost, Hooker's attack was poised to succeed while Jackson's defense of the Dunker Church ridge appeared in chaos and ready to break. Success for both generals turned on but one question—who could first push reinforcements into the fight? Forces which had fought to control the Cornfield so far were both largely spent, their ranks thin and those still fighting exhausted and low on ammunition. Gibbon's and Phelps's Brigades might take the Dunker Church, breaking Lee's line, but were unlikely to hold that gain against a determined Confederate counterattack. Similarly, Jackson's men might hold on, but thousands of fresh Yankee troops waited near the North Woods.

Hooker, however, had expected this moment all morning and was ready to strike. Immediately after ordering Doubleday and Ricketts forward, Hooker advanced the two remaining brigades of Meade's Division in their wake. That foresight put reinforcements within a short march of the Cornfield's northern fence at just the right moment. Hooker's planning, however, was undone as the Federals became victims of their own success. Taking the battle to the very doorstep of Lee's line meant Jackson's reinforcements were already close at hand, too, aided by the Confederacy's possession of interior lines. If Jackson's and Hooker's reinforcements began moving at the same moment, Jackson would certainly win the race. Given this, the moment had arrived for Stonewall to collect John Bell Hood's promise made the night before.[1]

***

Hood's men had been enjoying a break from the front lines and their first opportunity to cook in nearly three days. The previous night, after retiring behind the Dunker Church, Hood's men had formed to draw rations. A 4th Texas veteran recalled being issued the only food available, "scorched beef and corn;" the same fare they'd been eating for days, they nonetheless filled empty haversacks. About four that morning, the Southern boys were roused from sleep to draw more rations from their recently arrived commissary wagons—obtained personally by Hood—which contained mostly flour and little else, although a few lucky men also received bacon. Soon small fires appeared and men cooked biscuits and johnnycakes on their ramrods, on slabs of bark torn from trees, on their gum and wool blankets, or any other way in which to get them cooked quickly. Still, so hungry were Hood's men that many who received bacon ate it raw. Even as the nearby fighting intensified, and Yankee shells intermittently interrupted their meals, men continued cooking and eating. Once they would have complained about such fare and conditions, but at that moment it was nearly a feast.[2]

Complaining would begin soon enough, though, because suddenly Hood's men were called into ranks. Some men abandoned their fires and rations for duty, but most ate what they could—cooked or not—or shoved whatever remained into their haversacks. Some Texans ate their half-cooked breakfast from ramrods as they moved but fall into ranks they did and within minutes Hood's Division was ready to advance.[3]

What started this commotion was General Lawton's messenger finding Hood. The weary staffer saluted Hood, reporting "General Lawton sends you his compliments, with the request that you come to his support!" For Hood, monitoring the fighting since dawn and having received Lawton's warning to be ready, the call for help was no surprise. When the aide added that General Lawton was wounded, Hood knew it was time to act.[4]

Hood's Division contained two brigades, totaling roughly 2000 men. Colonel William T. Wofford from the 18th Georgia commanded Hood's former brigade. Known not by its formal names—Hood's Brigade or Wofford's Brigade—but as the Texas Brigade, it consisted of the 1st, 4th, and 5th Texas, 18th Georgia, and South Carolina's Hampton Legion. This last unit added additional color to the brigade; using the title "Legion," rather than "Regiment," was meant to evoke the power and might of a Roman Legion, even though the Hampton Legion now mustered only 77 men. The 4th Alabama's Colonel Evander M. Law led Hood's other brigade, consisting of the 4th Alabama, 6th North Carolina, and 2nd and 11th Mississippi. Despite its eclectic composition, Hood's Division was one of Lee's very best divisions in an army full of tough, fighting units.

As Hood's Division formed, Union shelling intensified, which many in the ranks believed was specifically targeting them. Although almost certainly mistaken—most were likely fired by Union artillery across Antietam Creek, beyond view of the forming Confederates—the shells began exacting a toll, so Hood moved his two columns forward at once. Law's Brigade advanced first, pressing from the woods, past the church, across the roadbed, and into the clover field beyond. Here Hood's men had their first view this day of the Cornfield, which they were about to enter. A soldier in the 4th Texas recalled "[R]ight here, when we reached the top of the hill, was the hottest place I ever saw on this earth or want to see hereafter. There were shot, shells, and Minie balls sweeping the face of the earth; legs, arms, and

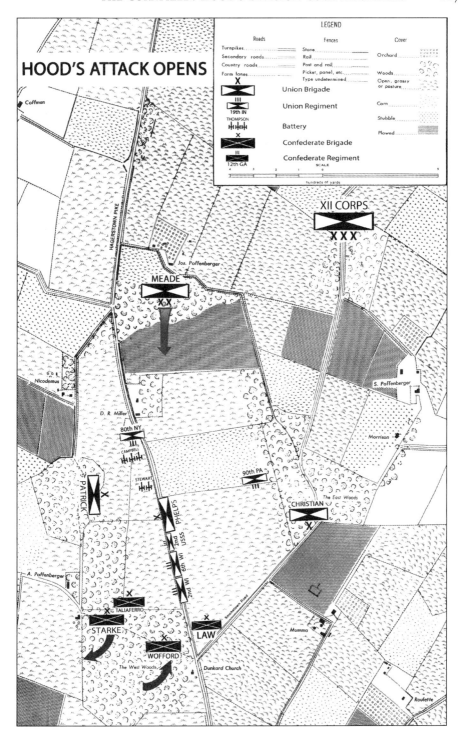

other parts of human bodies were flying in the air like straw in a whirlwind. The dogs of war were loose, and 'havoc' was their cry."[5]

The tactical situation facing Hood was no more encouraging. The flight of Starke's and Taliaferro's Brigades had exposed his front and reaching the Pike, Hood discovered that the Confederate position at the Cornfield was held by almost nothing at all—Lawton's command had dissolved into chaos. Only Harry Hays stood firm in the Confederate rear opposite the Cornfield, along with about 40 of his men. Hood advised Hays "to retire, replenish his cartridge boxes, and reassemble his command," which he immediately did. Then Hood's Division readied for battle. It was just 7:00 in the morning.[6]

Once across the road, Colonel Law shifted his brigade from a column into a battle front facing north, a formation placing the 3rd Mississippi on the left, with the 11th Mississippi and the 6th North Carolina, respectively, to their right. Law gave the order in such haste, though, that he failed to allow sufficient space for his entire brigade to deploy. With literally no place to go, the 4th Alabama moved "by the flank," right into the Smoketown Road's bed. Another reason for this crowding was that Wofford's deploying Texas Brigade, on Law's left, had left too little room for the Alabamians. Wofford's Brigade had followed Law's men to this point but stopped to form its battle line just north of the Dunker Church. Once deployed, the 5th Texas held the brigade's right flank, pinned on the Hagerstown Pike, with the 4th and 1st Texas, 18th Georgia, respectively, to their left. The Hampton Legion held the brigade's left flank. Barely had the division formed in battle lines when it began moving north toward the Yankees.[7]

Hood's quick action meant the Confederacy struck first in bringing reinforcements into battle before the Dunker Church. For years after the battle of Antietam, many of Hood's surviving veterans claimed their division commander's deployment and advance had been rash and ill-prepared, explaining the confusion and high casualties the Texas Brigade suffered in the Cornfield. At least some of this criticism probably stems from Hood's lackluster performance in the 1864 Atlanta Campaign, fights and mistakes that had yet to occur in 1862. Whatever these veterans thought, however, Hood's swift action—well-prepared or not—clearly turned the battle's tide in the South's favor at a critical moment.

Hood's Division now formed one extended line, nearly spanning the width of the Cornfield and reaching across the Hagerstown Pike and nearly through the West Woods. Nonetheless, this unity was short-lived. Barely had they formed, when Hood sent Law's Brigade marching gradually northeastward to strike Yankees holding the southeastern end of the Cornfield. At the same moment, Hood ordered the Texas Brigade forward almost due north to hit Union troops holding the southwestern end of the Cornfield. At first it was a slight thing, barely noticeable to those in ranks, but soon it became obvious—Hood had spilt his division into two. Not only were the two brigades moving in very different directions, but they were about to begin two nearly independent fights. Hood may have felt justified in splitting his force so because he was reacting to the immediate Union threat, which itself was widely divided. Regardless, this decision would soon significantly affect their battle. For now, though, Hood's massive division was about to overwhelm some very determined Yankees.[8]

***

"A long and steady line of rebel grey, unbroken by the fugitives who fly before us, comes sweeping down through the woods and around the church," recalled Major Dawes. Those in Gibbon's ranks who saw the Texas Brigade rolling toward them knew the tables had just turned. The cost of driving away Starke's and Taliaferro's men had gradually dissolved their unit cohesion and the Iron Brigade and Phelps's command now resembled a chaotic mass. Reaching the fence on the Hagerstown Pike restored some order, but not enough, and when Hood's men appeared on their exposed left flank, they opened fire. "They raise the yell and fire," remembered Rufus Dawes, "It is like a scythe running through our line." The enfilading fire swept away men's lives and what little order that existed in the Iron Brigade's ranks. Without prompting, Gibbon's men ran.[9]

"It is a race for life that each man runs for the cornfield," continued Dawes, "[b]ack to the corn, and back through the corn, the headlong flight continues." As the Union line broke, dozens of wounded men remained to survive as best they could. Silas Howard, from the 2nd US Sharpshooters's Company E, couldn't move but was determined to do what he could to help his comrades. Stripping the falling block mechanism from his Sharps repeating rifle, Howard flung the vital piece of machinery as far as possible hoping to deny the Rebs his high-tech weapon.[10]

***

Wofford pushed his Texans into the void and up the long slope of the shattered Cornfield, maintaining order and dress despite having been so quickly thrown into this fight. They had driven the Yankees back 600 or so yards when Wofford's left-most units—the Hampton Legion and 18th Georgia—suddenly stopped, stalled by two Union artillery pieces on a rise across the Hagerstown Pike pouring deadly canister rounds into Wofford's left flank. In response, the Hampton Legion's Lieutenant Colonel Gary and the 18th Georgia's Lieutenant Colonel Ruff moved their regiments' front left to face and return fire on the guns. What they faced was Lieutenant Stewart's section of the 4th US Artillery and its 80th New York infantry support. The Union men probably couldn't appreciate it but opening this unexpected fire on Wofford's flank had stripped the Confederate counterattack of its momentum, stalling it in an instant. Stewart's artillerists and the New Yorkers had duplicated the situation that robbed Gibbon's attacking brigade of success only half an hour or so earlier.[11]

Until those Yankee guns were silenced, Hood's advance was at risk. For the 18th Georgia and the Hampton Legion men, though, silencing the guns was more an act of simple survival than deliberate tactical maneuvering. Lieutenant Colonel Ruff knew the best way to get rid of these guns was to attack their weakest point—the men crewing them. Ruff quickly pulled his best marksmen from the ranks, sending them across the road to snipe at Stewart's 4th US gunners. Within minutes their deadly work began taking a toll on Stewart's crews.[12]

Colonel Wofford could see that his attack was stalling because his left flank was stuck on something. "I rode hastily to them (Hampton's Legion and the 18th Georgia), urging them forward, when I saw two full regiments, one in their front and other partly to their left." What Wofford observed across the road almost certainly was the 19th Indiana and 7th Wisconsin emerging from the West Woods to the south of Stewart's guns and the nearby 80th New York. With such a force in front and a Yankee battery tearing at their flank, the men of the Hampton Legion and the 18th Georgia could barely hold their ground—without immediate help, even continuing that might be impossible. Racing to the right of his line, Wofford found Lieutenant Colonel Work and ordered his 1st Texas from the center to the left to confront the threat there. Wofford's thinking was sound; the center faced only scattered infantry fire, but the left was now hard pressed. Wofford intended the 1st Texas to advance a few dozen yards forward—creating maneuver room—before driving through the Cornfield to the 18th Georgia's right, heading at the flank of the Yankee battery and two infantry regiments threatening his brigade's left. Work instantly set in motion the 1st Texas's move.[13]

General Hood, too, watched the Texas Brigade's attack stall. From the rear, Hood could see—probably even before Wofford—the Yankee regiments emerging from the West Woods to threaten Wofford's left, so the reason for the brigade's halt was no mystery. While Wofford rode left to investigate, Hood rode right to act. Being behind his division, Hood similarly could see the right of Wofford's line was unopposed, making these ideal reinforcements for the threatened left and Hood instantly ordered Lieutenant Colonel B. F. Carter to take his 4th Texas there. Moving at the left oblique, the Texans soon reached the Hagerstown Pike, where Hood once again joined them and ordered Carter to deploy left of the Hampton Legion. Once finished deploying, Wofford's Brigade would be in a radically different position than that taken upon deploying for battle. The 1st Texas would hold the right flank, with the 18th Georgia, Hampton Legion, and 4th Texas on its left. The brigade no longer faced north but nearly west now and only the 1st Texas continued moving north. Moreover, the Texas Brigade had lost one of its regiments completely. After ordering the 4th Texas left, Hood decided the 1st Texas had things there well in hand and sent the 5th Texas to the far right of the Cornfield to support Law's

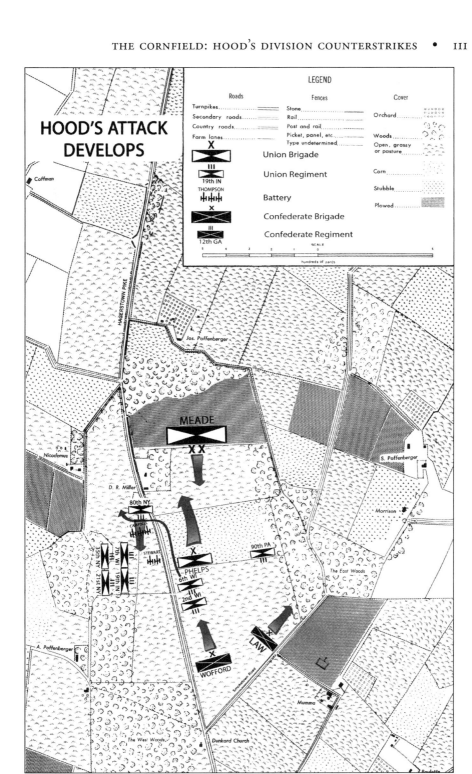

Brigade. The 5th Texas would walk forever out of the Texas Brigade's fight and into a completely different reality in the East Woods.[14]

Hood and Wofford certainly intended that their respective actions would protect the Texas Brigade and improve prospects for success. These good intentions, however, were little more than that. Wofford, responding to the threat on his left flank, deployed his troops to blunt that threat and get his counterattack back on track. Hood was doing nearly the same thing, albeit by moving a different regiment. Ultimately, these movements were complementary, putting regiments into different spots and bolstering the strength of Wofford's threatened line. However, Hood unnecessarily duplicated Wofford's role, serving at times not as a division leader but rather as a second commander of the Texas Brigade. Occurring at a critical moment, this command confusion fatally stalled Wofford's attack and resulted in additional significant, unnecessary casualties. Law and his brigade fared better because Hood had given clear directions, taking them far away and preventing Hood from interfering further with Law's actions. Perhaps the most devastating harm of Hood's misplaced attention to his old brigade was it robbed the division of its commander at critical moments, leaving no one to oversee the wider fight.

***

A short time before, the 90th Pennsylvania boys across the Cornfield had watched events to their right with concern. A large enemy force crossed the road and although Gibbon's and Phelps's Brigades were there to deal with that threat to their left and Christian's Brigade was nearby in the East Woods, the 90th now was the only Union force in the southeast portion of the Cornfield. Unexpectedly, a column of troops appeared from a concealed position on the Pennsylvanians's left, moving across the field toward their right, probably removing any sense of security the 90th men felt. To Christian's 26th and 94th New York, this column seemed to be walking behind the Mumma farmhouse, now consumed in flames and bellowing smoke into the morning sky. In ordinary circumstances, the burning house and tower of smoke would capture the New Yorkers's rapt attention, but today, these marching troops were of greater interest. This mysterious column was Colquitt's Brigade, another unit of D. H. Hill's Division, moving to support Hood's troops just beginning their counterattack into the Cornfield. Of more immediate concern to the 90th Pennsylvania, though, was Evander Law's Brigade which now headed right at them.[15]

***

Across the open field, Laws's men advanced, dressing their lines as best they could amidst the incessant Yankee shelling. Thompson's Battery was almost certainly what troubled Law's men not, as some later claimed, Campbell's guns then quite busy with Wofford's attacking brigade. Atop a rise by the East Woods, the battery poured a deadly accurate fire into the Rebels with spherical case shot—timed or impact-fused cannon balls. Even amidst this fire, Law's men advanced toward their objective.[16]

The deadly intensity of Thompson's fire proved too much for at least one of Law's men. The 4th Alabama's Private Joseph Frame suddenly broke from the ranks and started calmly for the rear, probably hoping others in the regiment would be too busy to bother with him. Lieutenant James Stewart, however, grabbed Frame's coat and ordered the private at gunpoint back into line. Frame, though, dropped to the ground and refused to move. With more vital duties before him, Frame's disgusted officer gave the private a swift kick and rejoined his regiment. As Private Frame raced to safety, his former regiment pressed on toward the enemy.

Nearing the East Woods, Colonel Law found himself facing two Yankee threats—one the regiment in the corn and another in the woods to his right. How to address these disparate threats was solved by news that the 5th Texas was on its way. Detaching the 4th Alabama to join the Texans in clearing the Yankees from the woods, Law ordered his remaining three regiments ahead at the left oblique, which took them in a northeasterly direction and right at the 90th Pennsylvania.[17]

***

The 90th Pennsylvania poured volley after volley into the advancing enemy but on pressed Law's men, surging up to and around the Pennsylvanians's flanks. As the 90th's Major Alfred Sellers noted, "solitary and alone, we gave and took our medicine." "We were at this time losing men rapidly," remembered Lieutenant George Watson of Company H, "and only a few minutes thus engaged, when it was observed that we being outflanked on our right, there we directed our fire." Firing on the threatened right flank did nothing to save the similarly threatened left, while the center of Law's line was nearly on top of the Pennsylvanians. As the two lines merged, casualties grew at an alarming rate. Men were shot but unable to say by whom, the enemy or their own ranks. Every company of the 90th Pennsylvania suffered casualties here. Despite this carnage, what occupied many of the Pennsylvanians was a threat to their colors.[18]

Four paces before the regiment's position—as dictated by the drill manual, though perhaps not common sense—stood its color guard. In theory, placing them before the main line allowed the two ranks to preserve alignment while also looking generally forward toward their objective. Working well on the parade ground, in battle this made the color guard—already a choice target—a most deadly unit in which to serve. The 90th's color guard had remained at its exposed post since leaving the East Woods and was now closest to the enemy, as was the regiment's loved national flag. As the flanks were being turned a volley felled color-bearer Corporal Theodore Mason, who had been cheering on his firing comrades. As Mason fell dead to the ground, so followed his charge, the national color. Seeing an opportunity, several Rebs swarmed forward from Law's center, grabbing the flag before tripping over each other to get their prize safely to the rear. At that same moment, though, 10 or so men from the center of the 90th bolted to reclaim their flag, launching a small, very personal battle within the larger fight in the Cornfield. Desperate, hand-to-hand fighting erupted. Private William H. Paul of the 90th's Company E recalled, "We clashed with a shock, and a sharp hand-to-hand fight ensued in which two of our men were killed and five so severely wounded that they were unable to be of further assistance." Paul, however, was committed to the task and not thinking about his actions so much as getting back that flag. "A Rebel had already seized the colors but I grasped them and with one supreme effort wrenched the precious banner from his hold," before sprinting away to safety. This act of heroism borne perhaps of bravery or maybe unthinking rashness, earned William Paul the Medal of Honor.[19]

Their flag and honor regained, the 90th Pennsylvania withdrew toward the East Woods and safety when Colonel Lyle, who remained at his post with the regiment despite being severely wounded in the side, ordered a retreat. The 90th's veterans would claim their retreat had been orderly; "the color bearer walking backward, the men turning and firing until it entered the woods, when it hurriedly pushed through them…" Not everyone remembered it so, and Private John Howell from Company B recalled "the line was in retreat or falling back. I was in between the two fires. Some of us heard the order to retreat and some of us did not." This uncertainty earned Howell a nearly fatal wound in the back of his head, but he was hardly alone. Final returns revealed the regiment had lost nearly half of its 200-man roster in the Cornfield.[20]

As the 90th Pennsylvania slipped hurriedly into the woods, it opened the eastern end of the Cornfield to Confederate control once again. Yankees held the southern end of the East Woods and Law's position could not be secured until these troops were driven from that key spot. At the same time, Thompson's Federal battery continued raining shells onto Law's ranks. Without pause, Evander Law set his brigade in motion to reduce these twin threats.

***

Ordering his three regiments forward into the southern end of the Cornfield—taking ground the Pennsylvanians had so stoutly defended only moments ago—Law suddenly halted the 6th North Carolina, and 2nd and 11th Mississippi in response to an order from General Hood, who directed the pause to provide the 4th Alabama and 5th Texas time to move into position. Although it only took the Alabamians three or so minutes to arrive—moving up the road in a column—and the Texans an additional two or so minutes, to the rest of Law's men it must have seemed to take hours because they had to endure both Thompson's artillery and the volleys of Christian's infantry from the East Woods. Law's North Carolinians and Mississippians weren't the only ones suffering during this transition, though, because the 4th

Alabama lost its commander, Captain Lawrence Scruggs, to fire from the woods while moving into position. [21]

To their rear, the 21st Georgia still clung to the ground, trying desperately to hold on against fire from Christian's men hidden in the East Woods. They had no idea how desperate their situation was; the rest of Trimble's Brigade had long ago pulled back to safety, leaving the isolated 21st behind. With the regiment's commander, Major Glover, wounded, Captain James Nisbet suddenly found himself in charge of this very bad situation. Only moments, before he'd been knocked to the ground and had just regained consciousness. Now Nisbet was pinned like the rest of his men, unable to advance or retreat. Looking around, Nisbet realized someone was calling his name and waving frantically. Scrambling on all fours, he almost reached the regiment's center where he saw Lieutenant James Blevins, now in charge of his own former Company H, fall with a severe, profusely bleeding shoulder wound. The 21st's new commander had just sent the lieutenant away for medical help when Company C's Captain Merrill Castleberry scurried over to ask what to do next. Barely had he asked his question when a Yankee ball plunged into Castleberry's open mouth, exiting through the back of his head. Horrified, Nisbet propped the dying man's head on an abandoned cartridge box to stem the bleeding and keep him from drowning in his own blood, when suddenly someone called out "They are running!" Glancing up from his grisly act of charity, Nisbet realized it was true. Ordering the men up, he led them forward across the Smoketown Road to what Nisbet thought was Lawton's right flank. Though marching back into the fight, apparently being any place else was preferable to remaining where they were. [22]

Law hastily added the 21st Georgia to his force, pushing them forward on the right of the 4th Alabama and then joining the 5th Texas to farther extend his right. Now Law had in effect two distinct three-regiment brigades at his disposal, one heading into the East Woods and the other ready to push northward into the Cornfield. This intentional divide grew wider during their brief pause because Law's left-most regiments had drifted obliquely left, leaving them facing nearly northward. Splitting his brigade into two parts was risky, but a calculated action. Although the Yankees would possess the better terrain in each of Law's coming fights, Law's two forces enjoyed both the attacker's momentum and the mass of greater numbers. The Mississippians and North Carolinians moving northward into the Cornfield carried some 889 well-trained men against a single Union battery—the only Federal force there after the 90th Pennsylvania's retreat. The right half of Law's command—headed for the East Woods—numbered 463 experienced fighters, while the three remaining regiments of Christian's Brigade numbered 681 men. Readying his left-most force to head north and deepen the Confederacy's hold on the Cornfield, Law ordered the right-hand force east to retake the East Woods. [23]

Law's Texans, Georgians, and Alabamians poured into the East Woods as three separate living streams, each coming from slightly different directions. Once across the wood line, though, these three flows merged into one, mighty torrent of Confederate force. The right-most regiments of Christian's Brigade never really had a chance. The 88th Pennsylvania tried shifting its front to meet the surging enemy but to no avail. They barely fired a few scattered volleys before Law's front ranks were upon them, forcing a quick retreat. Breaking from the right, Christian's men fled from the woods. Charles McClenthen of the 26th New York later claimed his regiment's retreat "was done without any more haste in confusion, than would have attended the same movement upon battalion drill," a recollection that is probably more creative than accurate. As Christian's Pennsylvanians and New Yorkers flowed out of the East Woods, Law's Texans, Georgians, and Alabamians flooded into their former position. Law's three regiments quickly halted, reformed their lines, and sought cover behind the trees and rock outcroppings that littered the woodlot. Perhaps they stopped because their commanders realized every eastward step took them farther from the rest of Law's Brigade—their only reinforcements—or because they lacked orders to do more than clear the woods of Yankees; regardless, their halt was critically important for Southern prospects in the battle. For at that moment, Law's men had both removed the Union threat to the right flank of Hood's advancing counterattack in the Cornfield and secured control over the southern end of the East Woods. If Law's men didn't really appreciate what they'd just done, neither apparently did General Hooker.[24]

***

Had the battle followed Hooker's original plan, most of the fighting would have occurred some 700 yards away on the slope of the Dunker Church ridge and the East Woods would have been little more than a backdrop for Union artillery. However, in creating a salient extending across the southern end of the Cornfield, Stonewall Jackson forced Hooker's corps to instead fight for control of an unanticipated, intermediate goal—Miller's Cornfield. It was becoming increasingly clear that without controlling the Cornfield, the Union attack simply couldn't reach its main objective on the Dunker Church ridge. Now Law's hold on the southern end of the East Woods added another unanticipated, intermediate objective because control of the Cornfield simply wasn't possible without first owning the East Woods. Holding the East Woods gave the South an anchor for the right flank of its salient, as well as a strong position from which to contest hold of the Cornfield itself. Even if Hood's counterattack failed and the Union moved to retake the Cornfield—as had happened to Lawton barely an hour earlier— it would have to contend with fire on both flanks, coming from the main Confederate line on the Dunker Church ridge, as well as from Law's men in the East Woods. Hooker now had to secure two intermediate objectives in turn, before attacking his main objective. The Union attack was stuck even deeper in the morass of a tactical bog.

Across the Cornfield to the west, the sniping fire of the 18th Georgia's skirmishers exacted an increasingly high human toll from the 4th US Artillery and Lieutenant Stewart suddenly realized that fresh men were available to replenish his section's thinning crews if he could get to them in time. Wheeling his horse, the lieutenant sought Miller's haystacks and the men there guarding the section's caissons and horses. When the Georgians killed his mount, throwing the lieutenant roughly to the ground, Stewart jumped to his feet and raced to gather any available replacement gunners. Within seconds, he was rushing this second-string gun crew into action.[25]

Ordering his new gunners into their roles, Stewart glanced to the rear and beheld a welcome sight. Captain Joseph Campbell and the rest of the 4th US Battery B were speeding down the pike toward their position. Deploying immediately left of Stewart's section, the remaining four guns at once added firepower to Stewart's hold on this vital position. These fresh guns and crews also gave the 18th Georgia's riflemen new targets at which to aim, however.[26]

His guns deployed just where he wanted them, Captain Joseph Campbell dismounted. At that same moment, the captain's bugler, John Cook—having been detailed to Lieutenant Stewart—reported to the new senior officer on the field. Before even acknowledging the boy's presence, a volley tore into Joe Campbell's shoulder and his horse, killing the poor animal and wounding the battery's commander. Instinctively, the bugler grabbed his wounded commander and helped him to the rear. The two soldiers made it as far as D. R. Miller's haystacks, which had become a makeshift haven for the 4th US Artillery's wounded. "The two straw stacks offered some kind of shelter for our wounded" recalled John Cook years later, "and it was a sickening sight to see those poor, maimed, and crippled fellows, crowding on top of one another…" John Cook made sure his commander got the care his rank suggested he deserved and placed Captain Campbell in the care of a driver. But John Cook's work wasn't done yet.

Before parting, Captain Campbell ordered John to alert Lieutenant Stewart that he now commanded the battery. John, without hesitation, returned to the battery's exposed position to relay this message. Even completing this dangerous task didn't end the boy's work. The battery was running thin on manpower, even with the new guns in place, and John noticed a Number 6 or 7 man from one of the gun's crews lying dead with a full ammunition pouch still wrapped around his shoulders. Knowing this meant that one of the guns was at risk, John swung his bugle over his shoulder and wrested the leather pouch from the dead man. From that moment until Campbell's Battery moved to the rear, the bugler worked a gun alongside the adults. It was an act that earned John Cook—who had turned 15 years old barely a month before—the Medal of Honor.[27]

The Georgian sharpshooters' accurate fire now wrought its deadly work on the crews of Campbell's other four guns. Returns would show the battery lost 38 men and 27 horses, but what mattered at that moment was what these casualties meant for the Union's hold on this position. Losing so many men and horses put the battery at risk of being overrun and surrendering its position and guns. General Gibbon, watching from nearby, knew all this well enough but his strong reaction to the sight was personal. After all, this was his old battery, which the general referred to in reports not by its modern name of "Campbell's Battery" or by its formal, military title of "the 4th US Artillery, Battery B" but instead as "Gibbon's Battery." In his mind, that's what it was and would always be and at that moment, Gibbon's Battery was dying.[28]

Seeing the left-most gun's captain fall—leaving no one to command or aim the brass Napoleon—Gibbon sprang without thinking to the piece. Ordering the remaining crew to load a double round of canister, Gibbon aimed the gun and fired into the face of the 18th Georgia and Hampton Legion, which were trying desperately to advance on the guns. Again and again, Gibbon ordered the crew to load and fire their huge shotguns into the advancing enemy. So close were the Rebels, that the battery's rounds tore up the ground and blasted the post-and-rail fence bordering the Hagerstown Pike into splinters.

John Gibbon knew this stalemate couldn't long continue and decided to act. Seeing a body of troops reorganizing in the swale on the northern end of the Cornfield, Gibbon determined they would become infantry support for his battery. Racing across the road, Gibbon found Major Dawes, holding the Wisconsin state color and rallying his men after retreating from Wofford's advance. Gibbon ordered, "Here, major, move your men over, we must save those guns!" His face streaked with gunpowder and sweat, the general pointed to the rear of his battery before returning to them. With that, Rufus Dawes ordered his now-ragged command—what remained of the 2nd and 6th Wisconsin—to "Right face, forward march!" and the line surged across the road into position on the 80th New York's right. Gibbon's guns had received their much-needed help.[29]

***

Colonel Wofford, however, was already a step ahead of John Gibbon. The 4th Texas's arrival on the Texas Brigade's left extended Wofford's front well beyond the right flank of the 4th US Battery's position. All he needed now do was push his Texas Brigade quickly across the Hagerstown Pike to eliminate the Yankee artillery, and just maybe take these guns in the process. Before Wofford could put any of this into action, though, another Union officer made known his presence on the field.[30]

As the 4th Texas moved into its new position at the Hagerstown Pike—the highest ground on this part of the field—it drew unexpected fire from somewhere ahead, across the road. Lieutenant Colonel Benjamin Carter hurried the regiment's left wheel movement and once on the roadbed, ordered it to open fire. However, the enemy was in a skirmish formation and so concealed by terrain and rock ledges that few, if any, of the 4th Texas could see who they were shooting at. Stewart's artillery

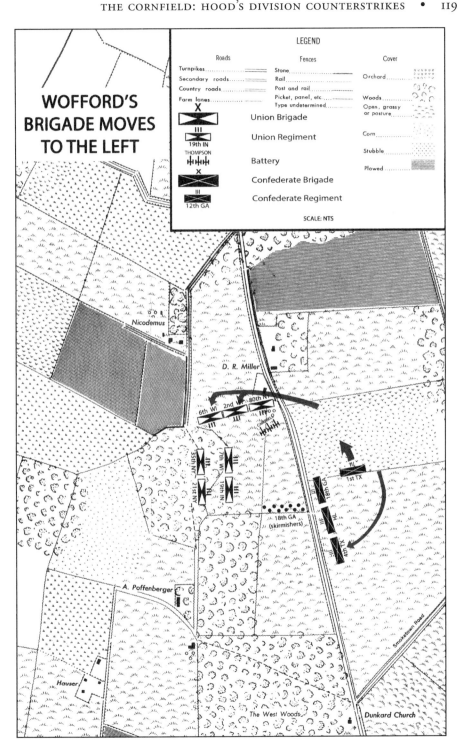

WOFFORD'S
BRIGADE MOVES
TO THE LEFT

LEGEND

Roads	Fences	Cover
Turnpikes	Stone	Orchard
Secondary roads	Rail	
Country roads	Post and rail	Woods
Farm lanes	Picket, panel, etc.	Open, grassy or pasture
	Type undetermined	Corn
		Stubble
		Plowed

Union Brigade

Union Regiment

Battery

Confederate Brigade

Confederate Regiment

SCALE: NTS

on their right continued tearing holes in the Southern line, and if this was bad, things were about to get much worse. Looking across the shattered remains of the Hagerstown Pike's fence, Colonel Carter noted fresh troops surging from the West Woods. These weren't ragged, disorganized troops rallied from recent fighting; they moved in neat, organized formations suggesting they were fresh. Rather than flanking the Union guns, Carter and his Texans now were themselves about to be flanked.[31]

***

After a long, arcing march, Gibbon's 19th Indiana and 7th Wisconsin, with Patrick's Brigade close behind, reached the edge of the West Woods just as Wofford's advance on Stewart's guns began. As Federal reinforcements entered the open field, S. D. Lee's guns on the Dunker Church ridge caught their range and poured a deadly fire into the blue troops. One shell sent 19th Indiana veteran Bob Patterson flying, while another threw Company E's Clint Anthony head over heels through the ranks. Despite other casualties, the Union force pressed on to the post and rail fence bordering the Hagerstown Pike, immediately opening fire on the 4th Texas only a few yards away. Deepening the Union's hold on this spot, the 7th Wisconsin men slid into the cover of a swale behind a rock ledge near the road, opening their own solid fire into the nearby Texans.[32]

***

"I found the enemy in heavy force…" wrote the 4th Texas's Lieutenant Colonel Carter, understating the deadly situation his regiment faced. They couldn't stay here long but retiring would expose the flank of the Hampton Legion, then preoccupied with its own fight against Gibbon's other regiments and Stewart's guns and the 80th New York. Carter, though, seized upon an idea that might save his command and preserve the brigade's flank. Wheeling the 4th to the left again, astride the Hagerstown Pike facing north, put Carter's regiment on the advancing 7th Wisconsin's exposed right flank, turning the tables on the attacking Yankees. Barely had the Texans begun moving, though, when Carter realized he had committed a grave error. "The movement, however, exposed us so much that we fell back directly…" he explained in his official report. Born of sheer desperation, the retreat probably killed any hope Wofford had of holding this spot.[33]

***

Seeing the Rebs falling back, the 19th Indiana and 7th Wisconsin men begged their officers to attack. The 19th Indiana's Colonel Alois Bachman saw it, too; drawing his sword and clutching his hat in his fist Bachman called out, "Boys, the command is no longer forward, but now it is follow me!" At that, Gibbon's two regiments surged ahead at the double-quick into position on the enemy's flank. Bachman's action was one of bravado and military necessity because using the manual-prescribed commands would have taken considerable time, allowing the wheeling Texans to beat his command into position. Such adaptation wasn't brilliant military thinking but rather the mark of an experienced, skilled citizen-officer. With Union troops poring over the road and into the Cornfield beyond, Bachman was about to slice a deadly hole in Wofford's enemy line.[34]

The 19th's George Finney wrote of that moment, "As the regiment gained the top of the hill they were greeted by a terrible volley of musketry from a brigade of Rebel infantry. For a moment the line staggered." They'd reached the high ground in the Cornfield held only moments before by the 4th Texas, whose desperate firing stopped Bachman's command in it tracks. Even though not fully on their flank, the 4th Texas's fire was so effective it convinced Finney they faced an entire Confederate brigade. Regardless, Gibbon's men returned the Texans volleys until reinforcements from Patrick's Brigade arrived to shore up their position. "The clarion voice of Bachman was heard urging his men to hold the hill until reinforcements could come up. The men rallying to his call began to fire into the dense mass of rebels in front; for five minutes they held the hill ... In those five minutes, one-third of the line had fallen. Still Bachman cheered on his men." In the midst of that hailstorm, a round struck the colonel's elbow, shattering his arm and spinning him around, into a spot where another ball pierced his body. Alois Bachman had broken Wofford's line, but paid for this feat with his life.[35]

Captain William Dudley assumed command of the 19th Indiana and quickly adjusted its position to protect Bachman's gains. Retiring the 19th to the Hagerstown Pike brought it in line with the 7th Wisconsin on their left and the newly arrived men of Patrick's Brigade. Colonel William Findley Rogers led Buffalo's own 21st New York up on the Indianans's left, while the 35th and 23rd New York each moved forward farther to the left. In the confusion, the 21st briefly crossed the road and advanced into the corn, seeking to align on Dudley's flank, but quickly halted and fell back as Dudley, too, moved his 19th regiment back to the road.[36]

Amidst this firing, though, one man in the 21st had something else on his mind. "[J]ust after we had fallen back, a stray shot struck a large fat pig," recalled Lieutenant Halsey, "which had been grunting about in the rear of our line, apparently indifferent as to the result of the fight. One of our boys taking in the situation at a glance, having, in all this excitement, presence of mind sufficient to feel the presence of an appetite, resolved that 'his porkship' should die a NATURAL death; dropping his musket he rushes to the spot with drawn sheath knife and with the practiced hand of a professional butcher brings the lingering sickness of Mr. Pig to an abrupt termination. Rolling him into a ditch 'to await further developments,' he runs back and resumes his place in line." That such a scene could occur amidst the desperate fighting along the Hagerstown Pike is a testament both the 21st New York's veteran status and to the importance of food to a hungry soldier.[37]

With this dinner secure, Patrick's regiments swept into line on the 19th Indiana's left, reinforcing Union control of the Hagerstown Pike. This infantry and fire from the remaining 4th US Artillery guns spelled doom for many in the 18th Georgia and Hampton Legion, still holding on in the corn. If things looked bad to those in the Texas Brigade's center, the situation was about to get even worse for the men on Wofford's right.[38]

**

As the 4th Texas arrived on Wofford's left, their comrades in the 1st Texas headed toward the brigade's right after Lieutenant Colonel Phillip A. Work led his regiment cleanly through its change of direction. These were veteran troops who had faced down Yankees in nearly every battle on the Peninsula, at the second battle of Manassas, and three days earlier atop South Mountain; if General Hood could trust any troops to perform under fire, it was the 1st Texas. Hood now wanted them to march due north and post on the 18th Georgia's right flank to stabilize Wofford's line and in response, the Texans pushed over the Cornfield's shattered southern fence and deeper into the remains of the field itself. Barely after stepping amidst the husks of corn, the 1st Texas attracted fire from Ransom's Battery C of the 5th US Artillery, posted by General Hooker atop the ridge overlooking the Cornfield from the north. The scattered case shot fired by Ransom's Napoleons couldn't stop these veterans, however, and deeper into the corn they went. Approaching some Union infantry, without prompting, the Yankees scattered and broke for the rear. The Texans were scoring a tremendous victory and had barely fired a shot. If this pace kept up, they might break the Union's hold on this spot single-handedly! Seeing the enemy fleeing, the men continued forward with a will all their own, pressing deeper and deeper into the Cornfield and farther and farther from their appointed post on the 18th Georgia's right. Flush with victory, the men of the 1st Texas had no idea what a disaster they had just set in motion.[39]

The cause of this tremendous error was simple—Lieutenant Colonel Work and his officers had lost control of the regiment. Years later, defenders of the 1st Texas would claim they'd not gotten word of Hood's orders or that those orders had been unclear. Hood commented that the 1st Texas had "slipped the bridle and got away from the command," which is likely closest to the truth. Colonel Work explained in his report that "[a]s soon as the regiment became engaged with the enemy in the corn-field, it became impossible to restrain the men, and they rushed forward, pressing the enemy…" Work had committed a military commander's gravest failure, letting his fighting machine morph into an uncontrolled, surging mob. Swept along by the situation, Lieutenant Colonel Work did little more than hoping for the best and as events would soon prove, it was a vain hope indeed.[40]

Hood might have been cheered by the situation facing Law's Brigade, were he able to divert attention from Wofford's sorry state. Having sent his right-hand force into the East Woods, Colonel Law restarted the northward attack by his brigade's left. Pressing deeper into the Cornfield and up the rise, the 6th North Carolina held the right—guiding along the edge of the East Woods—while the 11th Mississippi formed the center and the 2nd Mississippi carried the advancing line's left flank; the weakest position of all because of the growing gap between Hood's two brigades. Watching from across the field, General Hood could see them advancing at the same moment that Wofford's men were running headlong into Gibbon's position across the road. When Stonewall's adjutant Captain Alexander "Sandie" Pendleton appeared looking for an update, Hood replied "Tell General Jackson unless I get reinforcements I must be forced back, but I am going on while I can." Whatever was later said about Hood's command of the situation in the Cornfield, this certainly was an accurate summary of his division's state then. As events would soon demonstrate, Hood's glance into the future too proved more prescient than he might have wished.[41]

Law's three regiments swept northward through the fallen remains of the Cornfield. Suddenly, stout fire from Union troops holding the northern end of the field found them. These were 100 or so men from Duryee's Brigade's 104th and 105th New York, who had been holding this spot since being driven back early in the battle. Despite their determination, Law's larger force easily brushed the New Yorkers away toward the North Woods, where the rest of their brigade waited. Law's regiments now became the target of Matthews's Battery, posted on the ridge beyond the Cornfield's northern fence, which poured a terrible, double-shotted fire into the North Carolinians and Mississippians. Still, on Law's men came like the battle-tested veterans they were, perhaps driven by the idea that reaching the field's northern end might permit driving off the exposed guns or killing their crews where they stood. Reaching that spot, however, revealed a sight that staggered Law's men—Meade's fresh division of the I Corps. Hood's gains in the Cornfield were about to be tested as never before.[42]

***

After stepping from safety in the North Woods, Meade had prepared his division to move quickly in reinforcing Doubleday's and Ricketts's attacking brigades. Colonel Albert Magilton's Brigade of Pennsylvania Reserves held the left of Meade's position, while Lieutenant Colonel Robert Anderson's Brigade deployed on the right. Because both brigades were deployed in a "column of battalions in mass"—each battalion forming one behind another, to speed their advance and offer flexibility when ready to fire—there was considerable space between the two formations. Into this gap, Meade placed Ransom's Battery, moving ahead of the Pennsylvania Reserves, it deployed in nearly the center of the grassy field overlooking the Cornfield. Upon receiving Hooker's order to advance, Meade started his two columns forward but barely had they reached musket range of the Cornfield when Meade must have realized his division's mission had changed. No longer would Meade be reinforcing gains from a Union attack, instead he would be stopping a Confederate counterattack. Meade later recalled that he found the Cornfield in Rebel hands, "the possession of which the enemy warmly disputed."[43]

Meade halted his command in a swale in D. R. Miller's grassy field, using this natural cover to conceal his two brigades from the enemy, while reconnoitering the ground and situation before him. Such effective use of natural terrain demonstrated Meade's skill as a field commander, foreshadowing events less than a year in the future at Gettysburg when the general would again skillfully exploit the ground to meet tactical objectives. For now, though, what greeted Meade in the Cornfield wasn't encouraging and he recalled "I saw the enemy were driving our men from the corn-field." Nonetheless, this told George Meade what he needed to know. "I immediately deployed both brigades and forming line of battle along the fence bordering the corn-field, for the purpose of covering the withdrawal of our people and resisting the farther advance of the enemy." Barking orders, Meade quickly had Anderson's Brigade anchoring its right on the Hagerstown Pike where the 9th Pennsylvania Reserves formed for battle. Once in place, the 11th and 12th Pennsylvania Reserves formed to their left, extending the brigade's control nearly to the center of the open field. On their left deployed Magilton's Brigade, with the 7th Pennsylvania Reserves on the right maintaining contact with Anderson's left-most regiment, with the 4th, 3rd, and 8th Reserves filling the rest of Meade's line to the left. In barely a minute, Meade's formation stretched from the Hagerstown Pike to the East Woods. Almost as quickly, it moved from the fleeting cover between the two swells of ground and up the slope toward the Cornfield as one force.[44]

Reaching the ridge's crest and the northern edge of the Cornfield, Meade could now see in full detail what faced his command. On the right, directly ahead of Anderson's Brigade, was a single regiment, while a brigade—Wofford's—engaged Patrick's men at the road, fighting mostly perpendicular to his line. The situation on the left was far less encouraging, where a large body of Confederate troops held the northern end of the Cornfield, as well as the East Woods to his left. Meade's two brigades could cover Gibbon's retreat but might themselves be at risk from this threat on their left.

Throughout Meade's advance, General Hooker—who probably had no intention of using his last fresh I Corps division in a defensive role—worked feverishly providing support. Hooker directed Ransom's Battery to fire on Hood's advancing lines, probably to weaken this infantry before meeting Meade's Pennsylvania Reserves, then turned to securing Meade's flanks. Detaching the 10th Pennsylvania Reserves, Hooker ordered it across the Hagerstown Pike and beyond the right flank of Patrick's Brigade, reinforcing Patrick and ensuring Meade's right flank wasn't dislodged by an unexpected attack from the rear. To secure Meade's left flank, Hooker sent Meade a dispatch directing him to "detach a brigade to reinforce our troops in the woods on the left."[45]

This order to Meade was certainly well intended but revealed just how poor a grasp Hooker had of the situation because there was no longer any body of "our troops" in the East Woods for Meade to reinforce. The only Union presence there were dead or wounded men in blue or those left behind by now-retired regiments. A simple glance toward the woods would have shown Hooker the truth—any Union troops there should have been resisting Law's freely advancing Confederates. Regardless why it was so, the flawed order would soon bring Meade's Division to the brink of disaster.

Probably expecting to be fighting on the Dunker Church ridge, Hooker had failed to appreciate how important these woods might become if his plans didn't go as intended. Although the battle had been unfolding for over an hour in a way that made the East Woods a vital position for securing the Union left flank, Hooker had done nothing to reflect this change. Worse, once Seymour's Brigade had been pulled out, no Union force entering the East Woods, neither Hartsuff's nor Christian's Brigades, had been assigned the specific task of holding it. In fact, Hooker's order to Meade was the first time all day he'd acted to ensure the Union's hold on the woods. This effort was too little, too late, though, and Hooker's failure would continue bedeviling his tactical plans, undermining completing the critical first step of McClellan's battle plan.

Complying with Hooker's orders, Meade directed Magilton's Brigade to move "by the left flank" into the northern end of the East Woods. Magilton's Brigade had barely begun moving when Law's Confederates poured "a dreadful fire" into them from the Cornfield. Formed in a column facing left, Magilton's men were unable to return this fire and could do little more than endure it and keep moving toward cover. This all proved too much for the badly exposed middle of Magilton's line, though; the 3rd and 4th Pennsylvania Reserves responded in that most human of ways—they ran. In broken disorder, the two regiments fled to the rear, while their officers cursed and struggled to restore order. Fortunately for the fleeing Pennsylvanians, their comrades in the 8th Reserves had nearly completed moving into the woods and as the regiments on their right dissolved, the 8th was facing front to fight.[46]

***

Seeing their opponents melt away before them, Law's two Mississippi regiments surged forward—without any orders—into the gap. Men of the 2nd and 11th Mississippi scrambling over the broken remains of the Cornfield's northern fence into position. General Meade watched this disaster unfold, describing that "the gap made by the withdrawal of Magilton was soon filled by the enemy, whose infantry advanced boldly through the corn-field…" Meade rode feverishly to throw forward the only immediate help he had, Ransom's Battery C of the 5th US Artillery. Within seconds the battery's four 12-pound Napoleons were reoriented and firing into the rapidly filling gap.[47]

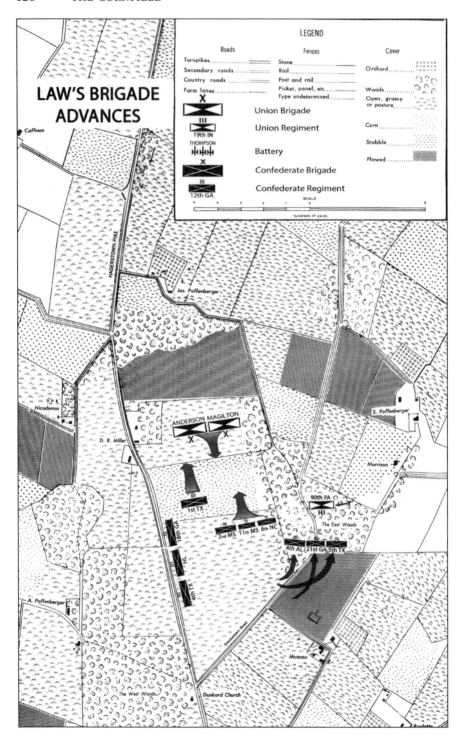

Even before Ransom's artillery opened, though, the situation had turned against the surging Mississippians. The 11th Mississippi men discovered a gap of their own had opened on their right because the 6th North Carolina was no longer there. The North Carolinians remained glued to their previous post, locked in a desperate firefight with the 150 8th Pennsylvania Reserves men, now deployed in the northwestern end of the East Woods. So intense was this fight that it drove Private Frank Holsinger of the 8th Pennsylvania Reserves to run away in fear, while Company F's Corporal George Horton held fast to the regiment's flag. When a Confederate ball shot away part of Horton's foot, bringing both him and the flag to the ground, Horton raised himself up by jabbing the staff into the ground for support. Seconds later, however, the corporal fell dead, and the regiment's flag was nowhere to be found.[48]

Things on the left of the Mississippians's line looked little better. Barely had the 2nd Mississippi men crossed the fence when flanking fire from the left stopped them in their tracks. This fire came from Magilton's 7th Pennsylvania Reserves which, being last in the brigade's long column, had been cut off by the Mississippians's charge. As the Mississippians surged into the gap before them, the 7th Reserves "refused the left" and opened a direct and deadly fire on the attacking enemy. Law's men were taking fire from both flanks, as well as from Ransom's Battery in front. It was a situation that could not remain so for very long.[49]

At that critical moment the only link between Law's advancing brigade on the right and Wofford's stalled men on Hood's left was the 1st Texas, which alone was pressing deeper into the corn and driving the enemy before them. Cresting the ridge, the Texans drew artillery fire from the right-most guns of Ransom's Battery. Still, Work's Texans pressed bravely on, firing at those Yankees they could see through the remaining, scattered patches of standing corn. The 1st Texas neared the Cornfield's northern fence, only 30 yards away, when seemingly out of the very ground Meade's Pennsylvania Reserves arose to pour a solid wall of fire into them.

***

Lieutenant Colonel Robert Anderson's men had waited for this moment now for some time and warned by retreating New Yorkers and Wisconsinites that the enemy was coming right for them Anderson had ordered his command to lie down. Springing to their feet, the Pennsylvanians's fire rolled into the Texans from their right; the 12th Pennsylvania Reserves fired first, followed by the 11th Reserves's own volley. Still reeling from this shock, another volley swept through the 1st Texas from the 9th Pennsylvania Reserves on the far left, firing at the left oblique. Work's Texans had walked into a firestorm.[50]

***

The Texans tried holding their ground. Company K's Private Hanks recalled spotting a Pennsylvanian wearing a double-breasted coat, rising from behind his fence-rail breastwork to fire. Taking aim, Hanks thought "I am going to see you killed" and fired, but he would never know if he hit his mark—a Yankee ball tore through his own upper chest, forcing Hanks to the rear for medical help. Others in the 1st Texas suffered similar fates and its ranks were thinning fast. In only a few minutes, eight men were killed holding the regimental colors. Work knew his regiment couldn't stay here long and sent his adjutant, Sergeant Shropshire, to the rear for approval to pull the 1st Texas back. Moments after Shropshire departed, the regiment simply melted away, "ordered" back by Yankee fire of Anderson's Brigade. To remain would have been suicide.[51]

They raced away in such confusion that it took considerable time before Work and his men realized they'd lost their beloved regimental color, a Lone Star flag of Texas, made from the wedding dress worn by the wife of the regiment's first commander, former US senator Colonel Wigfall. Worse, though, was the loss of men forming the regiment's lifeblood. Only 56 1st Texas men survived those moments before Anderson's Brigade. At muster in the morning, Lieutenant Colonel Work discovered that of the 226 men he'd marched into the Cornfield, 170 had been killed or wounded. It would be for later historians to figure that 82.3 percent of the regiment fell in the Cornfield. The 1st Texas had marched in a regiment and emerged as barely four squads.[52]

As the 1st Texas broke, it shredded the only link holding together the two halves of Hood's attack. On Hood's right flank, Colonel Law had run out of options. "Our loses up to this time had been very heavy; the troops now confronting the enemy were insufficient to cover properly one-fourth of the line of battle; our ammunition was expended; the men had been fighting long and desperately, and were exhausted from want of food and rest. It was evident that this state of affairs could not long continue. No support was at hand. To remain stationary or advance without [ammunition] would have caused a useless butchery, and I adopted the only alternative—that of falling back to the woods from which I first advanced." Law's three forward-most regiments retreated though the corn, retracing their path to the Dunker Church.[53]

The situation on Hood's left was even worse. When the 19th Indiana and 21st New York swept up to take the Hagerstown Pike, Wofford had the 18th Georgia move its right back, deeper into the corn, to avoid having its flank turned. Without the 1st Texas securing the Georgians's right, Wofford, too, was out of choices. "By this time, our brigade having suffered so greatly, I was satisfied they could neither advance nor hold their position much longer without re-inforcements." Seeing retreat was the only option, Wofford rode to General Hood, who ordered the brigade to withdraw. Before the colonel could return to pass along Hood's order, however, his men began retreating on their own. Seeing he could do little more than guide the movement already underway, Wofford recalled "I ordered them back under cover of

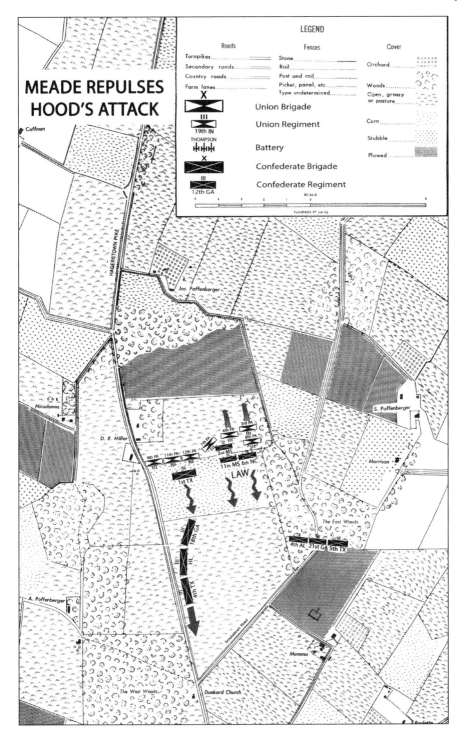

the woods to the left of the church, where we halted and waited for support, none arriving." As Hood's two brigades pulled back to the rear and safety, Lee and the Army of Northern Virginia once again lost control of the Cornfield.[54]

In the war's aftermath there was plenty of finger pointing in assigning blame for this lost opportunity. Hood, Wofford, and Law blamed the lack of reinforcements—Jackson's responsibility—for having to fall back while many others pointed directly at Hood, claiming his attack had been too hasty and poorly planned. It seems clear the lynchpin of Hood's advance became the 1st Texas's attack; its success might have become a turning point for the South, a moment of unplanned, soldier-driven bravado that was the right action, in the right place, at the right time. This was not to be. The 1st Texas's movement to Wofford's right flank was uncoordinated and poorly executed, leaving it out of position where and when it was needed most. Its spontaneous attack through the corn—when the men "slipped the bridle and got away from the command," as Hood colorfully described—represented a complete command breakdown. Lieutenant Colonel Work and his officers should have stopped the unplanned attack and ordered the regiment to its intended location; instead, they were either temporarily impotent leaders or—worse—allowed the men to seize command. When driven from the corn, the 1st Texas's failure collapsed the center of Hood's line, abandoning a role the Texans probably never knew they'd been playing. Lacking an intended purpose or unexpected success, the 170 men of the 1st who were killed or wounded in that attack died to no purpose. Worse, this result was caused by a leadership and command failure reaching from their regimental commander, through division commander General Hood, all the way to Stonewall Jackson. In the end, all those 170 casualties earned the 1st Texas was the "honor" of having the highest casualty percentage figure for any single regiment—on either side—of the entire war.[55]

In many respects, the reasons the 1st Texas's attack failed reflect the same problems plaguing Hood's larger assault into the Cornfield. Hood moved quickly into battle, putting his division in the right place at the right time to turn back Gibbon's Union attack and secure Jackson's salient south of the Cornfield. Had Hood been content with these achievements, his division's actions at Antietam would today be judged a success that had also prepared Hood's Division to meet the advance of Meade's fresh brigades. Instead, Hood chose to push beyond defensive goals and launched a wider counterattack into the Cornfield, a tremendous gamble the Confederacy lost because Hood's command mismanagement early-on surrendered control of the fight's direction and momentum. Despite Hood's initial success against Gibbon and the 90th Pennsylvania, he should have anticipated the looming threat of large numbers of fresh Union troops and acted accordingly. The fate of Lawton's, Trimble's, and Hays's Brigades should have warned Hood to the presence of unseen reinforcements; instead, Hood pressed on to counterattack, playing right into Hooker's advantages of greater manpower and mass once Meade's Division entered the fight. Hood acknowledged this in his postwar memoir, writing "Not far distant in our front were drawn up, in close array, heavy columns of Federal infantry; not less than two corps were in sight to oppose my small command, numbering approximately, two thousand effectives. However, with the trusty Law on my right, in the edge of the woods, and the gallant Colonel Wofford in command of the Texas Brigade on the left, near the pike, we moved forward to the assault." Was it overconfidence bordering on hubris that propelled Hood's advance or the common military assumption that securing the initiative can overcome manpower and firepower deficiencies of an attack? Regardless why it was so, Hood chose poorly.

Having decided to counterattack, Hood's success turned on his and his subordinate commanders' abilities. Although Colonels Law and Wofford were generally effective under fire, controlling their brigades in the whirlwind of battle and exploiting opportunities when possible, the same cannot be said for General Hood. Hood's first error occurred when dividing his division before a numerically superior enemy, moving Wofford's Brigade left against Gibbon and Patrick, while sending Law's Brigade right toward the East Woods. Had Hood's goal been modest and defensive, this deployment would have been completely appropriate. In shifting to the offensive, however, Hood's action created two separate brigade-sized forces, robbing his division's attack of mass and surrendering offensive initiative to the Yankees by reacting to their deployments. Moreover, Hood never tried reuniting his divided force to undo this error; instead, Hood let the situation spiral out of his grasp, focusing his command energy instead on overseeing Wofford's struggling brigade on the left. Regardless why this was so, at the most critical moments in the division's advance Hood was not directing his entire command but rather trying to be both a division and a brigade commander. As a result, command confusion erupted on the left as both Hood and Wofford moved the brigade's various regiments into place, frequently at cross purposes. Hood's misplaced command role left his critical center empty until the 1st Texas unknowingly filled it. This command confusion also probably explains in part how the 1st Texas drifted unchecked so far forward that it "slipped the bridle." The division's commander, who should have been monitoring his entire attack's progress and making adjustments to ensure success, was doing no such thing much of the time. When the situation slipped completely beyond control—when the 1st Texas's repulse collapsed the center—Hood wasn't in a position to do more than retreat. Hood's shortcomings as a senior commander were evident, even in late 1862. [56]

Stonewall Jackson, too, should shoulder some blame for Hood's counterattack's failure and the resulting catastrophic casualties. The result of Lawton's, Trimble's, and Hays's actions should have taught Jackson that his men could hold the Cornfield through firepower alone, rather than having to physically occupy the position, which had proven to be an impossible task for both sides so far. Even if Jackson hadn't appreciated this fact, it remains unclear why he permitted Hood's counterattack to proceed given that Lee had adopted a defensive approach for the battle's early phase.

Worse, Jackson failed to reinforce Hood—even after he called for support—or recall his division, dooming the assault which he'd at least tacitly approved.

***

If Hooker felt any relief watching Hood's men surrender the Cornfield, it should have been cold comfort to the general. Now sometime past 7:30 in the morning, the fight had been underway for nearly two hours and had cost the Union thousands of casualties, yet Hooker had rather little to show for the effort. Instead of struggling for the high ground on the Dunker Church ridge, Hooker and his corps had been forced to fight for control of the Cornfield and its surrounding ground, which from the start should have been under Union control. Worse, Hooker had been required to spend all three of his I Corps divisions just to reach this point; only a single brigade—Anderson's—remained in a condition or position to join the advance toward the Dunker Church.

The limitations and failings of Hooker's original plan had become obvious, but the general was slow to observe them or adjust. Hooker stubbornly remained committed to attacking on a north–south axis—from the North Woods toward the Dunker Church—which limited his force's maneuvering room to never more than 800 yards and prevented attacking in units larger than brigades. He by now grasped the importance of the Cornfield as a distinct position, necessary to secure and utilize in obtaining his objective, but this awareness had come too late; his men had fought all morning in consequence of this error and would continue paying for Hooker's failing. Even so, Hooker—like his counterpart Stonewall Jackson—failed to appreciate that thanks to the range and effectiveness of then-modern small arms and artillery, his forces could control the Cornfield through firepower alone, without physically occupying it. Having similarly missed the East Woods's importance, Hooker now appreciated that striking the Dunker Church position was impossible without first possessing that key position, too. Hooker's illusion that the Union held the woods—the 8th Pennsylvania Reserves had only a toehold there; three Confederate regiments controlled the lot—would have to first be shattered before the Union could control the Cornfield, much less reach the Dunker Church ridge.[57]

If Hooker's plan wasn't well crafted, its implementation only made things worse. Hooker apparently failed to explain to his division and brigade commanders how important was making their respective attacks in concert, unintentionally surrendering his greater manpower and firepower mass. Beyond starting at roughly the same time, neither Doubleday nor Ricketts coordinated their attacks' timing, a command failure that set the stage for similarly uncoordinated moves and attacks by Duryee's, Hartsuff's, and Christian's Brigades on the left. It was Hooker's role to ensure such coordination both before and during the fighting. Although active throughout the I Corps attack in moving troops and artillery into position, Hooker was so focused on such basic functions that he nearly abrogated his role as senior Union commander on the field and left Doubleday and Ricketts largely on their own. Hooker's command failings were the root of the I Corps's dire situation at 7:30 that morning, which so far had prevented the Union from reaching any of McClellan's battle objectives.

***

Even so, at that time, Joe Hooker might have thought things were finally looking up. The Rebs were streaming to the rear, abandoning the Cornfield, and for a change, Union troops were positioned to hold it, if not finally reach the Dunker Church ridge. So now the fight would change. The Union I Corps and Confederate divisions of Lawton and Hood withdrew from the stage to make way for the XII Corps and D. H. Hill's Division. It was a role that few who'd watched their fellow players perform that morning probably relished. Nonetheless, their show would now go on.

CHAPTER 8

The Cornfield: Mansfield Wrests Order from Chaos

Sometime before 7:00 that morning, Joe Hooker played the last card in his hand, ordering forward Mansfield's XII Corps of 7,500 mostly green troops. Division commander Brigadier General Alpheus Williams recalled that "At first dawn of the day the cannon began its work. Gen. Hooker's command was about a mile in front of us and it was his corps upon which the attack began. By a common impulse our men stood to arms. They had slept in ranks and the matter of toilet was not tedious, nor did we have time to linger over the breakfast table." The 10th Maine's Major John Gould wrote "We slept quietly in the furrows till 5 O'clock in the morning and then a sharp rattle of musketry precisely like that which had served as a 'good night' to us brought every man to his feet. Without so much as peeping into our haversacks we broke stacks and waited for orders." Edmund Brown of the 27th Indiana's Company C described many XII Corps soldiers' experiences that morning. "While we wait, many of the men pour water out of their canteens into their little tin pails, and make themselves a cup of coffee, over the small fires we have been permitted to kindle since daylight. With this black coffee and the crackers and raw pork in their haversacks, they eat a soldier's luncheon. It seems certain that we must very soon join in the battle. Few, if any, can forget that this may be the last food they will taste in this world, or the last, as well men. In fact, for that reason some of the more excitable ones cannot eat a mouthful. Others, not overburdened with sentiment, banteringly allege that they intend to eat all the more on that account. Yet, in one way or another, it is clearly revealed that the situation has awakened grave apprehensions with all."[1]

The XII Corps marched into battle that morning with a new commander, General Joseph Mansfield, who only five days before replaced the corps' first chief, controversial, politically appointed General Nathaniel Banks. Born on December 22, 1803 in New Haven, Connecticut, Joseph King Fenno Mansfield graduated second in West Point's Class of 1822 and was assigned to the Engineer Corps. By the Mexican War's 1846 advent, Mansfield had been promoted only twice, remaining a captain for eight long years. Service in Mexico, though, earned Joseph three brevet promotions, reaching colonel for actions at the 1847 battle of Buena Vista; a rank he retained in the peacetime Regular Army. Appointed the army's Inspector General in 1853, overseeing management of many far-flung forts and posts, by 1861 Mansfield commanded the Department of Washington and was promoted to brigadier general. Departing the capital on October to head a Department of Virginia brigade, by July 1862 Mansfield earned a division in the VII Corps and promotion to major general. Joseph Mansfield's meteoric late-career rise continued on September 15, this time to lead the newly formed XII Corps.

The XII Corps also entered battle that morning with rather little leadership cohesion. Mansfield's two days in command was certainly too brief a period for him to personally assess his officers and units, much less to build rapport with them. Similarly, most XII Corps senior officers were only just beginning to size up their new commander. General Williams—relieved to relinquish command of the corps—wrote five days later that although the very vision of an experienced soldier, Mansfield appeared "fussy" and "had a very nervous temperament and a very impatient manner." Contemporaries and modern historians have attributed this "fussiness" at Antietam to Mansfield's lack of confidence in his inexperienced officers and men—Williams's Division alone contained five new regiments which had never experienced combat—and lacking personal experience with the corps, Mansfield apparently adopted West Point's longstanding prejudice disparaging the skill and reliability of volunteer units. Just as likely, however, Mansfield's unsettled state probably reflects uncertainty in his own abilities because September 17 marked his first time commanding an entire army corps and the first time in 15 years Mansfield commanded troops in battle. That was General Williams's explanation for Mansfield's state, arguing "he had never before commanded large bodies of troops." Whatever the cause, General Mansfield led his corps toward imminent battle lacking full confidence in his men or perhaps in his own ability to command so large a unit. It was a very dangerous combination.[2]

Nearing the East Woods and sounds of battle, Williams's First Division advanced in the lead, followed by Brigadier General George S. Greene's Second Division. Advancing in a "column of battalions in mass"—each regiment deployed in a battle front, one in front of another—the XII Corps moved in a narrow but deep formation, reaching some 20 lines to the rear. Mansfield also directed his regiments to form only six paces apart, another measure meant to ensure cohesion, tighter command, and flexibility ahead of whatever battle brought. Nonetheless, this formation made the corps a nearly solid mass and an easier target for Confederate artillery. Williams argued as much to his new corps commander, fairly begging him to deploy in battle formation to increase their prospect of reaching the front in one piece. Mansfield, however, would not yield. "I could not move him," recalled Williams, "He was positive that all the new regiments would run away." Mansfield's fears led him to advance slowly, despite marching directly toward S. D. Lee's artillery before the Dunker Church, which instantly opened on them. Worse, Mansfield repeatedly stopped to dress lines, to detach troops for securing woodlots on its flanks and to recall those detachments to rejoin the main body, ensuring the corps advanced as one mass. This agonizing pace permitted the men to boil coffee, but at a terrible price. It took nearly half an hour for the XII Corps be near enough to aid Hooker's fight; as Hood's Confederates were entering the Cornfield, Mansfield was just riding forward to reconnoiter the situation and find General Hooker to receive orders.[3]

With Mansfield away, General Williams confronted the immediate threats facing the corps, and Hooker's I Corps men—probably from Ricketts's Division—surging back in a steady stream through its ranks firmed Williams's resolve to act. To limit the damage from enemy artillery fire and infantry volleys from within the East Woods, Williams wisely ordered his men to lie down. Still, it was a tough place to be. A 10th Maine soldier recalled "It may look like sport now, but it was hard and dismal enough then. You remember the flight of one great solid shot, that went jumping along fifty yards or more at a bound, plowing up cart loads of dirt, and landing at last in the [Samuel Poffenberger] cornfield … Some poor fellow in our midst, to vent his agony, called out 'over the fence, out!' and then there was a sickly, silly grin in response, from a number who would show their indifference and their love of the ridiculous. But it was no place for mirth."[4]

Brigadier General Samuel W. Crawford similarly disliked his command being a static target and ordered his green, huge 125th Pennsylvania forward to the East Woods, perhaps to drive away the Rebel infantry fire or maybe to just do "something." Colonel Jacob Higgins, commanding the 125th, recalled "I was then ordered into the woods … by General Crawford, then to throw out skirmishers and again advance through the woods until I reached the other side of the timber, and then deploy in a line of battle and advance through the fields and there halt. At this place my command was exposed to a most terrific fire of musketry, shot, and shell." Unknowingly, Higgins's Pennsylvanians walked right into the fight between Law's troops and Magilton's Brigade. Their mere presence, though, helped convince Evander Law to withdraw his force back toward the main Confederate line. The 125th Pennsylvania didn't fire a shot while in the East Woods; barely there for five minutes, it was recalled to its original position east of the woods. Nonetheless, the 125th suffered its first casualty while falling back. Those Pennsylvanians who reflected on the regiment's first loss might have realized just how important were those woods. It was a lesson General Hooker, too, was only just learning.[5]

Mansfield found Hooker, probably shortly after 7:00 and received his orders. The sight of Union troops littering the Cornfield before them made it painfully obvious that the I Corps was being badly handled by Jackson's troops. Still, Union attackers had a foothold in the Cornfield, and Hooker intended that the XII Corps now shore up what the I Corps had gained by its blood. Mansfield was to deploy Williams's leading division across the northern end of the Cornfield before immediately advancing to support Anderson's Brigade, then preparing to cross the northern fence into the Cornfield. Williams's entire division would deploy, in two lines, the first consisting of his new regiments of the 124th, 125th, and 128th Pennsylvania. The second line, advancing immediately behind the first, comprised the "old" regiments of the 46th Pennsylvania, 28th New York, and 10th Maine. Greene's Division would at the same time swing to Williams's left, driving through the East Woods to strike the right flank of any Confederates resisting Williams's advance through the corn. Mansfield rode back to deploy his corps and await Hooker's final directive to advance.[6]

It wasn't just the arrival of reinforcements that stood poised to turn the battle's tide, but also how Hooker planned to use them. Reprising his initial pincer approach, Hooker this time would use Williams's and Greene's entire divisions rather than the smaller brigades employed in Ricketts's and Doubleday's assaults. Doing so gave Hooker's attack the mass his earlier assaults had lacked. Hooker also enjoyed, for a change, good timing; Hood's attack had just then been turned back, opening a clear path to the Dunker Church ridge. Hooker was learning and adapting, and if Mansfield moved quickly, the XII Corps might take the Cornfield and reach the Dunker Church ridge, breaking Lee's line and completing the first phase of General McClellan's battle plan.

In the barely 15 minutes since Hooker and Mansfield parted, however, Joe Hooker changed his plans. Crawford's Brigade had already begun deploying when Mansfield countermanded the move, ordering it into a column ahead of its altered role. Hooker's revised plan had Crawford's three veteran Maine, New York, and Pennsylvania regiments deploying on the brigade's left, while the three massive, green Pennsylvania regiments would hold the right. Once so deployed, Williams's Division would control ground from the East Woods on their left to the Hagerstown Pike on their right. Brigadier General George H. Gordon's Brigade would advance behind the untested Pennsylvanians, providing the veteran support Crawford's "old" regiments no longer offered. Greene's Division would still execute its flanking attack but begin moving only once Williams's attack was well underway. In effect, Hooker traded his pincer movement for a "one-two punch," that—if it worked—could clear both the Cornfield and the East Woods of Rebels and put the Union attack on track to hit the Dunker Church ridge.[7]

Hooker never explained this sudden change, but it almost certainly reflected his realization that the Confederate hold of the East Woods threatened this—or any—Union attack through the Cornfield. Law's three detached regiments—the 4th Alabama, 21st Georgia, and 5th Texas—had been in the woods for nearly half an hour by then and perhaps the unexpected repulse of Magilton's Brigade awakened Hooker to the threat. Perhaps Mansfield had given Hooker a fresh view—from the eastern side of the East Woods—which he'd lacked before. Regardless, General Hooker had decided to secure this unexpected, additional intermediate objective by driving the Confederates out of the East Woods before launching his new attack.

This change came with a price, however. Taking the East Woods first prevented Hooker from using the full mass of his two XII Corps divisions to strike the

Confederate position on the Dunker Church ridge. Nor would this mass hit Jackson's salient in the Cornfield in front and flank in one large, coordinated attack. Instead, Hooker and Mansfield would have to juggle the timing of two related but different attacks and only then—using what was left of the XII Corps—fight on together to achieve McClellan's first objective. Once again, the battle had evolved in expected ways and Hooker's response was to diffuse his fighting power. Only time and skillful execution would tell if Hooker's performance met McClellan's expectations.

***

As Hood's Texans fell back toward the Dunker Church, the reinforcements he'd so longed for finally arrived. Their movement had been set in motion only a short time before in response to General Daniel Harvey Hill's ride to Cemetery Hill. There Lee approved Hill committing his entire 5,500-man force to supporting Jackson's fight in the Cornfield. D. H. Hill had secured what he wanted, although this came at the cost of Hill's mount's life when a Federal artillery round famously severed its front legs, creating a tragic-comic moment when the general was briefly trapped in the saddle, to the morbid delight of Lee and Longstreet. Nonetheless, sometime shortly after 7:00, Hill ordered his left-most brigade—Ripley's—forward to aid Confederate attackers. Although Hood's Division had been repulsed by the time Ripley arrived, the need for reinforcements remained just as great and many of Ripley's men were glad to finally be moving, no longer stationary targets for Union artillery. General Ripley recalled "the enemy from his batteries on the eastern bank of the Antietam opened a severe enfilading fire on the troops of my command, the position which we had been ordered to occupy being in full view of nearly all his batteries. This fire inflicted serious loss before the troops were called into positive action…"[8]

Ripley had earlier ordered his men to set fire to Samuel Mumma's house and buildings, which sat to his brigade's immediate north, "to prevent them being used of by the enemy." What use Ripley worried the house would be put to by Union troops, then nowhere near the farm, was never fully explained but perhaps the frustration of being a passive target prompted it. Although largely pointless, the act gave Ripley's troops something—anything—to do to control their deadly situation and fate. Regardless, Ripley's fire caused more problems than it might have solved. The fire's intense heat created confusion in Ripley's ranks, according to one member of the 44th Georgia, which took some time to fix and which certainly slowed its advance. Worse, Ripley had unknowingly given Union officers—and every other soldier, to historians' benefit—an unmistakable, obvious landmark on which to orient their position for the rest of the battle. Finally moving into the fight, Ripley's men had to march around the burning farm buildings, reforming at the southern end of Sam Mumma's plowed field to await their next move.[9]

Once in Mumma's plowed field, Ripley readied his 1,439-man brigade to attack. His left was held by the 4th Georgia, with the 44th Georgia, 1st and 3rd North Carolina to the right. Barely after dressing their lines, Yankees appeared in the woods to their front and opened fire. "We … were murderously assailed by the enemy concealed in a piece of woods a short distance in front. Our loss was fearful," recalled a 4th Georgia soldier. Ripley's regiments returned fire, but the contest was unequal; the Federals enjoyed cover from both the woods and a worm fence pulled down into a hasty breastwork, as well as a slightly elevated position that partially blocked Ripley's fire. Ripley's Brigade, moreover, fought in the center of an open field which offered no protection at all and the toll paid by Ripley's Brigade soon included General Ripley himself. Initially Ripley ignored the literal pain in his neck but soon this wound poured blood down his uniform coat, forcing the general to seek medical help or collapse on the spot. Turning command over to the 4th Georgia's Colonel George Doles, Ripley departed the fight.[10]

The Yankees Ripley's men fought were the left-most regiments of Christian's Brigade, then still holding the Federal left in the East Woods. It took little prodding to get Christian's men to leave their position, however, and Doles pushed his command forward into the wooded void. Doles didn't know it, but Law's three detached regiments were already moving into the East Woods's southern end, making this advance moot. Barely had Ripley's men started forward, though, when their division commander, D. H. Hill, rode up to save them.[11]

Ripley's men were about halfway to their objective when Hill halted the brigade, issuing new orders and a new objective. Facing "By the left flank"—moving them from a battle front into a long column, still as organized by General Ripley—they started northwestward. Now going to reinforce the Confederate hold on the Cornfield—Hill was supporting Hood's counterattacking division—Ripley's men marched toward the very center of that nightmare. Across the Smoketown Road they pressed, brushing the southern tip of the East Woods, walking four abreast in one long column into the deadly Cornfield. The situation there, however, had almost completely changed since General Hill redirected Ripley's Brigade, and Hood's Confederates no longer held the critical Cornfield; it was now owned by the Yankees of Anderson's Brigade.

***

Anderson was ordered into the Cornfield not by Generals Hooker or Meade—then on the left helping reform Magilton's scattered brigade—but rather by John Gibbon, who saw opportunity and acted on his own initiative. Racing eastward across the Hagerstown Pike, Gibbon found Lieutenant Colonel Anderson and ordered his brigade forward through the Cornfield, pursuing Hood's disintegrating line. Anderson's three regiments advanced in unison; the 9th Pennsylvania Reserves on the right bordering the Hagerstown Pike, with the 11th and 12th Reserves to their left, reaching almost to the Cornfield's center. Barely had Anderson's advance started before the attack began unraveling, however.[12]

The 9th Pennsylvania, within view of Gibbon's men across the road, pressed swiftly forward and was soon standing in the grassy field beyond the Cornfield's southern fence. Only then did the 9th Reserves men discover that the 11th Pennsylvania was no longer to their left, having stopped nearly in the center of the Cornfield. Worse, the 12th Reserves, holding the brigade's left flank, had halted even farther back in the corn, closer now to the Cornfield's northern fence than to the rest of its brigade. Lieutenant Colonel Anderson probably then wished his 10th Pennsylvania Reserves was still with the brigade, rather than engaged in an isolated firefight with Brigadier General Jubal Early's Brigade on the far left of the Confederate line. Meade had detached the 10th long ago to watch the Union's extreme right flank; it offered the brigade no help in its moment of need. Even so, Anderson's imperfect advance had retaken the Cornfield for the Union. Now, all that was needed to cement this gain were reinforcements.[13]

Gibbon had reassured Anderson at the outset that unlike every other Union force taking the Cornfield, his would be well-supported when the time came. Pointing across the Hagerstown Pike toward his own command and Patrick's Brigade, Gibbon promised they would join Anderson's advance. As Anderson readied his men, John Gibbon had returned to prepare his own and Patrick's men to offer support. Gibbon had much to do at that moment.[14]

For one thing, Gibbon's own men were no longer in the advanced position on the Hagerstown Pike where he'd left them. Barely after driving away Wofford's Brigade from the Hagerstown Pike, a line of Confederate infantry appeared to the 19th Indiana, holding Gibbon's right flank on the road. This unexpected threat was a consolidated command of scattered units and lost men from Starke's Division, gathered by Colonel Stafford. Stafford had watched Gibbon's enemy troops sweep past his ragged command to the road, in the process exposing their unprotected flank. Jumping at this opportunity, Stafford pushed his command northward along the Pike's edge toward the 19th Indiana's exposed right. The Hoosiers at that moment were so preoccupied with Wofford's fleeing men across the road that they failed to notice Stafford's troops until they were barely 100 yards away; instantly the Southerners poured a shocking and staggering fire on the 19th Indiana's right and rear, aided by shells from Jeb Stuart's Horse Artillery. The unprepared Indianans scrambled back to a less-exposed position on the West Woods's ridge, where a limestone ledge served as a hasty defensive position. With Gibbon's right flank collapsing, the 7th Wisconsin and Patrick's Brigade, too, fell back and Gibbon's only artillery support similarly vanished. As Stafford's cobbled-together Southern infantry force neared Stewart's Battery, deployed on the Hagerstown Pike's western side, Gibbon quickly ordered it to safety near Miller's barn. Despite Gibbon's good intentions, Anderson's men were on their own to hold the Cornfield against whatever the Confederates threw at them next. They would not have to wait long to see just what that was.[15]

***

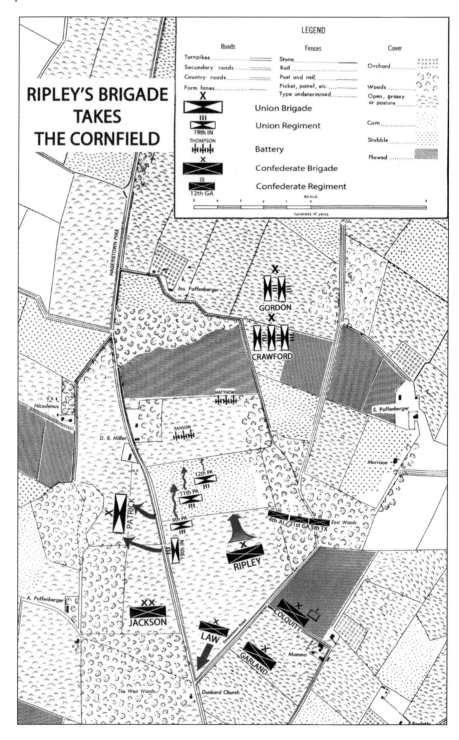

RIPLEY'S BRIGADE
TAKES
THE CORNFIELD

When Ripley's Brigade stopped atop the ridge north of the Smoketown Road, it stretched across nearly the entire width of the grassy field south of the Cornfield. The simple command "Front!" instantly faced the entire line northwards toward the corn, revealing to Doles's men what they now faced. The "immense cornfield seemed literally alive with Yankees," recalled a 4th Georgia man, and barely could that sink in before General Hill ordered the entire brigade forward. Up the gradual rise they marched, toward the southern end of the Cornfield.

The 4th Georgia, on the left of Doles's line, was the first to slam into Union troops. These were Anderson's 9th Pennsylvania Reserves, who had advanced beyond the brigade's other regiments, all the way to the Cornfield's southern fence. The Pennsylvanians opened fire instantly, halting the left of Doles's Brigade in its tracks and opening a firefight in which both sides paid a fearful price. "The regiment suffered a great loss here," remembered a 4th Georgian, "had three color-bearers shot in a few minutes." Nonetheless, the rest of the brigade continued forward, moving into the void created by Anderson's hesitant 11th and 12th Pennsylvania. Both Anderson's Federal Brigade and Doles's Confederates found themselves in the undesirable position of having one flank pinned in place, while the opposite flank extended too far forward, creating a mirrored stair-step formation. It was a situation that couldn't remain so for long.

***

It was the Pennsylvanians who blinked first. Unlike Doles's fresh troops, the 9th had fought to reach this exposed spot and was running out of steam. On top of that, the retreat of Patrick's Brigade and the 19th Indiana had exposed the 9th's right flank, while the stalled 11th and 12th Pennsylvania Reserves had uncovered its left. Retreat was a matter of simple survival. Although the regiment carried away two captured Rebel flags, as the 9th Pennsylvania fell back through the corn with the rest of Anderson's Brigade, the move signaled the failure of Meade's attack. Backward moved Meade's Pennsylvania Reserves, once again offering control of the Cornfield to the Confederates, who were only too happy to accept the offer.[16]

***

Doles ordered Ripley's Brigade forward once more, halting about 50 yards south of the Cornfield's southern fence. Given the morning's events, Doles might have questioned the wisdom of trying to hold the Cornfield at all but, once again, position determined the colonel's next actions. Halting there aligned the right of Ripley's Brigade with the left of Law's regiments holding the East Woods. Doles's left, too, aligned with Stafford's command, although it was too far away to physically connect with Ripley's Brigade. This wide gap was quickly filled when Doles pulled several

1st North Carolina companies from the line's secure center, sending them to deploy left of the 4th Georgia, facing due west and perpendicular to his main line. Doles probably sought to avoid another Union flanking move, which had swept aside the gains of Wofford's Brigade and triggered the failure of Hood's attack only minutes before. Although Ripley's Brigade didn't physically occupy the Cornfield, it possessed that key spot by firepower. So great was this firepower that it drove Ransom's 5th US Artillery, Battery C Redlegs to the unthinkable—abandoning their guns on the field. Regardless how they held it, the Confederates once again owned the Cornfield.[17]

***

Beyond the East Woods, Mansfield was setting Hooker's revised orders in motion. To first clear the East Woods, Mansfield deployed Crawford's veteran regiments on each side of the woods, before sending them largely in unison to sweep the enemy from their protected position. The 10th Maine held the left flank on the eastern side, while the equally experienced 28th New York and 46th Pennsylvania secured the right flank on the western edge of the woods in the Cornfield. His flanks secured by dependable veterans, the huge, inexperienced 128th Pennsylvania would drive through the center of the woods toward its ultimate goal, reaching the Cornfield to link the left of Crawford's new regiments with the right of his veteran units. This plan would get the 128th into position quickly and flush out any Confederates still holding on in the woods' northern end. Probably to ensure each disparate part of this important advance moved as planned, Mansfield personally led Crawford's veteran regiments into position before launching his assault into the East Woods. A common-sense decision, it would soon yield significant—and deadly—consequences. Once he'd pushed the Maine men into the small cornfield adjacent to the northeastern end of the East Woods, before they advanced at the "left oblique" diagonally across the field, Mansfield rode off to deploy the right half of Crawford's Brigade.[18]

Greene's 2,404-man division meanwhile moved gradually into the void created as Williams's units deployed. Lieutenant Colonel Hector Tyndale's First Brigade led the column, followed by Goodrich's Third Brigade, while Colonel Henry J. Stainrook's Second Brigade brought up the rear. After stopping repeatedly during the halting advance—their third or fourth pause—General Mansfield suddenly appeared, excitedly ordering Greene to bring his command forward as quickly as possible. The men repacked tin cups and slid coffee bags into their haversacks, falling in for yet another move. As Mansfield raced away from the reforming column, he probably had little idea just how fortunate was his timing or significant his order bringing Greene's Division into the fight.[19]

Next finding the 28th New York and 46th Pennsylvania, Mansfield led them through the gap between the North and East Woods. Nearing the northern point of

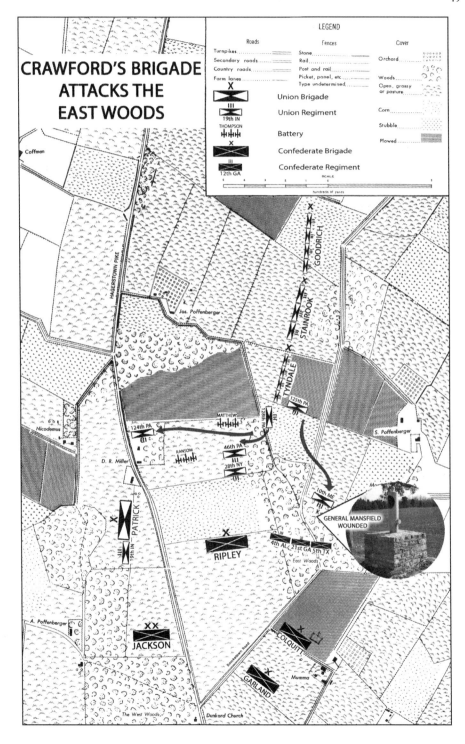

CRAWFORD'S BRIGADE ATTACKS THE EAST WOODS

LEGEND

Roads	Fences	Cover
Turnpikes	Stone	Orchard
Secondary roads	Rail	
Country roads	Post and rail	
Farm lanes	Picket, panel, etc.	Woods
	Type undetermined	Open, grassy or pasture

X
III
19th IN
Union Brigade

Union Regiment

THOMPSON
Battery

X
Confederate Brigade

III
12th GA
Confederate Regiment

Corn

Stubble

Plowed

SCALE

hundreds of yards

Coffman

GOODRICH

STAINROOK

HAGERSTOWN PIKE

Jos. Poffenberger

TYNDALE

125th PA

S. Poffenberger

MATTHEWS

12th PA

124th PA

Nicodemus

RANSOM

46th PA

28th NY

D. R. Miller

10th ME

GENERAL MANSFIELD WOUNDED

PATRICK

19th IN

RIPLEY

4th AL 21st GA 5th TX

East Woods

A. Poffenberger

XX
JACKSON

COLQUITT

GARLAND

Mumma

Smoketown Road

The West Woods

Dunkard Church

the East Woods, both regiments moved into a battle front and pressed on, guiding their left on the East Woods's western edge. Taking Rebel fire nearly at once, it was clear they were in for a rough time. Reaching nearly to the Cornfield's northern fence, enemy fire intensified and forced a halt to fight for this spot. Crawford's two now-isolated regiments instantly became the main target of both the 4th Alabama—covered in the woods—and the 1st and 3rd North Carolina; the right two regiments of Ripley's Brigade across the open Cornfield. Here, the two small regiments—the 28th New York numbered only 63 men; the 46th had but 150 men on duty—halted and opened a "lively fire," as the 46th's Lieutenant Colonel James Selfridge noted. They alone would have to hold this deadly spot until Mansfield could shove the rest of Crawford's Brigade into position, starting his attack on the East Woods in earnest. With these two experienced regiments holding on, Mansfield raced back to finish deploying his attack.[20]

Galloping to the center, Mansfield set the heart of his assault in motion. The 128th men moved timidly and awkwardly into the Morrison cornfield, however, toward the East Woods. "[A]s the regiment was new and inexperienced ... there was much confusion in accomplishing the movement," reported Major Joel Wanner. Deployed in a column, as directed by Mansfield, and so unable to return the Rebs's fire, the 128th—probably by its sheer size—drove Confederate skirmishers out of the corn to the safety of the East Woods, from which the enemy again opened fire on them. In that instant, the 128th Pennsylvanians became combat veterans. The first volleys felled several enlisted men in the column's front ranks, as well as several officers who were out front and exposed by leading the unsteady men into their first fight. Their commander, Colonel Croasdale, was killed instantly when a ball shattered his head, while the 128th's second-in-command took two rounds in his arm; blood loss and growing pain soon forced him to surrender command to Major Wanner. His inexperience matching the regiment's, Wanner recalled "I endeavored to finish the deployment but it being the first time the regiment had ever been under fire, I found it impossible to do so in the confusion and excitement."[21]

With the 128th Pennsylvania advancing in the center, Mansfield continued his feverish ride left. Reaching a small hillock at the southern end of Morrison's cornfield, Mansfield joined General Crawford and staff in reviewing Crawford's deployment. Barely had Mansfield taken stock of the scene when a disturbing sight appeared. The 10th Maine was holding Crawford's left flank as instructed but deployed in a battle line, contrary to Mansfield's orders.

Colonel Beal had made this change on his own initiative, an act of simple survival. "We were under fire and advancing at a brisk walk closed in mass, that is ten ranks deep (or fifteen ranks counting file closers). We were almost as good a target as a barn," wrote John Gould. "The fire of the enemy became more galling every step we took, and one man after another fell, so that at length Col. Beal could not endure to see his command so uselessly butchered, and without obtaining consent of the

General he ordered us to deploy into one line…" So ordered, Companies G and I and the 10th's color guard continued marching straight ahead, while each company to their rear peeled left or right—depending on their placement in the column of companies—until clearing the main body's respective flanks. Facing "front," each company rejoined the main line anchored by Companies G and I. Once in a battle line, the 10th Maine pressed to the East Woods's eastern fence, pushing 5th Texas's skirmishers before them back into the woods.[22]

Beal had barely finished overseeing the move when a Confederate ball split open his mount's head, sending the terrified horse spinning out of control and into the regiment's second-in-command, his hooves slamming Lieutenant Colonel Fillebrown's stomach and chest. Then another Rebel ball tore into Colonel Beal's legs. In an instant, the 10th Maine changed command three times.

Adding to the confusion, upon reaching the wood line the 10th men strayed from their line to exploit the natural cover offered by the ground and woods. Companies C and F, on the left, "refused the left" to protect against being flanked from that direction, taking cover behind a rock ledge. The regiment's remaining eight companies pressed toward the woods, although in seeking cover many men were already deep into the woods and beyond the regiment's guiding colors. This state risked destroying the regiment's cohesion and organization; worse, some Maine men inadvertently began firing into their own ranks. It was this dangerous sight that caught General Mansfield's attention.[23]

Instantly, Mansfield spurred his mount and raced to undo this disaster. Down the hill he tore, through the 10th Maine's ranks, all the while frantically waving his hat—so intensely he flung away his hat cord—and calling them to cease firing. Reaching the left-most company, C, Mansfield halted to take stock of his efforts. Widely ignoring his order, men in Company C began pleading with the general. Company C's Captain Jordan and Sergeant Burnham frantically pointed toward grey-clad men in the woods, only yards away. Apparently, seeing rifles aimed at them convinced Mansfield of his error and he calmly told Captain Jordan, "Yes, yes, you are right." Then, as if to drive home the point, a hail of gunfire showered the group.

Mansfield wheeled his horse gently to the right, starting back the way he'd come. He periodically stopped at breaks in the crushed fence line, apparently looking for a clear spot through which to lead his mount, but the horse refused to step into the tangle of shattered fence rails or to try jumping over them. Onlookers didn't know it, but the general's huge horse had been badly wounded in the hail of gunfire and certainly was terrified. Probably sensing his mount's fear, Mansfield dismounted to walk him through the obstacle on a lead. It was a measure of Joseph Mansfield's character that despite the unfolding chaos, rather than whipping or spurring his wounded companion he personally led the frightened animal where he needed it to go. It was something he'd been doing with his XII Corps men all morning.

Once past the obstacle, Mansfield tried climbing atop his horse, but it was clear to those in the 10th Maine who witnessed the scene that something was terribly wrong. The general hadn't the strength to remount his horse. John Gould recalled "his coat blew open, and I saw that blood was streaming down the right side of his vest." Gould suggested finding a surgeon and Mansfield quickly agreed. Casting about for help, Gould grabbed Company F's Sergeant Joe Merrill and the young black servant of a I Corps officer. The servant was in this deadly spot searching for an officer's lost frying pan, probably left behind when Seymour's Brigade pulled from the East Woods, but he agreed to help carry General Mansfield rearward for medical help.

Once clear of the East Woods, other 10th Maine men rushed to help their wounded corps commander. A five-man squad soon created a stretcher by rolling blankets around muskets and carried General Mansfield to Sam Poffenberger's gate, though they could carry him no farther. Flagging down an ambulance wagon, they hoisted Mansfield onboard and then returned to the fight. Taken to the Line farmhouse, he spent the rest of the day fighting for his life. Like too many of his men, General Joseph Mansfield lost this fight early the next morning.[24]

When Mansfield fell in battle, so might the Union's prospects have once again fallen. General Mansfield was the second most senior Union commander on the field and had been posting Crawford's regiments in a very specific way, which perhaps only he understood. His loss might have spelled yet more command confusion and disaster for the Union troops struggling to complete McClellan's attack on the Confederate left—but it did not. Fortune smiled twice on the Union in those few minutes after Mansfield's wounding. Not only had the XII Corps's new commander, Alpheus Williams, learned personally from General Hooker what to do in the evolving fight, but the transition between corps commanders lasted fewer than five minutes. "I had parted with Gen. Mansfield but a moment before this and in five minutes afterward his staff officer reported to me that he was mortally wounded and the command of the corps devolved on me," Williams recalled. It was a bit of luck the Yankees badly needed at that moment. Nonetheless, this was due not to dumb luck, but rather to Joseph Mansfield's skillful and effective command in the field. Even had the command gap lasted longer, the XII Corps probably would have continued functioning as planned because Mansfield apparently had told his subordinate division and brigade commanders precisely what they should do, if not perhaps even sharing the broad outlines of Hooker's plan with them. This clear, effective communication ensured that when Mansfield was suddenly removed from the fight, all was in place and officers need only continue moving and fighting within Mansfield's directed framework. It was perhaps General Mansfield's final gift to his men and to his country.

CHAPTER 9

The Cornfield: Williams Turns the Tide

Alpheus Williams, the XII Corps's new commander, stood in the plowed field below the North Woods "taking directions from General Hooker … amidst a very unpleasant shower of bullets…" when "up rode a general officer begging for immediate assistance to protect a battery," Williams recalled. "He was very earnest and absorbed in the subject, as you may well suppose, and began to plead energetically, when he suddenly stopped, extended his hand, and very calmly said, "How are you?" It was General Meade. He darted away, and I saw him no more that day." This odd juxtaposition of frenzy and civility in many respects typifies this very atypical day.[1]

Williams wasted no time stepping into Mansfield's role. "I began at once to deploy the new regiments," reported Williams. "The old ones had already gotten themselves into line. Taking hold of one, I directed Gens. Crawford and Gordon to direct the others." Crawford deployed the 125th Pennsylvania atop a small hill overlooking the northern end of the East Woods, in the immediate center and rear of Crawford's line, acting as a reserve. General Gordon was occupied with moving his brigade forward as Williams had ordered and never mentioned interacting with the 128th Pennsylvania—then already advancing in Crawford's center, as directed by General Mansfield—and it remains unclear if Gordon knew he'd been tasked with overseeing this regiment's deployment. Williams himself started the 124th Pennsylvania across the fields below the North Woods, heading toward the Hagerstown Pike.[2]

Moving still formed in a "column in mass," the 124th crossed Miller's plowed field until reaching the Hagerstown Pike where "[w]e were soon formed in line of battle at right angles to the turnpike…" recalled Sergeant Charles Broomhall of Company D. The reality of this moment suddenly hit the 124th's new soldiers. "A good number of wounded were now passing to the rear and this was the first sight of battle we had seen and the blood also, and it shook the nerves of some of the boys. The shells crashing through the trees and fluttering overhead as well as the musketry in advance to the left, all contributed to mark the time, and place, fixed in one's memory forever." For now, Sergeant Broomhall and the 124th simply had to hold this spot, the XII Corps's right flank, and await their brigade's clearing the East Woods before restarting Hooker's attack through the Cornfield.[3]

At that moment, in the northern end of the East Woods, the 124th's veteran counterparts were doing their best to carry out Hooker's revised plan. The 46th Pennsylvania and 28th New York held Crawford's right, while the 10th Maine anchored the brigade's left, but all three regiments were stuck in place, lacking the men or firepower to press any deeper into the woods or the Cornfield. The 28th New York's Chandler Gillam recalled "It was a hard fight ... the balls whistled very close to me some of the time. I could feel the wind of them they came so near my face." Suddenly, the 128th Pennsylvania pushed into the northern end of the East Woods—reinforcements had arrived! Barely had the 128th passed behind the 28th New York and 46th Pennsylvania, though, when it nearly dissolved into chaos and stopped, still deployed in the vulnerable column formation. The 46th Pennsylvania's Colonel Joseph Knipe could see something was very wrong—he might have guessed Colonel Croasdale was dead—and ran from his own regiment into the 128th's swirling mass. "At this moment, seeing the uselessness of a regiment in that position, I took the responsibility of getting it into line of battle the best way circumstances would admit," reported Knipe.[4]

Knipe not only restored order to the 128th Pennsylvania, he also directed its first attack before shifting command to Major Joel Wanner and returning to his regiment. Perhaps fearing delay would only permit the green men to run, Knipe threw them headlong into an attack "to dislodge the enemy," Wanner explained. Stepping over the remains of the Cornfield's northern fence, they rushed into the corn toward Ripley's Confederates, who intensified their fire. Knipe brought his 46th Pennsylvania forward on the 128th's left, probably hoping to support his fellow Keystone State men in driving through the corn. The 46th only made it to the Cornfield's northern fence before its depleted state forced a halt. Nonetheless, it opened on Ripley's men and the left of Law's 4th Alabama, which extended out of the East Woods.[5]

***

Colonel Doles struggled to stop the Yankees from reaching deeper into the Cornfield. His brigade had driven off Union troops threatening its left flank but now that threat hovered across the Hagerstown Pike, promising to return at any moment. His right was just as threatened; to improve its state, Doles pulled his line back to connect with Law's men in the East Woods. Before this was complete, however, a mass of Union troops was seen surging within the northern end of the East Woods, prompting the 3rd North Carolina on Dole's far right to change front to the right, meeting this new threat head on. The 3rd had just begun shifting when a huge Yankee force started toward it through the Cornfield.[6]

***

The 128th Pennsylvania "started off in gallant style," wrote Major Wanner, "cheering as they moved, and penetrated the corn field." Nearing the Cornfield's southern end, though, the regiment suddenly stopped in its tracks. Nearing the shifting right of Ripley's line brought them near Law's 4th Alabama, still concealed in the East Woods, which along with the 3rd North Carolina poured a deadly crossfire into the Pennsylvanians. The 128th's Frederick Crouse recalled hugging the ground to avoid the fire, then "we would load rise up and bang away." Soon, though, this fire was too much for the new Federals and "in consequence of the overpowering numbers of the enemy concealed, [we] were compelled to fall back…," recorded Major Wanner. The 128th Pennsylvania retreated from the Cornfield into the East Woods, halting in the center of Crawford's position holding the northern end of the vital woods. Although the 128th's charge had failed to retake the Cornfield, it nonetheless weakened Ripley's Brigade to the point of breaking—the 3rd North Carolina's confusion and poor position cost the regiment its colonel and "many killed and wounded"—and drained what was left of their ammunition. It was a matter of time before Ripley's Brigade had to surrender the Cornfield.[7]

Although Crawford's Brigade hadn't secured the East Woods—Law's Texans, Georgians, and Alabamians remained firmly entrenched there—it nonetheless had completed the crucial first step toward this end. The Union now possessed the East Woods's northern end, from which it might clear the entire lot. This small but important gain would become the turning point to getting Hooker's attack back on track.

Gordon's Brigade, meanwhile, having followed Crawford's Brigade to the front—save the 13th New Jersey, which Mansfield held back to secure the column's right—also came through the gap between the North and East Woods into the plowed field. Still, Gordon's command faced a moment of confusion; first sent right to support a battery, the general received new orders instead sending his brigade forward again. Advancing at the double-quick—a moderate jogging pace, not a flat-out run—toward Crawford's position, once past the North Woods, Gordon deployed his brigade for battle.[8]

Immediately after starting forward, one of Hooker's staffers arrived and begged Gordon to hurry. "It was apparent from the steady approach of the sound of musketry, that the enemy were advancing," reported Gordon, pressing his command more rapidly forward. Once deployed, Gordon's 2nd Massachusetts held his right flank, reaching nearly to the Hagerstown Pike. Behind them, taking the center, came the 3rd Wisconsin, while the 27th Indiana held the left flank with its left nearly touching the East Woods. The 107th New York remained behind by the East Woods, acting as the brigade's reserve. The 13th New Jersey's return from detached duty further swelled Gordon's reserve to a full third of his command's fighting power.[9]

General Gordon had expected to support Crawford's three green Pennsylvania regiments, as Williams had ordered, but upon arriving beheld a sight that suggested his orders had changed. Instead of the raw Pennsylvanians, Gordon saw before him nothing but a yawning void. Enemy troops were deployed across the shattered Cornfield but the only Union forces there were scattered across the length and depth of the fields in no apparent order. To his right and rear, by the Hagerstown Pike, stood one unit—the 124th Pennsylvania—while other Union troops held the woods on his brigade's far left. Gordon mistakenly believed this to be Greene's Division; it was in fact Crawford's Brigade fighting for the East Woods. Regardless why this state existed, Gordon's military instinct was to fill that gap as quickly as possible.[10]

Gordon rushed his center three regiments forward into the gap, advancing to the ridge running eastward from D. R. Miller's house before stopping. Hooker's force now stretched from the limestone ridge on the Hagerstown Pike's west side, across the width of the northern edge of the Cornfield, through to the opposite side of the East Woods. It was a strong position and exactly what Hooker needed to launch the next part of his plan for sweeping the East Woods clear of Rebels. Now, all hinged on getting General Greene's Division onto the field and into the right place. At that moment, that's exactly what Alpheus Williams was trying so desperately to do.[11]

Until Williams got Greene's Division moving, Crawford's and Gordon's men simply had to hold on where they were. Most officers in such a situation would welcome Gordon's reinforcements, but not the 46th Pennsylvania's Joseph Knipe. Now commanding the First Brigade—replacing Crawford, elevated to command Williams's Division—Knipe struggled to hold the East Woods and Cornfield until Greene arrived, his ranks thinned by the recent fighting and Confederate artillery fire attracted when Gordon's fresh 27th Indiana appeared only yards away. These shells meant for the 27th fell among the 46th's ranks instead, rapidly winnowing the Pennsylvanians's lines. Ordering his brigade back, Knipe explained that "This position would have been held, and the advance continued in face of the leaden hail which was fast decimating our ranks, had it not been for the Twenty-seventh Indiana forming in our rear and exposing us to a fire from a quarter unexpected." Knipe had a point, but the 27th Indiana and Gordon's other regiments too paid a heavy price for their immobile state.[12]

Edmund Brown of the 27th Indiana's Company C recalled the frustration of having to impotently stand amidst this firestorm. "The difficulty is to see the enemy. He is lying down among the corn. Another difficulty is that our own men have not entirely withdrawn from our front. But the men of the Twenty-seventh coolly stand with their muskets at a ready, and when they clearly recognize a soldier in grey, they take deliberate aim, and fire…" Challenging as this was, an unexpected enemy force appeared in their front, testing Gordon's men in a new and more deadly way.[13]

***

Ripley's Brigade had repulsed the advancing 128th Pennsylvania but just barely. Had the 128th been a battle-tested veteran regiment, its size alone might have broken the Confederate hold on the Cornfield. Colonel Doles might not have understood why this huge Yankees force had retreated, but he probably didn't care; more pressing was the weakened and increasingly disorganized state of his brigade. This situation begged for reinforcements and if this was Doles's thought, he need only have looked to the rear to find his wish granted.

Cutting across the grassy field came Colquitt's Brigade. Colquitt's command had literally followed in Ripley's Brigade's footsteps to this point. The 13th Alabama led the advance, followed by the 23rd, 28th, 27th, and the 6th Georgia regiments, still ordered as deployed late the previous night. Moving increasingly northward, Colquitt's Brigade broke from Ripley's path to guide along the western edge of the East Woods until, once past the right of Ripley's 3rd North Carolina, Colquitt's 13th Alabama moved "By files, left" and led the column across the front of Ripley's line. Colquitt's Brigade gradually formed a protective human wall in front of Ripley's weakened formation. Barely had Colquitt's Brigade formed in earnest, when Colonel Doles faced his brigade left and marched quickly off the field, toward the Dunker Church. Ripley's Brigade had done its duty; now it was Colquitt's Brigade's turn to secure the South's hold on the Cornfield.[14]

The appearance of fresh infantry offered opportunities for the artillery of both sides. S. D. Lee had watched in frustration as Hood's Division lost the Cornfield for want of support; the proximity of the clashing infantry forces kept his nearby guns from helping Hood for fear of killing friend and foe alike. Colquitt's new position holding the Cornfield, however, changed the situation. "I advanced two guns of Moody's Battery some 300 yards into a plowed field, where I could use them," Lee explained. Captain Moody and Lieutenant John B. Gorey—commanding these guns— instantly began raining deadly explosive rounds down on the men of Gordon's static brigade in their exposed, vulnerable position.[15]

***

General Gordon quickly had his artillery respond in kind. As Gordon's infantry swept to the Cornfield's edge, Ransom's 5th US Artillery Battery C men sprinted to retake their guns, which remained just where they'd left them after the 3rd North Carolina had driven them away. Their honor restored, Ransom's men charged their guns with canister and tore into Colquitt's line, adding to the withering effect of Gordon's infantry fire. At the same moment, Lieutenant Stewart brought Campbell's Battery back onto the field, deploying in almost the same spot in the plowed field below the North Woods from which the battery supported Gibbon's earlier attack. Gibbon had ordered them here apparently unaware that Gordon's 3rd Wisconsin was nearly in front of the battery's new post, leaving Stewart's artillerymen little more

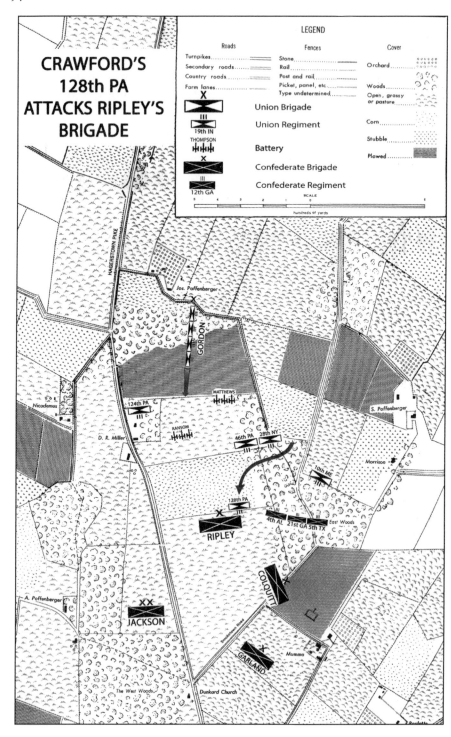

than targets for Rebel fire. Stewart ordered his guns loaded with canister, before sending the limbers and horses to the rear, then commanded his men to lie down between the guns. Using the ground's slight rise as a natural entrenchment, they waited. Next, Cothran's 1st New York Light Artillery, Battery M, rolled up behind Ransom's re-manned guns and immediately opened on the Rebels, while Matthews's Battery continued pouring shells into Colquitt's men holding the Cornfield. Gordon's Brigade now fought supported by a wall of four Union batteries.[16]

***

Colonel Colquitt, however, wasted little time getting his brigade deeper into the fight. Stepping over the southern fence's remains, it pressed through the broken Cornfield and over wounded men strewn across the ground like chaff after the harvest. The 3rd Wisconsin's Julian Hinkley watched from across the Cornfield, recalling "The Confederate infantry moved steadily across the corn-field, while the decimated brigade in its path fell back step by step. The enemy were handicapped by the fact that they were moving diagonally across our front, instead of directly toward us, and our fire was terribly severe…" The 6th Georgia's Benjamin Witcher recalled "I remember when coming into position being under fire we got into some confusion when the Col. ordered guides to the line, and dressed his Regt. This order coming at this time quieted all confusion and the Regt. was a cool as on dress parade…" It was perhaps this temporary calm that shifted Witcher's attention to an odd threat, recalling "[b]etween us and [the enemy] were several cows who were running about frantically and I remember I was more afraid just then of being run over by a cow than of being hit by a bullet…" Colonel Colquitt, however, remained focused on the enemy and may have hoped that moving so quickly would secure his command's hold on the Cornfield before the fresh Yankee brigade across the field could move to stop him. Colquitt's line reached the very center of the Cornfield before Gordon's nearly overwhelming infantry and artillery firepower stopped the brigade in its tracks. It might have been at that moment that Colquitt realized what had happened during his advance.[17]

***

As Colquitt's Confederates advanced, the right of Gordon's Brigade moved, too. Barely had the 2nd Massachusetts formed Gordon's right at the Hagerstown Pike, when it was pushed 75 yards forward to a new position along the southern fence of Miller's orchard. With fighting raging to the left in the corn, the 2nd deployed at an angle along the orchard's southeast corner, effectively "refusing the left" to face the fighting. Next, the massive 124th Pennsylvania swept southward along the Hagerstown Pike and nearly over its position, stopping finally at the northern end of the Cornfield. For now, the 124th would anchor the right of Union forces opposing the Cornfield, but not so the 2nd Massachusetts. Once the Pennsylvanians cleared their front, Colquitt's line appeared and the Bay Staters opened fire.[18]

***

The 2nd's fire played havoc with Colquitt's advance, stopping his left while the nearly unopposed right pressed ever deeper into the Cornfield. Worse, a fresh Yankee threat emerged from the East Woods as the 6th Georgia—holding Colquitt's right flank—reached the Cornfield's northern end. Colquitt's Brigade now faced steady fire on its front and both flanks. Ranks thinning fast, the five minutes there must have seemed like hours. The colonel now played a dangerous waiting game, betting he could hold on until the promised reinforcements of Garland's Brigade arrived on his right to bolster Southern possession of the Cornfield. For now, Colquitt could do little else.[19]

It was about 7:30 in the morning and Confederate hold on the Cornfield now depended on Garland's Brigade quickly getting into place on Colquitt's right. Colonel Duncan K. McRae—replacing General Garland, killed at South Mountain—recalled receiving D. H. Hill's orders to move "to the support of Colquitt, who was then about engaging the enemy on our left front." But, McRae added, they were also "cautioned by Gen'l. Hill not to fire upon Colquitt who might be in our front." With these two directives in mind, McRae led his brigade—the 5th, 12th, 13th, 20th, and 23rd North Carolina—across Mumma's plowed field toward Colquitt's right. Stepping off in good order, it would be about the last thing that would go right for McRae's command this day.[20]

Barely had McRae's force reached the East Woods when things started unraveling. "Here a state of confusion ensued which it is difficult to portray," the 5th North Carolina's Captain Thomas Garrett recalled. Advancing into the woods, "the movements of the brigade ... were vacillating and unsteady, obliquing to the right and left [until it] came upon a ledge of rock and earth, forming a fine natural breastwork." McRae's line halted and opened fire. These odd movements resulted from the brigade being unnerved even before entering the fight. Whether from having to withstand enemy artillery fire, the lingering effects of desperate fighting at South Mountain, or the loss of their commander, the men of Garland's Brigade weren't behaving like the battle-hardened veterans they were, but rather as shaky and unsteady as any of the green XII Corps regiments fighting Colquitt's men yards away.[21]

Suddenly, McRae's shaken command encountered an unexpected body of troops. Some considered them the enemy and opened fire, others were sure they were fellow Confederates and a cry rose up to cease firing. "[U]naccountbly to me, an order was given to cease firing—that General Ripley's brigade was in front. This produced great confusion...," McRae noted. What Garland's Brigade had found was the 4th Alabama,

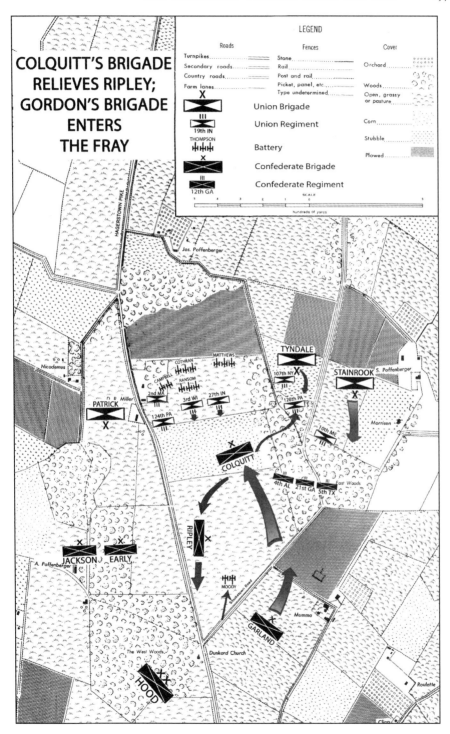

COLQUITT'S BRIGADE
RELIEVES RIPLEY;
GORDON'S BRIGADE
ENTERS
THE FRAY

LEGEND

Roads

Turnpikes
Secondary roads
Country roads
Farm lanes

Fences

Stone
Rail
Post and rail
Picket, panel, etc.
Type undetermined

Cover

Orchard
Woods
Open, grassy or pasture
Corn
Stubble
Plowed

Union Brigade

Union Regiment

Battery

Confederate Brigade

Confederate Regiment

SCALE
hundreds of yards

21st Georgia, and 5th Texas, still fighting in the East Woods of their own accord. Until this moment, their presence had been of nothing but benefit to Confederate prospects.

Occupying the East Woods, while their respective brigades had been driven back, time and again they'd denied the Union control of this ground and the Cornfield, too. All this had been done without formal leadership or orders from Hood, Hill, Jackson or any other senior Southern officer directing this fight. It was a marvelous piece of soldering and command skill. Now, however, these same attributes would spell their downfall and the undoing of very much more. Lacking command coordination, these three regiments were right where no one in Garland's Brigade expected any Confederate troops to be. This uncertainty spurred cacophony within the ranks; repeated and conflicting orders were shouted though only some emanated from the brigade's officers.[22]

***

As Garland's Brigade moved to Colquitt's aid, so Greene's Division entered the fight. Arriving as General Williams assumed command, Williams ordered Greene to post his division's right on the farm lane leading from the East Woods to the North Woods, his left extending toward the burning Mumma farm buildings. Once deployed, Greene was to start his whole division forward as one—advancing and wheeling gradually to the right, pivoting on Gordon's Brigade's left in the East Woods—to hit the Rebels in flank. [23]

Certainly, some of those fighting on both sides in Miller's Cornfield that day were progeny of men who fought alongside George Washington in the Revolution. Few, however, enjoyed a stronger such connection than did Brigadier General George Sears Greene, a descendant of Washington's trusted, influential colleague Major General Nathanael Greene. Born in Apponaug, Rhode Island, on May 6, 1801, George graduated second in the West Point Class of 1823—ahead of General Mansfield—Greene served in the artillery after a brief stint as a West Point professor. While posted to Maine's Fort Stevens, George lost his entire family to illness—probably tuberculosis—prompting Greene to resign his commission and enter the business world to escape the loneliness of army life. As a civil engineer, Greene built railroads in six states and designed the water systems in Washington, Detroit, and other cities. With the advent of Civil War, Greene returned to army life, commanding the 60th New York. Rising quickly, Greene held a series of increasingly important commands, most recently of Geary's Division when that officer was wounded at the battle of Cedar Mountain. Once again, now at Antietam, a Greene would play a central role in his nation's history.

Greene's task was complicated even before reaching the field when Williams detached Goodrich's Brigade from his division. Williams was fulfilling an earlier pledge to Gibbon, who had pled for reinforcements for Doubleday's bruised command on the far right. Though an important role, shoring up the Union right cost Greene one third of his manpower mass, risking fatally diminishing the striking power of his assault. Greene would make do with only 1,519 men to carry out his attack.[24]

Lieutenant Colonel Hector Tyndale's First Brigade led the column, moving south across the plowed field heading for the East Woods. Tyndale had good reason to be elsewhere at this moment, having built a thriving Philadelphia ceramics' import house before the war and facing his Quaker mother's opposition to his military service. During a business trip in Paris, he'd heard Lincoln's call, however, and returned home to join the 28th Pennsylvania; an odyssey which brought him to this deadly spot. Moving ever closer to the woods, Tyndale's men heard and saw the fighting but had no idea what they were really in for. Still, Tyndale's regiments quickly deployed from the right on Gordon's left-most regiment. First the 66th Ohio moved up, followed by the 7th Ohio, and finally the 28th Pennsylvania; a veteran regiment by length of service which nonetheless marched into its first battle. The 10th Maine, meanwhile, moved out of Tyndale's way, as earlier ordered. Once in position, the 28th Pennsylvania fired a volley that "sounded like one gun" and surged into the vacant northern end of the East Woods.

Through the smoke, Captain John Hannah, leading the right-most company in Colquitt's 6th Georgia, raced to find his commander—Lieutenant Colonel James M. Newton—to warn about the unfolding Yankee attack. Before Newton could act, though, the 66th Ohio's first volley tore through the Georgians's ranks, sweeping away both officers in a stroke. Regardless where their support—Garland's Brigade—was, Colquitt's men were now caught in a vice tightening on them with increasing speed and fury.[25]

As Tyndale's 28th Pennsylvania pushed deeper into the no-man's land of the East Woods's northern end, the two Ohio regiments moved at the right oblique out of the woods and into confusion. The 66th Ohio's Lieutenant Colonel Eugene Powell and 7th Ohio's Major Orin Crane carefully watched the two regiments advance up a slight hill. Peering through low-hanging smoke, Powell saw a body of troops and ordered his men to open fire. "No!" shouted Crane, "they are our men" and for a moment the Ohio regiments teetered on the edge of command chaos. To resolve the dispute, Powell rode frantically to the 66th, where a hasty volley resolved the question—they were Confederates. Meanwhile, the 28th Pennsylvania continued its grand right wheel, firing volleys as it advanced. Tyndale's progress was slow but, unlike so many of Hooker's earlier attacks, moved consistently forward. Key to this progress was that rather than simply marching swiftly ahead, Tyndale's regiments kept up a nearly constant routine of firing and advancing, edging their way forward. The Ohioans and the 28th Pennsylvania pushed nearly to a position from which they could unleash an enfilading fire on Colquitt's right flank in the Cornfield ahead. Moving deeper into the East

Woods, the 66th Ohio's Eugene Powell found it "beyond description ... dead men were literally piled upon and across each other." The task of securing the East Woods for the Union was being completed just to their left, however, and to accomplish it Tyndale's men wouldn't have to fire a shot.[26]

***

At that moment in the East Woods's southern end, McRae's control of Garland's Brigade was rapidly slipping away. His officers were struggling furiously to restore order when the final blow came. A body of enemy troops surged into the East Woods—Tyndale's Ohioans and Pennsylvanians—and headed toward the brigade's left flank, held by the 5th North Carolina. The 5th's new regimental commander was quick to assign blame for what happened next. "Captain T. P. Thompson, Company G, came up to me in a very excited manner and tone cried out to me 'They are flanking us! See, yonder's a whole brigade!' I ordered him to keep silent and return to his place. The men before this were far from being cool, but, when this act of indiscretion occurred, they began to break and run." Run they did, back the way they had come onto the field, back toward the Mumma farm they raced. Jumping fences and bodies and rock piles, dodging around trees, the Southern boys sprinted for their lives in no particular order. A captain in the 5th Texas ordered his men to fire on their fleeing comrades but then thought better of it. Confronting an officer in Garland's Brigade, the Texan demanded to know his name and regiment. "I'll be damned if I will tell you!" he snapped before joining his fleeing men. McRae and his officers tried rallying the men, but it was too late, they'd lost control—nothing would restore order to the mob that had once been Garland's Brigade.[27]

***

As McRae's men broke, the final shoe of Hooker's XII Corps attack dropped. Stainrook's Brigade appeared on Tyndale's left, shifting from a column into one, long battle line—"By company, into line" was the command—its regiments poured into the fight one after another. The 111th Pennsylvania deployed first, guiding toward Tyndale's left-most regiment. The 3rd Maryland followed next, in the center, while the 102nd Pennsylvania ran to post on the brigade's left. To Confederates defending the East Woods, it appeared as if barely had one regiment arrived when another emerged on its left, adding to their momentum and making it seem the attacker's resources knew no limit.

To Stainrook's men, though, this move was anything but smooth. As intended, the 111th Pennsylvania swung into place on the brigade's right—left of Tyndale's 28th Pennsylvania—and immediately opened fire to cover the rest of the brigade's deployment. The 3rd Maryland and 102nd New York, however, misjudged the

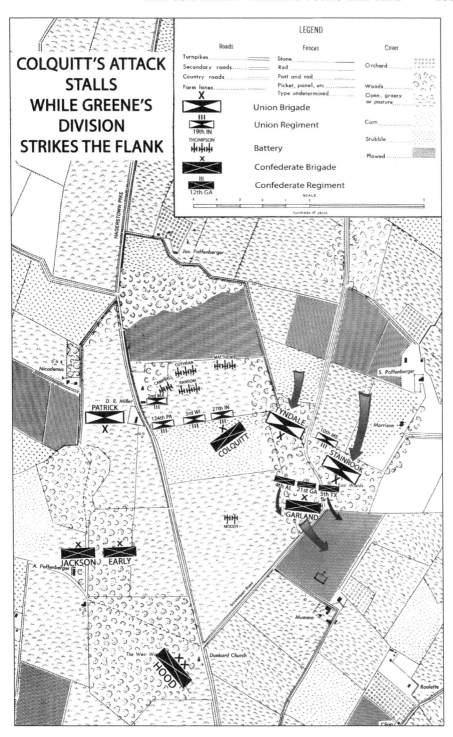

COLQUITT'S ATTACK
STALLS
WHILE GREENE'S
DIVISION
STRIKES THE FLANK

LEGEND

Roads	Fences	Cover
Turnpikes	Stone	Orchard
Secondary roads	Rail	Woods
Country roads	Post and rail	Open, grassy or pasture
Farm lanes	Picket, panel, etc.	Corn
	Type undetermined	Stubble
		Plowed

Union Brigade

Union Regiment

Battery

Confederate Brigade

Confederate Regiment

SCALE

hundreds of yards

available open space and crashed into each other. Confederate fire added to the chaos, suggesting the wheels were coming off Stainrook's attack just as it was beginning. Suddenly, though, the two regiments' officers were out in front amidst a hail of Rebel fire with their swords drawn, wresting the two lines once again in order—and it worked. Shifting leftward opened sufficient room and the three regiments formed one, long brigade line. With that, the whole of Stainrook's command advanced to the woods.[28]

"We advanced and fired as we deployed" recalled the 111th Pennsylvania's Major Thomas Walker, "and by the time we reached the woods were in line, closing up on the left of the First Brigade. We swept the rebels from the woods, taking a large number of prisoners…" Stainrook's attack gained momentum with each step, even as men in Law's cobbled-together brigade repeatedly stopped to fire at the oncoming line. This resistance was having an effect, of course, such as that suffered by the 102nd New York's Captain M. Eugene Cornell, who was shot through the head, and the 3rd Maryland's 19-year-old Captain W. A. Hacker, badly wounded in the chest. On top of the casualties, many in Stainrook's ranks were shocked by their first sight of the East Woods. "The dead, wounded and dying, were strewn about us on every hand," recalled the 3rd Maryland's chaplain, "and it was a sickening sight to behold; and we could hear the cries of the latter, as they writhed in their pains, we could hear above the din of battle. The enemy in retiring had left them, strewn in every direction over the field." Still, on pressed Stainrook's men, driving through the East Woods without halt and into the grassy field beyond.[29]

As Greene's Division swept through the East Woods, Gordon's Brigade advanced, too. Seeing blue-clad lines appear in the Cornfield's northern end, Gordon's officers ordered a "cease, fire" to avoid hitting their comrades. Fixing bayonets, the 27th Indiana and 3rd Wisconsin went to "charge, bayonet!" and "At the command, our line moves forward," recalled the 27th's Edmund Brown. "Down the modest slope to the tragic fence, over that and on, between the bloody corn rows, with their cut and hacked corn-stalks, advancing our left as we go…"[30]

Right of Gordon's position, the 2nd Massachusetts swept out of Miller's orchard heading for Colquitt's men in the Cornfield. The 2nd's Captain Robert Gould Shaw—who later commanded the 54th Massachusetts and enjoys modern fame in the 1989 film *Glory*—recalled "[T]he Brigade advanced through the cornfield in front, which, until then, had been occupied by the enemy; it was full of their dead and wounded … Beyond the cornfield was a large open field, and such a mass of dead and wounded men, mostly Rebels, as were lying there, I never saw before; it was a terrible sight, and our men had to be careful to avoid treading on them; many were mangled and torn to bits by artillery, but most of them had been wounded by infantry fire." Charles Morse recalled of the moment "[W]e swept forward with a rush which carried us through the cornfield and into the open field beyond." Their immediate target was the 11th Mississippi—from Law's Brigade, which had remained to fight—which now ran for its very existence. Having already lost two regimental commanders, the 11th's suffering increased when a 2nd Massachusetts sergeant grabbed from the regiment's latest wounded color-bearer its beloved flag, sprinting away with the prize. Crawford's 124th Pennsylvania too advanced, joining with Gordon's Brigade. Halting briefly at Miller's orchard to drop backpacks and blanket rolls, the Pennsylvanians quickly continued forward, guiding right through the corn until reaching the Hagerstown Pike.[31]

Once through the East Woods, Greene's men realigned their formations on the move and pressed forward. The 111th Pennsylvania's Captain John Boyle remembered "The roar of the heavy batteries, the scream and explosion of the shells, and the sharp rattle of the musketry fire enveloped the field and deafened the ear. But amid it all the word 'forward' was passed, and from the skirting of the first woods the line moved forward again across the open, up the slope and to[ward] the left of the church, the enemy giving way slowly, sullenly, and steadily." First Sergeant Lawrence Wilson from the 7th Ohio's Company D remembered emerging from the East Woods when "Sergt. Jere G. Claflin, of Company A … was wounded, being hit on the shin-bone as he was crossing a fallen tree, and for a few minutes the air was blue with expletives from him on account of the severe pain occasioned by the wound." Greene's Division swept Confederates from the Cornfield as efficiently as they'd done when clearing the East Woods and those who resisted were rewarded with failure and death. "[A] line of the enemy [was] drawn up along a fence, in the edge of a corn-field. We immediately opened fire upon the enemy, who soon broke," reported the 66th Ohio's Lieutenant Colonel Eugene Powell. "From the woods the enemy retired to a corn-field, followed by us, and while in the corn our regiment engaged a Georgia regiment in hand-to-hand combat, using clubbed guns, a portion of the men having no bayonets. The enemy at this point was severely punished," Major John Collins of the 5th Ohio dryly reported. No matter how valiantly the Southerners tried, all their result was the same—failure. Greene's lines swept steadily, inexorably forward toward the slope of the Hagerstown Pike.[32]

***

It was too much for Confederates holding the Cornfield. Their right was turned and the enemy advanced in front, too. S. D. Lee's artillery was of no help either; having been pulled away from before the Dunker Church earlier to refit. D. H. Hill would shortly send them even farther to the rear and safety. The vice squeezing them from right and front turned rapidly into a noose and men reacted as anyone would in such a spot—they fled. First in ones and twos, then in greater numbers, until Colquitt's entire brigade melted into a fleeing mass. Colquitt's line broke apart from right to left, sweeping with it Ripley's 3rd North Carolina and elements of the 1st North Carolina, which had remained behind and was moving to bolster

Colquitt's left. To save the brigade's reputation, Colonel Colquitt and his officers later claimed General D. H. Hill had ordered the retreat to the Dunker Church ridge. Even Colquitt, however, gently admitted the situation's reality writing, "The enemy closed in upon the right so near that our ranks were scarcely distinguishable. At the same time his front line advanced. My men stood firm until every field officer but one had fallen, and then made the best of their way out." The 27th Indiana's Edmund Brown was less charitable, recalling "we see our antagonists rise up and move briskly away, without any regard to order."[33]

The color-bearer of Colquitt's 13th Alabama stopped to rally his fleeing comrades but found only dishonor for his effort when the 5th Ohio's John P. Murphy seized the 13th's cherished flag, earning his new nation's highest honor, the Congressional Medal of Honor. The 6th Georgia's Private Benjamin Witcher also sought to stand just beyond the East Woods, recalling "a comrade by my side suggested we had better leave as that [Federal] line is going to charge, but noticing the men lying along the fence I replied no, we have a line, let them come, but, says he, these men are all wounded & dead and shook several to convince me; then, says I, the quicker we get out of this the better … At this time the Federal line fired & killed one of the four & wounded two others, so I came out alone bringing one wounded … to [the Dunker] church in [the] West Wood. I saw no other troops of ours until I got to the church."[34]

Colquitt repeatedly tried rallying the men "making the best of their way out," until settling for gathering his shattered brigade beyond the safety of the West Woods. Stonewall Jackson, D. H. Hill, Hood, and others similarly sought to restore order to the scattered Confederate defenders from the Cornfield. The teeming mass, racing back the same route they'd taken into the fight, resisted these efforts. Law's remaining troops from the East Woods, too, fled. The 5th Texas and 4th Alabama men ran south toward the smoldering Mumma farm buildings, before turning west toward the Dunker Church. As the last Rebels crossed the Hagerstown Pike, they surrendered control of the Cornfield to the Union once again.[35]

***

This time, though, it would be different. The Cornfield changed hands and the Confederacy would never again completely control this decisive spot. As XII Corps regiments swept across the broken fields of corn, grass, and plowed earth, they set the stage for Union victory—finally. At long last it appeared General Hooker would be able to break the Confederate left and hold on to the key high ground and ridge dominating the Confederate position surrounding Sharpsburg. Perhaps General McClellan's first goal would finally be achieved, enabling step two—turning the Confederate right—all in preparation for a grand thrust at breaking the Southern center, just north of town.

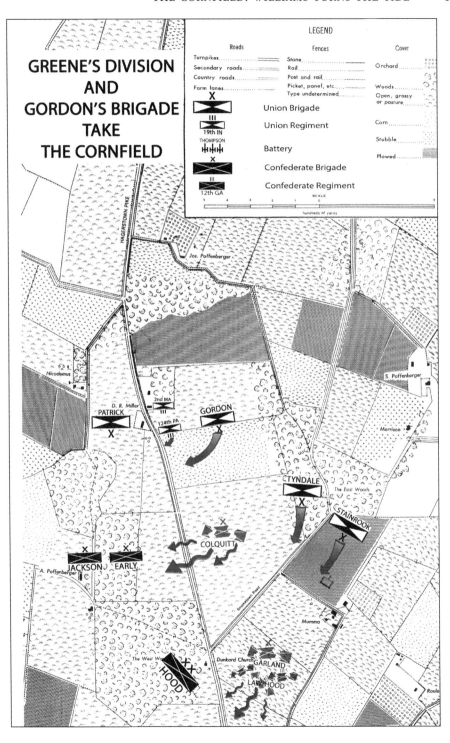

GREENE'S DIVISION AND GORDON'S BRIGADE TAKE THE CORNFIELD

***

Historians and Confederate Antietam veterans alike have blamed the dissolution of Garland's Brigade for the failure of D. H. Hill's forces to hold the Cornfield. Colonel Colquitt, too, laid blame for his command's failure to hold its position in the Cornfield directly on Garland's Brigade. "In the mean time Garland's brigade, which had been ordered to my right, had given way, and the enemy was advancing unchecked … With steady supports upon the right we could yet maintain our position." General Hill rolled blame even farther downhill, squarely onto the 5th North Carolina's Captain Thompson. Colonel McRae's reputation was spared in his superiors' and fellow officers' accounts, probably because he had struggled to regain control and was wounded in the stampede. Undoubtedly, Garland's Brigade became a scapegoat for the Confederacy finally losing control of the Cornfield; nonetheless, its officers'—from Colonel McRae on down—failure to preserve order in the face of an enemy assault set the stage for a potentially massive Southern defeat.[36]

Colonel Colquitt, too, bears some responsibility. His brigade's angled position lacked any secure connection with Law's force in the East Woods and was vulnerable from the start. Had the 2nd Massachusetts and the 124th Pennsylvania pushed beyond Miller's orchard, they might have turned Colquitt's left and completely cut the brigade off from the main Confederate line. Worse, once both flanks began collapsing, Colquitt's inaction risked his command being completely enveloped. Colquitt admits in his official report that this nearly happened, explaining that "we were exposed to a fire from all sides and nearly surrounded." Despite blaming Garland's collapse and his left-most regiments' failure to advance fully for this situation, Colquitt's own lapsed leadership is as much or more to blame; he alone was responsible for adjusting the brigade's position to counter these developments. Instead, Colquitt let events unfold, permitting command to slip from his grasp as surely as Colonel McRae lost hold of Garland's Brigade. When Greene's line swung through the East Woods threatening his right, Colquitt's lapsed leadership left his brigade in the worst possible position for defending its hold on the Cornfield.[37]

Numbers, however, suggest the odds were stacked against the Confederates from the start. Colquitt's, Garland's, and Law's patchwork brigade brought to the field 2,529 men; a force that was much diminished by time it faced the 6,855 Union troops in Williams's and Greene's fresher XII Corps divisions. Lacking numbers, Jackson all morning had skillfully exploited his interior lines to move reinforcements and employed operational initiative, counterattacking quickly to seize or retain initiative in blunting Union's assaults. This new Union attack, however, would test Jackson's approach as never before.

***

The change that enabled finally securing the Cornfield for the Union was Hooker's revised tactical approach to the XII Corps assault, which integrated the Union's greater manpower and firepower mass with more skillful maneuver. Finally aware that he could employ entire divisions—not just brigades—as his maneuver force, Hooker's adaptation increased the mass of his assault. At the same time, coordinating and combining pressure from the front—Gordon's advance—with Green's turning assault on the Confederate right created conditions Southern forces had not yet seen this day. Alone, either of these changes might have fallen short, but employed together, they became an overwhelming, irresistible force that negated the Confederacy's advantages of interior lines and initiative.

Hooker was finally living up to the trust General McClellan had placed in him. The opening battle phase's chief tactical architect consciously changed his approach mid-fight, taking risks and looking for opportunities to achieve victory, however that came. Hooker's physical presence amidst his fight too was critical to these changes and success in the Cornfield. Once aware the opening attacks had failed, Hooker left his headquarters at the J. Poffenberger house and ranged over the entire field, personally reconnoitering the ground, the enemy's evolving position and condition, and the state of the overall fight; he also personally placed infantry and artillery units to suit his purposes. In so doing, Hooker gathered intelligence that enabled innovations in the XII Corps's assault and which provided an inspiring personal example, showing his officers and men that their commander shared their risks and deadly experience.

At the same time, Hooker's change was too little, too late. Despite being poised for a tactical breakthrough, Hooker's earlier failures hovered over the battle, dimming the Union's prospects. Failed tactical approaches resulted in one-sixth or more of McClellan's fighting force being spent and "combat ineffective." In human terms, the I Corps attack had been costly, indeed. Total casualties numbered 2,589—of 9,438 engaged—of which 417 were killed outright in the fight to this point. Looked at another way, 27 percent of Hooker's I Corps command was destroyed, and an unknown additional percentage was lost in helping the wounded or had fled. As bad, Hooker's failed use of the I Corps had cost the Union critical time. It had taken nearly two hours to reach this point and Hooker had yet to complete McClellan's goal for his key part to the Union's battle plan. Nearly a quarter of the available daylight—sunrise was 5:53 and sunset 6:07—was gone and the Union had gained little during this period. Thanks to Hooker's shortcomings, McClellan had only nine hours remaining and nearly ten thousand fewer men remaining to use in defeating Lee's army.[38]

***

None of these explanations and excuses mattered that morning, however. What counted—from the lowest private in the ranks to Generals McClellan and Lee—was that the Union XII Corps was sweeping through the Cornfield and grassy field to its south toward the Dunker Church, while Confederate brigades that had been holding the Yankees away from this objective since well before dawn were fleeing. The Cornfield was finally decisively in Union hands. Now that it was, everything turned on what Joe Hooker and his Federal troops would do with it.

CHAPTER 10

The Cornfield: Union Success Weighs in the Balance

All morning, General McClellan remained at his Pry House headquarters, probably monitoring the battle's progress but certainly otherwise remaining quite apart from these events. As the battle intensified—while his men died by the score only a mile away—George McClellan remained indoors and unavailable to anyone but his staff. Even the arrival of General Sumner and his son and adjutant, Captain Samuel S. Sumner, shortly after 6:00 didn't break McClellan's isolation, leaving the army's second-ranking officer on the field that day to wait for his orders and for his commander to appear. Captain Sumner commented "I don't know if General McClellan was asleep or engaged inside. I know General Sumner was uneasy and impatient … we remained outside Headquarters for some time, quite an hour or more as I remember it."[1]

McClellan emerged shortly after 7:20, not in person but rather in the form of orders. Although bearing General Randolph B. Marcy's signature and carried by an aide, they nonetheless held General McClellan's considerable weight and authority. "The Comdg. General directs that you move Sedgwick and French across the creek by the fords which Capt. Custer will point out to you," they read. "You will cross in as solid a mass as possible and communicate with Genl. Hooker immediately. Genl. Richardson's Division will not cross till further orders. You will cross your artillery over the bridge and halt after you cross until you ascertain if Genl. Hooker wants assistance." These orders finally provided Sumner the clear direction he'd looked for since the previous evening.[2]

By 8:30, McClellan dictated an update—one to Sumner and another to Hooker—bearing the signature of McClellan's assistant adjutant general Colonel Albert V. Colburn, which Sumner received while en route to the front. "General Hooker appears to be driving the enemy rapidly," it read, "If he does not require your assistance on his right, please push left through the ravine at the head of which the house was burned this morning, getting possession of the woods to the right as soon as possible & push on towards Sharpsburg and a little to its rear as rapidly as possible. Use your artillery freely." Reflecting that by 8:30 McClellan finally had intelligence of the battle's state, it also indicates his preference for Sumner and his

II Corps striking toward Lee's center, developing what Hooker had presumably achieved.[3]

At first glance, the two orders to Sumner might suggest McClellan was innovating in response to the unfolding battle; in fact, they reflect the opposite. Sending some of Sumner's batteries across the Upper Bridge the previous evening to support Hooker suggests they were moving ahead of their corps, indicating McClellan had already decided to cross the II Corps on his position's right. Directing Sumner's corps to cross and wait to learn if Hooker needed help before acting could have reflected a situation-driven, mid-battle adaptation, positioning the corps to play a flexible role in whatever phase of the battle it was most needed. Instead, roles supporting Hooker on the right and driving toward the Confederate middle hewed closely to McClellan's original battle plan. Placing Sumner's II Corps first at Hooker's disposal probably reflects McClellan's priority in completing the battle's first phase, necessary before unleashing subsequent phases. Finding Hooker had already completed his work allowed Sumner to lay groundwork for the attack in the center, as McClellan had probably planned from the start.[4]

By mid-morning, McClellan probably believed his battle was unfolding largely according to plan and he moved to ensure it continued doing so. By 8:00, McClellan apparently had intelligence indicating Hooker's attack on Lee's left flank had been at least partially successful. Although what this intelligence was exactly and how he obtained it remains a mystery, it nonetheless became the lynchpin that prompted McClellan to unleash the second phase of his battle plan; the assault on Lee's opposite flank. Sometime before 7:00 that morning, McClellan had sent word to Burnside to prepare his IX Corps to move against the bridge but—reflecting McClellan's focus on carefully sequencing his attacks—to await further orders before moving. This came around 8:00 when McClellan sent Burnside a message—through the Topographical Engineers's Lieutenant Wilson—directing him to open his attack on Lee's right flank. Given the timing in which these two flanking attacks were launched, McClellan might well have intended that his 8:30 order to Sumner would support and enable striking Lee's center. McClellan might even have considered that if things continued so smoothly, victory might be his by midday or early afternoon.[5]

Such considerations were at that moment beyond General Sumner's concern, however. Sumner and his son quickly rode to where Sedgwick's and French's Divisions were bivouacked behind the Pry House and within minutes men were up and forming their lines to march. They'd been waiting since before dawn, so there was little to do but fall in and await their turn to move. Private George Beidelman of the 71st Pennsylvania's Company C—part of Howard's Brigade in Sedgwick's Division—recalled "Reveille long before daylight, with orders to make coffee and be ready to march in an hour. But we did not go until sunrise." The 69th Pennsylvania was ordered to unsling knapsacks and leave them in a pile, guarded by a few chosen for the duty. The Irishmen of the 69th knew that this meant hard fighting lay ahead;

this itself didn't trouble them, but the only previous time they'd left behind knapsacks in such a manner had been at Savage's Station and that battle hadn't gone well at all for them. Regardless, the II Corps began flowing toward Pry's Ford to cross the creek. George Beidelman recalled "we had to ford a creek, which was about knee deep; but we didn't mind at all." Apparently, a few men of the 108th New York did mind, though, and were severely upbraided by their officers for stopping to remove their shoes and socks. Regardless if they splashed unconcernedly through the creek or sought to stay dry, the men of the II Corps were moving ever closer toward the sounds of battle.[6]

The situation into which Sumner's men marched, which had recently been so promising, once again hung in the balance. Although Greene's Division and Gordon's Brigade held the Cornfield and were poised to strike the Confederate main line, two critical realities had stopped them. The first was a simple lack of ammunition. "After pressing them closely for a distance of one-half mile, we were obliged to slacken our fire, as our ammunition had given out…" reported the 7th Ohio's Major Crane, echoing both of Greene's brigade commanders. No matter how much Greene's officers and men wished to continue pressing the attack, until being resupplied, they simply hadn't the means to do so.[7]

The other obstacle stalling their attack was the fence running the length of the Hagerstown Pike. General Crawford described it as "A fine wooden fence which skirted the road and proved a very serious obstacle to our farther advance." So far, most fences the XII Corps encountered were what the soldiers called a "worm fence," comprised of fence rails piled on each other in a zig-zag fashion. Gravity largely held these fences in place, and they were easily torn apart. This, however, was a post-and-rail fence, which consisted of a post, secured vertically into the ground, through which six holes were bored, each hole holding the ends of a rail connecting the posts. This deceptively simple design was what made the fence such an obstacle. The interlocking rails left no weak points on which to twist the fence apart and the two posts of each section were deeply secured into the ground to prevent large animals like cattle and horses from breaking through. Tearing down the fence required significant, coordinated effort because—unlike worm fences—no one man could accomplish this by himself. This same fence had hindered Gibbon's Brigade during its earlier Union advance down the Hagerstown Pike. Nonetheless, although troublesome to Lee's troops fleeing the XII Corps—men had climbed the fence or dashed through one of its growing number of artillery-generated gaps—the fence had been no obstacle to Hood's Division and other Confederate units. Why then had the Hagerstown Pike's fence become such an impediment that it stopped the Union assault in its tracks?[8]

What made the fence "a great obstruction to our rapid pursuit, checking our line until the enemy could bring up his strong re-enforcements," as General Williams described, was the presence of nearby enemy rifle fire. Confederate Brigadier General

John G. Walker thought it was such when his men encountered the fence and fire combination later that morning. "Colonel Manning and [three of his regiments] dashed forward in gallant style…," Walker explained, "driving the enemy before him like sheep, until, arriving at a long line of strong post and rail fences, behind which heavy masses of the enemy's infantry were lying, their advance was checked." The want of ammunition and the challenge of crossing the fence under heavy, nearby fire now protected the Hagerstown Pike from the Union advance more effectively than any of the Confederate units then on the field.[9]

***

Across the Pike, Stonewall Jackson and his officers worked tirelessly to shore up what remained of the Confederate main line. By 8:15 or so, however, Jackson had thrown nearly all his available brigades and divisions into the fight. Now, with the Union XII Corps advancing and his own advanced line crumbling, Jackson turned to his last fresh brigade—that of Brigadier General Jubal Early.

Early's men began the day behind the West Woods, spread across the Alfred Poffenberger farm. Barely had the battle started when Jackson ordered it left to support Stuart's cavalry and horse artillery, holding Nicodemus Heights and the true left flank of Lee's position. While the fighting raged for nearly three hours, Early's Brigade had been largely spectators to the carnage going on through the woods in their front. Sometime after 7:00—as Meade's Division and Patrick's Brigade pressed the Confederate line—however, Stuart concluded that his artillery on the Heights was of no further use because the two lines were so close they simply couldn't fire without risking hitting Southern boys. Moreover, Patrick's Brigade, then in the West Woods, was dangerously close to cutting his command's link to the rest of Lee's line. Remaining on Nicodemus Heights was suddenly too risky, so he ordered Early and his brigade back to its starting point near the West Woods.[10]

As Early's men faced right and formed a column to move, Stuart informed Early of Lawton's wounding and that Jackson wanted him to assume command of Lawton's Division. Leaving behind the 13th Virginia to support Stuart's moving artillery, Early and his brigade started off, heading toward more of a role than they could imagine.[11]

Barely had Early's Brigade reached its intended post when the enemy advanced in its front. While his new division was nowhere to be seen, Early found Colonels Grigsby and Stafford from Jackson's Division feverishly reforming the 300 or so scattered men left in their combined commands. Grigsby eventually got his brigade in line, clearing way for Early's men to move into position perpendicular to the Hagerstown Pike, its left on a rock ledge and right on Grigsby's reformed line. This critical task completed—and brigade command passed to the 49th Virginia's Colonel Smith—General Early raced to where Lawton's Division had been the night before.[12]

Scanning the woods and fields for his new command revealed nothing of Lawton's Division. About that time Early learned, probably from officers on the scene, that the division had taken a beating in the Cornfield and was now reforming somewhere in the rear. Although deserving of a break, Early dispatched Major J. P. Wilson from Lawton's staff to bring Lawton's Division immediately forward. Early, meanwhile, surveyed the situation before him. Across the Hagerstown Pike, two Confederate brigades had collapsed and were racing his way. Worse, Union troops were advancing on both flanks in numbers Early couldn't match—the situation was bad and getting worse by the second and Early needed reinforcements soon. Only Jackson might offer that help and in a flash Early was off to find him.[13]

Reaching Jackson, Early warned that the Southern position in the Cornfield had broken and was crumbling toward Jackson's main line, pressed by advancing Union troops. Jackson promised reinforcements and directed Early to hold the line at all costs until they could arrive. Having secured what he'd come for, Early raced back to his command and Grigsby's Stonewall Brigade—reinforced by Stafford's men—which now were all that held the center of Jackson's line.[14]

Once again, Union and Confederate forces fighting at the Cornfield entered into a race for reinforcements. Jackson clearly knew fresh troops were already on their way, which probably explains why he calmly and confidently assured Early that help was coming, despite having no such troops at hand. Those reinforcements—McLaws's and Walker's Divisions—had done almost no fighting this day and were ordered to Jackson's center around 9:00, probably in response to Hood's plea for help. Although Hood's fight in the Cornfield was lost by the time McLaws and Walker were put in motion—McLaws from the center behind Lee's headquarters; Walker from the still-placid Confederate right—they would now play for Early and Jackson the role they'd been unable to perform for Hood. Only a few hundred yards across the Hagerstown Pike, the Union's reinforcements, too, were anxiously anticipated. Hooker knew the II Corps was on its way, though probably not that it was then racing directly toward the East Woods. All now weighed on which side first put these fresh men into the fight.[15]

It was the South which struck first. At roughly 8:30, Brigadier General Robert E. Rodes's command was ordered from Sharpsburg to the left, supporting the brigades of Ripley, Colquitt, and Garland, then entangled in the Cornfield and East Woods. The order almost at once became moot, however. "I had hardly begun the movement before it was evident that [Colquitt and Garland] had met with a reverse, and that the best service I could render them and the field generally would be to form a line in rear of them and endeavor to rally them before attacking or being attacked," Rodes noted, "Major-General [D.H.] Hill held the same view, for at this moment I received an order from him to halt and form line of battle in the hollow of an old and narrow road just beyond the orchard." Hill added that "three of my brigades had been broken and much demoralized, and all of the artillery had been withdrawn from my front." Apparently, loss of the East Woods and the XII

Corps's advance convinced Daniel Hill that these 850 fresh men were best used in holding a second defensive line before Sharpsburg. Although the fight would soon find them—the "old and narrow road" in which Rodes's men waited is better known as "Bloody Lane"—for now, these reinforcements would not shore up Jackson's line or help Jubal Early on the far left.[16]

As reinforcements surged toward the front, an odd lull settled over the Cornfield and the contested woodlots of Miller's farm. General Williams described the break matter-of-factly, noting "the firing on both sides wholly ceased." Although men on the front lines may have lacked a reason to continue firing, much remained for Generals Jackson and Hooker to do preparing for the fighting's inevitable return. Although Jackson could do little more than steady his line and wait for reinforcements, Hooker had some important new realities to consider in weighing what to do next.[17]

***

Hooker's Union forces now possessed the Cornfield and nearby ground standing before Jackson's main line on the Dunker Church ridge. Gone was the Confederate salient that had turned the Cornfield into a killing ground and with it had disappeared the strategic depth Jackson had depended on all morning to keep Hooker's attacks from his main position. Now it was Hooker's Union troops that enjoyed strategic depth, allowing Sumner's Union reinforcements to march largely unfettered across the Cornfield and nearby ground to strike directly at Jackson's main line. Confederate artillery fire would slow, but was unlikely to stop, advancing Federals. Not having to fight their way forward also meant Union reinforcements would arrive fresh and with full supplies of ammunition with which to strike Jackson's main position. It was a critical turnabout, if Hooker could hold and exploit this hard-won ground.

Hooker also had to consider how to exploit the changed axis of his attack, altered by the evolution of the Cornfield fight and the XII Corps's advance. No longer were Union forces attacking in a generally north-south direction but rather from east to west. Regardless if this change was intended in Hooker's revised attack plan or was an unintentional benefit of Greene's swinging-gate maneuver and advance, it now gave Hooker important advantages that his earlier approach lacked. Hooker's II Corps reinforcements could strike Jackson's Confederates in a simple, straightforward frontal attack launched from nearer the enemy than had come in any earlier Union assaults. Union attackers also could do so without exposing their vulnerable flanks to enemy fire; a weakness that had dogged and undermined Hooker's attackers all morning.

The XII Corps, too, offered new possibilities for attacking Jackson. Although tired and short on ammunition, the corps held a wide front along the Hagerstown Pike. Greene's Division occupied the position's left facing west, its left pinned on Mumma's farm lane—bordering the small Clipp farm cornfield—extending north to hold the

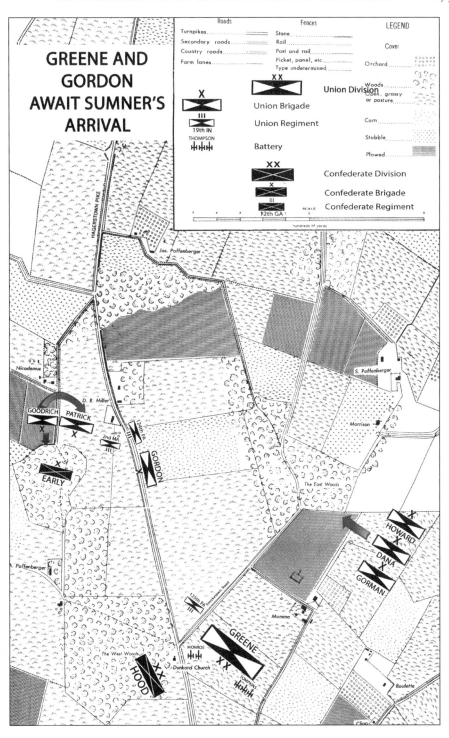

GREENE AND
GORDON
AWAIT SUMNER'S
ARRIVAL

Roads
Turnpikes
Secondary roads
Country roads
Farm lanes

Fences
Stone
Rail
Post and rail
Picket, panel, etc
Type undetermined

LEGEND

Cover

Orchard

Union Division

Woods
Open, grassy
or pasture

Union Brigade

Corn

Union Regiment

Stubble

Battery

Plowed

Confederate Division

Confederate Brigade

Confederate Regiment

SCALE
hundreds of yards

Smoketown Road–Hagerstown Pike intersection near the Dunker Church. On the right, Gordon's Brigade and Crawford's 124th Pennsylvania faced south holding a broad front, running from the East Woods, across the southern end of the Cornfield, to its right on the high ground at the Hagerstown Pike. Although facing different directions and with poorly secured flanks, the position's greatest failing was a gaping hole between the two Union commands. Probably a result of the uncoordinated—and perhaps unplanned—pursuit of retreating Confederates through the Cornfield. Hooker apparently planned to throw his II Corps reinforcements thorough it to strike Jackson's line; Greene's and Gordon's commands would secure the flanks of this attack. Hooker almost certainly worried the Confederates would seek to exploit this weakness as an invitation to push through their own troops, threatening his new and still-weak line and stealing back the battle's offensive momentum. Although unable to make Sumner's reinforcements appear faster, Hooker, Greene, and Gordon worked to secure their positions.[18]

Gordon's immediate challenge was eliminating the confusion remaining from taking the Cornfield. Probably seeking to address this by restoring order to his ranks, Gordon quickly shifted his command into two lines. When completed, the still-fresh 2nd Massachusetts and 107th New York held the front, with the battle-worn 3rd Wisconsin and 27th Indiana posted behind, and the large 124th Pennsylvania securing the line's right along the Hagerstown Pike.[19]

Supporting Greene's Division was even more challenging because until Sumner arrived only artillery was available for this task, so Hooker and his staff dashed about the field finding any available batteries to help. Near the North Woods, Hooker found two batteries, Captain John A. Monroe's Battery D of the 1st Rhode Island Artillery and Lieutenant Frederick Edgell's Battery A of the New Hampshire Light Artillery, adding 12 brass Napoleons to the cause. Hooker sent Edgell's Battery to a spot northwest of the burning Mumma farm buildings; Monroe's Battery was ordered to a rise left of Greene's position (the site of today's Antietam Battlefield visitor center). This deployment suggests Hooker intended Monroe to provide short-range support to Greene, while Edgell could fire longer-range rounds into the West Woods beyond.

Arriving behind Greene's position, Captain Monroe ordered his caissons to remain in the rear, while the then-nearby 125th Pennsylvania removed fence rails to clear the battery's path to the front. Riding forward, Captain Monroe saw the woods ahead alive with Rebels; things became worse when moments later Greene advised in a low voice that he was unable to offer infantry support because his men were armed only with bayonets. Nonetheless, Monroe ordered "In battery!," sending his six guns into position facing south toward Sharpsburg. Now Greene had at least something resembling reinforcements securing his left flank.[20]

A nearby occurrence, however, instantly changed the very course of this fight, if not the war itself. This event wasn't caused by Jubal Early or Edwin Sumner, nor was it the result of a momentous decision or the "fog of war." Rather, it was the simple act of one man, doing his routine duty in this very extraordinary situation, firing a single musket ball which found as its stopping place General Hooker's foot.[21]

Hooker must have known of the wound instantly. Putting himself at risk all morning, General Williams noted in recording their last encounter "While we were talking the dust of the ploughed ground was knocked up in little spurts all around us, marking the spot where musket balls struck." The 125th Pennsylvania's Colonel Higgins might have observed Hooker's wounding, writing "General Hooker came up to me and inquired if any troops were in the woods in front. I replied, "None but rebels" and that my command was in the front. While talking to me, his horse was shot by some of the enemy's sharpshooters. I remarked to him that his horse was shot. He replied "I see," turned and went away." Hooker ignored the wound and continued preparing for the II Corps's arrival and resumption of full-scale battle. Before long, though, the blood loss became too great for even "Fighting Joe" Hooker to ignore. Returning from the 125th's position, Hooker fell from his saddle and his staff was immediately upon him. Removing a boot, one staff officer poured out a stream of blood, prompting a surgeon to order Hooker immediately borne to the rear on a stretcher.[22]

Well to the rear, McClellan finally emerged from the Pry House sometime after 7:20, joining his staff on the lawn in monitoring Hooker's progress as best he could, given the limits of terrain—ridges west of the Antietam and the East Woods blocked McClellan's view of all but the southern end of the morning's fighting—and the flow of information. David Strother of McClellan's staff recorded "[Generals Porter and McClellan] sat together during the morning in a redan of fence rails, Porter continually using the glass and reporting observations, McClellan smoking and sending orders. His manner was quiet, cool, and soldierly, his voice low-toned ... The intense excitement under his manner was also very apparent." McClellan had good reason to be anxious. All his plans hinged on the success of Hooker's attack; he apparently believed events were going his way—his orders to Sumner implied as much—and that Hooker's efforts were bearing fruit.[23]

It was now that the crushing weakness of McClellan's plans and command style were called to account. The two men bearing Hooker from the field to the Pry House hospital carried away the only man aware of McClellan's overall battle plan and who could ensure its first phase came to fruition. The one other man who knew this plan and could guide it toward reality remained safely in the rear, watching and smoking. The torch of McClellan's vital first battle phase was about to pass to a new leader and soon enough it would be clear just how clumsily that passing had occurred.[24]

CHAPTER II

The Cornfield's Influence:
Sumner Assaults the West Woods

General Sumner and his II Corps staff rode directly west around 9:00 toward the sound of firing, when they came upon Hooker being carried to the rear on a stretcher. The two may have talked as Hooker lapsed in and out of consciousness—Hooker recalled the conversation, though Sumner never mentioned it—but if so, Sumner apparently gained no clearer sense of what awaited his corps, of Hooker's tactical approach, or of McClellan's overall plan. Regardless, Sumner must have known that he was now the ranking officer on the field and in command of the Union's attack on the Confederate left.[1]

In some respects, Major General Edwin Vose Sumner was the ideal man to step into Hooker's central role at this moment in the fight. Born on January 30, 1797 in Boston, Massachusetts, Sumner completed West Point in 1819, before serving in the Black Hawk War and Mexico. Still bearing his Old Army nickname, "Bull"—because his booming voice could be heard over the din of battle, though other accounts claim the name was really "Bull-head," resulting from a musket ball reportedly once having bounced off his thick head—Sumner was the only commander the II Corps had ever known and had built it into a first-rate fighting unit, earning McClellan's praised in a June 2 letter to Secretary of War Stanton. Nonetheless, McClellan harbored reservations about Sumner. Not only had the prospect of serving under Sumner in the 1st US Cavalry probably played a role in McClellan leaving the army in 1857, but on May 6, McClellan wrote Mary Ellen that "Sumner has proved that he was even a greater fool than I supposed & had come within an ace of having us defeated" and on June 11 reassured her he was taking care of himself because should he be disabled army command might fall to Sumner, who "would ruin things in about two days…" Regardless what McClellan might have wished, his battle plan's fate was now in Sumner's hands.[2]

Barely had Sumner and staff started forward again when an aide, sent to find someone in command of the I Corps and gauge the situation, returned. Finding only General Ricketts and his beaten division behind the East Woods, he reported Ricketts "could not raise 300 men of the corps." Minutes later, a rider from headquarters appeared bearing McClellan's two 8:30 dispatches. Atop his mount, Sumner read, probably for the first time, McClellan's intelligence that Hooker was "driving the enemy rapidly" and orders that if possible, the II Corps should secure "possession of the woods to the right [of the burning buildings] ... & push on towards Sharpsburg and a little to its rear as rapidly as possible." Sumner may also have read Hooker's dispatch: "Genl. Sumner has been directed (if you do not require him to assist you on the right) to move up on your left and push rapidly forward toward Sharpsburg. P.S. Keep the Genl. fully posted by means of his aides." Although these orders made clear McClellan's preference that the II Corps develop Hooker's successful attack, none of this squared with Ricketts's report. Sumner apparently needed more intelligence about the state of Hooker's attack before deciding what to do next.[3]

Immediately behind Sumner, Sedgwick's Division of 5,698 men and two batteries advanced, bearing 12 guns. Sedgwick's three brigades each crossed the ford below the Upper Bridge, before resuming the three parallel division formation used since leaving their Keedysville bivouac; Gorman's Brigade formed the left-most column with Dana's and Howard's Brigades to the right. Moving quickly, within a mile or so of the East Woods they halted briefly to deploy in a battle front, probably in response to nearing the sounds and sight of battle beyond the East Woods. Facing "Front" placed Gorman's Brigade in the front line of the three-brigade-deep formation—a "column of brigades" in the manual—with Dana's and Howard's Brigades standing immediately behind. Facing southwest, this tight formation—General Howard recalled they were no more than "60 to 70 paces apart"—started off again at the double-quick in the general direction of Sharpsburg. This southwestward course made perfect sense at that moment, reflecting McClellan's orders sending Sumner's corps in exactly this direction unless needed farther to the right to aid Hooker.[4]

"[W]e advanced in three lines of battle," recalled the 19th Massachusetts's Captain Jack Adams in Dana's center brigade, "over hills and fences, through fields, under a terrible fire of artillery." Despite the swift march, some in Howard's 72nd Pennsylvania found the Neikirk farm's orchard— "fairly bending with loads of ripe, luscious fruit," recalled one—too tempting to pass up. Grabbing what fruit they could, men rejoined the ranks marching "with arms at 'right shoulder shift,' went on at a quick step eating apples." Others weren't so carefree, though, and Captain Adams recalled that to calm the men, "Colonel Hinks halted us, put us through the manual of arms, ending with parade rest. Having become steady, we moved forward..."[5]

Eagerly awaiting them were Williams's XII Corps men. Just as Hooker had personally shifted artillery to support Greene, Williams moved available infantry to support Gordon and keep the Rebels busy until the II Corps arrived. Patrick's I Corps brigade remained behind a small rock ledge across the Hagerstown Pike using the break to eat breakfast and boil coffee amidst scattered artillery and musket fire, prompting a nearby artillery officer to comment that "it was about the coolest thing he had seen during the war." Patrick's respite would prove short-lived when the brigade soon became part of Williams's time-buying distraction.[6]

In a move that diverted the enemy's attention and relieved the pressure facing Gordon's men, Williams ordered forward Goodrich's Third Brigade in response to Gibbon's plea for support. They headed toward the northern end of the West Woods past Patrick's men, who scrambled into line while swilling down coffee and kicking fires dead, unaware their general had advised Colonel Goodrich to wait until the two brigades could act together. The 21st New York's Colonel William F. Rogers similarly cautioned "I warned him if he determined to move on to dismount as he was a conspicuous mark." Ignoring Rogers's advice, Goodrich pushed across the field on Patrick's right, into the woods itself. Almost immediately, Early's and Grigsby's Confederates, holding Lee's left flank and hidden deeper in the woods, poured fire into them.[7]

One of Patrick's 35th New Yorkers recalled "An awful crash of musketry followed—the brigade gave way and came fleeing toward us. We were ordered forward to the cliff again, and taking position, we returned fire." Patrick's men surged forward to the rock ledge, while Goodrich's men rallied behind. Sergeant Theodore Nagle, from the 21st New York's Company C, recorded "the order came, 'Twenty-first, fall in! Forward!!' and we passed through this big crowd going pell mell to the rear, we in proper order to the front. I was never more proud of our little regiment. When we had passed the last of the retreating regiment [Nagle apparently mistook Goodrich's Brigade for one of Williams's large, new regiments], we deployed in line of battle, advanced a short distance. The rebels had not followed in force and what did was stopped with a few shots." Patrick's action saved Goodrich's unit but not its commander. Colonel William B. Goodrich was killed in the West Woods and command passed to the 78th New York's Lieutenant Colonel Austin. One 35th New Yorker recorded "the stampede was stopped for a moment but our right was being flanked by a large force." He might well have seen this in his mind years later, but at that moment Early's and Grigsby's men were in no condition to make such a move.[8]

Williams also ordered the 124th Pennsylvania forward from the Cornfield, probably to support Goodrich and Patrick. Guiding right on the Hagerstown Pike, the 124th advanced until halted by fire from Early's concealed men and a nearby Confederate battery. Lieutenant Colonel Litzenberg—commanding for only half an hour—ordered Major Isaac Haldeman to take Companies A, D, and F across the Pike and drive away the unseen foe. Haldeman's force pressed through the Pike's fences into D. R. Miller's barnyard, then directly into the West Woods. They'd gone about 100 yards when the enemy—still hidden by smoke—made his presence painfully clear. "We quickly found that the rebels were in the woods for they opened on us," recalled Company D's First Sergeant Broomhall. "They were behind rails and everything they could put up, while we were out in the open field." The 124th's regimental historian Robert Green added, "[t]he enemy had a great advantage of position; clouds obscured the sky; smoke hung near the ground, and the gloom of the woods was so increased that it was difficult to see one of the enemy even when he stepped from cover, while the Union troops could be distinctly seen on their elevation against the horizon. Perceiving they were fighting at a great disadvantage, and not receiving any orders to advance, the men fell back to the turnpike … where the crest of the hill and the slight bank along the side of the turnpike afforded some protection, and from this point they fired when any of the enemy appeared in sight." Although Haldeman's probe failed to clear the enemy fire, the 124th was probably performing exactly the role Williams wanted—tying up Early and Grigsby and buying time for II Corps reinforcements to appear.[9]

The 125th Pennsylvania too re-entered the fight. Since aligning on Greene's right across the Smoketown Road, they'd done little more than tear holes in the road's fences for Monroe's and Edgell's Batteries to cross through in supporting Greene. Then Lieutenant Witman of Crawford's staff appeared with orders sending the 125th forward to hold the West Woods at all hazards. The order's timing was fortuitous because Monroe's nearby battery had just silenced the enemy artillery which had so troubled the 125th's prone men; instantly the Pennsylvanians were up and moving forward. The South Carolina and Georgia skirmishers from Hood's weary division melted away before the Yankee mass, and up to the deadly fence they pushed. This time, though, there was no enemy fire making the fence impenetrable so they surged through and over it. The road they crossed was littered with dead and wounded Confederates, including the 6th Georgia's Lieutenant Colonel Newton, who begged the 125th's passing colonel for "stimulants or morphine." With neither to offer, Colonel Higgins recalled, the Georgian cried "I am shot through. Oh, God, I must die" and rolled over and did as predicted. Reaching the West Woods's eastern edge, Higgins ordered Company G forward among the trees in skirmish order and detached Company B to move left to secure the Dunker Church. Higgins next sent his brother, a lieutenant in Company B, riding back to inform General Crawford of what they'd just done and warn that without reinforcements they must eventually be flanked and driven back. The 125th Pennsylvania had just accomplished what no other Federal unit—regardless of size or skill—had been able to do all morning—secure a hold on the Dunker Church ridge within the Army of Northern Virginia's lines.[10]

The intelligence Colonel Higgins had just gathered would have greatly benefitted Sumner and other Union generals. A single regiment—albeit a large one—had just reached the objective of McClellan's first battle phase nearly unopposed, suggesting the Confederates were vulnerable here and lacked ready reinforcements to close the breach. Company B men found the Dunker Church a hospital full of wounded, but no nearby troops to contest their presence. More significantly, Company G's Captain John McKeage and his men reached the woods' western end unopposed to observe the open fields beyond; these first Union men to glimpse Lee's rear area now knew that no Confederate reinforcements awaited anywhere. This intelligence might have changed the battle and the war, but it went no further than Colonel Higgins if he appreciated the find. Preoccupied with their immediate tactical situation, Higgins and the 125th simply tried to hold on until reinforcements finally arrived.[11]

Making this and much more possible was General Williams and his subordinates who effectively prepared the field for the arrival of Sumner's II Corps, although historians have largely overlooked their contribution. Hooker's sudden departure had created a command gap that invited disaster; instead, Williams, Gordon, Crawford, and Greene worked in concert—even if unplanned—holding together the Union gains until Sumner's fresh troops appeared. Their efforts ensured an open position into which Sumner might drive his reinforcements, just as Hooker probably planned, and their constant small attacks kept Rebels on the defensive, preventing any counterattack to again turn the tables on the Union. Their effective leadership also preserved order within the battered Union ranks and maintained the North's offensive momentum. All that prevented the Union from completing McClellan's vital first phase of this fight was exploiting these gains.

***

Jubal Early returned from meeting with Jackson to a situation even worse than the bad one he'd left. The attack on his left—by Goodrich and Patrick—remained underway and a huge body of reinforcements—the 124th Pennsylvania—had appeared in the Cornfield. Worse, Union troops were in the West Woods itself near the Dunker Church—the 125th Pennsylvania—threatening his right flank, too. Understanding his predicament, Early was determined to hold on. "I saw the vast importance of maintaining my ground, for, had the enemy gotten possession of this woods, the heights immediately in rear which commanded the rear of our whole line, would have fallen into his hands," Early explained, "I determined to wait for the re-enforcements promised by General Jackson…" Until they arrived, Early would make do with units at hand and he welcomed a battery deploying near the Dunker Church until his acting adjutant-general, Major Hale, cautioned that the battery appeared to be a Union crew. Disbelieving, Early rode right and at the edge of the woods peered across the open field. This confirmed the battery's allegiance—it was very probably Monroe's Federal battery—and let Early for the first time observe Greene's Division hovering across the Pike. Early knew this situation was "exceedingly critical:" the gap between his two thin brigades fairly begged to be breached by the enemy.[12]

Early's only remaining option required further spreading his paper-thin force to cover more ground. Racing to his brigade, Early faced them "by the right flank" into a right-facing column headed toward the Dunker Church, whenever possible passing behind the many limestone ledges to conceal the move. Everything Early now did was fraught with risk—his force was outnumbered, divided before a larger foe, and vulnerable to destruction if its flank-exposing movement was discovered before deploying for battle. Like his Union counterpart Alpheus Williams, Jubal Early looked desperately to the rear for reinforcements. Neither general knew it, but at about 9:15 in the morning, the South was about to win this latest race of the reinforcements.[13]

First to arrive was Colonel George T. "Tige" Anderson's Brigade from D. R. Jones's Division, which spent the morning in the Confederate center amidst gravestones on Cemetery Hill supporting the Washington Artillery. General Lee directed Anderson's Brigade left toward the sound of the firing to support Hood, but lacking a guide, they waited briefly until Hood appeared to lead them around his scattered division to the immediate north of the Dunker Church. Tige Anderson's Brigade brought some 478 men to the Confederate left, just as the main body of Lee's promised reinforcements appeared.[14]

McLaws's Division swept up from the south with 2,725 men and seven fresh guns. Crossing the Potomac overnight with the aid of torches, they'd arrived exhausted and hungry before dawn, just as the battle was just getting underway far to their left. McLaws halted his two divisions—Special Order No. 191 attached General Richard H. Anderson's Division to McLaws—just west of Sharpsburg and rode into town to find General Lee and guidance. Finding Longstreet instead, McLaws was directed to send Anderson's Division forward through Sharpsburg over the hill—into Lee's center—to await further orders. With Anderson underway, McLaws found Lee at his headquarters, dressing for the day, who sent McLaws's Division to a spot one quarter mile west of Sharpsburg—protected from the Union artillery then dismantling the town—to await further orders. There, McLaws's Division took a well-deserved and much needed rest, and the general turned his horse loose to graze before himself laying down to rest in the tall grass. The coming hours would prove McLaws and his men needed all the energy they could muster.[15]

McLaws's and Tige Anderson's move left had its genesis in General Hood's plea for support, carried to headquarters by Sandie Pendleton. Lee had resisted moving more forces to the left flank—he'd earlier sent D. H. Hill's Division—but this message apparently softened Lee's stand and adjutant Major Walter H. Taylor was dispatched to direct McLaws's Division left.[16]

Taylor was unable to find McLaws—apparently deep asleep in the tall grass, hidden from view—and passed to McLaws's adjutant-general Lee's orders sending the division left to support Jackson. In his absence, McLaws's staff ordered the division—comprised of the brigades of Barksdale, Kershaw, Semmes, and Cobb, though Lieutenant Colonel Christopher C. Sanders now commanded the latter—northeastward. Behind came the batteries of Manly, Read, Macon, McCarthy, and Carlton. As the division began moving, a staff officer found and awakened McLaws, who joined his command at the western edge of town and ordered it left onto the road leading north to the hamlet of New Industry. But after clearing the northern end of Sharpsburg McLaws abandoned the road, sending his division into the fields, directly toward the sound of battle. Pausing to unsling knapsacks, McLaws's Division was once again marching into a fight.[17]

Like Tige Anderson minutes before, General Hood provided McLaws intelligence of the situation and directed his division to where it was most needed. Arriving Southern reinforcements had little or no idea what they faced and less understanding of the rapidly unfolding situation in the West Woods or the Hagerstown Pike, as Lafayette McLaws admitted in his report writing "I was, of course, entirely ignorant of the ground and of the location of the troops." With his own division safely in the rear, John Bell Hood had remained to guide these reinforcements into place, serving as the glue holding together the uncertain, shifting Confederate line at that key moment and ensuring that every Confederate unit counted as quickly as possible. Underappreciated by historians, this role was vital to ensuring Confederate victory in the race for reinforcements.[18]

McLaws moved his troops at the double-quick toward the woods. Probably unaware that Anderson's Brigade and Early's men were already pushing back the 125th Pennsylvania's skirmishers and Patrick's Brigade, McLaws responded first to the large enemy formation across the Hagerstown Pike. McLaws couldn't know these men—Greene's Division of the XII Corps—lacked ammunition and were hardly the threat they appeared, so he pushed his first arriving unit, Cobb's Brigade, forward toward the enemy across the Pike. Using Cobb's Brigade as an anchor on the right, McLaws would throw each arriving brigade—Kershaw's, Barksdale's, and Semmes's, in turn—increasingly to the left.[19]

Appearing at the right moment, it suddenly seemed that might be the only thing going General McLaws's way. First, Lieutenant Colonel Sanders led Cobb's Brigade forward so quickly and without knowing where it was to go, that he literally marched his men out of the fight; moving far to the right, Cobb's Brigade completely missed Greene's Division and stopped only after running into D. H. Hill's troops, where Sanders posted them left of Rodes's Brigade. McLaws—unaware of the error—would soon miss these men. Worse, General Jackson appeared and ordered one of McLaws's brigades to the far left to support Stuart's hold on the true Confederate left flank. Dragging his heels, McLaws finally ordered his last brigade, of Brigadier General Paul J. Semmes, to this task. These two events stripped away one third of McLaws force, leaving only three brigades to confront the large Union force before him.

Given this, McLaws must have been heartened to learn Brigadier General John G. Walker's Division was arriving, too. Consisting of Colonel Van H. Manning's Brigade—Walker's former command—and Brigadier General Robert Ransom's Brigade, Walker brought an additional 3,627 men and six artillery pieces to the fight. The last of Lee's reinforcements, the division's unintentionally staggered arrival threw another well-timed punch at the enemy.[20]

***

The 125th's Company G skirmishers under Captain McKeage, holding the Union's forward-most position, had no idea how vulnerable they were at that moment. Hiding behind trees and hugging the ground for cover, they suddenly observed "[a] large column formed in the field in its front … advance[ing] toward it, carrying their guns at right shoulder shift." These were likely Tige Anderson's men, heading right for the Pennsylvanians's position and enduring Company G's scattered fire from the woods. First Sergeant Andrews of Anderson's 1st Georgia Regulars recalled "We marched in line of battle through a large field to a heavy timbered piece of woods that was occupied by the enemy. On reaching the woods, the enemy's sharpshooters opened on us from behind trees. Gen. Anderson gave the order 'Sharpshooters to the front,' which was quickly obeyed by the men springing out of ranks and dashing to the front." Pausing briefly while a body of McLaws's troops rushed northward across his front, Anderson instantly sent his 1st, 7th, and 9th Georgia toward the wood line. Reaching the fence line, the Georgians "tore it down and formed an obstruction by piling up the rails lengthwise so that we would lie down and shoot over them," recalled Sergeant Andrews. As bad as this was for McKeage's men, the arrival of Brigadier General Joseph B. Kershaw's Brigade—the 2nd, 3rd and 7th South Carolina—made things much worse for the Pennsylvanians.[21]

Kershaw, with only one of his three regiments yet available, apparently resisted McLaws's orders to throw forward Colonel John Kennedy's 2nd South Carolina. As incentive, McLaws claimed guns of an abandoned Confederate battery remained near the church awaiting recapture. Although McLaws may have invented this story, the 253 men of Kershaw's 2nd South Carolina instantly advanced at the double-quick past Anderson's Brigade on their right, over the fence, into the West Woods toward the left flank of the 125th Pennsylvania's skirmishers. Facing Tige Anderson's fresh brigade in front, Kershaw's 2nd South Carolina on the left, the Pennsylvanians's situation became instantly worse when Early's 49th Virginia—leading his column—swung into position and opened fire on its right. Company G now faced elements of every Confederate force then in the West Woods.[22]

McKeage's Company G "did what it could to hold in check the column, as well as the force on the right, which was endeavoring to and did finally connect with the column moving towards it from the field…" Behind them at the Dunker Church, Colonel Higgins and the rest of the 125th Pennsylvania knew instantly who had won the latest reinforcement race. Higgins recalled the skirmishers to consolidate his line; the last hope of holding this advanced position until reinforced. Ordering his reunited regiment to fire on Early's men and the South Carolinians, Higgins 125th was joined by Monroe's Battery, a combined fire that was deadly and sufficient; it halted the Rebel advance and wounded the 49th Virginia's Colonel William "Extra Billy" Smith. Having bought the Union additional time, Higgins looked anxiously to the rear for any sign of much–needed help.[23]

Sumner could still mitigate having lost the latest reinforcement race by bringing his greater manpower mass to bear and undoing the enemy's advantage in position and timing. Peering across the shattered Cornfield for the first time, Sumner beheld a scene littered with dead and wounded men and animals, plowed by deadly artillery fire. He also could see Union troops holding the field's far side, Greene's Division on the left and, well to their right, Gordon's Brigade; between them was a large gap seemingly designed for his use. Captain Samuel Sumner explained his father's dilemma and decision at that moment; "[H]e found the Twelfth Corps in a precarious position. This placed him in an awkward situation. If he halted and withdrew the Twelfth Corps, it meant virtual abandonment of the attack and consequent disarrangement of the battle plan. If the Twelfth Corps was to be supported in its advanced position, it had to be done without delay. He decided to advance, and Sedgwick's Division was formed for attack."[24]

Historians and Antietam veterans alike have criticized Sumner for attacking rashly, particularly for not awaiting the appearance of French's Division to support Sedgwick's assault, and in hindsight, such criticism seems obvious given the attack's result. At that moment, however, it was anything but obvious to Sumner that waiting—for more intelligence of the enemy's position or for French to arrive—was the right course. As Captain Sumner makes clear, the general believed waiting risked losing the XII Corps's gains and whatever momentum Hooker had secured through the lives of his I and XII Corps's casualties in taking the Cornfield. Moreover, Captain Sumner's comments suggest the general had witnessed French's arrival, sending the captain to direct French into position supporting Sedgwick. What Sumner knew of the situation in the woods and Lee's reinforcements remains unknown, but from what we know of Sumner's thinking, attacking quickly clearly appeared the right course.[25]

Sumner also chose to launch a frontal assault at the Confederate line in the West Woods, enabling both decisions by ordering Sedgwick's Division to advance in the "column of brigades"—each of the three brigades deployed in battle fronts, advancing one behind the other—in which it was already formed, without deploying skirmishers. Although the formation's single-brigade front gained maneuverability at the expense of striking mass, its real power lay in creating flexibility once engaged, easing throwing one or both reinforcing brigades into the fight where and when they were most needed. Having engaged the enemy line, Sumner and Sedgewick could quickly develop the fight—pushing the remaining two brigades to the left, to the right, or one on each flank—wherever the Rebel line appeared weakest at that moment. A highly flexible formation, it packed considerable mass and firepower into a compact front.[26]

Although the formation carried inherent risks, Sumner must have considered them manageable. Its compact nature particularly made the division vulnerable to artillery fire and exposed both flanks while advancing, but here, the Union's control of the Cornfield, and Greene's and Gordon's advanced positions on the Cornfield's western end, would mitigate any immediate Confederate infantry threat. Nearing the enemy in the West Woods revitalized this vulnerability but Sumner apparently planned to use French's Division to secure Sedgwick's left; the flank nearest the Confederate center and the direction from which enemy reinforcements would most likely appear. Checking on French's Division, Sumner found it advancing but moving "too far to the left, and not in position to connect with Sedgwick…" In response, Sumner directed his son to carry "an urgent order to French to make a vigorous attack in order to aid the advance of the leading division." General Sumner then returned to guiding Sedgwick into place, secure that French's Third Division would soon appear. As events would show, it was trust sadly misplaced.[27]

The 34th New York's Colonel James Suiter described the division's arrival in the Cornfield: "Arriving near the battlefield, we were moved by the right flank through a piece of timber in three columns … [and a]rriving at the open field, we were again ordered in line of battle…" Brigadier General Willis A. Gorman's Brigade comprised the first line; its right was held by the 1st Minnesota, with the 82nd New York, 15th Massachusetts and 34th New York to the left. Second in line was Brigadier General Napoleon J. T. Dana's Brigade; from the right, the 19th and 20th Massachusetts, 59th and 42nd New York, and 7th Michigan. Last came Brigadier General Oliver O. Howard's Brigade, consisting of the 71st, 106th, 69th, and 72nd Pennsylvania from right to left. Sumner directed the three brigades to move closely together while advancing, leaving only 50 to 75 yards between each brigade during the rapid advance, which began shortly after 9:00 in the morning.[28]

Emerging from the East Woods intensified the artillery fire Sedgwick's brigades were enduring, but it was the sight of I and XII Corps men littering the Cornfield which burned indelible scenes into their minds. The 71st Pennsylvania's Lieutenant John Rogers recalled even 20 years later that "[w]hole windrows of the rebel dead lay behind demolished rail fences, stumps, clumps of bush, or any object which offered the least protection as they made the most desperate and determined fight and were shot down in their tracks and our brave boys rushed over them in hot pursuit after the living foe. … The rebels lay everywhere," was how Lieutenant Benjamin Hibbs described it, "Many were in their last agony, and only asked us not to tread on them. Some asked for water but we had not the time, for we were advancing in line of battle." Gorman's men were first to fully experience the Cornfield's carnage and it unnerved many. Corporal Edward Walker from the 1st Minnesota's Company D remembered, "Our men and Secesh lay as they fell, many begged us for a drink of water, others telling us not to tread on them and it was difficult to march over the ground without stepping on some man. We passed a spot were Secesh had their line of battle and the dead lay in rows as they fell. I never could have believed [it] had I not seen it. Here we passed fragments of regiments that had been in the fighting in the morning, they cheered us as we passed."[29]

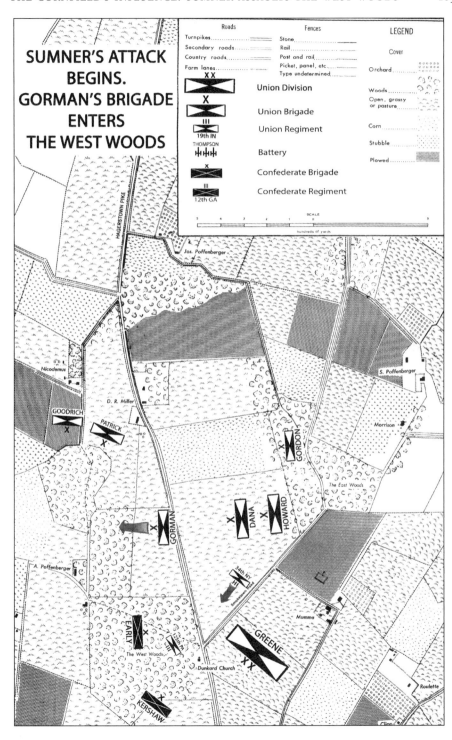

SUMNER'S ATTACK
BEGINS.
GORMAN'S BRIGADE
ENTERS
THE WEST WOODS

Roads
Turnpikes
Secondary roads
Country roads
Farm lanes

XX — Union Division
X — Union Brigade
III 19th IN — Union Regiment
THOMPSON — Battery
X — Confederate Brigade
III 12th GA — Confederate Regiment

Fences
Stone
Rail
Post and rail
Picket, panel, etc.
Type undetermined

LEGEND
Cover
Orchard
Woods
Open, grassy or pasture
Corn
Stubble
Plowed

SCALE
hundreds of yards

The Cornfield and its surrounding ground remained a chaotic mess which now complicated Sumner's ordered plans in ways he couldn't imagine. Although Gorman's Brigade continued advancing once clear of the East Woods, once in the open, General Dana suddenly halted his command. Observing a line of men lying down in his front, Dana assumed this was Gorman's Brigade and ordered his entire brigade similarly to the ground to ensure he maintained the directed interval. It remains unclear what Dana saw—perhaps the 124th Pennsylvania, straggling portions of Gordon's Brigade, or even a line of dead men—but regardless, as a result, Gorman's command continued forward alone through the Cornfield, risking repeating the disastrous experience of Duryee's Brigade. Dana had become the latest officer victimized by the Cornfield's confusion and undulating terrain.[30]

Next Howard, too, was thrown by the chaotic Cornfield. Emerging from the East Woods, Howard received Sumner's order to send a regiment right to aid what Sumner assumed were Mansfield's troops. It remains unclear who Sumner sought to support or why he decided to do so as his assault was just getting underway; regardless, Howard detached the 71st Pennsylvania. Within a few minutes, though, the 71st returned for similarly mysterious reasons and Howard halted the brigade so they could rejoin the formation. This brief halt further spread out Sumner's formation and undid his plans for a tight, united advance.[31]

Facing no opposition, Gorman's Brigade passed swiftly through the Cornfield, guiding gradually to the right—away from the Dunker Church and toward where Patrick's Brigade was posted. No record of an order or decision to move right was recorded but linking Sedgwick's right with Patrick both protected the division's vulnerable right flank and cleared space on Sedgwick's left for French's Division when it arrived. Soon Gorman's men came upon their first physical obstacle—the Hagerstown Pike fences. "We now crossed the turnpike, had to climb two fences, this was the place they were last drove from, the fences are perfectly riddled with bullets. Our men lay thick here, it was a hard place to carry," wrote the 1st Minnesota's Corporal Walker. Thanks to the I and XII Corps's sacrifice, these fences were no longer a deadly impediment.[32]

Once across the Hagerstown Pike's second fence, Gorman's men caught their first rifle fire. One round hit the 1st Minnesota's color-bearer, Sergeant Sam Bloomer, ripping apart his knee and driving him to the ground just west of the fence. So swift was Gorman's advance that no one stopped to help Bloomer or pick up his precious flag; Bloomer dragged himself to the shelter of a tree near the Dunker Church, where he tore the flag from its staff and hid it in his blouse. Without the 1st Minnesota's colors, Gorman's regiments quickly redressed their lines, returned fire, and pressed toward the West Woods.[33]

Worse than losing a flag, Gorman discovered on reaching the Pike he'd lost the regiment holding his left flank. The 34th New York had started forward with the brigade but missed the rightward shift and still guiding along the Smoketown Road found itself headed straight for the Dunker Church, alone. "For some cause to me unknown, I had become detached from my brigade..." explained the regiment's Colonel James A. Suiter, ignoring that attending to such details was precisely his job. Regardless, once over the Hagerstown Pike fences and into the West Woods, Suiter and his officers spied a line of troops they believed to be Union. After Company C's Lieutenant Wallace confirmed this, Suiter pushed the 34th forward, forming between these friendly troops and the church building. Suiter's blunder unintentionally provided the lonely 125th Pennsylvania its long-awaited reinforcements, adding 311 muskets to the 125th's fire on Early's, Kershaw's, and Anderson's Brigades. More importantly, though, the 34th New York now held the vulnerable left flank of Sumner's attack as it stretched ever deeper into the West Woods.[34]

As Sumner's forces advanced, the Cornfield and the related ground between the East and West Woods finally fulfilled the role Hooker assumed it would play when crafting his original attack plan. No longer would they be killing grounds to be fought over; instead the Cornfield and grassy field to its south would provide the strategic depth the Union attack needed to succeed. Union troops could cross it unimpeded and fall back into the Union-controlled Cornfield if the attack in the West Woods failed. For Confederates, however, this ground now posed an immediate threat which could only be eliminated by restoring it to Southern control. Determining which side exploited this ground now lay in the hands of Sumner's Union attackers and Confederates under McLaws and Early.

Building on momentum gained by moving unopposed through the Cornfield Gorman's men pushed deeper into the West Woods, sweeping away remaining Rebel skirmishers. Reaching the woods' western edge, they halted at a worm fence running its length. Ahead, the terrain sloped gently down to a low point where Alfred Poffenberger's house and farm buildings stood, then rose again gradually to another cornfield and finally to the opposite ridge on which the next woodlot started. It was likely the Confederate troops on the opposite ridgeline halted Gorman's advance, though—Pelham's Battery of six guns in the cornfield's far northern end, supported by the remaining 13th Virginia companies and Grigsby's Stonewall Brigade in the corn behind the Poffenberger home. Gorman's Brigade had just taken a large portion of the West Woods and found the main Confederate line, but they now had to hold it.[35]

The 1st Minnesota's Corporal Walker explained what happened next: "As soon as we got into the proper position both sides commenced peppering one another. Our company fired a few shots at the artillerymen, but the distance was so great we directed most of our shots at the rebel colors, they came down several times, but the men stuck to them well ... We kept firing at what we considered the best marks, every man firing at will, we could see their wounded hobbling to the rear and some that wasn't wounded, but they seemed to have plenty of reinforcements."[36]

As if on cue, Dana's Brigade appeared behind them, although their advance had come with considerable challenges. Crossing the Cornfield and Hagerstown Pike unopposed, barely after entering the woods, Dana's left-most regiment, the 7th Michigan, unexpectedly confronted the enemy. Breaking from the formation, the Michiganders executed a "left wheel" maneuver that faced them toward the enemy before opening a vigorous fire, joining the 125th Pennsylvania and 34th New York facing Barksdale's Brigade. General Dana recalled "hardly had my left regiment entered the woods when a tremendous musketry fire opened on my left and front, apparently perpendicular to my line of march and flanking the first line." Dana may have been the first senior Union officer to discover that Sedgwick's Division's position had already been turned. Probably reflecting this awareness, Dana reinforced the left by detaching his 42nd New York to post on the 7th Michigan's left, then remaining to oversee his two detached regiments while the brigade's remaining three regiments continued forward toward Gorman's position. Responsibility for overseeing Sumner's increasingly thin and weak left flank had now fallen to General Dana.[37]

Dana's main force arrived to find itself blocked by Gorman's line, leaving Dana's Brigade as little more than patient targets. Lieutenant Henry Ropes of Dana's 20th Massachusetts summed up their situation, "Our line was advanced close to the first, exposing us to an equal fire, while we could not fire at all because of our first line." This bad situation became worse when Howard's Brigade halted immediately behind Dana's line. All three of Sedgwick's brigades were now jammed together in, or nearly in, the West Woods. Lieutenant Ropes added "The third line was finally advanced close to the second; all the time we stood up and were shot down without being able to reply."[38]

The situation was worse than the lieutenant knew because Sedgwick's Division had walked into a trap of its superiors' making. Sumner had crowded Sedgwick's three brigades into a heavily wooded box 600 yards deep by 900 yards wide, bounded in front and left by nearly two enemy divisions and in the rear by two fences which would slow a retreat under fire. The only maneuvering room lay outside the box to the front and right, where the 13th Virginia supporting Pelham's Battery and some widely scattered cavalry held the true left flank of Lee's line. Pushing just one of Sedgwick's three brigades past that small force might have turned Lee's left to break and begin rolling up the Southern line. But this scenario was not to be.[39]

This was the moment the battle began slipping from General Sumner's grasp, perhaps irreversibly. Attacking quickly had given Sumner's assault momentum but success depended on skillful execution when the two lines met. Sumner needed to deftly oversee the attack, guiding Sedgwick's Division at key moments and adapting quickly to the rapidly shifting tactical situation as the fight progressed. Any mistake—misreading the Confederate position and developing the attack on the wrong flank—would be potentially disastrous. What Sumner actually did at this critical moment was far worse than making a mistake—he did nothing. Sumner made no adjustments at all as Sedgwick's three brigades continued jamming themselves into the West Woods box, letting the attack flow on of its own accord with no guidance or correction. Now a new race had begun, hinging on who would first discover and react to Sumner's tremendous error, the general himself or his Confederate opponents.

Sumner's situation unknowingly grew worse because the threat facing Gorman's three-regiment front suddenly increased when the Stonewall Brigade—now commanded by Major H. J. Williams of the 5th Virginia—appeared to support the 13th Virginia. Even worse for Sumner, Confederate artillery—Brockenbrough, Raine, and Poague from left to right—appeared on the opposite ridge to Grigsby's right, pouring fire on Sedgwick's three tightly packed brigades and on Dana's force holding the left. Sumner's men desperately needed French's reinforcements to appear, but across the West Woods, Lafayette McLaws was about to unleash a fury on Sumner's command that would undo all his efforts.[40]

***

Abandoning his planned blocking force approach, McLaws instead threw a two-pronged assault on Sumner's vulnerable flanks. The attack on Sumner's right flank fell to General Paul Semmes's Brigade. Deploying the 32nd Virginia on his right—with the 10th Georgia, 15th Virginia, and 53rd Georgia to the left—Semmes's Brigade swept northward right of the Hauser farm; the 53rd Georgia advancing through the Hauser family's apple orchard. Semmes's men caught their first Yankee fire from Gorman's 15th Massachusetts and 82nd New York and Semmes briefly had his brigade return this "galling fire," about which the 32nd Virginia's J. T Parham remembered "both of my jacket sleeves were bespotted with the blood and brains of comrades near me…" Not yet in position, Semmes's Brigade pushed on, men climbing the fence east of the Hauser house before pressing into a stubble field where they fell with each step. In response, Semmes ordered a dead run until reaching the Alfred Poffenberger farm, where the brigade reformed behind the barn and a series of low rock ledges. This cover allowed Semmes to fire on the Yankees at close range but, more importantly, he was now squarely on Gorman's right, turning the right flank of Sumner's stalled force.[41]

As Semmes passed the Hauser farm, McLaws launched the main assault on the Union left by waving a white handkerchief over his head. Barksdale's Brigade—from left, the 13th, 18th, 17th, and 21st Mississippi—pushed through Anderson's Brigade and over the West Woods's southern fence, removing them from the terrible, raking fire of Monroe's and Tompkins's Union batteries on their right. At the same time, Kershaw's remaining regiments wheeled slightly right, starting toward the right flank of the forward-deployed 2nd South Carolina.[42]

***

Through the woods, Dana's cobbled-together brigade held on for dear life. Seeing the enemy advancing through the woods, the 34th New York's Colonel Suiter had his

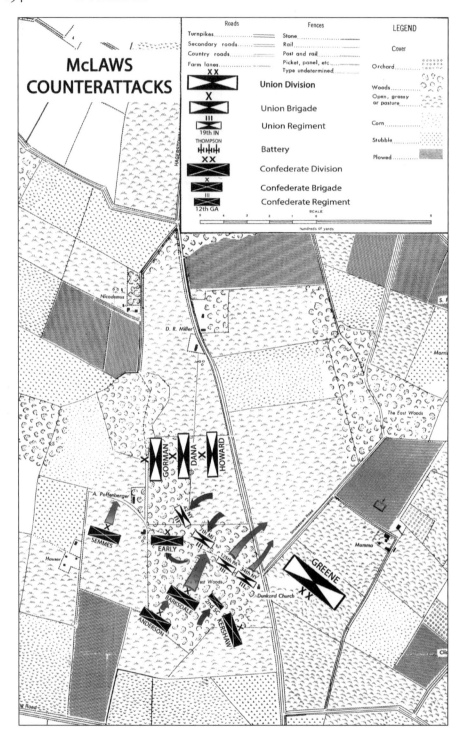

regiment "refuse the left" until they touched the church building. Once completed, the regiment's line resembled a large, flattened, inverted V, overlapping with the 125th Pennsylvania on their right. Dana's own 7th Michigan and the 42nd New York were then moving into position on the 125th's right to strengthen the line, but just as Dana was forming his line, it shattered into hundreds of running, panicked pieces.

Barksdale's Brigade had caused this by pushing onto the 125th Pennsylvania's right before Dana could get the 7th Michigan there. Here, Barksdale's Brigade quickly loosed six full volleys into the right of the skittish Pennsylvanians while Kershaw's 2nd South Carolina advanced to threaten the Pennsylvanians's left, too. Facing threats in front and on both flanks was too much for the green troops—the 125th Pennsylvania men fled. Only by relaying the flag—wounded Color Sergeant George A. Simpson passed it to Company C's Sergeant Walter Greenland before Captain Wallace sprint it away to safety—did the 125th retain its honor. A Confederate officer later observed the captain must have led a charmed life because 100 rifles fired at him during his run. The 2nd South Carolina's Robert Shand recalled that "We yelled and charged and they broke and fled, veering in our front towards our right and out into the open field beyond the church." The Pennsylvanians fled through an artillery gauntlet of Tompkins's Battery A, 1st Rhode Island—which replaced Monroe's Battery on Greene's left across the Pike—until the gunners could wait no longer. When Rebels appeared through the woods Tompkins's canister-charged guns fired, tearing apart the bodies of friend and foe alike. "[M]en were falling as thick and fast as leaves in autumn," remembered the 125th's historian.[43]

Dana's force holding the Union left was in deep trouble. The 34th New York fired a volley that briefly halted the 2nd South Carolina, but with the 125th Pennsylvania gone the New Yorkers's right was uncovered and Barksdale's fire swept it away, too. Dana's 7th Michigan held on, though, and the general rushed the 42nd New York toward its left, hoping to plug the gap before Barksdale's Confederates closed it for him. Barely had the 42nd begun moving, though, when Barksdale's Brigade—laying down behind a rock ledge—loosed a volley that tore huge gaps in the New Yorkers's formation. Recovering from this, Dana's line still faced a reinforced enemy as Kershaw's 3rd South Carolina and Tige Anderson's men opened on the 7th Michigan's still-exposed left flank.[44]

The firing in and around the Dunker Church had been intense for nearly half an hour and even General Dana received a leg wound in the maelstrom. When pain finally forced Dana rearward, he passed command of Sumner's left to the 7th Michigan's Colonel Norman Hall. Dana apparently offered Hall no guidance about what to do next—"I had received no orders whatsoever on the field," Hall recalled—creating a command vacuum at the very moment the 42nd New York and 7th Michigan disintegrated. Even the appearance of reinforcements—the 72nd Pennsylvania, from Howard's Brigade, entered the woods but fired a single volley before withdrawing—couldn't stem the tide. Barksdale took the gap created by clearing the 34th New York and 125th Pennsylvania and tore it asunder. Sumner's left flank was completely open and exposed.[45]

Sumner, meanwhile, rode to the division's right after learning of Semmes's threat there. Sumner enquired how the 15th Massachusetts was fairing, and Colonel John W. Kimball replied, a bit optimistically, "We are holding our ground and slowly gaining, but losing heavily as you can see." Barely had this conversation occurred when the sound of tremendous fire and fleeing troops appeared on the division's far left. Sumner now realized the enemy was not just on his flanks but advancing into his rear. "My God, we must get out of this!" Sumner exclaimed to Kimball as he raced away.[46]

Sumner sped left and upon reaching Howard's Philadelphia Brigade began issuing orders in such haste and to no one in particular, so that the men took it to be groundwork for a charge. Up they rose, cheering while fixing bayonets for the expected attack. Sumner sped back along the line, however, making it clear this was not to be. "Back boys, for God's sake back, you are in a bad fix!" he reputedly warned. Sumner next rode excitedly to Howard, his hat off and gesturing wildly. Though Sumner's words were lost amid the battle noise, Howard knew what was wanted and instantly faced his brigade by the rear, heading them for the Pike and safety in the securely Union-held Cornfield.[47]

The scene facing Sumner's remaining force was desperate, bordering on chaos. McLaws's men poured in volley after deadly volley, firing so intense that General Sedgwick was wounded three times, his horse killed beneath him. Like Hooker, Sedgwick succumbed to blood loss and retreated to join Woodruff's Battery, before eventually leaving the field for medical care. Gorman's fire slowed Semmes's advance which gave the men a sense of purpose and control, but not so Dana's Brigade; it remained trapped by circumstance—blocked by Gorman's line from firing, lacking orders to retreat—despite their path to safety being open by Howard's withdrawal. The 59th New York, holding Dana's left, was wavering and perhaps out of frustration or simple fear men began firing through the 15th Massachusetts in their front as enemy targets appeared, felling 15th men until Sumner stopped it with a stream of invective. One unfortunate, Sergeant Jonathan Stowe, wrote in his diary amidst the swirl of fighting "Battle Oh horrid battle. What sights I have seen. I am wounded! And am afraid shall be again as shells fly past me every few seconds carrying way limbs from the trees … Am in severe pain. How the shells fly. I do sincerely hope I shall not be wounded again."[48]

Sumner seized control of Dana's Brigade, too—the 20th Massachusetts's Colonel Lee refused to assume command—ordering it out of this private hell "by the right flank," northward toward the Nicodemus farm where Goodrich's and Patrick's men still held on. As the 19th Massachusetts moved away, the 20th faced by the rear rank and blindly fired a few rounds. Doing so may have been cathartic—the 20th had been little more than targets for half an hour—but it attracted fire from Anderson's

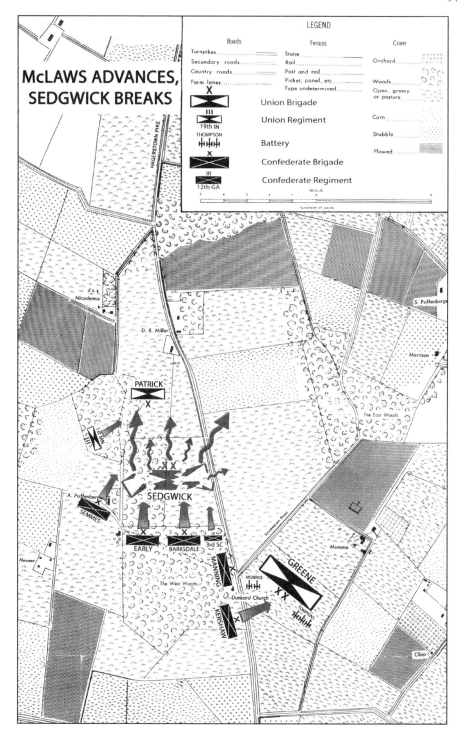

LEGEND

Roads	Fences	Cover
Turnpikes	Stone	Orchard
Secondary roads	Rail	
Country roads	Post and rail	Woods
Farm lanes	Picket, panel, etc.	Open, grassy or pasture
	Type undetermined	Corn

Union Brigade

19th IN — Union Regiment

THOMPSON — Battery

Confederate Brigade

12th GA — Confederate Regiment

Stubble

Plowed

SCALE

hundreds of yards

McLAWS ADVANCES, SEDGWICK BREAKS

Confederate brigade, now firmly in control of the northern West Woods above the Dunker Church. So terrifying was Anderson's fire that the 20th Massachusetts broke, trampling men of the 19th Massachusetts in racing through its still-ordered ranks.[49]

Although Gorman's Brigade held its ground and covered Dana's retreat, chaos infected his ranks too. As Gorman explained "The attack of the enemy on the flank was so sudden and in such overwhelming force that I have no time to lose, for my command could have been completely enveloped and probably captured, as the enemy was moving not only upon my left flank but also forcing a column toward my right, the two lines having both moved from their position before either of my three right regiments changed theirs." When a large portion of Gorman's 82nd New York fled, once again trampling men in Dana's 19th Massachusetts, Gorman ordered a rapid "fighting retreat," moving and then halting to fire, before again moving. During the chaotic move once more the hard-luck 19th Massachusetts was trampled, this time by the 1st Minnesota. After going 200 yards Gorman rushed the 1st Minnesota—still mostly intact—behind a low stone wall, followed on their left by his 82nd New York and 15th Massachusetts.[50]

Gorman re-formed his force left of Patrick's Brigade—still holding on north of the West Woods after an hour—but Sedgwick's other troops fled on in confusion and disorder. The 21st New York's Colonel William F. Rogers in Patrick's Brigade recalled "It was a complete route [sic], and they passed on out of our sight." The 35th New York's Private Louis C. Greenleaf echoed Rogers "they fell back from the woods [and] broke through our lines in spite of all that we could do to stop them." As Sedgwick's II Corps division streamed back toward the Cornfield, the North Woods, and the East Woods it signaled the final collapse of Sumner's once-promising attack.[51]

Although Sedgwick's fleeing men might have wondered where French's Division was at that moment, General Sumner probably knew and early on had made a decision ensuring it would be of no help in the West Woods. By the time Captain Sumner found General French, his division was already engaged with the enemy, though not where or how General Sumner had intended. The position French stumbled onto held three Confederate brigades under D. H. Hill—including Colquitt's, which had earlier fought in the Cornfield—deployed in a sunken farm road now serving as hasty earthworks. Joining French in this fight would be Israel Richardson's command—Sumner's third division of 3,743 fresh, battle-tested men—which completed what French was unable to, though at the cost of Richardson's and many of his men's lives. By day's end, the road they fought for had a new name—"Bloody Lane"—and had claimed roughly 5,500 American casualties.[52]

Presented with a decision to direct French to disengage and follow his original orders supporting Sedgwick or to let events decide the battle's course, Sumner once again chose the latter. Leaving French to continue the unintended fight at the Sunken Road divided Sumner's II Corp force, dissipating the mass and power of his attack. This decision stole from Sedgewick reinforcements which might have made the critical difference in the West Woods, while leaving French—and eventually Richardson—to fight a costly engagement disconnected from Sumner's wider plans for the Union right, robbing the Sunken Road fight of meaning or purpose. In doing so, Sumner unknowingly largely wasted the lives and sacrifice of those men who fought so well and so valiantly there.[53]

With the West Woods returned to Confederate control, the Cornfield and its nearby terrain once again became the key to Antietam's outcome, this time by protecting the Union right from collapse. Despite failing in the West Woods, Sumner successfully exploited the hard-won Cornfield's strategic depth and the extended range of Union artillery to protect his retreating force and hold off McLaws's advancing troops. Just as Sedgwick's line was breaking, Sumner had sent his artillery chief, Major Francis N. Clarke, racing toward the East Woods in search of idle batteries. Clarke first sent Lieutenant George A. Woodruff's Battery I of the 1st US Artillery racing across the grassy field at a gallop, heading for the Hagerstown Pike and dodging the scattered remains of Sedgwick's fleeing division. Woodruff deployed his battery near the western end of the grassy field, firing as the enemy appeared. Cothran's Battery M, 1st New York Light Artillery—which followed Woodruff forward without orders—deployed on Woodruff's right, extending and strengthening this steel line. Soon Sumner's 7th Michigan and 72nd Pennsylvania rallied behind the guns, adding their firepower. Union hopes now depended on these ten artillery pieces and their meager infantry support stemming the Confederate tide.[54]

✳✳✳

Sumner probably had no idea how close he was to again losing the precious Cornfield. Driving straight for the Cornfield's western edge came Confederate units flush with victory. Kershaw's 3rd South Carolina stepped into the open, grassy strip bordering the Hagerstown Pike, joined on the left by Barksdale's 13th and 18th Mississippi and Early's Brigade. Semmes's Brigade, too, pushed northeast through the West Woods—on Barksdale's left—heading straight for the Miller home. With unrelenting momentum borne of success, Southern victors chased Sumner's broken command.[55]

✳✳✳

The 3rd South Carolina and Barksdale's Brigade advanced northward along the West Woods's edge, with nothing at all to check them, until fire from Woodruff's and Cothran's Union artillery on their right suddenly shattered any hope of easy victory, single-handedly halting Barksdale's drive. "[T]he ... shell and canister thinned their ranks to such an extent, that when the infantry was met, their galling fire forced Barksdale to retire in great disorder," recalled the brigade's historian. The 1st Mississippi's Private Edward Burruss was less charitable, recalling "In falling back ... what almost amounted to a panic seemed to seize on the men..." It wouldn't completely save Sumner, but his artillery reserve bought critical time and stopped nearly a third of the Confederate counterattack.[56]

Semmes's Brigade moved in roughly the same direction on Barksdale's left, driving remaining Yankees from the West Woods's northern end, though unevenly. The 32nd Virginia advanced too far and suddenly found itself alone until the 10th Georgia swept forward on their left, renewing the counterattack. Driving northward again, Semmes's Brigade pushed Gorman's scattered Union troops before it like fleeing sheep.[57]

***

Amidst this calamity, remnants of Hooker's battle-worn I Corps provided the cover, protecting Gorman's retreating men. General Gibbon had pushed forward from the North Woods those few units still in fighting condition, using his own tired Iron Brigade to rally some of Sumner's troops at the North Woods. Nearer the West Woods, Patrick's Brigade held on, firing as targets appeared and quickly running through their scant remaining ammunition.[58]

Securing Patrick's right, Gorman's 1st Minnesota was soon joined by the rallying 19th Massachusetts and 82nd New York, deploying on the 1st's flanks. This cobbled-together Union line stretched from the Pike westward nearly to the woods, but a simple glance right would prove their efforts were for naught. There, Stuart's artillery and Early's 13th Virginia infantry support, sent north by Stuart to join the chase, pressed around the 82nd New York's right, holding the Union line's right flank. Patrick's Brigade too found its right turned by Semmes's left-most regiment, the 53rd Georgia, which pressed into the gap between Patrick's and Gorman's lines. Nonetheless, Union Colonel Alfred Sully—now commanding this default brigade—calmly moved his force rearward to a stronger position on a slight rise nearer the North Woods. Patrick's remaining men, too, fell back in generally good order, but out of ammunition and with thinned ranks, they kept going until within the safety of the North Woods.[59]

Once again, Union artillery from the Cornfield area opened to save the day; this time halting Semmes's counterattack. This fire probably came from Stewart's section of Campbell's Battery, which earlier faced Hood's Division along the Hagerstown Pike. Gibbon had posted it on the edge of Miller's orchard and left of Reynolds's Battery, along the ridge north of the Cornfield. Stewart quickly discovered Reynolds's position being pounded by Rebel batteries across the road, which were obscured by thick smoke and impossible to target with counter fire. When enemy infantry appeared in the road, though, Stewart had his target. "I ordered my guns to be loaded," he recorded, "The enemy commenced to fall back on the same road, I waited until I saw four stands of the enemy's colors directly in front of my section,

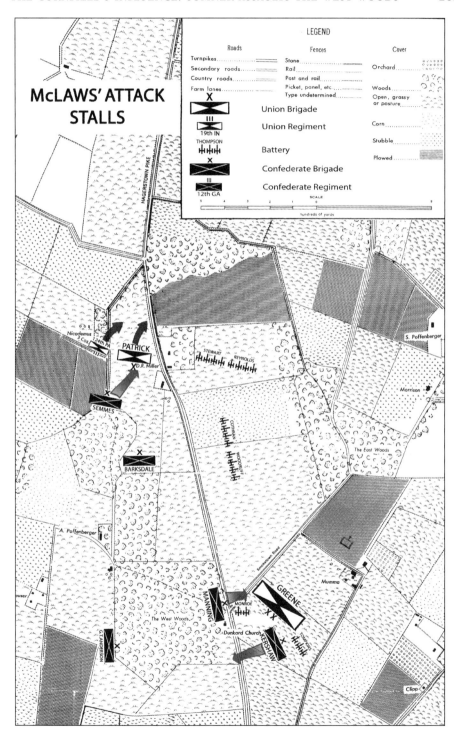

McLAWS' ATTACK
STALLS

LEGEND

Roads
Turnpikes
Secondary roads
Country roads
Farm lanes

Fences
Stone
Rail
Post and rail
Picket, panel, etc.
Type undetermined

Cover
Orchard
Woods
Open, grassy
or pasture
Corn
Stubble
Plowed

Union Brigade

Union Regiment
19th IN
THOMPSON

Battery

Confederate Brigade

Confederate Regiment
12th GA

SCALE
hundreds of yards

and then commenced firing with canister, which scattered the enemy in every direction." As Semmes's men raced away in disorder, Jackson's counterattack came to a sputtering end.[60]

Nonetheless, in a spectacular bit of bad timing, Sumner's infantry reinforcements appeared as Confederate forces retook the West Woods. Summoned at the height of Sedgwick's attack—reflecting his knowledge that French's Division wasn't coming—Sumner had dispatched a staff officer rearward to search for any available troops. The officer found General Williams and breathlessly reported "General Sumner directs you to send to the front all of your command immediately available," before racing away. Williams turned to General Gordon who sent his only available units, the 13th New Jersey and 2nd Massachusetts. Stepping from the East Woods, these regiments traced Sedgwick's path through the Cornfield and toward the Pike. They couldn't know that the success they were to reinforce had simply vanished.

Although the 2nd Massachusetts had seen combat, the 13th New Jersey men were fresh fish about to experience their baptism by fire. "We were ordered forward!" recalled Joseph Crowell, "[o]ver eight hundred strong, in battle front, we proceeded. The officers ordered us to 'dress to the right,' but it was a straggling line. The z-z-z-ip of the bullets could be heard whistling past us. And a moment later the first man of Company K fell. … The feeling of seeing one of our own men fall out this way was indescribable. And the pitiless, relentless order was 'Forward! The cannon balls and shells struck around us, tearing up the earth, and sometimes ricocheting or bouncing along the ground a great distance, like a flat stone skims across the water of a pond. Wounded men lay everywhere. Some were writhing and kicking. Others lay still. Some of the human forms were already quiet in death. The number of dead horses was enormous. They seemed to lie everywhere. But it was still 'Forward!' We climbed over a rail fence. It was the road, [w]e did not take this road, however, for the order was still 'Forward!' We climbed over the fence on the other side of the road. We marched some fifteen or twenty feet into what was then a meadow. We could not see any of the enemy, although their bullets were whistling past our heads. The rebels seemed to be in a woods on the other side of the meadow." Having crossed both the Hagerstown Pike fences, the two regiments stood before the West Woods probably facing Early's Brigade, itself reforming after falling back from McLaws's just-failed counterattack. The retreating Confederates might have given Gordon's men some hope of success.[61]

"Suddenly something occurred that seemed supernatural," continued Crowell. "A vast number of the enemy appeared to rise straight out of the solid earth, and they poured into us a deadly volley of leaden hail." Crowell and the 13th had discovered one of Antietam's many natural rock ledges, behind which Early's men took refuge. "They fired into us a murderous volley. Surprised, demoralized, we wavered and fell back and made for the first fence, on the nearest side of the road! …[T]he green and inexperienced Thirteenth Regiment broke and with one accord made for the fence." On their left, the 2nd Massachusetts retired too, having realized they were on a deadly fool's errand. Fortunately for Gordon's Federals, Early's men apparently had fired a brigade volley, requiring all to reload. "A cessation, for a few moments, not entirely, but partially, of the firing, enabled us to collect our shattered senses as we gazed over the meadow we had just left." The 13th left nine dead and 60 wounded—including Crowell's Company K commander, Captain Irish—all casualties of a single Rebel volley. For better or worse, the 13th New Jersey had become Civil War combat veterans.[62]

Retreating through the Cornfield, Crowell recorded that Union artillery there again made the difference, now saving Gordon's fleeing troops. "[T]he enemy made his appearance in full force on the other side of the turnpike. Then our artillery opened upon them in good shape. The enemy was given a hot dose of shot and shell and shrapnel and canister … and the enemy was promptly sent back to his shelter at the edge of the woods."[63]

Sumner's Cornfield-centered artillery line had grown considerably during the advance of Gordon's regiments, to 33 guns of seven batteries and nearly all possessed full ammunition stocks. On the left, Tompkins's Battery held Greene's left flank, while Woodruff's guns held his right, both facing the West Woods. Next on the right was Cothran's Battery, commanding the West Woods's northern end, while Knap's Battery E, Pennsylvania Light Artillery, and Bruen's 10th (Excelsior) Battery of New York Light Artillery both held the Cornfield before the East Woods. Securing the line's right was Stewart's section, backed up by Reynolds's Battery. So formidable was this artillery line that it dissuaded McLaws from trying to retake the Cornfield. "The artillery of the enemy was so far superior to our own in weight of metal, character of guns and numbers, and in quality of ammunition, that there was but very little to be gained by opposing ours to it, and I therefore did not renew the attempt after the first experiment," he wrote. Federal artillery centered on the Cornfield was now the backbone of the Union right; a secure position on which the broken infantry could rally.[64]

**

Still, Southern prospects for retaking the Cornfield were probably undone by a simple lack of coordination. Although McLaws's swift advance into battle skillfully turned an uncoordinated rush of reinforcements into a coordinated counterattack that halted and turned back Sumner's Union assault, it quickly collapsed into disorder. First Barksdale's and Semmes's advances stalled after an uncoordinated rush exposed their flanks to Union artillery fire. On the right, Anderson's and Kershaw's commands each advanced in isolation against Greene's terrain-entrenched infantry and artillery. In all likelihood, however, neither McLaws nor Jackson probably intended to push the counterattack beyond retaking the West Woods because both operated here under Lee's "tactical defense" approach, at least initially. Regardless why it was so, the failure to more fully exploit the West Woods victory was a lost opportunity for the South.[65]

***

It was approaching 10:30 in the morning and General McClellan remained no closer to completing his battle plan's first phase than he'd been four hours earlier. Both the Union I and the XII Corps were spent, while Sumner's II Corps was rapidly heading down the same path. Abandoning the offensive McClellan's orders directed, Sumner was instead shoring up the Union right against a Confederate counterattack, leaving McClellan's plan stalled. McClellan, however, was blissfully unaware of this and staff officer Lieutenant Colonel David Strother recalled "McClellan was in high spirits. "It is the most beautiful field I ever saw," he exclaimed, "and the grandest battle! If we whip them today it will wipe out Bull Run forever."[66]

McClellan's mistaken impression of success probably derived from the limited, inaccurate intelligence he possessed then. Apparently lacking updates from Hooker or Sumner at the front, McClellan's understanding was limited to what he and his staff could observe from their Pry House forward headquarters, which suggested all was well. Staff officer Lieutenant James H. Wilson recalled "[F]rom McClellan's headquarters it was a thrilling sight. With flags flying and the long unfaltering lines rising and falling as they crossed the rolling fields, it looked as though nothing could stop them … [although t]he interval between echelons was too great and their flanks were too much exposed." Strother remembered "The fire of Sumner was tremendous, and after some time of suspense the debris of the Rebel column was seen fleeing disorganized back across the open ground, followed by a storm of shells and balls. A brigade of ours followed them cheering, but stopped in a sheltered hollow short of the wood from whence they kept up a skirmishing fire. The Irish brigade made a gallant rush on the center and forced the enemy back behind his batteries. Graham's Battery then advanced most gallantly under a tremendous fire of at least forty guns and took position at short range, whence he opened on the enemy with effect. This position he held for some time, driving the enemy infantry still farther back." Wilson's account of the Irish Brigade's advance—marked by its highly visible green regimental flags—accurately describes French's and Richardson's series of attacks and perhaps the presence of Greene's Division; it does not, however, reflect Sedgwick's more compact formation which, in any case, was obscured from McClellan's view by terrain.[67]

Several diverse sources reinforce this. Captain George Noyes from Doubleday's staff briefly visiting the Pry house early that morning recalled "I could not distinguish a single battery, nor discern the movements of a single brigade, nor see a single battalion of the men in gray. Smoke-clouds leaped in sudden fury from ridges crowned with cannon, or lay thin and dim upon the valleys, or rose lazily up over the trees; all else was concealed…" Edwin Forbes's 1862 sketch of the battlefield visibly reinforces Noyes's description of a limited view, depicting nothing beyond the ridge on which rests today's NPS visitors center. Forbes depicts all this limited view allowed of fighting on the Union right—smoke rising over the trees but nothing more. That McClellan's Pry House headquarters is depicted in Forbes's drawing indicates he sketched from a higher elevation, reinforcing that McClellan couldn't have directly observed any of Hooker's, Mansfield's, or Sumner's actions in the Cornfield, East Woods, or West Woods. Modern US Geologic Survey and the US Department of Agriculture's Forest Service topographic mapping and imaging software provides a modern perspective reinforcing the limited view of the Cornfield area from the Pry House. What McClellan could see—described by Wilson and Strouther—however, suggested all was going according to plan and the general may have assumed French's and Richardson's Sunken Road fighting reflected the most optimistic option given Hooker in his 8:30 orders, sending Sumner's corps toward Sharpsburg. Remaining isolated at headquarters had created an inaccurate impression that McClellan's battle was progressing as desired.[68]

Regardless what McClellan believed, by 10:30 both armies had suffered considerable casualties with rather little to show for it. Since dawn, Union forces had gained only modest ground against a determined Confederate defense of the Sharpsburg ridge and both lines remained largely where they had been the previous night. Only the Cornfield and its surrounding ground between the East and West Woods had changed hands and the strength of Union control there grew with each passing hour, and as the unfolding battle soon proved, this single gain was to became increasingly significant to Antietam's outcome.[69]

CHAPTER 12

The Cornfield's Influence: Greene's Division Takes the Ridge

McClellan's misplaced confidence in his plan's success was brought to earth upon receiving his first accurate intelligence from the front, sometime late that morning. This may have come after 8:30 from McClellan's aide Major Herbert von Hammerstein, who wrote "General ~~Sumner~~ Hooker is wounded in the foot. General Sumner is coming up. The enemy is driven on our left and retiring, they open briskly on the right. General Mansfield is killed." Probably McClellan's first hint of Hooker and Mansfield's fates, it also was the first indication of the XII Corps's success. A second message, from aide William S. Albert, reiterated Hammerstein's information but with a more ominous tone. "Hooker wounded and left the field. Sumner is OK. Things look blue." Although McClellan might already have received intelligence from the forward signal post at Hooker's headquarters, wig-wagged to the Pry House signal station, these messages nonetheless showed events were not progressing as McClellan had earlier believed or hoped. Albert's message probably was McClellan's first indication that the headstrong, impetuous Sumner—whom McClellan kept from independent command in this battle—was now in charge of the swirling situation on the Union right. Perhaps reflecting this concern and these two updates, at 9:10 McClellan had Colonel Ruggles send Sumner a message cautioning "General McClellan desires you to be very careful how you advance, as he fears our right is suffering." As the message was created, however, Sumner's troops were already engaged in the West Woods.[1]

Whatever McClellan knew or perceived about the battle's course then, he probably had no idea that hope for completing his critical first phase now lay with Greene's single division. It had been the swinging door which, working in concert with Williams's Division, brought the XII Corps to the Confederate line's doorstep in the West Woods, but no further. Rather than enemy resistance, it was want of ammunition—spent clearing the East Woods and advancing to this point—which halted Greene's advance. Greene used this break to secure his division's position—his left anchored on Mumma's cornfield, his right on the Smoketown Road—and nearly all those remaining of his original 2,404-man force concealed behind the military crest of an otherwise unremarkable rise in the Mumma farm's rolling ground.

Nonetheless, Greene's Division could only watch as Sumner's attacking division drove deep into the West Woods on its right.

Once again, possession of the Cornfield and its nearby ground was key to enabling Union operations, allowing Greene's Division to hold an advanced position barely 200 yards from the enemy's main line despite lacking ammunition. The appearance of the ammunition wagon, however, meant Greene's Division would soon rejoin the battle and men eagerly refilled their cartridges boxes for what lay ahead.

Greene's Division had been enjoying the support of two Union batteries during its forced respite. Monroe's Battery D, 1st Rhode Island Artillery, had been ordered by Hooker during the XII Corps's advance to "take a position as near the wood as the ground would permit;" the battery deployed on the high ground across the road from the Dunker Church and opened immediately on the Confederates in the West Woods. Soon Tompkins's Battery A, 1st Rhode Island Light Artillery, appeared; Greene may have personally led it into position on his right, in advance of his infantry line. Tompkins's appearance permitted Monroe's weary battery to retire, but together they protected Greene's vulnerable men and one of Thompkins's artillerists reportedly promised Greene's men as he rode past "[w]e will stand by you while there is shot in the locker."[2]

***

Facing Greene across the Hagerstown Pike was Kershaw's Brigade, the right-most portion of McLaws's counterattacking force. General Kershaw faced considerable challenges from the outset; chiefly, his regiments' delayed arrivals forced launching his portion of the counterattack piecemeal if he was to match McLaws's pace. Moreover, Kershaw's opponent—Greene's Division—was nearly due east across the Hagerstown Pike and disconnected from Sedgwick's Yankees well to the north, requiring him to advance under fire over open ground before engaging the enemy. These realities delayed and diminished the striking power of Kershaw's effort, which also would stand largely on its own, apart from the wider Confederate counterattack.

Kershaw's force nonetheless quickly advanced, making solid gains thanks to the 2nd South Carolina. Spearheading Kershaw's advance, the 2nd pushed the 34th New York from the West Woods's southern end before halting to await the rest of the brigade. This position just north of the Dunker Church enabled the 2nd to pour a destructive flanking fire into Sedgwick's retreating troops and serve as an anchor for Kershaw's portion of the counterattack—until Union artillery appeared in its front.[3]

Union guns across the pike—Monroe's Battery—poured deadly fire into Kershaw's men forming on the high ground by the church. Kershaw had his men return volley after volley into the Union line across the road, but the stubborn Yankees refused to move away. Answering with his own artillery—Read's Battery, posted right and behind the West Woods's edge—resulted in little more than drawing additional Union shelling, costing the South 20 men, horses, and a gun abandoned a few minutes later. Perhaps thinking these Federals couldn't take much more of this close quarter fighting either, Kershaw pushed forward his infantry.[4]

Colonel David Aiken's 7th and the 8th South Carolina advanced swiftly across the Pike's two fences and up the slight rise, heading toward the crest behind which the enemy waited. When 30 yards from Greene's line, though, a fresh Union battery—Tompkins's—appeared, firing into their ranks from point-blank range. This fire stalled the South Carolinians, who sought shelter in a swale in front of their objective. Only then did officers realize their commands had drifted apart during the advance, creating a considerable gap between the 7th and 8th South Carolina that needed to be closed somehow. Before any of this could be sorted out, the 3rd South Carolina swept forward on the left, following Kershaw's orders to "pass over Colonel Aiken's regiment, and try to carry the works behind which the enemy…" stood, heading left of Tompkins's Battery and probably seeking the gap between Tompkins's and Monroe's positions. If this was their objective, they never made it. Colonel Nance's 3rd South Carolina reached only as far as Kershaw's other regiments before ordering his men "to lie down under cover of the hill in front, while I kept a strict watch for any demonstration of our forces in his front." Kershaw's stalled line was being ripped apart by Union artillery fire from only yards away—this situation could not remain so for long. "No sooner did we gain the top of the hill than they opened a most murderous fire of grape and shells from batteries on our right, front, and left," recorded one of Kershaw's 7th South Carolinians, "[o]f all the cannonading I have ever experienced, this was the most destructive. It seemed almost whole lines would melt away at once…" Finally, the tactical logjam broke when the 8th South Carolina pulled back, prompting Nance to explain that the line "that just before advanced in such admirable style" began moving back, leaving no option but to retire, too. As Kershaw's Brigade retreated, Greene's infantry and the two Union batteries remained unmoved.[5]

Kershaw's reinforcements, Manning's Brigade, were nonetheless already in motion. Wounded Colonel Manning had moments before passed command to the 46th North Carolina's Colonel E. D. Hall and despite missing the 3rd Arkansas and 27th North Carolina—Walker detached them to close a gap between the West Woods and Longstreet's Sunken Road troops—the 48th North Carolina, 30th Virginia, and the 46th North Carolina pushed across the Hagerstown Pike just north of the Dunker Church. Hall's command headed left of where Kershaw's Brigade had been. Had Kershaw held for a few minutes longer the two brigades might have acted in unison—Kershaw holding the enemy in place, while Manning turned Greene's right—but with Kershaw's infantry gone, Union artillery focused its considerable power on Manning's advancing line alone.[6]

**

Manning's Brigade advanced swiftly, in good order, striking left of the Union artillery while Greene's infantry responded by advancing to the very axles of Monroe's and Thompkins's guns. While the cannon spewed canister rounds, Greene's men poured nearly constant rifle fire into Manning's advancing men. Still, on came the Southerners, suggesting to the 111th Pennsylvania's John Boyle that "[it] looked for a few minutes as if it would be a hand-to-hand struggle," and then, suddenly, as Boyle remembered the charging line simply "disappeared." In seconds, Manning's line was gone and what remained was racing for the rear in disorder.[7]

With his front suddenly clear, Greene ordered his division into the void, across the Hagerstown Pike and into the West Woods itself. Sweeping around the Dunker Church about 10:30, Greene's Division once more established Union hold on the ridge and—for the third time that morning—was poised to secure McClellan's vital first phase goal. Now it was General Greene's turn to face the daunting challenge of holding it.[8]

Greene quickly deployed his division to protect this unexpected gain. Forming an arc facing front and left, regiments exploited the slight terrain swells to improve their position. Two companies of the 102nd New York and 3rd Maryland held the division's left flank, their left on the Hagerstown Pike itself. On the 3rd's right and similarly facing south toward Sharpsburg was the 111th Pennsylvania. To their right, Greene's line turned abruptly right, a position held by the 28th Pennsylvania. Two companies faced south alongside the 111th, while the remaining companies faced southwestward. On the Pennsylvanians's right stood the small 5th and 7th Ohio regiments, holding the rest of the slope. Anchoring the line from behind was Tompkins's Battery, with the remaining 102nd New York as its infantry support.[9]

***

If securing this spot challenged Greene, General Kershaw faced a very different struggle. His now-reforming brigade's disordered flight had opened a considerable gap in the center of this part of Lee's line and, lacking reinforcements, there was little Kershaw could do about it. The depth of Kershaw's failure is best expressed by his report, which opens with a series of excuses "[o]wing to the exigencies of the service, my command were without their usual supply of subsistence from Monday morning, September 13 until the night of the 17th. They were also under arms or marching nearly the whole of the nights of Monday and Tuesday, arriving at Sharpsburg at daylight on Wednesday morning, September 17. As a consequence, many had become exhausted and fallen out on the wayside, and all were worn and jaded." After describing his brigade's movements and his own role in taking the West Woods, Kershaw turns to the uncomfortable subject of his defense of the Dunker Church position. "About this time, the enemy was heavily re-enforced and our line fell back to the woods, which was never afterward taken from us." Kershaw's heavily sugar-coated explanation fails to note that his new position on the Reel farm—well behind the main Confederate line—gave the Union control of ground in the center of this part of Lee's line. Kershaw may have done his best, but his failure offered only potential disaster for the Confederacy.[10]

***

As Greene prepared for whatever the Rebs might do next, he certainly assessed the ground and enemy facing his command. To the left, Southern units were reforming on the edge of a cornfield at the base of a long slope that gradually dropped toward town. Whatever faced Greene's right was concealed by the thick West Woods and should the enemy strike there, Greene lacked ready reinforcements. In response, Greene apparently sent a staff officer to the rear to appeal for support.[11]

Minutes later, Maryland's Purnell Legion came to Greene's aid, posting in the rear and center of Greene's angled formation to act as a reserve. Shortly, the 13th New Jersey also appeared, allowing Greene to retire the small, worn 5th and 7th Ohio from his front line, sending them back to where the division had begun its attack to serve as additional reinforcements if needed. Replacing the battered Ohioans in holding Greene's right, the larger, fresher 13th New Jersey was better suited for this job, but it couldn't address all the vulnerabilities on Greene's right.[12]

General Greene, however, was blissfully unaware just how vulnerable his right flank remained because he apparently believed Sedgwick's Division was supporting him there. Greene's belief derived from having seen it advance beyond view into the West Woods, as well as somehow completely missing Sedgwick's repulse. Confident that Sedgwick secured his right, Greene had ordered his division forward against Kershaw's fleeing brigade, apparently assuming that doing so lengthened and straightened the overall Federal line and supported Sedgwick's and Sumner's advanced position.

On Greene's right, however, the 13th New Jersey's Colonel Ezra Carman knew the truth and sent Greene—then attending to his left flank—a message warning of the danger. Within minutes, Carman's adjutant, Major Charles A. Hopkins, returned with Greene's verbal reply "Tell your colonel not to be uneasy about his flank. The whole of Sedgwick's Division is in the woods on his right." Carman later understood Greene's perspective, writing in his massive Antietam study "Greene had good reason for his belief; he had repulsed two brigades of McLaws's right. He had seen Barksdale's Brigade, the 3rd South Carolina, and a stream of stragglers going through the woods to seek shelter beyond them. There was a cessation of infantry fire on the right, and he concluded that the whole of the Confederate line had been repulsed." That understanding was years in the future, though; then convinced the Rebels were in the woods just yards from his position, Carman somehow had to correct General Greene's mistaken view.[13]

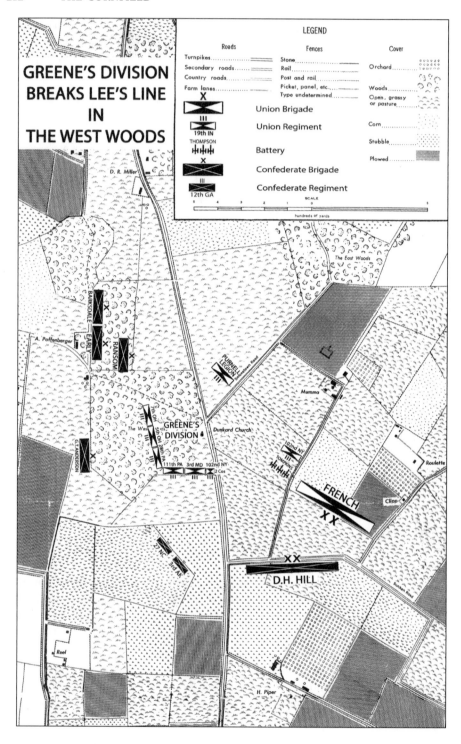

GREENE'S DIVISION
BREAKS LEE'S LINE
IN
THE WEST WOODS

LEGEND

Roads	Fences	Cover
Turnpikes	Stone	Orchard
Secondary roads	Rail	
Country roads	Post and rail	
Farm lanes	Picket, panel, etc.	Woods
	Type undetermined	Open, grassy or pasture

Union Brigade

19th IN — Union Regiment

THOMPSON — Battery

Confederate Brigade

12th GA — Confederate Regiment

Corn

Stubble

Plowed

SCALE
5 4 3 2 1 0   5
hundreds of yards

D. R. Miller

The East Woods

BARKSDALE

A. Poffenberger

EARL

RANSOM

PURNEL LEGION

Mumma

The West Woods

GREENE'S DIVISION

Dunkard Church

102nd NY

Roulette

ANDERSON

111th PA   3rd MD   102nd NY
2 Cos

FRENCH

Clipp

2? NC 3rd AK

D.H. HILL

Sunken Road

Reel

H. Piper

Seeing sunlight glinting off musket barrels of Rebels shifting right toward his flank and rear convinced Carman to again try persuading Greene of the truth. What Carman probably saw were Tige Anderson's men, now joined by the 46th North Carolina. Major Hopkins returned to Greene on the left, this time adding the 13th New Jersey's colonel was absolutely sure the position Greene assumed Sedgwick occupied was in fact held by Rebels. Minutes later Major Hopkins returned, escorted by General Greene himself. Carman recalled "He made a hurried examination of the position, insisted that Sedgwick was on the right, told [me] that [I] was surely mistaken in the idea that the enemy were in the woods on the right, and gave stringent orders that the men should under no circumstance be permitted to fire to the right." Reiterating that the greatest threat was to the left, Greene ordered Carman to direct his regiment's fire at the left oblique—angling slightly left—and returned to his opposite flank. Carman had once again failed.[14]

Retuning left, Greene met a staff officer bearing guidance from General Williams at XII Corps headquarters. Almost offhandedly Greene commented to Williams's aide that officers on his right were under the "delusion that Sedgwick had been driven from the woods." Startled, the aide replied, "Why, yes, general. Did you not know it?" As Greene related to Colonel Carman several days later, his "response was more picturesquely sulphurous than polite." Greene now realized how perilous his position really was. Both flanks were exposed and he was well in advance of the main Union line—his position by the Dunker Church didn't support the overall Union position on the ridge, it was only an exposed, solitary toehold. Greene instantly knew that without reinforcements—all that could be spared—his men couldn't hold on for long against even a modest attack. Greene apparently believed only he was able to obtain the needed reinforcements in time; an aide's plea or written appeal could easily fall on Williams's deaf ears at headquarters, wasting precious time. With that, General Greene spurred his horse and raced for the rear.[15]

Leaving his command in the midst of battle was a risk but a calculated one. After all, his division had been on the ridge in the center of Lee's line for over an hour now without being pushed back. Greene had good reason to be unhappy as he rode away but at least he now knew his command's true situation. The same could hardly be said for General McClellan.

Aware of Hooker's wounding, Mansfield's death, and having received Albert's pessimistic readout, such setbacks probably held less influence than McClellan's personal observation of what appeared to be progress by French's, Richardson's, and Greene's Divisions. By judging these attacks by their appearance alone, McClellan might well have believed the sequencing of his battle couldn't be unfolding any better and with this mistaken belief, George McClellan moved his unshakable battle plan forward.[16]

The battle's second phase was launched by McClellan's 8:00 order to Burnside, which reached IX Corps's commander Jacob Cox at roughly 9:00. Shortly after that, Cox ordered the 11th Connecticut to cross and hold the Lower Bridge, while Brigadier

General Isaac Rodman's force probed left in search of Snavely's Ford to turn the Rebel position at the bridge. Just as with the Cornfield action, McClellan's presence at his headquarters afforded no view of the Lower Bridge area and he remained blissfully unaware for nearly two hours of that assault's progress. By 10:00, however, it was increasingly clear that events on the Union left were not going according to plan, so McClellan directed the first of a series of efforts to prod Burnside into action. "After some time had elapsed, not hearing from him, I dispatched an aide to ascertain what had been done," McClellan recorded. When the aide reported that "but little progress had been made," McClellan once more dispatched the aide with orders for Burnside to attack and take the bridge "at all hazards." The aide returning again with the same dispiriting news that the Lower Bridge remained in Rebel hands, McClellan sent his Inspector-General Colonel Delos B. Sacket to reiterate the orders and threaten Burnside's removal if the bridge wasn't taken immediately; moreover, Sackett would remain until the task was complete. Not until 1:00 that afternoon did Burnside's IX Corps secure the Lower Bridge for use in the more important Union attack on Lee's right flank position along the Harpers Ferry Road south of town. Union ineptness and Confederate skill in exploiting terrain as a "force multiplier" had allowed a mere 400 men—Toombs's Brigade's 2nd, 20th and 50th Georgia regiments—to further throw McClellan's battle plan into disarray. And just as in the Cornfield, McClellan's plan was again stalled by failing to take an intermediate objective, in this case the bridge.[17]

With the second phase presumably underway on the Union left, McClellan turned to preparing the attack in the center by advancing Union cavalry across the Antietam. As General Pleasonton reported, "On the morning of the 17th instant, after the commencement of the action on the right, I was directed by Major-General McClellan, verbally, to advance with my division of cavalry and horse batteries of artillery on the turnpike toward Sharpsburg, to some suitable position beyond the bridge over the Antietam Creek, and support the left of Sumner's line of battle with my force."[18]

***

Pleasonton's six cavalry regiments and four batteries of horse artillery crossed the Middle Bridge and halted while 4th Pennsylvania Cavalry skirmishers and a section of John Tidball's Battery probed ahead until encountering resistance. Roughly 100 men from George Anderson's Brigade, commanded by the 1st Georgia Regulars's Captain Hansford D. D. Twiggs, faced the Pennsylvanians. Twigg's command was here to watch for just such a Union advance across the Middle Bridge and he'd posted 20 of his best shots in an advanced position behind a low stone wall. Skirmishing erupted between the two lines, reinforcing the Union hold across the bridge and testing the thin line of Confederate defenders.[19]

***

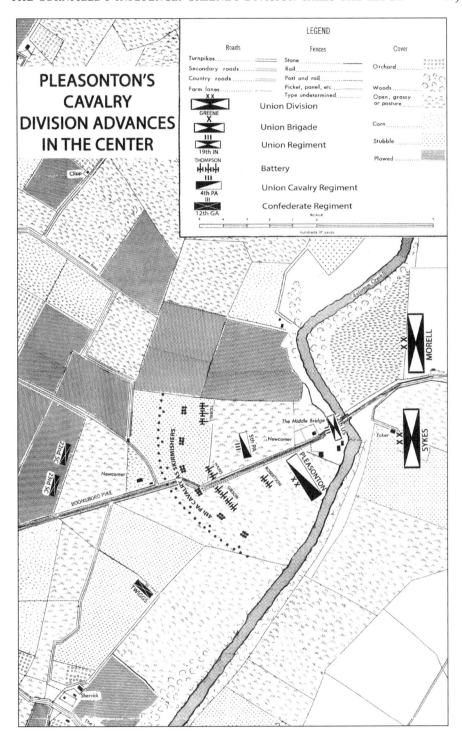

At 11:45, McClellan composed a dispatch to Pleasonton advising "Do not expose your batteries without necessity unless they are inflicting on the enemy a loss commensurate with what we suffer. How goes it with you[?]," adding in a postscript "Can you do any good by a cavalry charge?" Despite that by 1862 massed cavalry charges belonged in Napoleon's day, McClellan apparently considered using the shock and speed of his mounted arm to break a hole in Lee's center, which the V Corps and its US Regulars could plunge through and widen. Suggesting such an attack was McClellan's objective, shortly thereafter Pleasonton's cavalry was reinforced by the 2nd/10th US Infantry and, at 1:00 that afternoon, General Sykes advanced the 12th US Infantry's Second Battalion. By 1:30 or so, the stage appeared set to launch McClellan's third battle phase, the main attack on Lee's weakened center. This attack would never occur, however, because of two midday events that once again centered on the Cornfield.[20]

The first event was intelligence arriving at Headquarters finally revealing to McClellan the true situation in and around the Cornfield. At 11:00, Sumner composed his first direct communication to McClellan since taking the field: "Re-enforcements are badly wanted," it read, "Our troops are giving way. I am hunting for French's and Slocum's Divisions. If you know where they are, send them immediately." Troops giving way? Reinforcements badly wanted? This is not how the situation had appeared when viewed from headquarters. Now, however, McClellan knew right from the source that things on the right were not just "blue," but perhaps turning against him. The dispatch's last line was perhaps the most sobering to McClellan because although Sumner might be forgiven for not knowing the location of Solcum's Division—the first VI Corps reinforcements, then en route to the front—having lost track of French's Division suggested Sumner was losing control of the situation on the Union's right. At about the same time this message arrived, McClellan's staff officer Major Nelson Henry Davis—carrying orders to Sumner, he was to "ascertain the condition of affairs under his [Sumner's] command"—returned from the Union right. Davis reported Sumner appeared badly shaken and exclaimed "Sir, my troops have suffered severely, they have been repulsed—the new troops broke, sir, and straggled to the rear—Hooker's troops are scattered badly and demoralized—but sir, I have rallied these troops in the woods and behind the fences and got them in line—Sir, tell the general I will _try_ and hold my position—tell him sir, I _will_ hold it, I _will_ hold it sir." All this new intelligence fairly screamed a wake-up call at McClellan, that events on the Union right—his vital first battle phase—were turning against him.[21]

This intelligence probably sparked the second event, which would end in the Cornfield early in the afternoon, when around noon McClellan finally left his headquarters to survey the condition of his troops and battle. Cheers rose up from the ranks, allowing men to track McClellan's progress by the sound, and his presence inspired many who needed the boost. John Smith of the 118th Pennsylvania recalled that "[r]egardless of the flying, bursting missiles, there he sat astride his splendid charger, glass in hand, calmly reviewing the mighty hosts."[22]

At 11:30, Union success once again weighed in the balance as General Greene rode away in search of help. Before departing, Greene placed Lieutenant Colonel Tyndale in temporary command of the division and brought forward the only remaining reinforcements at hand. First, Owen's 1st Rhode Island Artillery, Battery G, replaced Thompkins's Battery, which had run low on ammunition. Deploying on nearly the same spot, Owen's men provided Greene's Division counterbattery fire targeting Rebel guns—probably Read's Battery—lining the ridge that ran from the Reel cornfield toward town, which had been troubling Greene's men for some time.[23]

Next to arrive was Lieutenant James D. McGill's two-gun section from Knap's Battery E, Pennsylvania Light Artillery, led forward by the general's son and aide Lieutenant Charles T. Greene. Racing up the Smoketown Road, it deployed on open, high ground overlooking Greene's advanced position. The section instantly began raining shells onto Rebel infantry, which had for some time been firing into Greene's flank from a cornfield across the Hagerstown Pike.[24]

***

Beyond the Dunker Church and West Woods, Confederate commanders, too, scrambled to prepare. Kershaw's and Barksdale's broken brigades reformed beyond the Reel cornfield's western edge, shielded by Manning's Brigade's 27th North Carolina and 3rd Arkansas deployed along the cornfield's opposite side nearer the Yankees. Deploying so along the cornfield's edge—which angled southeast toward the Hagerstown Pike—perfectly positioned the two regiments to fire into Greene's exposed left flank. Nonetheless, the Carolinians and Arkansans were nearly alone here; Kershaw's and Barksdale's men were 400 yards behind, while Cobb's and G. T. Anderson's Brigades were 150 yards to their right.

Lee had few options left to resist Greene's incursion, reflecting his line's vulnerability at midday. To fill the void immediately beyond the church Lee was forced to recall Hood's weary division from the rear. Hood's men deserved a rest and more—after fighting in the Cornfield, the battered Texans were barely up to this vital task—but again they moved forward to secure the West Woods's western end. Well left of the church was Ransom's Brigade, with Armistead's, Early's and a portion of Barksdale's Brigades. Barksdale's and Armistead's commands held a second line at the northern edge of the West Woods, while Early still held the woods' eastern edge, with Ransom's four regiments to his right. This was a thin defensive force, but as events soon revealed, it was quite up to the task at hand.[25]

***

Throughout the nearly two hours Greene's Division held the West Woods's southern end, it had been constantly under fire. John Boyle, adjutant of the 111th Pennsylvania, recalled "[w]ithout nervousness or haste the men monotonously loaded and discharged their pieces, and the officers walked back and forth shouting orders or alertly watching the field. Every moment men went down, some with wounds so slight that they were unheeded, some to be disabled for life, and some to rise no more. Throats were parched with thirst. Faces were blackened with smoke, lips were smeared and cracked with the powder from bitten cartridges. The guns were so hot that their brass bands were discolored. Belts sagged loosely over empty stomachs. Hands were swollen with the incessant use of the ramrod. Shoulders were lamed by the recoil of the pieces. Noon came and went, but there was not lull in the storm." Greene's other regiments fared roughly the same and the pressure to hold on until help arrived was tremendous.[26]

The constant fighting was steadily wearing away Greene's infantry line, though. Under Tyndale's command, the division had driven the two Confederate regiments back into the Reel corn; these Rebels, however, simply reformed and straightened their lines for another advance. While these enemy regiments remained, the division's weak left was at risk; infantry fire hadn't cleared the threat away, so perhaps artillery would do the trick. At just that moment, two fresh guns unlimbered across the road, fairly offering their services.

Barely had McGill's two guns opened from their high ground spot when Tyndale appeared to order them forward to the very center of Greene's advanced position across the road. Lieutenant McGill formally objected, adding that being so close to the enemy's infantry fire put his horses at risk and without their power his men certainly couldn't quickly get the guns to safety. McGill didn't need to add that this move threw away the advantage provided by the guns' range and, more troubling, put them across the Hagerstown Pike's post and rail fences—even a modest enemy advance might take his guns. Tyndale would hear none of this, though, and repeated his order to cross the road and dislodge the Rebs on the northern end of the Reel cornfield. Likely cursing the folly of this decision, McGill limbered up his two guns before moving northward nearly 100 yards to find a gap in the fence through which to pass. Sending only one gun forward, McGill held the second in the road until specific orders forced him to place that gun, too, in immediate danger. McGill's concern was well placed and in but a few minutes, he would learn just how much so.

***

The infantry so troubling Tyndale from the Reel cornfield, now commanded by the 27th North Carolina's Colonel John R. Cooke, was biding its time. Although the corn provided some cover, the two regiments had endured a constant stream of Yankee fire, so the appearance of a Union gun on the slight rise in his front meant trouble. Fire from this single nearby gun would tear his men to bits—it had to go. Cooke ordered the 27th North Carolina's left-most four companies forward to the fence, opening fire that began felling artillerymen and horses—four men and three horses, it turned out—but still the gun remained, and something more had to be done. General Longstreet had observed Cooke's dilemma and sent orders directing that Cooke charge the enemy in his front, working in concert with Cobb's Brigade, now commanded by Lieutenant Colonel William MacRae, which was already moving forward on their right.

***

Watching his forward-most gun's crew being felled by rifle fire, Lieutenant McGill must have taken grim satisfaction that he'd accurately warned Lieutenant Colonel Tyndale that this exposed position was no place for artillery. When a Rebel shell brought a huge limb crashing down, pinning his remaining horses, McGill might have considered things couldn't get much worse. If so, McGill was horribly mistaken for the 27th North Carolina and 3rd Arkansas soon sprang from the corn, headed right for Greene's unsupported left flank on the road.[27]

***

At nearly the same moment, in the West Wood's northern end, Ransom's Brigade began stirring. Brigadier General Robert Ransom, Jr.'s brigade had moved to the Confederate left with Walker's Division shortly after 9:00 that morning, joining the Confederate defense there. When Greene's Yankees retook the southern end of the woods, Ransom's command joined Early's Brigade to hold the enemy in check. Now the Federals remained, while Ransom was short a full quarter of his brigade because the 24th North Carolina hadn't returned from joining McLaws's earlier counterattack. Clearing this enemy from the woods would require every available musket so just as his Union counterpart General Greene had done, Ransom left in search of his errant regiment. Unknown to the still-absent Ransom, the 24th had returned about the time he departed. Nonetheless, the 24th North Carolina's timing couldn't have been better.[28]

Colonel Mathew W. Ransom, the general's older brother, had assumed command in the interim and with the 24th North Carolina's sudden reappearance the colonel may have assumed it was the sign for action, which the general may have ordered before departing. Perhaps the sight of two Union artillery pieces filing through the fence gap in the brigade's front convinced him something had to be done. Regardless why, Colonel Ransom instantly ordered forward his three right-most regiments—the 25th, 35th, and 49th North Carolina—toward the enemy's right flank.

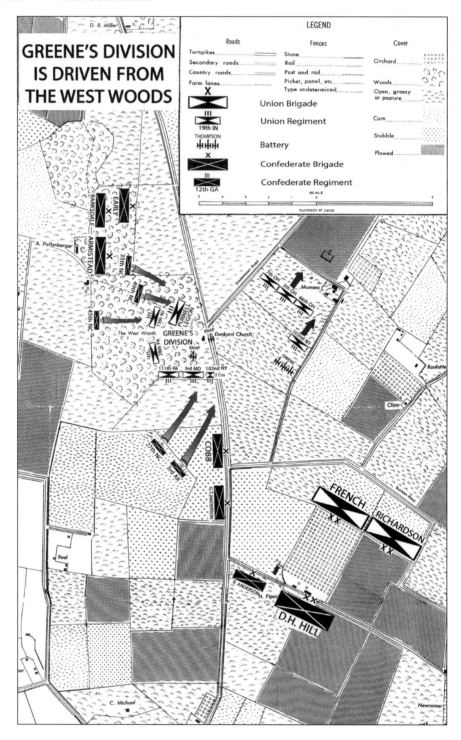

To hide its position, Ransom's Brigade had been exploiting both a ravine running northward from behind the church and the woods' thick foliage. Now Colonel Ransom used the ravine to conceal and guide the brigade's move toward the enemy's position near the church. The 49th North Carolina led the way with orders to "change front on the first company"—facing immediately to the right, pivoting on the first company—once clear of the ravine and charge for the church. The 35th and 25th North Carolina would follow immediately behind, executing the same orders in turn. As the 49th's front rank advanced, though, the thick woods quickly became a hindrance that slowed and confused the movement. As the 49th began changing front, the men discovered an unanticipated body of troops so effectively concealed by the dense woods that identifying them by uniform was impossible. In response, the 49th's Colonel Lee M. McAfee sent forward a captain on horseback to reconnoiter.[29]

***

At the same moment, the 13th New Jersey's adjutant Lieutenant Charles Hopkins watched the deep woods intently. Some time ago, Sergeant Warren—posted forward and right of the 13th's line to snipe at any enemy he found—called the lieutenant forward to alert him to Rebels moving in the woods where they weren't supposed to be. Passing this intelligence up the command chain brought reassurance that it was Sumner's II Corps, but now Hopkins wasn't so sure. Seeing sunlight reflecting off rifle barrels, Hopkins tried again; sending word to Colonel Carman, Hopkins ran forward down the hill to check his suspicion. Nearing the ravine, Hopkins spotted Ransom's Rebel column before racing back uphill through the woods for all he was worth, shouting the whole time, "They are rebs!"[30]

***

Through the woods Captain Cicero Dunham rode ahead of Ransom's advancing 49th North Carolina probing for the enemy. Nearing the unidentified body of troops, Dunham heard a voice call for his surrender; the 13th New Jersey was now aware of the nearby Confederates, thanks to Hopkins's warning only seconds before.[31]

The two opposing officers shared the experience of being caught between close lines of fire as the 13th New Jersey and 49th North Carolina opened on each other at nearly the same moment. Mounted Captain Dunham raced to safety behind his own lines but Charles Hopkins—on foot—could only drop to the ground while rounds zipped over his head. The 13th New Jersey, joined by the Purnell Legion, resolutely held Greene's right, while the 49th and 35th North Carolina—the latter moved into the front line just as firing began—sought nothing less than breaking that hold. Firing two quick volleys, Ransom's leading regiments charged. Why they did so remains uncertain; perhaps Colonel Ransom believed his brigade's position was so weak that only a rash act could save it. Maybe Ransom knew from earlier reconnaissance that the Yankees' exposed right flank lay ahead, and that quick, decisive action could carry the spot. Regardless, Ransom's men surged through the woods, up the ravine, and across the right of both the 13th New Jersey and the Purnell Legion.[32]

On Greene's left, Cooke's 27th North Carolina and 3rd Arkansas slammed into the 3rd Maryland, turning the division's left flank, too. Confederate attacks turned both of Greene's flanks at virtually the same moment, and had it been planned, it would have been a model of military skill and execution. General Longstreet had ordered Cooke's attack and Cobb's advance, but Ransom's assault was unplanned and unexpected. Regardless, the simultaneous Confederate attacks crushed Greene's Division, which broke into a thousand pieces, each racing for safety in the rear to escape the Rebel vise.[33]

***

Greene's hold on the West Woods collapsed in seconds. Orders to retreat weren't given or necessary; men simply looked around and knew it was time to run. The 13th New Jersey's Private J. O. Smith explained "[a]s I hurriedly made for the rail fence that skirted the road, I hastily debated with myself as to the better policy to pursue: whether to go for the gap in the fence through which we had entered, or go directly to and scale the fence. I reasoned that if I sought the opening the "rebs" would get there about the same time I could reach it, and I should be shot or captured sure. To my mind, there seemed little choice in these disasters. Again I thought, if I get on top of that fence, I'm a gone coon, for I shall present a glaring target to the now exultant and rapidly advancing foe. I finally concluded to chance the fence-top and on reaching it I threw my musket over into the road and scrambled to the top of the fence, when, alas! One of those big splinters that are prevalent in such crude material for fence building caught my haversack strap and momentarily held me a prisoner on the fence-top. Finding I could not disengage it, I slipped my head out of the strap and left my grub dangling on the fence for some hungry Johnny … Once more on terra firma, I regained my musket and went nimbly over the fence on the opposite side of the road with no further mishap. This brought me on the Mumma farm, and my course now lay over an open grass field rapidly sloping toward the ruins of the farm-houses that had occupied a sort of glen or gully." Like Private Smith, the rest of Greene's men surged over, under, or through the Hagerstown Pike fences toward safety.[34]

Lieutenant McGill tried getting his artillery away, too. McGill's gun remaining in the road was quickly driven away to rejoin the battery along the Smoketown Road. McGill's Number Two Gun—deployed closest to the Rebs—however had to be left behind, the only artillery the XII Corps lost during the war. The remaining men of Gun Two had the presence of mind during their retreat to grab an abandoned Rebel gun—probably one of S. D. Lee's pieces—which was there for the taking.

Manhandling it to the rear, they could at least claim to have come out of the fight even. As Corporal James P. Stewart later wrote "We had a good many horses killed and lost Number 2 Gun, but we have a Rebel Gun in it's [sic] place ... But James Marshall was shot in the side, he affected a piercing shriek and fell dead. Wm. Anderson was shot in the elbow and made a narrow escape, Saml. Clark was also shot in the arm, ball still in shoulder, Sergeant Shaw, wounded in side, John Lewis also wounded in three places, very severe."[35]

Nearby, a sound caused Captain Owen to glance right only to see Union infantry flying rearward. Moments before, Owen had planned to move his battery closer to offer these men better support—exploiting a lull in enemy firing from the cornfield—but now getting away was his only hope. Working furiously, Owen hastily limbered up his Battery G and headed for the smoldering Mumma buildings. As Owen's Battery and Greene's men fled, they peeled back the flanking guard of French's Division before the Sunken Road.[36]

Greene's Division fled with no one in command. Lieutenant Colonel Tyndale, already nursing a hip wound, caught a second round in his ankle that brought him to the ground amidst the chaos. General Greene, meanwhile, remained absent; having failed to pry reinforcements from Williams, Greene was next sent—"ordered," he explained—to General Hancock, who now commanded Richardson's II Corps division. Riding farther to the Union left, Greene found Hancock busy repulsing an attack on his own right flank, which Greene couldn't know had been enabled by his own division's collapse. At that moment a messenger from XII Corps headquarters notified Greene, to his horror, that his division had been driven from the West Woods. Once again, any immediate prospect for completing McClellan's first battle phase—and hope for Union victory on the right—seemed lost.[37]

***

From his location behind D. H. Hill's Division, Longstreet certainly could see Cooke's and Cobb's advance, as well as Greene's collapse. What he almost certainly couldn't see or have appreciated was the attack by Ransom's North Carolinians on Greene's opposite flank in the West Woods. Having turned the Union right, the 48th and 35th North Carolina drove the 13th New Jersey and the Purnell Legion from the woods and across the Pike, themselves pressing to the western fence. A few men climbed the fences, too, chasing the fleeing enemy but barely had they crossed when Federal artillery opened from the grassy field across the road. These were the remaining guns of Knap's Battery and Thomas's Batteries A and C of the 4th US Artillery; the latter having just moved up to Knap's aid. At such short range, the shells tore the ground around the Carolinians, stalling their advance and taking a fearful toll on Ransom's lines. Colonel Ransom quickly ordered his two regiments back to the West Woods's cover and here they would remain. Not so, however, Cooke's and MacRae's commands on the other side of the church.[38]

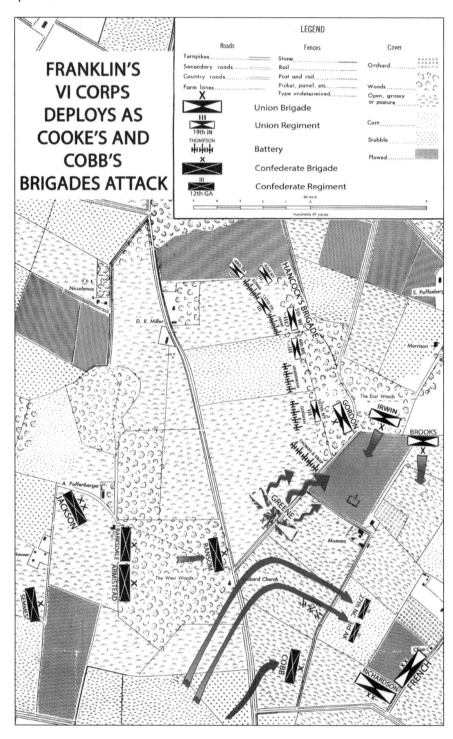

FRANKLIN'S
VI CORPS
DEPLOYS AS
COOKE'S AND
COBB'S
BRIGADES ATTACK

LEGEND

Roads	Fences	Cover
Turnpikes	Stone	
Secondary roads	Rail	Orchard
Country roads	Post and rail	
Farm lanes	Picket, panel, etc.	Woods
	Type undetermined	Open, grassy or pasture

Union Brigade

19th IN   Union Regiment

THOMPSON   Battery

Confederate Brigade

12th GA   Confederate Regiment

Corn

Stubble

Plowed

SCALE

hundreds of yards

Cooke's regiments and Cobb's Brigade swept over the high ground around the church, following the retreating Yankees eastward. Unfortunately, Cooke and MacRae didn't stop to dress their lines and restore order once over the fences, rather letting the men press on in disordered clumps. Barely had Cooke regained control of his color guards—chided, the 27th North Carolina's color-bearer lamely offered "Colonel, I can't let that Arkansas fellow get ahead of me"—when he realized his command was well left of Cobb's Brigade, which had wheeled right to face the enemy there. Ordering a "right wheel," Cooke's regiments soon joined MacRae's more organized command at the fences bordering the Mumma cornfield. Though now reunited and maximizing its striking power, Longstreet's advance would go no further. Facing Cooke and MacRae's men was Brigadier General Nathan Kimball's Brigade from French's Division, still recovering from its earlier attack on the Sunken Road. Seeing the advancing enemy, Kimball ordered his 14th Indiana and 8th Ohio to change front, facing the two regiments right and putting them in the very position MacRae's men sought to take. At the same moment a large, apparently fresh Yankee force—Irwin's Brigade of the VI Corps—appeared headed right for them from the direction of the Mumma farm buildings. Longstreet's force had been under artillery fire since crossing the road and their halt only made the Union batteries' job that much easier. In an exposed position, enduring artillery fire and facing a soon-to-be-reinforced concealed foe was too much for Cooke's rattled regiments. Even before Irwin's Brigade reached them, Cooke's men fled, leaving McRae little choice but to send Cobb's Brigade rearward, too. Longstreet's disjointed counterattack had failed and, worse, MacRae marched away with only 50 or so of the nearly 250 men with which he'd started.[39]

***

Once again, Union control of the ground between the East and West Woods, secured by victory in the Cornfield, proved decisive. It had provided Greene's men a secure staging area from which to strike and take the West Woods and created the possibility of supporting Greene's gains with easily advanced reinforcements. When driven back, the position provided the depth that protected Greene's retreating and broken division during its time of greatest vulnerability. This Union strategic depth also blunted Longstreet's sole counterattack, drawing it deep beyond the South's limited means of supporting an advance. That the Union continued holding the Cornfield and its surrounding ground was the good news.

The bad news was that Greene's repulse represented yet another failure to complete McClellan's first battle phase. Greene's bold, if ill-timed advance into the West Woods had failed for lack of support to reinforce its gains, failure that fell squarely on the shoulders of General Sumner—now commanding the Federal right, he continued functioning instead as barely a corps commander—and General Williams, who struggled to lead the XII Corps even in its defensive stance. McClellan, too, continued reinforcing failure and undermining his own plan by inaction. Once again, the combination of McClellan's singly focused mindset and operational failure by his immediate subordinates was robbing the Union of hope for victory.

At the same time, McClellan had one more card in his hand to play on the Union right. Throughout Greene's time in the West Woods, General William Franklin and his VI Corps had moved steadily toward the fighting. Now it was their turn to weigh in the balance of completing McClellan's key first battle phase, an opportunity once again made possible by the Union's hold on the precious Cornfield and its nearby ground.

CHAPTER 13

The Cornfield's Influence: Franklin's Moment and the VI Corps Arrive

McClellan drew his final card on the Union right shortly after 10:00, when the first VI Corps troops appeared on the Boonsboro Pike behind army headquarters. They'd marched that morning at 5:30, leaving Pleasant Valley where the corps had been guarding the army's flank from an anticipated attack by Lee which never materialized. After two days consisting largely of rest, Franklin's corps made good time in reaching the front. Major General William F. "Baldy" Smith's Second Division led the march, followed by Major General Henry Slocum's First Division. Darius Couch's attached IV Corps division, however, remained away following McClellan's orders to occupy Maryland Heights.[1]

Even without nearly a third of his force, Franklin's corps was large and capable. Smith's Division held 5,569 infantrymen and 16 artillery pieces, while Slocum's Division boasted 3,692 infantry and 20 guns. Combined they gave Franklin 9,261 infantrymen and 36 guns to throw into the fight. The VI Corps moreover was comprised of battle-tested veterans; they had fought up and down the Virginia peninsula, endured the second battle of Manassas, and broken Lee's hold on South Mountain in McClellan's greatest victory to date. The corps' only weak spot, the green 137th Pennsylvania's 681 men, were nonetheless assigned to a brigade with experienced, proven fighters from Maine, New York, Pennsylvania, and Wisconsin commanded by capable veteran Brigadier General Winfield Scott Hancock. The VI Corps's arrival gave McClellan a large, experienced, well-rested force at just the moment reinforcements were most needed, to potentially face a Confederate enemy greatly weakened by the day's fighting. The VI Corps was indeed a potential game-changing force.[2]

McClellan directed Franklin sometime before 3:30 that morning to begin his march, an order critics point to as evidence of McClellan's "slows" and some VI Corps men agreed. Typical was a soldier in Colonel William H. Irwin's 20th New York who recalled "We received no orders to move until 3 AM on September 17. Again, we did not move immediately. Only after we had coffee and breakfast did we break camp and begin our march at 5:30 AM." McClellan, however, probably wanted the corps at the front no earlier than mid- to late-morning, to avoid overcrowding and further clogging the Boonsboro Pike with men and wagons. Like all such movements before entering battle this day, McClellan had carefully planned and prepared the VI Corps's appearance, whatever the purpose of its timing.[3]

Nearing army headquarters, Franklin's men caught a first hint of what awaited them. The 4th Vermont's Captain John Conline recalled "Our ears were greeted by the deafening roar of about 200 pieces of artillery; hissing, exploding shells filled the air, and the rapid fire of musketry was also heard at intervals at various points in front. From an artistic standpoint, the spectacle was grand beyond description." The 7th Maine's Major Hyde recalled a sense of foreboding, noting "the diapason of the artillery and the rattle of small arms grew louder, we all felt we had got to brace ourselves, for the trying moment." So ominous was the sight that Hyde "made our drummers and fifers arm themselves with guns picked up by the roadside, and join their companies." What most troubled the 27th New York's William Westervelt was "the Surguns and their assistants with their coats off and sleeves rooled up with their hands and amputating instruments all bloody looking more like "butchers" than "professional" men. I tried to get along without seeing them as it was a sight that tended more to unnerve me than going right into the fight but they were on all sides and look which way I would they were before me."[4]

Sometime during this march, McClellan sent the VI Corps to the Union right, clarifying an earlier dispatch cautioning Franklin to be "ready to support the attack on the right or left as might be required." What prompted this remains uncertain but reflects McClellan's linear-thinking determination to stick with his original approach and complete his plan's first phase. Upon arrival, McClellan immediately ordered Smith's Division right to support Sumner. Once over the Pry's ford crossing, Hancock's First Brigade replaced Irwin's command as the leading unit and off they went toward the sound of fighting. Reaching the East Woods about 11:00, Smith reported to General Sumner and given McClellan's earlier orders to take offensive action, these reinforcements might have seemed just the thing. Rather than presenting opportunity, however, Smith's fresh troops put Sumner in a bind.[5]

Two messages Sumner sent headquarters around that time suggest the mental and command struggle permeating his mind then. Sumner's 11:00 dispatch to McClellan—asking for news of French's and Slocum's whereabouts, more reinforcements, and cautioning that troops were "giving way"—may have been prompted by Smith's arrival. Sumner may have intended its uncertain, defeated tone to convey to McClellan the vulnerable, precarious state of the Union right just then—which from his recent experience certainly wasn't one to support an attack. A second message, sent on the 11:00 dispatch's heels, struck an opposite, aggressive tone, asking "Do you think it proper to countermand the order to send Slocum's Division to Richardson's support, as I shall need it on the right if I advance?" Taken at face value, these messages suggest Sumner was suddenly ready to attack, as McClellan directed. Viewed another way, the second message too may have been meant to prompt McClellan to rethink or rescind his earlier attack order by demonstrating that things on the far right—beyond McClellan's view—were more uncertain and vulnerable than he knew. Regardless of the messages' real objectives, Sumner's actions and deployments show that in his hands the VI Corps would prove to be a useless tool for achieving Union victory.[6]

Sumner quickly ordered Smith's Division into the Cornfield, deploying on the right of his line behind batteries before the East Woods. Barely had this move begun when Sumner changed his mind, sending staffer Lieutenant Colonel Joseph H. Taylor to direct two of Hancock's regiments to support Cothran's and Frank's Batteries. Smith understood Sumner's intentions but feared doing so nearly halved Hancock's Brigade and he didn't like it at all. Although Smith was probably unaware then, it was exactly this diffusion of Union manpower and firepower that had cost the army so dearly all morning. Smith decided to follow Sumner's orders, but he'd keep Hancock's entire First Brigade together in this new position to ensure that if ordered to attack, Smith could easily reassemble his entire division.[7]

Smith also reinforced his Cornfield position by moving up his artillery. Cowan's 1st Battery, New York Light Artillery posted right of Frank's position. Next Vanneman's Battery B, Maryland Artillery, slid into the gap between Cothran and Frank, created when Knap's Battery moved south to aid Greene's Division. Next, Hancock's infantry support appeared and with a few shouted commands it peeled into individual regimental formations, filling the gaps between batteries. The 49th Pennsylvania posted on the far right, beyond Cowan's guns. The 43rd New York and a detachment from the 137th Pennsylvania moved up between Cowan's and Frank's Batteries. On their left, the 6th Maine and 5th Wisconsin slid into place between Frank's and Cothran's Batteries. Once in place, Hancock's Brigade and these 16 guns provided an iron spine securing the Union hold on the Cornfield, the East Woods, and beyond.[8]

As solid as this position was, however, Smith's left flank remained vulnerable. Observing Confederate troops moving in his front—probably either Ransom's regiments or Cooke's and MacRae's advancing commands—Smith personally directed Irwin's Brigade into position on Hancock's left, filling the gap. First posting the 33rd and 77th New York as skirmishers to cover the move, next the German-speaking 20th New York emerged from the East Woods to anchor the right. Smith had an ulterior motive in using the 20th so because they "had behaved badly at White Oak Swamp" and he was determined they should redeem themselves, even if officers needed to prod the regiment forward at sword point. Advancing, they called out their unique regimental battle cry "Bahn Frei! Bahn Frei!;" even if the Rebs didn't understand it meant "Clear the way!" in German, this steadied the men for what lay ahead. Next the 7th Maine wheeled into position on their left, while the 49th New York deployed on their right. Wheeling slightly left, Irwin's Brigade drove straight at Cooke's and MacRae's advancing Rebels.[9]

The 20th New York instantly caught the worst of the fire; the 7th Maine's Major Hyde explained that they moved "in fine line, and looked so well that the whole fire of the enemy was being concentrated on them." Hyde noticed troops hiding behind the remaining Mumma barns and directed the 7th Maine to move at the left oblique to clear the obstacle. "[W]e charged them, tearing the rail fences down as we went" until the Southerners fled. So easily was this achieved that Hyde recalled not the charge, but "what had been a Confederate regiment of perhaps four hundred men. There they were, both ranks, file closers and officers as they fell, for so few had been survivors it seemed to me the whole regiment were lying there in death." These men were perhaps from Ripley's or Colquitt's Brigades; regardless, by then—nearly 1:00 in the afternoon—it seemed they'd come from a different circumstance, on a different field altogether. For Irwin's men, this fight was all too real and immediate, though, and once the 7th Maine returned, the brigade resumed its advance.[10]

Irwin pressed on, chasing Cooke's and MacRae's fleeing troops until encountering an unexpected challenge near the Hagerstown Pike. "A severe and unexpected volley from the woods on our right struck full on the Seventy-seventh and Thirty-third New York, which staggered them for a moment, but they closed up and faced by the rear rank, and poured in a close and scorching fire, driving back and scattering the enemy at this point … As soon as my line was formed, facing the belt of the woods and the open ground to its right, the men were ordered down." Lacking support, Irwin's Brigade lay down behind the same ridge Greene's Division had exploited an hour earlier. "Pickets were posted on the crest of a small hill along our front," Irwin recorded, "and all kept in readiness to hold firmly to the position or to attack."[11]

Despite their cover, Irwin's command remained close to the enemy—Ransom's Brigade in the West Woods and Cooke's and MacRae's rallying men, as well as scattered Confederate batteries—and began taking fire. The 20th New York remained the top Confederate target and soon Major Hyde realized why—the Germans' color guard defiantly waved their flag, taunting the Rebs. Racing over, Hyde advised Colonel von Vegesack to drop his colors a bit. "Let them wave; they are our glory," said the brave old Swede, and he kept on riding back and forth behind the regiment," recorded Hyde admiringly. Irwin's Brigade had unknowingly become the Union's latest, best hope for finally breaking Lee's line and taking the ridge above Sharpsburg. If the men had no idea they'd been put in this position, neither did their officers—or General Sumner. Once again, McClellan's plan stood on the brink of success, but no one in authority knew it or acted to finish the job.[12]

Smith next pushed Brigadier General W. T. H. Brooks's Second Brigade forward, deploying on Irwin's left; lacking orders to attack, Smith nonetheless positioned his division to reinforce Irwin's gains and position. Before Smith's aide found General Brooks, though, someone—probably Sumner—ordered his brigade farther left to support French's Division, reportedly heavily pressed and out of ammunition. Marching left around the smoldering Mumma buildings to French's right, Brooks instead "found that the enemy had been checked and repelled." His purpose for being there moot, Brooks returned to fill the gap between French's right and Irwin's left. Such command confusion was becoming increasingly common under Sumner's uncertain stewardship and it rankled Smith even days later. "As soon as the Third Brigade was established in its position, I sent back for the second Brigade (General Brooks's) to act as a support, but it had, without my knowledge or consent, been ordered away," Smith ranted. "It is not the first or second time during a battle that my command has been dispersed by orders from an officer superior in rank to the General Commanding this corps and I must assert that I have never known any good to arise from such a method of fighting a battle and I think the contrary rule should be adopted of keeping commands intact."[13]

Nonetheless, the North's last glimmer of hope for victory on the right was just then riding onto the field in the form of Major General William B. Franklin, who's dithering nearly cost the Union decisive victory at South Mountain. This performance and his role in losing Harpers Ferry might have crowded Franklin's thoughts before joining his deployed corps, perhaps replaced now by assessing the tactical situation facing his command. The specter of failure certainly lingered over Franklin, but this fight offered opportunity to undo any professional damage still clinging to his reputation from earlier events.

Franklin appeared behind the East Woods with staff in tow probably between 11:30 and 11:45. Finding General Sumner to receive his orders should have been a priority, but Franklin's report and later writings indicate he first sought General Smith to understand what his Second Division was doing. Upon learning that Smith's command was prepared to attack, with Irwin's Brigade poised like a knife aimed at the Dunker Church, Franklin decided to wait only for Slocum's First Division to complete deploying before attacking. This groundwork laid, Franklin sought General Sumner.[14]

Riding right, Franklin found Sumner at his headquarters busily wrestling with the battle's situation and deployment decisions but no longer conflicted about what should be done. "I found him at the head of his troops, but much depressed," Franklin later advised Congress, "[h]e told me that his whole corps was exhausted and could do nothing more that day." Receiving no direct guidance from Sumner, Franklin rode to find Slocum's Division as it neared the field.[15]

Nonetheless, guidance of a sort was even then on its way. Sometime shortly after 1:00, McClellan had learned that Burnside's IX Corps troops were across the Antietam and advancing against Lee's right flank. If this was so, then phase two of his battle plan was proceeding accordingly and, although phase one hadn't gone as originally intended, what mattered now was shoring up this "success" and avoiding surprise on the Union right. McClellan dispatched Lieutenant Wilson with a verbal dispatch advising Sumner "to get up his men and hold his position at all hazards, as Burnside had crossed and was advancing finely." This message firmly written in his mind, Wilson mounted his grey horse and started the 30-minute ride to find Sumner.[16]

Arriving at Sumner's headquarters on the Poffenberger farm shortly before Franklin departed, Wilson found the same beaten man that Franklin recalled. "I found Sumner glum and grim, surrounded by his staff and several division commanders, and, so far as I could judge, with little or no fight left in him." Repeating his by-now well-learned lines, Wilson wasn't at all prepared for Sumner's response. "Go back, young man, and ask General McClellan if I shall make a simultaneous advance with my whole line at the risk of not being able to rally a man on this side of the creek if I am driven back!"[17]

Wilson thought he understood what Sumner was driving at and with the blissful ignorance and self-confidence of youth, replied "General, from the tenor of the order I have just delivered, I will assume to say that General McClellan simply desires and expects you to hold your position for the present."[18]

Beyond requiring guidance from someone higher ranking than a lieutenant, Sumner apparently wanted orders that clearly, unmistakably removed any need to attack. Driving home the point, he ordered, "Go back, young man, and bring an answer to my question." With nothing more to say, Wilson mounted his horse and returned to the Pry House.

There Wilson repeated Sumner's question. Wilson remembered that in no mood for this, "McClellan retorted in sharp and impatient tones: 'Tell General Sumner to risk nothing. I expect him to hold his present position at every cost. This is the great battle of the war and every man must do his duty.'"

But then McClellan must have realized the implication of his statement, which clearly precluded Sumner from advancing. Only General Sumner could really know at that moment if attacking was the right move, and, after all, he still needed that ridge on which to deploy artillery to support the center attack. According to Lieutenant Wilson, "And then, as if changing his mind, he added, 'Tell the general to crowd every man and gun into ranks, and, if he thinks it practicable, he may advance Franklin to carry the woods in front, holding the rest of the line with his own command, assisted by those of Banks and Hooker.'" Once again, Wilson raced to find Sumner.

Exactly repeating McClellan's words, it must have taken mere seconds for Sumner to realize this was not at all what he wanted or needed from McClellan, who clearly didn't understand the situation here on the Union right. Sumner would have to try one more time convincing McClellan to directly order no attack. Sumner replied "Go back, young man, and tell General McClellan I have no command. Tell him my command, Banks's command and Hooker's command are all cut up and demoralized. Tell him General Franklin has the only organized command on this part of the field!" Once again, James Wilson raced rearward with Sumner's latest plea for release from responsibility.[19]

Meanwhile, Slocum's Division arrived. "On we went," wrote the 27th New York's Charles Fairchild from Bartlett's Brigade, "and, two miles farther, we reached the battle-field of Antietam, and were placed in line of battle; then loading our pieces, we moved forward across fields, through bits of wood and over fences, continually passing the dead, in blue or gray, and meeting stretcher-carriers with wounded, on their way to the rear." Preceding Bartlett's command were the brigades of Colonel Alfred T. A. Torbert and Brigadier General John Newton, which were immediately thrown into line between Smith's now-divided brigades. Newton's Brigade slid through the East Woods and deployed along its western edge, its right reaching nearly to the left of Hancock's Brigade. Torbert's line moved next and quickly deployed astride the Smoketown Road on Newton's left. Though Torbert's left flank was hanging in the air in the Mumma's plowed field, a short march forward would bring them into line on Irwin's rightmost regiment. The deployment added five fresh brigades to the Union line, further strengthening the position centered on the Cornfield.[20]

Next Slocum's artillery raced up, strengthening the Union's iron hold on the Cornfield position and East Woods. First to move was Lieutenant Leonard Martin's Battery C of the 5th US Artillery, which deployed just right of the Mumma cemetery, before immediately opening on Cooke's reforming Confederates and their batteries on the ridge beyond. Next, Lieutenant Edward Williston guided the 2nd US Artillery's Battery D into place on Martin's right, taking up the rest of the Mumma's plowed field all the way to the Smoketown Road. As this was happening, Captain Josiah Porter's Battery A of the Massachusetts Light Artillery slid right off the Smoketown Road, replacing Thomas's Battery. Cothran's tired men, too, received welcome relief as Captain John Wolcott moved the Maryland Artillery's Battery A into their former position just below the Cornfield. Now Sumner possessed 44 guns—most rifled and nearly all from fresh batteries—to fulfill whatever clear orders McClellan sent next through Lieutenant Wilson.[21]

***

Confederate officers across the Hagerstown Pike, too, used the lull that had appeared to adjust their lines. Ransom's, Barksdale's, and Armistead's Brigades held the West Woods, backed up by the remnants of Jackson's Division. Stuart's largely unscathed cavalry held the far-left flank of Lee's line, as it had all day. Cobb's Brigade and Tige Anderson's command returned to their previous spots on the Hagerstown Pike, linking Jackson's line to Longstreet's men in the Piper farm fields. This adjusted line, however, remained terribly fragile. Each Confederate brigade—every single one—had been in the field and fighting for hours; men were tired and low on ammunition, ranks thinned by casualties. They remained all Lee had available to stop McClellan's next prospective attack on the left. Despite all this, these Southern troops were hardly ready to give up on this fight.[22]

***

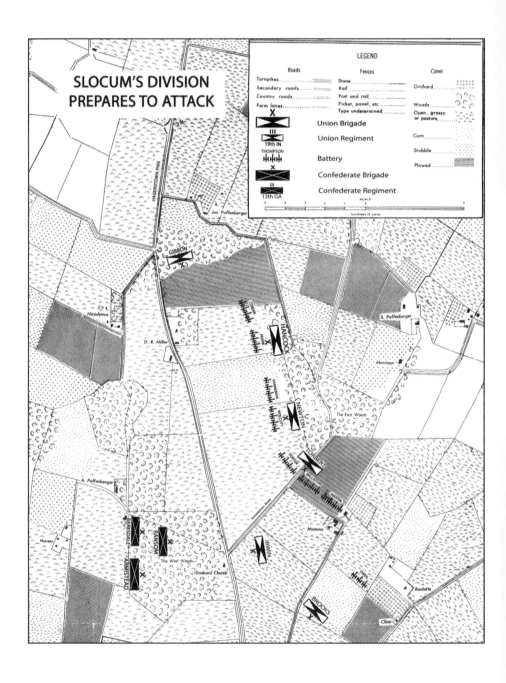

SLOCUM'S DIVISION PREPARES TO ATTACK

LEGEND

Roads
Turnpikes
Secondary roads
Country roads
Farm lanes

Fences
Stone
Rail
Post and rail
Picket, panel, etc.
Type undetermined

Cover
Orchard
Woods
Open, grassy or pasture
Corn
Stubble
Plowed

Union Brigade

19th IN Union Regiment

THOMPSON Battery

Confederate Brigade

12th GA Confederate Regiment

General Franklin was at that moment planning to test such Confederate resolve. Working with a will, Franklin checked Smith's positions, monitored and determined "sufficient" Slocum's progress, and considered the position and pace of the artillery's fire as well. Franklin intended to send Slocum's Division forward to attack the Dunker Church position in a classic "two up, one back" assault—Torbert's and Newton's Brigades attacking, supported by Bartlett—aided by all 44 guns of the artillery line centered on the Cornfield. Smith's three already nearby brigades of his First Division would be the ready reserve to support Slocum. Only two things prevented launching this attack—alerting Sumner of his plan and bringing up Bartlett's Brigade, his sole remaining undeployed unit. With all in motion, Franklin sent off two staffers, one headed to General Sumner and the other to find Colonel Joseph Bartlett. Franklin was poised to save both his career and the Union victory here on the right.[23]

Franklin waited impatiently for his two aides to return. When Bartlett's Brigade hove into view, Franklin must have felt a mix of anxiousness and relief for he was now, finally, poised to strike and directed the brigade into its supporting post in the center of Slocum's two-brigade attacking front. Then disaster struck—General Sumner himself rode up. If Franklin considered it a bad sign that Sumner was now here in response to his dispatch, he was quite right.

Sumner implored Franklin to abandon his attack. The situation on the Union right was still in terrible danger, he explained, and attacking was simply too risky. Franklin's corps was the only fresh force on that part of the field, Sumner continued, and if it was defeated the entire Union right "would be entirely routed." Still, Sumner hadn't ordered the attack abandoned, so Franklin pushed back. "I informed him that I thought it a very necessary thing to do, and told him I would prefer to make the attack unless he assumed the responsibility of forbidding it." Franklin had pressed the issue as far as he dared and in response, Sumner issued his final decision. "He assumed the responsibility, and ordered me not to make it," Franklin recalled. Being robbed of this opportunity must have tremendously frustrated Franklin.[24]

With shells screaming overhead and thousands awaiting their orders, the irony was certainly lost on Franklin and Sumner that they were playing just the opposite roles from those they usually chose. Here was cautious, careful, plodding William Franklin, now all aggression and optimism, seeing opportunity in a tight spot and itching to attack. Facing him in this standoff was the ever-impetuous, too eager to attack "Bull" Sumner, now cowed and broken in spirit, capable only of defense, if not longing for a retreat that might end this danger. It was truly "the world turned upside down."[25]

Rank and command hierarchy notwithstanding, their standoff continued for what must have seemed an agonizing eternity. Both knew only General McClellan could really resolve this dispute, and luckily at that very moment, the general's staffer, Major Hammerstein, appeared. Franklin asked the major to tell McClellan of the situation and explain that he favored attack. Presumably, Sumner agreed to this approach and would have added his own reasons for not attacking. With that, Major Hammerstein raced away to find McClellan, the final arbiter to this fight within a battle.[26]

Then, as if on cue, General McClellan himself rode up. His sudden appearance neither the result of Major Hammerstein's nor Lieutenant Wilson's efforts, but probably driven by the mounting intelligence arriving at the Pry House that things were going poorly on the right. Regardless why he was there, McClellan had thrust himself into the center of commanding this battle—finally.[27]

The three men must have been studies in contrast at that moment, standing amidst the swirl of battle and the stink of death. Sumner, slightly disheveled and sweaty from his exertions of the last hours; Franklin edgy and frustrated, his voice rising in anticipation of the fight as he tried desperately to win this debate; and McClellan all rationality and arbitration, sitting above this dispute as judge and jury. The meeting, held perhaps somewhere near the southern end of the Cornfield, was in one sense simply a heated conversation between three colleagues; in reality, it was a debate that might determine the fate of a nation.

After listening patiently to his opposing subordinates, McClellan rendered his verdict. "General Sumner expressed the most decided opinion against another attempt during that day to assault the enemy's position in front, as portions of our troops were so much scattered and demoralized," McClellan later explained. "In view of these circumstances, after making changes in the position of some of the troops, I directed the different commanders to hold their positions…" General Franklin remembered the moment a bit differently, telling a Congressional Committee "[T]he general himself came up and stated that things had gone well on all the other parts of the field, that he was afraid to risk the day by another attack there on the right at that time." Regardless how the conversation actually went, the result was the same—there would be no VI Corps attack.[28]

It was a watershed moment in the battle. General McClellan himself decided there would be no final assault to complete a task that had claimed some 8,817 Union casualties—including 1,575 killed—that warm September day, all before 2:00 in the afternoon. McClellan's decision meant that at the cost of nearly 9000 casualties, the Union had gained control of about three hundred yards of Maryland farmland it had not held at dawn. No more would the Union utilize the depth offered by its costly acquisition of the Cornfield and its surrounding ground to launch an assault to secure victory. Still, the Union's control of the Cornfield's three hundred yards would yet influence the battle of Antietam's course, even if in ways that General McClellan wouldn't fully appreciate.

CHAPTER 14

The Cornfield's Influence:
The South Seeks the Offensive

General McClellan returned from the Cornfield meeting and prepared a message at 1:25, his last of the day to General Halleck and Washington. "We are in the midst of the most terrible battle of the war, perhaps of history—thus far it looks well but I have great odds against me," McClellan wrote, "Hurry up all the troops possible. Our loss has been terrific, but we have gained much ground. I have thrown the mass of the Army on their left flank, Burnside is now attacking their right & I hold my small reserve consisting of Porters (5th Corps) ready to attack the center as soon as the flank movements are developed. I hope that God will give us a glorious victory." Perhaps meant to influence Washington's understanding of the fight for his own ends, McClellan's message more importantly shows that at 1:25 he remained committed to his original battle plan.[1]

Having declared his first phase complete by ordering Franklin to stand down on the right, McClellan turned his attention to the second phase—striking Lee's opposite flank. Just as on the right, the attack from the Union left wasn't going as swiftly or successfully as originally hoped because after seizing the Lower Bridge by 1:00, Burnside took nearly two hours getting his IX Corps into position. Along with McClellan's decision on the Union right, this created a lull in the battle, which General Lee exploited to prepare his own force to finally go on the offensive. Just as McClellan had, Lee planned to attack his enemy's right flank.

**

In fact, Lee, Jackson, and Longstreet were each independently planning assaults on the Union right. A testament both to their shared aggressive approach and command unity, attacking and defeating McClellan's army was a daunting task given the Army of Northern Virginia's state at that moment, and that the Union line centered on the Cornfield had swelled with fresh batteries and infantry. Any attack now would only come with a considerable price and at great risk.[2]

Jackson at that moment was behind Barksdale's line in the rear of the West Woods, sitting casually on his mount with a leg thrown over his saddle's pommel while plucking and eating apples from one of the Poffenbergers' fruit trees. When General Walker arrived to report an enemy force—certainly Irwin's Brigade—advancing toward Cooke's two regiments. Jackson seemed to ignore Walker's report, instead asking "Can you spare me a regiment and a battery?" Walker offered the capable 49th North Carolina, and French's and Branch's batteries, though cautioning they lacked long-range ammunition.[3]

Jackson then shared his attack plan with Walker. After an opening flanking attack on the Union right, Jackson's entire force would strike directly at the Yankees in the Cornfield and its surrounding ground. Stuart would lead the flanking force—although the ground precluded using cavalry, Jackson explained, Stuart had offered his services—which would include Walker's three units. He was cobbling together four or five thousand men for Stuart, Jackson continued, and Walker should return to prepare his division to join the frontal assault. Swinging his foot back into the stirrup, Jackson boldly stated his objective, "We'll drive McClellan into the Potomac." Ignoring that to do so would require reversing positions on the field, the comment impressed on Walker the seriousness and aggressiveness of Jackson's plan. Walker next "reported General Jackson's order to my brigade commanders, and directed them to listen for the sound of Stuart's guns."[4]

Longstreet's plan similarly drew on his first-hand experience but focused instead on ground farther to the right. As Longstreet later explained, "At one or two points near our centre were dead angles into which I rode from time to time for closer observation of the enemy when his active aggression was suspended. General Burnside was busy at his crossing, but no report of progress had been sent me. One of my rides towards the Dunker chapel revealed efforts of the enemy to renew his work on that part of the field. Our troops were ordered to be ready to receive it. Its non-aggression suggested an opportunity for the Confederates, and I ordered McLaws and Walker to prepare to assault. Hood was back in position with his brigades, and Jackson was reported on his way, all in full supply of ammunition. It seemed probable that by concealing our movements under cover of the wood from the massed batteries of Doubleday's artillery on the north, and the batteries of position on the east, we could draw our columns so near to the enemy in front before our move could be known that we would have but a few rods to march before we could mingle our ranks with those of the enemy; that our columns massed and in goodly numbers, pressing severely upon a single point, would give the enemy much trouble, and might cut him in two, and break up his battle arrangements at the lower bridge…"[5]

These competing plans might have created confusion and disaster for Lee's weakened army but Jackson's preparations soon eclipsed Longstreet's. As Walker recalled "About half-past three a staff-officer of General Longstreet brought me an order from that general to advance and attack the enemy in my front. As the execution of this order would materially interfere with Jackson's plans, I thought it my duty before beginning the movement to communicate with General Longstreet personally. I found him in rear of the position in which I had posted Cooke in the morning, and upon informing him of Jackson's intentions, he withdrew his order." Once again, the atmosphere of initiative permeating Lee's command had paid off because by seeking clarification—rather than blindly obeying—Walker defused a potentially disastrous command conflict. From 3:30 onward, the Army of Northern Virginia would pursue one attack plan—that probably formulated by Jackson and ordered by Lee.[6]

General Stuart was by then already heading northeastward toward the Federal right with Jackson's flanking force, consisting of seven cavalry regiments from Fitzhugh Lee's and Hampton's cavalry brigades and the 7th Virginia from Robertson's Brigade. Marching behind the horsemen was Walker's 48th North Carolina, the only available infantry, and three batteries. In addition to Walker's 12 guns of French's and Branch's Batteries, Stuart possessed six more guns—one from Poague's, two from Raine's, and three from Brockenbrough's Batteries—which formed a cobbled-together battery commanded by Major John Pelham.[7]

Stuart's force moved quickly and unbothered—probably unseen, too—by any Yankee resistance. Reaching the hamlet of New Industry, Stuart turned east toward the Yankees' right flank. It was hardly an ideal location; there the Potomac takes a nearly dead-eastern turn, limiting the depth of Stuart's position and threatening his command's security if Federals counterattacked. Stuart's presence here also greatly stretched his connection on the right to Jackson's main force in the West Woods. Nonetheless, a prominent ridge rising some 300 yards in front offered excellent ground for Stuart's artillery to support the attack. The position also was near the base of Nicodemus Heights—ground Stuart knew well—offering an anchor for Stuart's right, where additional batteries might support his cavalry assault.

Stuart quickly got to work, directing Pelham to advance his "battery" to the ridge, while French and Branch led their batteries toward Nicodemus Heights. Stuart next ordered Fitzhugh Lee's 4th Virginia Cavalry, leading the mounted column, northward to establish the attacking force's left flank. All was proceeding better than Stuart might have expected until, suddenly, it wasn't.[8]

Barely had Pelham's force deployed on the ridge when a terrific artillery barrage rained lead and hell down on them. "Along with six or eight other guns, under the direction of Major Pelham, an attempt was made to dislodge the enemy's batteries, but failed completely, being silenced in fifteen or twenty minutes by a most terrific fire," recalled William Poague who remained with his single gun's crew. Losing men and horses fast, Pelham abandoned the position and raced for the rear. As these targets disappeared, the Yankee gunners turned to fire on French's and Branch's men struggling to deploy on Nicodemus Heights. Even before the attack began, Stuart's artillery support had dissolved.[9]

***

Stuart's artillery was driven away by Union I Corps guns placed by acting corps commander Meade, now commanded in whole by General Doubleday. These approximately 30 guns formed in two lines on the Poffenberger farm—north of the North Woods, facing directly west—and complemented Sumner's artillery line centered in the Cornfield. Behind the artillery, Doubleday's Division, bruised and weakened but reformed, rested after being resupplied with ammunition. They'd been waiting here for several hours and when the Rebels appeared shortly before 4:00, back into action they went. Doubleday wrote, "[T]he enemy massed his infantry and opened fire with his artillery to force our position, but my thirty guns replied with such vigor and effect that the columns of attack melted away and the rebels gave up the attempt." Stuart preferred instead to blame the Potomac River for his retreat. "In endeavoring to pass along up the river bank, however, I found that the river made such an abrupt bend that the enemy's batteries were within 800 yards of the brink of the stream, which would have made it impossible to have succeeded in the movement proposed, and it was accordingly abandoned." Stuart's excuses aside, Northern soldiers clearly remained ready and willing to fight.[10]

***

At probably the same moment, Stuart's flanking force encountered Union opposition, Stonewall Jackson received his own reality check. Jackson planned his main attack to strike when Stuart's flanking assault got underway and to assemble the five or six thousand men needed, Jackson moved from regiment to regiment gathering what he could. Riding the Confederate lines then could not have been heartening. Thinned ranks, short on ammunition, scattered and tired, Jackson's force was weary and worn. Worse, Jackson apparently could see fresh Union infantry and artillery deploying in the Cornfield and beyond, jealously guarding his attack's objective.

Riding among Ransom's 35th North Carolina at the West Woods's eastern edge, Jackson ordered Private William S. Hood—no apparent relation to the general—to climb a nearby tall tree to collect some detailed intelligence about this force he was about to strike. Once near the top, Jackson directed Hood to count the flags he could see. "Who-e-e! There are oceans of them, General," reported Hood. Not satisfied with the accuracy of this, Jackson commanded "Count their flags." After Hood reached 39 Union colors, Jackson called him down. There would be no more Confederate counterattacks into the Cornfield this day.

"In the afternoon, in obedience to instructions from the commanding general, I moved to the left with a view of turning the Federal right, but I found his numerous artillery so judiciously established in their front and extending so near the Potomac, which makes here a remarkable bend ... as to render it inexpedient to hazard the attempt," reported Stonewall, mirroring Stuart's excuse. No matter how much Lee or Jackson wanted to attack, doing so at this moment would only have been suicide.

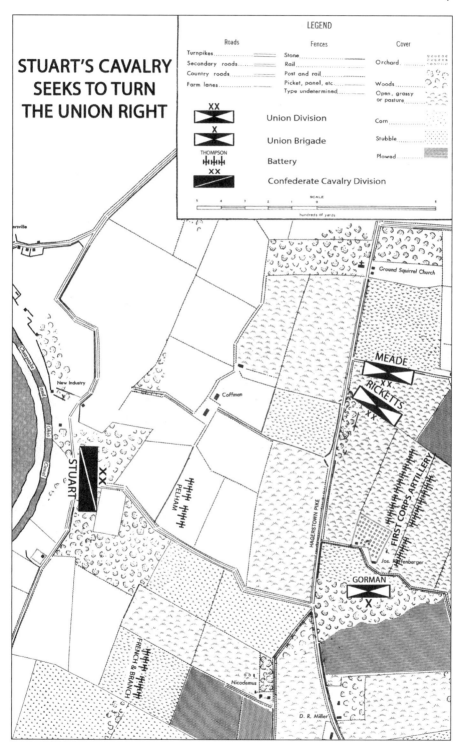

STUART'S CAVALRY SEEKS TO TURN THE UNION RIGHT

LEGEND

Roads	Fences	Cover
Turnpikes	Stone	Orchard
Secondary roads	Rail	
Country roads	Post and rail	
Farm lanes	Picket, panel, etc.	Woods
	Type undetermined	Open, grassy or pasture

Union Division

Union Brigade

THOMPSON Battery

Confederate Cavalry Division

Corn

Stubble

Plowed

SCALE

hundreds of yards

The Army of Northern Virginia was exhausted and thinned, while a large nearby Federal force remained fresh and formidable. Lee had waited too long in seeking the offensive and that door had slammed shut.[11]

It was, in fact, at this moment that the II Corps men of French's and Richardson's Divisions unknowingly redeemed the sacrifice they had been called on to make in "Bloody Lane." Stalling the Yankee attack had validated Confederate sacrifices there, but their Union counterparts' fight had been disconnected from any larger strategic objective and Sumner's failed leadership precluded exploiting their sacrifice to any gain or purpose. Still, their fighting, suffering, and dying did have a purpose, even if an unintended one. That is, because French and Richardson had struck D. H. Hill's Division in the Sunken Road, including those not involved in the morning's fighting in the Cornfield, Hill's men were as worn and battle-weary as the rest of Lee's army by mid-afternoon. When Stonewall Jackson sought fresh troops for his frontal attack, D. H. Hill's spent division was no longer available or up to the task.

Throughout the rest of the afternoon Federal lines centered on the Cornfield and the Southern position in the West Woods remained largely unchanged. The suffering and dying, however, continued because both sides' artillery opened on these stationary infantrymen and on their opposite numbers manning the guns. The 4th Vermont's John Conline, part of Brooks's Brigade before the Sunken Road, recalled "We were at once ordered to lie down, heads toward the enemy and resting on our knapsacks. While we were lying down the rebel infantry fire slackened in our front, but their artillery shelled us unmercifully for perhaps twenty-five minutes or more. One of their shells exploded about two feet from the ground and not more than twenty feet directly in front of me, and covered us with sand, gravel, and dirt. E. S. Cooper, the soldier next on my left in ranks, was struck on the top of the head by a piece of this shell and dangerously wounded and taken from the field." Hours of tension, lack of purposeful action, and remaining so near the enemy provided a new and perhaps more trying situation to the men of both armies around Miller's Cornfield.[12]

***

During this time occurred one of the most pointless actions of the entire war. Late that afternoon Jackson ordered Hood's Division and Hays's Brigade south to plug a gap on the Piper farm, prompting Slocum's artillery chief Captain Emory Upton to advance three guns of Captain John Wolcott's Battery A, 1st Maryland Light Artillery to plug a similar Union gap beyond the left of Hancock's left-most regiment in the Sunken Road. Halting the Confederate advance, the battery fired for half an hour until replaced by three guns of Lieutenant Edward Willison's Battery D, 2nd US Artillery. To drive away this threat, skirmishers from D. H. Hill's Division soon advanced through the Piper orchard, felling Yankee artillerymen and their horses.

Persuaded he must keep the battery "in full play," Colonel Irwin ordered the veteran 7th Maine's commander Major Thomas Hyde to "take your regiment and drive the enemy away from those trees and buildings."

Dumbfounded at this lopsided mission, Hyde saluted and replied "Colonel, I have seen a large force of rebels go in there. I should think two brigades." Irwin snapped back "Are you afraid to go, sir?!" before repeating the order. Hyde retorted "Give the order so the regiment can hear it, and we are ready, sir." Irwin did so and the 7th Maine readied to advance. First, though, Hyde ordered back young guidon bearers George Williams and Johnny Begg to spare them—or so he thought, because the boys both raced back into line once Hyde's back was turned.[13]

Hyde marched the 7th toward the Piper orchard, first crossing the Sunken Road so full of dead and wounded that Hyde recalled his horse having to step on bodies. Taking Confederate skirmish fire, Hyde ordered a charge toward the corner of the Piper barn, which dropped the 7th into a swale and safety. Emerging, Hyde's regiment found it had driven away the skirmishers they'd been sent there for but were now exposed, half a mile from Irwin's Brigade's support, and taking Confederate fire from a large force behind a stone wall near the Hagerstown Pike. Moving left into another swale brought relief but once on the next ridge Hyde spied a large enemy force lying down, awaiting the 7th Maine's advance. Retreating to the safety of Piper's orchard to secure his gain, Hyde expected infantry support but only received help from Williston's battery and Hexamer's Battery A of the New Jersey Light Artillery, which stalled advancing Rebels and allowed Hyde to slip his men out of this trap.[14]

Fifteen minutes after advancing only 73 7th Maine men returned, leaving 108 of their comrades strewn over the field of their pointless advance. These casualties included the boys who had snuck back into line; George Williams was killed in the advance and Johnny Begg spent the evening having an arm sawed off. Colonel Irwin praised "No words of mine can do justice to the firmness, intelligence, and heroic courage with which this regiment performed its dangerous task." Major Hyde perhaps more honestly judged "When we knew our efforts were resultant from no place or design at headquarters, but were from an inspiration of John Barleycorn in our brigade commander alone. I wished I had been old enough, or distinguished enough, to have dared to disobey orders."[15]

On the Union left flank, though, things were beginning to look up. After taking all morning to cross the Lower Bridge and three hours to prepare his assault, Burnside's attack began moving forward around 4:00 as a nearly unified force. Improving Federal prospects, his six large brigades extended well beyond the right of the five brigades of D. R. Jones's Confederate division defending Lee's right. Once again, as in the Cornfield, a race was on, though probably only General Lee and a very few of his senior officers really knew it. A. P. Hill had reported to Lee at his headquarters around 2:30 that his division was on its way from Harpers Ferry and from that moment on a contest existed between the speed of Burnside's attack and of the swiftness of Hill's men on the march. Whichever first reached its goal would win and, as in the Cornfield, the prize was no less than victory this day.

***

Jones's position along a ridge south of Sharpsburg provided the Confederate defense tactical depth and his artillery a long field of fire for slowing the advancing Yankees. Despite this barrage, Union troops swept up the gradually rising ground, eventually forcing Jones's line off the ridge in retreat. On Jones's left, men ran into Sharpsburg's streets and struggled to reform but even this bad situation couldn't compare to the situation on Jones's right. Drayton's and Kemper's Brigades fell back to the highest—and last—ridge below town. Along this ridge ran the Harpers Ferry Road—one of only two remaining routes Lee's army could take to Virginia and safety, as well as the road Hill's men would need to use in reaching the field. Within minutes, Toombs's Brigade, too, fell back to the final ridge as the Confederate right contracted and crumbled. But then, as if on cue, "up came Hill," and the situation south of town changed in an instant.

The 17-mile-march had wearied A. P. Hill's men, but they moved knowing the army's fate rested on their shoulders. Appearing unexpectedly on Burnside's now-exposed left flank, they moved directly into battle. Gregg's Brigade hit the green 16th Connecticut, which had been pushed out from the Union left, and as the 16th broke, it signaled a sea change. In almost an instant, the left of Burnside's advance stopped and men began falling back, stalling the entire attack to avoid exposing Burnside's entire line to a flanking attack. By sometime after 5:00 in the afternoon, Burnside's attack was over and with it closed the second phase of George McClellan's battle plan, successful in his eye or not.

***

McClellan's sole remaining prospect for victory now lay with the US Regulars of Porter's V Corps, holding the Union center at the Middle Bridge, and Pleasonton's cavalry. Though this portion of the field had been quiet most of the day, around 2:00 General Sykes reinforced his hold on the bridge and the position beyond it by ordering the 4th US Infantry's Captain Hiram Dryer to lead his regiment and the 14th US First Battalion across the creek, where he would assume command of all US Regular units west of the bridge. By 4:00—as Burnside's attack began within view to their left—the two Regular regiments discovered just how thinly held was the Confederate center. Captain Dryer's unordered move to attack this weakness was called off once it was discovered up the ranks and Pleasonton's plea to Fitz John Porter to provide infantry support for a cavalry attack was similarly stillborn.[16]

Sometime after 5:00, McClellan rode to the center to see the situation there and probably to determine if his battle plan's last phase—the main attack on the weakened Confederate center—should be launched. Between the positions of Taft's and Weed's Batteries, McClellan conferred with Generals Porter and Sykes, who respectively commanded the V Corps and the division of US Regulars which would make this final assault. At that moment, a note arrived from Captain Dryer, reporting the vulnerable state of the Confederate center; Sykes read the note before passing it to McClellan and Porter. What the three said wasn't recorded but Sykes later explained that "he remembered the circumstance very well and that he thought General McClellan was inclined to order in the Fifth Corps. But when he spoke of doing so, Porter said 'Remember, General! I command the last reserve of the last Army of the Republic.'" Regardless if Sykes meant to blame Porter for what happened next, history clearly records what George McClellan did.[17]

Through inaction McClellan called off the anticipated attack in the center, abandoning the battle plan he'd so determinedly clung to all day. The US Regulars would do nothing more to affect the battle's outcome and Union cavalry remained massed in the center, similarly unused. Although historians have repeatedly blamed Porter for McClellan's decision and growing caution—now bordering on command gridlock—it was McClellan alone who made this final decision. Porter's advice was simply that, which McClellan could have brushed aside. While Porter's cautious advice might have swayed McClellan at a critical moment, the lingering effects of visiting the Cornfield—seeing firsthand the battle's cost and the chaos now pervading his once-orderly plan—certainly also shook McClellan's confidence and probably contributed to his calling off this attack—just as he had earlier cancelled Franklin's attack to break the Confederate left. Regardless why, McClellan's decision doomed the battle of Antietam to being not the decisive battle of the war but, instead, just a major, bloody fight in a war full of costly fights. The men who had fought so hard and suffered so much had died in droves to make this battle matter, and when the moment of truth came, George McClellan denied them success.

Darkness covered the shattered remains of Sharpsburg's countryside and the fighting gradually sputtered to a painful, costly close. The struggle now shifted from one of armies and divisions maneuvering and killing to thousands of individual, personal battles as men fought simply to live—or, perhaps as often, to die and eternally gain the peace they'd been denied on September 17. These new fights centered on clinging to life, finding a friend or brother amid the hellish scene, or reaching a hospital to learn if fate called for the surrender of a limb or a life. Others sought only a drink of water to ease their suffering. A New Yorker, who spent the night amidst the battle's wreckage, recorded "The creeping dark of Sept. 17th, 1862 is now covering her vale over a horible scene. While thousands of Brave Heroes are at Rest. The Battlefield for miles is covered with Wounded Suffering and dieing groans of agony Help help Ephraim E. Brown Co C 64 N.Y.S.V the Lord have Mercy." Yet even amid such suffering and pain, many men were willing to endure this sacrifice as long as it made a difference, as long as it preserved the Union or led to Confederate independence. Only time would tell if they would get their wish.[18]

CHAPTER 15

"How Did They Remain and Live So Long?"

Men's shattered remains littered the ground from the North Woods to the fields south of Sharpsburg, but no place held more of these suffering, struggling forms than the Cornfield and its nearby ground. So searing was the horror of Antietam's aftermath that it burned into witnesses' consciousness, creating memories that refused to fade. The 2nd Massachusetts's Charles Morse remembered in 1892 that "In the morning of the day, the cornfield which is mentioned so prominently in all accounts of the battle, stood high with corn ready for the harvest, but before night it was level with the ground and thickly sprinkled with the dead of both armies." Writing his wife within days of the battle, the 23rd New York's Seymour Dexter could only say "The scene on the field of conflict is beyond description. In many places, the rebel dead were so thick that it seemed as through a battalion had laid down and never risen up."[1]

Though the two armies' soldiers differed on many issues—not least who won—one point upon which they agreed was the horrid sight dawn provided on September 18. A soldier in Kershaw's 2nd South Carolina wrote morning "broke with profound silence upon two exhausted armies and the sun scattered his bright rays over the vast heaps of the slain." Another 2nd veteran wrote "Around me are dead and wounded in horrid crowds," while the 21st Mississippi's Edward Burruss recalled there were "frequently places where for 50 or 60 yards you could step from one dead Yank to another & walk all over the ground without touching it with your foot." The 60th New York's John D. Stevens wrote in October of 1862 that "the battle on the 17th saw men fall in every direction … The bomb shells cut the tops of the trees right off. The limbs fell all around us and the pieces of shells. The next day the Rebels turned black as a nigger. We saw some without any head. Some without any arms. Some without any legs. Some shot through their guts. The battle was in the cornfield. There was a rebel to every corn hill. Their field was covered with Rebels and where we, we was, in the woods were covered with the Rebels and our men, too. And the ground was black with them. It took hard to see them lay there bleeding to death."[2]

What most impressed the 76th New York's Abram Smith was the contrast of Sharpsburg and the surrounding countryside before and after the battle. "Before the battle, the neighborhood in which it was fought, had been an interesting farming community. But a fortnight before, it had been dotted over with farm-houses filled with happy families, while the goddess of peace and plenty was about to fulfill with her golden promises. But how severely had this beautiful valley suffered. The houses and hungry soldiers had eaten up the cornfields and cereals. The fruit had been prematurely plucked. Every house, barn and outbuilding had been pierced by the shot and shells of the contending hosts; and now, the day after the battle, not a family remains in that recently so densely populated region. The little church standing by the roadside in an important position seems to have been the focal point where the wrath of the contending armies met, for a hundred cannon solid-shot have pierced it, while thousands of bullets have marred its sacred walls."[3]

John Whiteside, of Duryee's 105th New York, was viscerally scarred by the sight of the Cornfield the next day writing: "I availed myself of the earliest opportunity of going over the battle ground. Such a sight was too much for me. Others might pass by and see this sight with out being amased or overcome, but such a sight I never witnessed before and never want to do so again. Men lay in every shape and position, some places they lay piled across each other like fence rails. Others had their heads and necks twisted in different shapes, still others lay with one leg cocked up in the air and others with their hands twisted and turned in all shapes. Others had a ball in their fingers ready to load when they received the death bullet and when dead held it in the act of loading. Then to think of how they were shot, some had their heads blown off, others skulls broken and their brains dashed out, others faces shot off, others half their face gone, others blown to pieces. Oh! The sight of this battlefield makes my blood chill when I think of it."[4]

The 33rd New York's David Judd was scarred by the human suffering the battle caused, writing less than two years later, "One forgets the horrors of war in the roar of the artillery and shock of contending thousands, but when the field is afterwards surveyed, we realize how fearful, how terrible is the calamity. The falling back of the enemy left the battle-field of Antietam in our possession, with all its heart-rending and melancholy scenes. Scattered over a space of four miles, were men with uniforms of blue, and uniforms of gray, exhibiting all the fearful mutilations which the human body can suffer.

"Shot through the head, shot through the body, shot through the limbs, shot to the death, they lay stretched out together, wherever the surging to and fro of the contending armies had marked the line of battle. Approaching the field from the direction of Hagerstown, the first evidences of the conflict are seen, in a small grove [probably the North Woods] which had been cut to pieces by a hurricane of shot, and shell. Close by appears the debris of a once elegant farm house, literally shot down by our guns. Near the adjoining barn are several dead animals, killed in their stalls, or while grazing in the pastures. Advancing farther, the fences by the road-side are completely riddled with bullets. Here, for several moments, two contending regiments fought, divided from each other only by the width of the road, until both were nearly annihilated.

"Many, who fell forward on the fences, still remain in a standing posture, grasping in death the rails which had afforded them so frail a protection. Others lie stretched out upon the ground, fiercely clenching their muskets, and with countenances exhibiting all the savageness and ferocity which marks the warrior in the strife. Several of the wounded have crawled close into the fence corners to avoid the hot sun, or lain themselves out on a pallet of straw, gathered by their own hands from a stack close by. Of this number is a North Carolinian, who on being informed, as he is carried away to the hospital, that the wound is very severe, replies, "Cut off my leg, for, if you do not, I shall be exchanged…

"Farther on is a Federal soldier, who, though he has lost a leg, is consoling himself with the prospect of soon being in the bosom of his family. Alas for the poor New York boy lying near! No sight of home will ever greet him, for the death film already dims his eye, and the clammy sweat is gathering upon his brow.

"To the left and rear of this, is the corn-field through which … Sumner went to the relief of Hooker. The mangled corpses lie in heaps among the tall bare stalks, shorn of their leaves, as if by a hail storm. One long row of rebel dead lie in their outskirts of the field, almost as straight, and regular, as if they had fallen on dress parade. They were drawn up here to resist the charging party, who, reserving their fire until reaching the corn, then, discharged a volley, which bore down almost the whole line.

"Numerous are the evidences of the terribleness of our fire, when it was concentrated upon them, as the battle progressed. Dead cannoneers, dead infantrymen, and dead horses; exploded caissons, broken wheels, and fractured limbers; muskets, revolvers, and stilettos; round shot, sold shot and case shot, scattered promiscuously together! Could mortal live under such a concentrated fire? How did they remain and live so long?"[5]

Quickly burying the dead became both armies' top priority, seeking to limit the horrific sight and smell of rotting corpses. Some fallen were cared for by friends and relations who ventured onto the darkened field to bury relations, comrades, or beloved officers, sporadically creating makeshift "tombstones" to record their presence. Others—particularly Confederates left behind on the 19th—remained unburied for days, prompting Union surgeon Daniel Holt to recall that "the dead were almost wholly unburied, and the stench arising from it was such as to breed a pestilence." The 64th New York's Ephraim Brown participated in both burying the dead and looking for fallen friends, recording during the battle "William Wimple & I are Detailed to look after Our Dead. We took Ephraim Green … off under flag of truce & the Sharp Shooters whizzed 5 bullets at us … we then got Norman Foster William Fuller & John Orr & carried them back down the slope to a house & barn & buried them under a big apple tree … taking a good pine board from the barn & marking E Green inscription on & putting to his head." The next day, he added "today I was given detaile to burry the Dead Rebels ... 12 lengths of fence being counted off for my station & in 10 rods we have piled & buried 264." Burying the many horses, which had offered their own ultimate sacrifice for man's folly, added to the detail's challenges.[6]

Regardless how, most killed on the 17th were initially buried on the battlefield itself and D. R. Miller's property became home to many such graves. Several Southerners were buried within the Miller home's fences, while the West Woods and the farmyard abutting it became the site of 313 recorded graves. The Cornfield itself became the final resting place of at least 715 Confederates and Maryland's list of the dead recorded that even years after the battle some 18 trenches still "can all be seen, although the field has been plowed; buried shallow. Bones exposed in places; trappings, &c., can be seen." The Cornfield had become, in the truest sense, a cemetery.[7]

Many wounded on both sides spent an agonizing night of suffering and uncertainty on the field, unable to move and lost amidst the debris of battle. The 2nd Massachusetts's Lieutenant Colonel Wilder Dwight is probably typical of many that night, despite his life of privilege capped by a Harvard education. Dwight had begun writing his mother that morning, while waiting for Gordon's Brigade to go into battle, noting in careful penmanship "I write from the saddle to send you my love and to say that I am very well so far." Wounded by a ball that pierced his hip during fighting in the Cornfield, sometime later the colonel pulled out his unfinished letter. Staining the page with his blood, Wilder scrawled in sprawling, nearly unreadable script "Dearest Mother, I am wounded so as to be helpless. I think I die in victory. God defend our country. I trust in God and love you all to the last. Dearest love to father and my dear brothers. Our troops have left the part of the field where I lay." Wilder Dwight lingered for three days, dying Friday afternoon at Jacob Thomas's house in Sharpsburg.[8]

Those wounded who could move struggled to reach medical treatment. Typical of such experiences was that of the 31st Georgia's commander, Lieutenant Colonel John T. Crowder. Wounded early in the morning, while Lawton's Brigade had held the Cornfield, he was initially taken from the field and hidden behind a large rock to avoid his being hit by shells. When the brigade was driven toward the West Woods, the 31st's Lieutenant Judson Butts and Sergeant Sutton placed Crowder in a ravine behind the Dunker Church. As soon as the battle was over, the two raced back, finding Colonel Crowder weak from loss of blood. They next carried him to a road, flagging down a passing ambulance heading for the rear and a Confederate hospital. These two friends' efforts certainly saved their commander's life and Butts later wrote "There [the hospital] he struggled for a long time, just between life and death, but his wounds were at last healed and he was restored to his country."[9]

Another Confederate who made it to a field hospital was Private Ezra E. Stickley, Colonel Grigsby's orderly who had first wakened the Stonewall Brigade's men that morning. Barely had the battle begun when he was wounded by an artillery shell, nearly severing his right arm. Stickley made it to a nearby house—perhaps Alfred Poffenberger's—where surgeons stopped the bleeding long enough for him to stumble to a hospital in town where the surgeons removed his shattered right arm. Stickley spent the rest of the day hovering between life and death, before being moved by ambulance that evening to safety in the rear. Ezra Stickley never recorded if he saw any irony in the fact that he'd started the day troubled by the loss of a new right glove and, by nightfall, had lost his right arm as well.[10]

Corporal Austin Stearns of the 13th Massachusetts helped his friend Henry Gassett escape the maelstrom of the Cornfield to search for medical help. After resting for a time in the East Woods—Henry had been injured twice again, a flesh wound to his leg and a ball through his left shoulder—Stearns urged Gassett to gather his strength and continue on to the hospital. "[B]ut he, holding up his hand to shake, bade me good by and told me to save myself. I told him I would not go unless he went with me. He then said he would try." Advancing Rebel troops and the nearing sound of musket fire provided added incentive and off they headed. After much time, effort, and repeated rests, they reached medical help. "The hospital was only a field one at a farmhouse, where the Surgeons were to bind up the wounds before sending them farther away. I laid Henry in the front yard with a great many others and went to find a Surgeon or some of the boys, for I knew there must be several somewhere. I went up to the house and round to the back door but it was full of terribly wounded men, and finding some of our regiment there, I went back and out toward the barn and beyond to an immence straw stack; I found about a dozen of [Company] K men besides other from [the] regiment. Some had desperate wounds, and others were ministering to their wants as best they could. ... At the stack were Sergeants Greenwood shot through the shoulder, Fay through the arm. Cordwell hit on head with piece of shell. Corp'l Davenport through the foot, and Private Trask with a mortal wound in side and back by a piece of shell. I learned that Tom Gassett [older brother of Henry] and Hollis Holden were killed, Duke Wellington mortally wounded and left on the field, Cap't Hovey wounded and gone on with many others. ... I stayed with Henry two days and nights, taking the best care I could, and then I left for the regiment."[11]

One particularly inspiring such account of aiding a wounded man was recorded by the 13th New Jersey's Private Smith, who recalled that "A strong, sturdy-looking Reb was coming laboriously on with a Yank of no small proportions perched on his shoulders. Wonderingly I joined the group surrounding and accompanying them at every step, and then I learned why all this especial demonstration; why the Union soldiers cheered and again cheered this Confederate soldier, not because of the fact alone that he had brought into the hospital a sorely wounded Federal soldier, who must have died from hemorrhage had he been left on the field, but from the fact, that was palpable at a glance, that the Confederate too was wounded. He was totally blind; a Yankee bullet had passed directly across and destroyed both eyes, and the light for him had gone out forever. But on he marched, with his brother in misery perched on his sturdy shoulders. He would accept no assistance until his partner announced to him that they had reached their goal—the field hospital. It appears that they lay close together on the field, and after the roar of battle had been succeeded by that of a painfully intense silence that hangs over a hard-contested battle-field…" Later, Smith added "The groans of the wounded Yank reached the alert ears of his sightless Confederate neighbor, who called to him, asking him the nature and extent of his wounds. On learning the serious nature of them, he said 'Now, Yank, I can't see, or I'd get out of here mighty lively. Some darned Yank has shot away my eyes, but I feel otherwise as strong as ever. If you think you can get on my back and do the seeing, I will do the walking, and we'll sail into some hospital where we both can receive surgical treatment.' This programme had been followed and with complete success."[12]

Hospitals were welcome sights to the wounded, and the Army of the Potomac's Medical Director Jonathan Letterman had done his work well. Homes on the battlefield's edge—including D. R. Miller's barn, the Samuel Poffenberger farm (where Clara Barton labored), the Pry House, the Rohrbach home, Jacob Miller's farm, and the Hoffman buildings—served as aid stations and were crowded with wounded and dying men. Homes as far away as Keedysville, Smoketown, and Boonsboro received the overflow and worst cases for more lasting treatment. Nonetheless the 2nd Massachusetts's Charles Mills, who helped a wounded friend find a field hospital, recalled a sobering scene. "He was carried to an improvised hospital in a Barn [perhaps the Miller barn] where he was very soon attended upon by a Surgeon who relieved his anxiety as to the nature of his wounds and gave them all the dressing they needed. In this Barn he remained for two days surrounded by about two hundred wounded and dying men and with everything uncheerful and depressing, no officers whom he knew and but few of his men."[13]

Those remaining on the field between the lines that night would have gladly traded places with any man receiving hospital care, however bleak. The 1st Minnesota's Color Sergeant Sam Bloomer had spent the time since his wounding early in the West Woods fight with his back to a tree, praying that shells and flying splinters wouldn't finish off what having his knee blasted apart had started. Eventually a Rebel—who would turn out to be the 1st Georgia's First Sergeant W. H. Andrews—appeared who took pity on him. Andrews later wrote, I "wondered to myself if he was the color bearer I was so anxious to shoot in the first of the fight, Have no desire to harm him now. He is wounded and should do anything in my power to aid or assist him. Strange that while he was on his feet I would have killed him if I could, but now he is down at my mercy, have no animosity towards him." Andrews and his friends piled up cordwood around Bloomer, which the Minnesotan later recorded saved his life because "I have no doubt that more than a hundred bullets struck that barricade." Now, however, Bloomer was on his own and could do little more than pour water from his canteen onto his knee to keep clean his hideous wound. Remaining on the field until Thursday night, Confederates carried him to a barnyard where he remained another night. Next, he went to the hospital at the Hoffman farm were doctors amputated his leg on the 20th. Despite this suffering, Sam Bloomer survived and years later was reunited with Georgia's Sergeant Andrews, whose kindness had surely saved his life.[14]

Another such sufferer was the 15th Massachusetts's Sergeant Jonathan Stowe, wounded in the West Woods, who early on the 18th wrote in his diary "Misery acute, painful misery. How I suffered last night. It was the most painful of anything have ever experienced. My leg must be broken for I cannot help myself scarcely any. I remember talking and groaning all night. Many died in calling for help … Sgt. Johnson who lies on the other side of the log is calling for water. Carried off the field at 10 A.M. by the Rebs who show much kindness but devote much time to plundering the dead bodies of our men … Water very short. We suffer much." At midday, Stowe was taken to a field hospital at the Nicodemus house, where he lay with no treatment for a full day before being moved to one of the many Confederate field hospitals in Sharpsburg. There he laid in the house's yard under a rubber blanket as his only covering against the drizzle that fell that night. "Rebs retreat. Another painful night," he wrote on the 19th. As Union troops advanced into town Stowe and the other wounded—both Federal and Confederate—became the responsibility of Jonathan Letterman and his doctors. Moved indoors, the sergeant had his leg amputated and hung on until October 1, when he died. Those of both sides who shared Jonathan Stowe's fate, suffering the effects of horrific wounds for days without care, endured perhaps the greatest trials of all Antietam's thousands of casualties.[15]

Even those who had survived intact weren't free from such suffering and death. Not only would daylight likely bring more fighting, but dangers still stalked the fields around Sharpsburg like a specter, and in some cases in very much unexpected ways. The 13th New Jersey's Private Joseph Crowell counted himself lucky to have survived but found that duty still awaited and was sent with a group to guard some cattle, which were to be slaughtered for food in the morning. When not on guard duty, the men relaxed until their two-hour shift began. "We lighted a fire, cooked some coffee, and had a smoke before turning in for a rest. The conversation turned on the events of the day, and particularly on the death of Captain Irish. Then we began to talk about the wounded members of Company K. 'By the way,' said Browne, 'I got a little dose of it myself. Look at this.' He took off his cap and turned his face toward the camp fire. In the middle of his forehead there was a small round bruise, as if it had been hit with a stone. 'What is it?' I asked. 'I don't know. I think I must have been hit by a spent ball that bruised the skin without entering.' 'You're sure that it did not go into your brains?' I remarked laughingly. I had no more idea of such a thing than Curt did. 'No!' he answered good-naturedly. 'My brains are not as soft as that.' 'Does it hurt?' I asked. 'Not a bit,' was the answer, 'It is nothing—not worth talking about.' And none of us thought at the time that it was. Yet at that very moment there was a one-ounce bullet imbedded in Curt Browne's brain that afterward caused his death. He remained with the regiment for some days and then his head began to pain him so badly that he had to be sent to the hospital. He grew worse, but slowly, and he actually lived until the following March, when he died from the effects of the wound which was at first supposed by all to be so trivial." How many other such latent wounds lurked in the darkness that closed the horror of September 17?[16]

Those on both sides of the Cornfield who survived physically unhurt spent the night doing what soldiers do after battle, sleeping, resting, eating, struggling within their minds and with God about what had happened this day, and waiting to be told what to do next. Like many of his comrades, the 2nd South Carolina's Robert Shand decided to do a little shoe shopping, recalling "Early Thursday morning I went out among the Yankee dead to get a pair of shoes. I picked out my size and was in the act of removing them from his feet, when he opened his eyes and said 'Can't you wait until I'm dead?' I replied that I really thought he was dead and that even then I would not have disturbed him but for the fact that I was barefooted. I gave him water, and passed on; it was all I could do. I got my shoes from another, first making sure he was dead." Such efforts reflected that nearly everyone, North and South, expected the battle would be renewed on the 18th, sometime, somehow…[17]

***

McClellan spent the 17th's closing hours weighing his options. "The night … presented serious questions," he reported, "the morning brought with it grave responsibilities. To renew the attack again on the 18th or to defer it, with the chance of the enemy's retirement after a day of suspense, were the questions before me. A careful and anxious survey of the conditions of my command, and with the knowledge of the enemy's forces and position, failed to impress me with any reasonable certainty of success if I renewed the attack without re-enforcing columns. A view of the shattered state of some of the corps sufficed to deter me from pressing them into immediate action, and I felt that my duty to the army and the country forbade the risks involved in a hasty movement which might result in the loss of what had been gained the previous day."[18]

McClellan's "survey" ride once again took him to the Union right and the Cornfield, where he encountered General Franklin, who hadn't given up on launching an attack. "When General McClellan visited the right in the afternoon I showed him a position on the right of … [the West Wood]," recalled Franklin, "which I thought commanded the wood, and that if it could be taken we could drive the enemy from the wood by merely holding this point. I advised that we should make the attack on that place the next morning from General Sumner's position. I thought there was no doubt about our being able to carry it. We had plenty of artillery bearing upon it. We drove the enemy from there that afternoon, and I had no doubt that we would take that place the next morning, and I thought that would uncover the whole left of the enemy." Franklin was proposing to seize then-unoccupied Nicodemus Heights as an anchor for attacking Lee's left with his VI Corps; a variation of his earlier plan. Once again, it was the Union's possession of the Cornfield and its surrounding fields that made contemplating such an attack feasible in the first place—if McClellan would approve it.[19]

As night fell on the 17th, Franklin apparently believed McClellan had approved his plan. McClellan perhaps had even prepared groundwork for this attack, sending IV Corps division commander Major General Couch a message at midnight directing "march with your command to-morrow morning in time to report with it to Major General Franklin as soon after daylight as you can possibly do. Franklin is on the left of General Sumner." Franklin's attack, however, was never to be. Franklin later explained "I did not hear the direct reason of the General Commanding, but I have understood that the reason was that he expected some fifteen thousand new troops; those which would make the thing a certain thing, and he preferred to wait to make this attack on the right until these new troops came." McClellan offered a similar explanation; "I awaited the arrival of my re-enforcements … Of the re-enforcements, Couch's Division, although marching with commendable rapidity, was not in position until late in the morning; and Humphreys's Division of new troops, fatigued with forced marches, were arriving throughout the day, but were not available until near its close. Large re-enforcements from Pennsylvania, which were expected during the day, did not arrive at all." McClellan also cited artillery shortages to explain his inaction; "A large number of our heaviest and most efficient batteries had consumed all their ammunition on the 16th and 17th, and it was impossible to supply them until late on the following day."[20]

Although these undoubtedly were concerns, in all likelihood McClellan had independently decided against a "hasty" attack or any assault at all, because the tactical situation on the 18th was a fundamentally new reality that required a similarly new battle plan. Creating this required several hours or days of thoughtful consideration because George McClellan couldn't create plans on the fly; lacking adequate time to prepare and plan in the way that his mind required, McClellan probably never seriously considered Franklin's proposal. Instead of risking another attack, McClellan had reason to hope Lee and his army would simply slip away, leaving him the ground and a Maryland free of Confederate invaders. Rather than developing a new plan and preparing another assault, McClellan began stalling, slow-rolling his and his army's actions in order to give Lee time to leave—a departure that would ensure a Union victory.

McClellan's actions and writings on the 18th and 19th suggest this was so. At 8:00 in the morning of the 18th, he wrote General Halleck to highlight Antietam's gains, explain the current situation, and vaguely pledge "the battle probably will be renewed today. Send all the troops you can by the most expeditious route." The next day at 8:30, McClellan again wrote Halleck; "But little occurred yesterday except skirmishing, we being fully occupied in replenishing ammunition, taking care of the wounded, etc. Last night the enemy abandoned his position leaving his dead & wounded on the field. We are again in pursuit. I do not know whether he is falling back to an interior position or crossing the river. We may safely claim a complete victory." Gone from this second message was any suggestion of attack beyond promised "pursuit." By 10:30 on the 19th, McClellan claimed to Halleck "Pleasonton is driving the enemy across the river. Our victory was complete. The enemy is driven back into Virginia. Maryland and Pennsylvania are now safe." Despite implying his cavalry was pressing the enemy's retreat, McClellan had no intention of risking major battle again. Once aware Lee was retreating to escape rather than to fight—Confederates felled trees behind them to impede Federal pursuit—McClellan continued dragging his heels to ensure "complete victory" without battle, directing Porter sometime after noon to "mass [your] troops in readiness to move in any direction." Such tepid, vague orders reflect that McClellan was content with the "victory enough" of Lee's retreat.[21]

***

Lee, too, during the long night after the battle, weighed his next moves and what McClellan might be planning. "On the 18th we occupied the position of the preceding day, except in the center," he wrote "where our line was drawn in about 200 yards. Our ranks were increased by the arrival of a number of troops, who had not been engaged the day before and, though still too weak to assume the offensive, we awaited without apprehension the renewal of the attack." Lee clearly states he had no intention of attacking on the 18th; nonetheless, his report is dated August 19, 1863—nearly a year after Antietam—and may represent what actually happened, rather than Lee's thinking in the predawn hours of September 18.[22]

Another account, however, suggests Lee remained focused on somehow attacking that morning. Colonel S. D. Lee claimed in a manuscript written years after the war that early on the 18th General Lee sent him riding left, to report to Jackson in his field headquarters and provide artillery support for an attack Jackson's infantry was to launch against the Federal right in the Cornfield area. Riding together to the base of Nicodemus Heights, Jackson explained General Lee's intention.

"I wish you to take fifty pieces of artillery and crush that force which is the Federal right," directed Jackson, "Can you do it?" Although apparently unsure what Jackson was after, Colonel Lee well knew how to play this game. "Yes, General," was his enthusiastic reply, "Where will I get the fifty guns?" "How many do you have?" Jackson responded. Lee relied honestly; "About twelve out of the thirty I carried into action yesterday. My losses in men, horses and carriages have been great." Jackson's reply suggested 50 guns could be scrounged from various units in the field, prompting Lee to respond, "Shall I go after the guns?" Jackson shot back "No, not yet, Colonel Lee, can you crush the Federal right with 50 guns?"

The conversation's turn apparently caught Lee off guard. A quick glance across the Hagerstown Pike to the massive VI Corps presence centered on the Cornfield would answer the question but Lee had to say something. His reply was a masterwork of blended reality and expected military optimism. "General, I can try. I can do it if anyone can."

"That is not what I asked you, sir," replied Jackson. "If I give you 50 guns, can you crush the Federal right?" Both men knew artillery alone wasn't up to that task, being something only infantry could achieve.

Lee was being backed into a corner and running out of options. "General," he replied, "you seem to be more intent upon my giving you my technical opinion as an artillery officer, than my going after the guns and making the attempt."

"Yes, sir," Jackson countered, "and I want your positive opinion, yes or no."

Lee was trapped by the facts before his eyes and Jackson's skillful wordplay. There was nowhere left to run. "General, it cannot be done with 50 guns and the troops you have here." There. It was done. He could say nothing else. But was reality what General Jackson wanted?

"Let us ride back, Colonel," was Stonewall's only reply.

Lee's mind was troubled. Jackson had backed him into being the first to flinch and Lee knew that while this might help Jackson, it could only hurt him. He had to say something. "General, you forced me to say what I did unwillingly. If you give the fifty guns to any other artillery officer, I am ruined for life. I promise you that I will fight the guns to the last extremity, if you will only let me command them."

"It is all right, Colonel," Jackson reassured, "everybody knows that you are a brave officer and would fight the guns well. Go to General Lee and tell him what has occurred since you reported to me. Describe our ride to the hill, your examination of the Federal position, and my conversation about your crushing the Federal right with fifty guns, and my forcing you to give your opinion." Jackson had considered this all late on the 17th and knew the Confederate army was no more able now to carry out that attack than it had been yesterday. Colonel Lee had been set up and all he could do was hope General Lee would see through this bit of military theater.

Reporting to General Lee apparently had the effect both Jackson and Colonel Lee desired because the Confederate commander replied calmly, "Colonel, go and join your command."[23]

Colonel Lee's story remains in dispute, despite its first-hand provenance, but possibly both Lees's accounts are accurate. Colonel Lee's version tracks with the general's plan from late on the 17th, which Jackson and Stuart failed to implement for reasons General Lee still might not have understood even the next day. General Lee's September 21 letter to President Davis, written after crossing back into Virginia, in fact hints Lee might have sought the offensive early on the 18th. After explaining the army's rough condition, Lee states "it is still my desire to threaten a passage into Maryland, to occupy the enemy on this frontier, and, if my purpose cannot be accomplished, to draw them into the Valley, where I can attack to advantage." If after Antietam's losses and retreating to Virginia, Lee still sought to keep alive his Maryland Campaign, then attacking McClellan's right flank in the Cornfield early on September 18th might well have entered the Confederate general's thinking, if only fleetingly.[24]

Regardless, there would be no Confederate attack on the 18th. Orders directed the Confederate army to move after dark, west from Sharpsburg to cross at the Shepherdstown Ford into Virginia. Rain aided the night-time march, muffling the retreating army's sounds, and by morning, Lee and his men were gone. McClellan pressed forward a cautious cavalry and infantry probe only after 10:30 that next morning. McClellan's manufactured caution was unnecessary, however. The last gasp of Lee's Maryland Campaign was a small but sharp battle between Lee's rear, blocking forces under Brigadier General William Nelson Pendleton—though A. P. Hill directed the fighting— and elements of the First Division of Fitz John Porter's V Corps on September 19th and 20th. By contesting the Potomac crossing site, the battle of Shepherdstown bought Lee time to gather his scattered and battered army in Virginia, moving away in some order to fight another day. And this they would do in spades for nearly three more years.[25]

***

As Lee's weary army slogged its way deeper into Virginia and McClellan's men returned to camps on Antietam's banks, the battle's human cost was on nearly everyone's mind. Both Union and Confederate veterans of Antietam's horrors wrestled with the experience they'd just endured and adjusted to the loss of friends, brothers, and messmates. The first sense of how costly the fighting on September 17 had been began forming only hours after battle as clerks throughout each army conducted their routine paperwork, compiling muster rolls that recorded men who would never return. Loss totals wouldn't be fully aggregated until the quarterly collection of names and numbers of the deceased passed up the command chain to plan for coming food and equipment needs, rather to notify families or to mourn the fallen. When complete, this count revealed Antietam's fearful cost. The Union had accrued 12,401 casualties in driving Lee's army from Maryland. A total of 2,108 of these were killed outright, of 55,956 soldiers actually engaged in the fighting, representing 20 percent loses for the Union. Lee's foray into Maryland cost the Confederacy 9,298 casualties, of which 1,546 had been killed, costing Lee 25 percent of his army of 37,351. For the Union, Antietam was the costliest battle of the war to date; for the Confederacy, only the Seven Days fight cost more lives (even so, that rate was a lower percentage of overall troops engaged, a "mere" 21 percent).[26]

The cost to several individual regiments, too, was almost beyond understanding. Not surprisingly, the two regiments which paid the greatest price at Antietam both fought in the Cornfield. The 12th Massachusetts from Hartsuff's Brigade of Ricketts's I Corps division lost 46 killed, 165 wounded, and 10 missing of the 334 men who marched into the Cornfield; a 64 percent casualty rate. From the Confederacy, it was the 1st Texas of Wofford's Brigade, in Hood's Division, which paid the dearest price; of 211 soldiers who'd assembled at dawn, 50 were killed and 132 wounded, amounting to a stunning 82 percent casualty rate. This fact earns the hard-fighting Texans the "honor" of having paid the greatest human cost of any regiment—on either side—in a single battle during the entire war.[27]

America lost 3,654 men killed outright that single day and suffered 20,946 casualties on both sides, making September 17, 1862 the single bloodiest day in American history. As horrific as those numbers seem, most historians agree they remain too low, particularly of the total who gave their lives. Army accounting practices ensured that wounded men who lingered for weeks beyond the battle or who were moved to regional hospitals but later died of their wounds were never counted among Antietam's losses. Those who survived and lived into old age, but later died from their Antietam wounds were never counted in the battle's total, despite being victims as surely as if they'd dropped amidst D. R. Miller's shattered corn. Even with this skew in place, one quarter of Antietam's wounded died from their injuries. With such a costly butcher's bill Americans—then and now—are entitled to ask if this battle had to be fought and, if so, what did the Union or Confederacy secure in return? Did the sacrifice of lives attain anything but death and loss, and why, in God's name, did the price have to be this high?[28]

***

Antietam cost Lee and the South dearly, and the sad fact is that in the end they simply had nothing to show for it. Lee achieved none of the objectives set at the Maryland Campaign's start to advance either of the Confederacy's two tracks to independence. Despite Lee's claim to Davis immediately after Antietam that the battle ended with the Army of Northern Virginia "maintaining the ground," in truth nothing could hide the fact that this battle was not the decisive Confederate victory on Northern soil both leaders had wanted. No tactical draw would prompt Northern governors to demand President Lincoln end the conflict or to refuse sending more men to support Lincoln's war. Similarly, a stalemate wouldn't enrage Northern people or cause an uprising to force their governments, at any level, to stop the war. Only New York's largely impoverished Irish community, outraged by the Irish Brigade's casualties at the Sunken Road, openly opposed continuing the war in response to Antietam. Being socially and physically isolated from the general Union population, though, their outrage simply didn't resonate with most Americans. Lee's retreat into Virginia also meant his army wouldn't spend the winter in the North draining Yankee food and forage. Shenandoah Valley farmers would have to harvest and transport their crops despite the ever-looming threat of Federal troops again descending to deny food to Richmond and the Confederate army.[29]

Most importantly, this military draw wasn't the decisive battlefield victory needed to convince England or France to risk their own interests supporting the South by intervening in the war. Lee didn't need any news from Europe or the Northern papers to understand this. That would come later; President Davis acknowledged in 1863 that "In the course of this war our eyes have often been turned abroad...We have expected sometimes recognition, and sometimes intervention, at the hands of foreign nations; and we had a right to expect it ... but this I say: 'Put not your trust in princes,' and rest not your hopes on foreign nations. This war is ours; we must fight it out ourselves. And I feel some pride in knowing that, so far, we have done it without the good will of anybody." Though Confederate ministers in Europe continued working to secure recognition and intervention, it had become a fools' errand. The Southern failure at Antietam ensured there would be no "Confederate Saratoga;" that fact and the strategic impact of Lincoln's Emancipation Proclamation forever closed the door to foreign intervention. The only strategy left Richmond was to fight on, raising the North's cost of continuing the war to such levels that Northern governors and growing segments of an unhappy public would become the South's unknowing ally and new hope for a negotiated peace and independence. If this single-track strategy didn't work, the Confederacy faced nothing but failure ahead. Though few could really see it in late September 1862, after Antietam the writing was on the wall for the South.[30]

These strategic setbacks were bad enough, but worse for Lee was that Antietam had gained the South nothing of lasting military value, at the cost of nearly a quarter of his army. Such losses even in 1862 were straining the South's limited manpower pool needed to support the army. Only two weeks before, at the second battle of Manassas and at Chantilly, Lee had used up 18 percent of his army, all on the heels of expending 15 to 20 percent driving McClellan from before Richmond and off Virginia's peninsula. More men would, of course, fill the ranks—willingly or not—but the quality and dedication of these newer men never equaled the fighting spirit and skill of those who answered the South's call in 1861 and early 1862. Gone forever, too, were some of the best officers—like General Starke and Colonel Douglass—who led by example, willing to expose themselves to danger to get the job done. The Yankees faced these same problems, but the North had a larger population on which to draw and ports in New York, Boston, and Philadelphia were flooding with immigrants from Europe nearly each day. Thanks to the Union Navy's blockade, the

South had no such immigrant tide, further thinning Richmond's manpower pool ahead of the next battle.

The Union also had obtained little of immediate military value, really only two gains to show for its 11,648 casualties. The first, winnowing the opponent's ranks, was already being felt by Lee and was probably not at all appreciated by General McClellan and most other Northern leaders. Though eventually grinding down the South's manpower resources and ability to wage war would become the centerpiece of Northern war strategy, in late 1862 it was simply not an objective or seen as an important measure of military success. McClellan so little appreciated this that he never mentioned the human cost extracted from Lee at Antietam as a sign of success. Even in his 1887 memoir *McClellan's Own Story*—published long after Grant made wearing down the South's resource base central to his winning military strategy—McClellan failed to point out how many Confederates his Antietam battle had killed or removed from the war. This oversight is perhaps the last indication from the battle of Antietam of just how limited and linear George McClellan's operational thinking was.

Antietam's only other military gain McClellan could rightly claim was driving Lee's army from the North; a point he made early and often in spinning the result with Washington officials and the Northern public. McClellan's first report—penned on October 15, 1862—appears designed to record exactly what had happened at Antietam and why. "In the beginning of the month of September the safety of the National Capital was seriously endangered by the presence of a victorious enemy, who soon crossed into Maryland and then directly threatened Washington and Baltimore, while they occupied the soil of a loyal State and threatened an invasion of Pennsylvania. The army of the Union, inferior in numbers, wearied by long marches, deficient in various supplies, worn out by various battles, the last of which had not been successful, first covered by its movements the important cities of Washington and Baltimore, then boldly attacked the victorious enemy in their chosen strong position and drove them back, with all their superiority of numbers, into the State of Virginia, thus saving the loyal States from invasion…" Despite some outright lies and considerable misleading hyperbole in this explanation, McClellan was nonetheless largely correct; he and the Army of the Potomac had forced Lee and his enemy army back across the river, removing this threat from Union soil. This success, however, was quickly lost in a storm of criticism over McClellan's failure to pursue Lee's retreating, wounded army, letting it escape to fight another day. Compounding this error, McClellan chose to rest the Army of the Potomac on the Antietam battlefield for weeks, allowing Lee's army to recover unmolested. Not until October 26 would McClellan finally start his army south after the Confederates. Remaining so on the Maryland battlefield suggests McClellan was trying to remind Washington and the public that he and his army were the victors at Antietam because they alone held the ground. If this was McClellan's goal, he failed miserably.[31]

So great was the sense of failure hounding McClellan that he eventually found a scapegoat in Ambrose Burnside, who replaced him in command on November 7. As McClellan argued until his death, if Antietam hadn't lived up to expectations, it was because Burnside failed to press the attack on the afternoon of the battle. First officially noted in McClellan's second Official Report, written on August 4, 1863, Burnside's own massive failure commanding the army at the disastrous battle of Fredericksburg in December 1862 probably added credibility to McClellan's 1863 charges. That McClellan's post-war discourse on Antietam focused not on highlighting its success but rather on laying blame, suggests even George McClellan knew in his heart that, for its cost, Antietam should have bought the Union more than just driving Lee's army from Maryland.[32]

Ironically, it was exactly this military "success" Lincoln seized on to justify issuing his preliminary Emancipation Proclamation on September 22. As Lincoln explained at a cabinet meeting that day "The action of the army against the rebels has not been quite what I should have liked. But they have been driven out of Maryland, and Pennsylvania is no longer in danger of invasion." Antietam wasn't the victory Lincoln hoped for, but it was victory enough and with the stroke of a pen Lincoln did what George McClellan had failed to do—he fundamentally changed the war to the Union's advantage. No longer would the war seek only to end rebellion, it was now a war of liberation and freedom. The war would no longer seek to preserve the Union as it was, but rather restore the Union in order to transform that nation into something new and better. Lincoln's risky political act was a strategic masterstroke that made Antietam the springboard for permanently blocking one of the South's two-track paths to independence; by recasting the war as a fight for freedom, Lincoln forever shut the door to European intervention. Although initially sympathetic, British officials haughtily dismissed the Proclamation and stepped up efforts to intervene, but such moves were doomed. As the January 1, 1863 enactment date neared, growing numbers of working-class Britons took to the street cheering the prospect of slavery's end, making it simply impossible for London to move ahead with intervention on the South's behalf. By changing the war's nature and meeting a vital strategic goal, it was President Lincoln, not General McClellan, who redeemed the sacrifice of nearly 12,000 Union casualties who fell at Antietam.[33]

Lincoln's Proclamation and the battle's strategic implications aside, Antietam's military result had failed to live up to the expectations of both North and South. Like Lee, McClellan had to admit that the battle ended in stalemate, writing on October 15, 1863 that "We had attacked the enemy in position, driven them from their line on one flank and secured a footing within it on the other. Our forces slept that night conquerors on a field won by their valor and covered with the dead and wounded of the enemy." Despite his closing assertions, this is hardly the crowing of an undisputed war champion. In fact, both sides had expended tremendous resources—mostly human lives—that resulted in little more than marginal adjustments to their lines.

Both had failed to achieve measurable tactical gains at Antietam that could translate into strategic victory—but why?[34]

***

For the South, responsibility for this tactical failure rests on what was otherwise its greatest military asset, Lee and his senior command staff. Lee's first mistake made at Antietam occurred when he decided to stay and fight in Maryland in the first place. By countermanding the orders for McLaws to ready a return to Virginia—brought on by Jackson's unexpected Harpers Ferry success—he took a tremendous roll of the dice for his military prospects and the fate of his new nation. This was just the sort of risk Robert E. Lee excelled at taking; he'd done it before and would do it again. But Antietam's result proved he'd lost, and the Confederacy's cost for that miscalculation was exceptionally high. In retrospect, Lee probably would have been better served by following conventional military wisdom and taking the safer bet, returning to Virginia to re-enter Maryland and fight another day in another place. For once, Lee might have considered doing what George McClellan most likely would have done were their positions reversed, for it was probably a surer path to victory than the one he ultimately chose. Still, the decision to stay and fight only proved a poor choice because Lee and the South paid a proportionally higher cost for the battle of Antietam than did their enemy. Lee and his army had won when facing worse odds, so why did the Confederate performance at Antietam fall so short that it exposed the folly of Lee's decision to fight at all?

Having determined to fight, the South's military failure was chiefly caused by its inability to take the offensive, particularly in exploiting the various counterattacks launched during the day. Lee and his army had brilliantly executed the defensive part of Lee's plan, repeatedly fending off Yankee attacks though outnumbered, outgunned, and with their ability to use terrain constrained by having to remain largely static and on the defense. Nimbly shifting to the offensive was important because simply stopping Union attacks alone wasn't what Lee or anyone else believed would secure the decisive military victory the South needed from a battle in Maryland. Such strategic success could only come from a decisive win brought about by the Southern army on the offensive. This was probably why Lee sought late in the day to launch a coordinated attack on the Union's right flank—in the Cornfield and beyond the North Woods—using Stuart's cavalry/artillery and Jackson's infantry. Securing an offensive victory also probably explains why Lee would have wanted to attack early on September 18; the stillborn effort that Stonewall Jackson had opposed.

Although the South had numerous opportunities throughout the day to assume the offensive, chiefly in the Cornfield and its nearby ground, Confederate commanders never utilized any of these various counterattacks for that purpose. Advances or counterattacks by Lawton's and Hays's Brigades, by Hood's Division, by Ripley's

Brigade, by Colquitt's Brigade, by Garland's Brigade, by McLaws's Division, by Kershaw's Brigade, by Ransom's Brigade, and by Stuart's cavalry and artillery—as well as those Confederate strikes against Union troops in the Sunken Road and south of Sharpsburg, too—each came and went without senior commanders putting the wider Southern army on an offensive footing. Even those attacks possessing offensive momentum—like Hood's and McLaws's—quickly lost steam and stopped, not just for lack of possible reinforcements but because no one in authority provided the support needed to turn these opportunities into a serious offensive. Although in many previous battles the South's many aggressive, skilled battlefield commanders had exploited such opportunities to attack and achieve victory, neither Jackson, Longstreet, Hill, McLaws, Early, or any of the other senior officers at the division level and higher did so at Antietam. The cost of this inaction was that with each such missed opportunity the South remained on the defense, allowing the Union to regroup and attack again, and requiring the sacrifice of more and more Southern lives.

In all likelihood, however, senior Confederate officers failed to act because they were following General Lee's strategic intent. Lee deliberately adopted a defensive posture early on and he alone would decide if and when to shift to offensive operations. Because Lee apparently did not intend for his army to assume the offense during most of the battle—probably hoping McClellan would wear out and weaken his army—Jackson and other senior officers had no choice but to forego these repeated opportunities to genuinely attack, doing so simply did not align with Lee's strategic intent. When Lee finally tried to make this shift, it became apparent that defending the Cornfield and its nearby ground had cost the South too dearly, making a major attack so late in the day simply impossible. Although Confederate manpower and other resource limitations may have doomed this approach from the start, Lee had waited too long in seeking the offensive and it had cost the South any hope of military victory.

***

If McClellan could claim tactical victory because his army alone ultimately held the field, the Union nonetheless had missed a tremendous opportunity. With Lee and his army trapped in a vulnerable position, achieving decisive victory offered McClellan opportunity to fundamentally change the war's terms, if not end it right then and there between Antietam Creek and the Potomac River. After all, most historians agree that throughout the war the vitality and success of Lee's Army of Northern Virginia breathed life into an increasingly politically divided, economically isolated and morale-deficient Confederacy, keeping the Confederacy alive long after it might have otherwise collapsed. McClellan had the opportunity to make Antietam the war's pivotal turning point, sparing thousands of lives sacrificed to achieve in 1865 the same result possible in 1862—the Union preserved, the South defeated.

But this was not to be because the Union, too, failed to achieve most of its tactical goals at Antietam.

As architect of the Union's battle plan and one of the very few men able to guide or change its direction, General McClellan certainly bears the lion's share of responsibility for the Union failing to secure anything more of military value at Antietam. Although his many actions, inactions, and decisions made during the battle might seem to be triggers of this result, the factor most responsible is one McClellan probably didn't fully appreciate—that his innate mindset prevented him from successfully leading men to victory in the unpredictable, swirling ebb of battle. The impact of this cocktail of personal traits—his derivative and deductive mind, his excessive stubbornness, and his linear decision-making style—on McClellan's leadership chiefly explains why he failed to manage the Antietam fight to a successful end. Although excessive caution, political ambition, lacking or inaccurate intelligence, an overly ambitious plan, or incompetent or disloyal subordinates may have played a role, none of these factors had the fundamental impact on McClellan's leadership in battle that his innate mindset did. The general probably understood on some level his own mind, which explains why he had previously avoided personally directing an unfolding battle. Why he chose to personally plan and execute this particular battle may never be known, although pressure from Washington and his own ambition and ego may explain it. George McClellan shouldn't be criticized for facts of existence he couldn't control; the innate traits of the working of his mind. But McClellan put himself in a position that let those traits influence the course of a great battle, which required men to sacrifice their lives under his unable leadership, and for this, he can and should be held to account.

Even so, McClellan gave major tactical decision-making authority to his hand-picked subordinates and because he was incapable of such "leadership under fire," any hope for Union victory rested on their abilities and actions. Unfortunately for Federal prospects, McClellan's subordinates failed him early and often at Antietam. Hooker's inability to successfully oversee such a large, complicated assault and to quickly adapt to changed circumstances—foreshadowing his own shortcomings, exposed eight months later at the battle of Chancellorsville—cost the Union dearly and set the stage for failure. Other Union generals' command shortcomings, similarly, if in lesser ways, prevented Union success. Sumner's failure to fully utilize the depth offered by the Cornfield in executing and supporting the West Woods attack was the other most notable such failure. Mansfield, Williams, Franklin, and others of lesser rank also fell short, though in ways that did less harm to the Union's prospects for victory. McClellan's willingness to devolve decision-making authority might have empowered his subordinates and enabled success, but his disconnected, distant—both physical and operational—approach to managing the battle too often left his subordinates to guess if their actions worked in concert

266 • THE CORNFIELD

with McClellan's wider battle plan. Their failure simply compounded Union shortcomings at Antietam.

Nowhere was the impact of McClellan's command limitations—particularly his linear mindset—more evident or devastating to Union prospects than in and around the Cornfield. Despite the high cost, fighting there had succeeded in a way and was just good enough to meet McClellan's original goal for the opening attack. Union forces there had at several points managed to draw Confederate troops away from the center, had cost the South dearly in manpower, had caused the Confederate left to contract, had brought Union troops to the doorstep of Lee's main line, and had offered the Union control of high ground on Nicodemus Heights on which to place Federal artillery—all these developments resulting from Union actions in and around the Cornfield could have been built upon or exploited to achieve military success for the North at Antietam. This was what Lee or Grant would likely have seen, had they been in his place, but not General McClellan. Because the result didn't match his preconceived concept of success—breaking Lee's line and putting Union troops on the Dunker Church ridge—in the general's limited, linear mindset, Union action on the right appeared to have failed. Once finally personally engaged and aware of the battle's course, McClellan tried repeatedly to make the battle situation meet his own preconditions, never adapting to meet and exploit the battle's state as it was to achieve his goals. This failed approach required McClellan to spend over half his available forces to take one objective, which stuck the Union plan in place for hours at the cost of thousands of lives.

***

Military failure at Antietam for both North and South understandably came at the epicenter of the costliest fighting of the battle, that which occurred in and around the Cornfield. This ground had barely figured in the Union's initial tactical planning; to the extent it was considered at all by Federal leaders, Miller's Cornfield was nothing more than ground over which Union troops would pass to reach their objective—the Confederate position around the Dunker Church. It was Confederate General Jackson who first made the Cornfield matter by putting Southern brigades there out front of his main line, establishing extra fighting room—tactical depth, as modern military analysts term it—in which to slow any Yankee attack on troops near the Dunker Church.

Although historians have traditionally viewed the Cornfield fight as a limited, distinct event—a series of intense, back-and-forth early morning actions amidst the corn—what happened in Miller's Cornfield affected the fighting well beyond this place and time. The effects of the Cornfield fight became inherently interconnected to Antietam's wider course and outcome, influencing nearby actions in the East Woods, West Woods, and elsewhere to determine the Union's or Confederacy's ability to meet their strategic goals for fighting at Antietam in the first place. Further cementing the interrelation of the Cornfield, the East Woods, the West Woods, and the various fields between and around them is that all these locations were part of D. R. Miller's farm, suggesting Antietam's morning's actions might well be best named "The Fight for Miller's Farm."

The tenacious Confederate hold on the Cornfield not only stalled McClellan's plan and fixed the morning's fighting there, but eventual Union control of the Cornfield and the adjacent ground also enabled Sumner's assault on the West Woods that nearly broke Lee's line; made possible the advance of Greene's Division that seized the Dunker Church and nearly severed Lee's position; allowed Franklin's VI Corps to deploy for a potentially decisive attack; blunted repeated, if disjointed, Confederate counterattacks throughout the day; and prevented Lee from putting his army on the offense late in the day. Had Miller's Cornfield remained in Southern hands, none of these actions could have occurred as they did, and the battle's outcome might have been very different.

It was in the Cornfield itself that Union attackers encountered their first and most ferocious opposition, where they had to expend the most life to move toward reaching their first military objective. Reinforced by McClellan's linear determination to succeed there, as the fighting flowed and expanded throughout the day on the Union right/Confederate left it never spread far beyond D. R. Miller's deadly field. The numbers, too, tell of the central role the Cornfield and the fights that it spawned played in determining Antietam's outcome. Of the 9,298 men Lee lost at Antietam, roughly 7,000 fell in fighting in or around the Cornfield. McClellan, too, lost most of his men sacrificed at Antietam in fighting around the Cornfield, some 9,913 of his total 12,401 battle casualties. Both Lee and McClellan lost nearly two thirds of their armies in fighting around the Cornfield and this singular focus dimmed any hope—both in reality and in one general's mind—of succeeding on any other part of the field at Antietam. The struggle for the Cornfield and its related fights had simply bled both armies dry.

One month after the battle, the 97th New York's chaplain John Ferguson visited the Cornfield once again, recalling "evidence of terrible work was visible on the trees, fences & everything was pieced with balls & bullets & every house in Sharpsburg is pierced with cannon balls & shells. On the field are caps & clothes of all kinds pierced torn & bloody & near a cornfield in a lane this ground is still covered with blood pools dried on the hard path where they fell & laid in heaps..."[35]

Today, a visitor to D. R. Miller's Cornfield can walk once more over its subtle rises and soft earth, and as it has been since the first settlers cleared the land, this place is a farm field. Though today it is more often planted in grass, soybeans, or some other crop David Miller might never have heard of, periodically it once again is covered by tall, thick green cornstalks that rise over the heads of most who venture there. On a mid-September day, you can walk through the rows, smelling the pungent scent of plants alive and growing. You can hear the swallows darting overhead from nests in the nearby East Woods, listen as locusts drone in the late-summer sun, and hear the hum of gnats and flies that own the field in their own annoying way. You can feel the corn leaves as they brush over your clothes and face, sense the shifting dirt as it moves underfoot. If you look around, you can find yourself lost in the thick sea of green, led along by the direction of the corn in its long, straight rows. Without knowing where exactly you are, it would be easy to think this spot is no different than thousands of other cornfields in America. You might never know of the horror that occurred here, that on a single day this spot became the grave of thousands of American men who would never again see New York or Georgia or Massachusetts or Texas. For this isn't just another farm field—the events that occurred here have prevented it from ever being just another field. Those same events have presented us—the recipients of the gift given on this spot by our forefathers—a lifelong charge to preserve all that they did and to never forget the day when the fate of a nation turned on what happened in a simple Maryland cornfield.[36]

Order of Battle—Union and Confederate Forces Engaged in or Around The Cornfield

Army of the Potomac

Major General George B. McClellan

Headquarters Escort—Captain James B. McIntyre
    Independent Company, Oneida Cavalry (New York)–
Captain Daniel P. Mann
    4th US Cavalry, Company A—Lieutenant Thomas H. McCormick
    4th US Cavalry, Company E—Captain James B. McIntyre
    Engineer Battalion—Lieutenant Charles E. Cross
        2nd US Infantry, Companies E, F, H, and K—Captain George A.
                             Gordon
        8th US Infantry, Companies A, D, F, and G—Captain Royal T.
                             Frank
        19th US Infantry, Companies G and H—Captain Henry S. Welton
    Headquarters Guard—Major Granville O. Haller
        93rd New York—Lieutenant Colonel Benjamin C. Butler
    Quartermaster's Guard
        1st US Cavalry, Companies B, C, H, and I—Captain Marcus A.
                             Reno

I Corps—Major General Joseph Hooker (w)
    —Brigadier General George G. Meade
        Escort: 2nd New York Cavalry, Companies A, B, I, and K
            —Captain John E. Naylor
    First Division—Brigadier General Abner Doubleday

First Brigade—Colonel Walter E. Phelps
    22nd New York—Lieutenant Colonel John McKie, Jr.
    24th New York—Captain John D. O'Brian (w)
    30th New York—Colonel William M. Searing
        —Captain John M. Campbell
    84th New York (14th Militia)—Major William H. de
        Bevoise
    2nd US Sharpshooters—Colonel Henry A. V. Post (w)
Second Brigade—Brigadier General Abner Doubleday
    —Colonel William P. Wainwright (w 9/14)
    —Lieutenant Colonel J. William Hofmann
    7th Indiana—Major Ira G. Grover
    76th New York—Colonel William P. Wainwright
    —Captain John W. Young
    95th New York—Major Edward Pye
    56th Pennsylvania—Lieutenant Colonel J. William
        Hofmann
    —Captain Frederick Williams
Third Brigade—Brigadier General Marsena R. Patrick
    21st New York—Colonel William F. Rogers
    23rd New York—Colonel Henry C. Hoffman
    35th New York—Colonel Newton B. Lord
    80th New York (20th Militia)—Lieutenant Colonel
        Theodore B. Gates
Fourth Brigade—Brigadier General John Gibbon
    19th Indiana—Lieutenant Colonel Alois O. Bachman (k)
    —Captain William W. Dudley
    2nd Wisconsin—Lieutenant Colonel Thomas S. Allen (w)
    —Captain George B. Ely
    6th Wisconsin—Lieutenant Colonel Edward S. Bragg (w)
    —Major Rufus R. Dawes
    7th Wisconsin—Captain John R. Callis
Artillery—Captain J. Albert Monroe
    New Hampshire Light, First Battery—Lieutenant
        Frederick M. Edgell
    1st Rhode Island Light, Battery D—Captain J. Albert
        Monroe
    1st New York Light, Battery L—Captain John A. Reynolds
    4th US Artillery, Battery B—Captain Joseph B.
        Campbell (w)
        —Lieutenant James Stewart

Second Division—Brigadier General James B. Ricketts
  First Brigade—Brigadier General Abram Duryee
      97th New York—Major Charles Northrup
              —Captain R. S. Eggleston
      104th New York—Major Lewis C. Skinner
      105th New York—Colonel Howard Carroll (mw)
      107th Pennsylvania—Captain James MacThomson
  Second Brigade—Colonel William A. Christian (i)
          —Colonel Peter Lyle (w)
      26th New York—Lieutenant Colonel Richard H.
              Richardson
      94th New York—Lieutenant Colonel Calvin Littlefield
      88th Pennsylvania—Lieutenant Colonel George
              W. Gile (w)
              —Captain Henry R. Myers
      90th Pennsylvania—Colonel Peter Lyle
              —Lieutenant Colonel William A. Leech
  Third Brigade—Brigadier General George L. Hartsuff (w)
          —Colonel Richard Coulter
      16th Maine—Colonel Asa W. Wildes (detached on 9/12)
      12th Massachusetts—Major Elisha Burbank
              —Captain Benjamin F. Cook
      13th Massachusetts—Major J. Parker Gould
      83rd New York (9th Militia)—Lieutenant Colonel
              William Atterbury
      11th Pennsylvania—Colonel Richard Coulter
              —Captain David M. Cook
  Artillery
      1st Pennsylvania Light, Battery F—Captain Ezra W.
              Matthews
      Pennsylvania Light, Battery C—Captain James Thompson
Third Division—Brigadier General George G. Meade
      —Brigadier General Truman Seymour
  First Brigade—Brigadier General Truman Seymour
          —Colonel R. Biddle Roberts
      1st Pennsylvania Reserves—Colonel R. Biddle Roberts
              —Captain William C. Talley
      2nd Pennsylvania Reserves—Captain James N. Byrnes
      5th Pennsylvania Reserves—Colonel Joseph W. Fisher
      6th Pennsylvania Reserves—Colonel William Sinclair
      13th Pennsylvania Reserves (1st Rifles)

—Colonel Hugh W. McNeil (k)
—Captain Dennis McGee
Second Brigade—Colonel Albert L. Magilton
3rd Pennsylvania Reserves—Lieutenant Colonel John Clark
4th Pennsylvania Reserves—Major John Nyce
7th Pennsylvania Reserves—Major Chauncey A. Lyman
8th Pennsylvania Reserves—Major Silas M. Baily
Third Brigade—Lieutenant Colonel Robert Anderson
9th Pennsylvania Reserves—Captain Samuel B. Dick
10th Pennsylvania Reserves—Lieut. Col.
Adoniram J. Walner (w)
—Captain Jonathan P. Smith
11th Pennsylvania Reserves—Lieutenant Col.
Samuel M. Jackson
12th Pennsylvania Reserves—Captain Richard Gustin
Artillery
1st Pennsylvania Light, Battery A—Lieutenant John G. Simpson
1st Pennsylvania Light, Battery B—Captain James H. Cooper
6th US Artillery, Battery C—Captain Dunbar R. Ransom

II Corps—Major General Edwin V. Sumner
Second Division—Major General John Sedgwick (w)
—Brigadier General Oliver O. Howard
First Brigade—Brigadier General Willis A. Gorman
15th Massachusetts—Lieutenant Colonel John W. Kimball
1st Minnesota—Colonel Alfred Sully
34th New York—Colonel James A. Suiter
82nd New York (2nd Militia)—Colonel Henry W. Hudson
Massachusetts Sharpshooters, 1st Company
—Captain John Saunders (attached to 15th Massachusetts)
Minnesota Sharpshooters, 2nd Company—Captain William F. Russell (attached to 1st Minnesota)
Second Brigade—Brigadier Gen. Oliver O. Howard
—Colonel Joshua T. Owen
—Colonel De Witt C. Baxter
69th Pennsylvania—Colonel Joshua T. Owen
71st Pennsylvania—Colonel Isaac W. Wister (w)
—Lieutenant Colonel Richard P. Smith

—Captain Enoch E. Lewis
72nd Pennsylvania—Colonel De Witt C. Baxter
106th Pennsylvania—Colonel Turner G. Morehead
Third Brigade—Brigadier General Napoleon J. T. Dana (w)
—Colonel Norman J. Hall
19th Massachusetts—Colonel Edward W. Hinks (w)
—Lieutenant Colonel Arthur F.
Devereux
—Captain H. G. O. Weymouth
20th Massachusetts—Colonel William R. Lee
7th Michigan—Colonel Norman J. Hall
—Captain Charles J. Hunt
42nd New York—Lieutenant Colonel George N.
Bomford (w)
—Major James E. Mallon
59th New York—Colonel William L. Tidball
Artillery
1st Rhode Island Light, Battery A—Captain John A.
Tompkins
4th US, Battery I—Lieutenant George A. Woodruff
Unattached Artillery
1st New York Light, Battery G—Captain John D. Frank
1st Rhode Island Light, Battery B—Captain John G.
Hazard
1st Rhode Island Light, Battery G—Captain Charles D.
Owen

VI Corps—Major General William B. Franklin
First Division—Major General Henry W. Slocum
First Brigade—Colonel Alfred T. A. Torbert
1st New Jersey—Lieutenant Colonel Mark W. Collet
2nd New Jersey—Colonel Samuel L. Buck
3rd New Jersey—Colonel Henry W. Brown
4th New Jersey—Colonel William B. Hatch
Second Brigade—Colonel Joseph J. Bartlett
5th Maine—Colonel Nathaniel J. Jackson
16th New York—Lieutenant Colonel Joel J. Seaver
27th New York—Colonel Alexander D. Adams
96th Pennsylvania—Colonel Henry L. Cake
Third Brigade—Brigadier General John Newton
18th New York—Lieutenant Colonel George R. Myers

31st New York—Colonel Francis E. Pinto
32nd New York
95th Pennsylvania—Colonel Gustavus W. Town
Artillery—Captain Emory Upton
Maryland Light, Battery A—Captain John W. Wolcott
Massachusetts Light, Battery A—Captain Josiah Porter
New Jersey Light, Battery A—Captain William Hexamer
2nd US Artillery, Battery D—Lieutenant Edward B. Williston
Second Division—Major General William F. Smith
First Brigade—Brigadier General Winfield S. Hancock (detached to command of II Corps, First Division)
—Colonel Amasa Cobb
6th Maine—Colonel Hiram Burnham
43rd New York—Major John Wilson
49th Pennsylvania—Lieutenant Colonel William Brisbane
137th Pennsylvania—Colonel Henry M. Bossert
5th Wisconsin—Colonel Amasa Cobb
Second Brigade—Brigadier General W. T. H. Brooks
2nd Vermont—Major James H. Walbridge
3rd Vermont—Colonel Breed N. Hyde
4th Vermont—Lieutenant Colonel Charles B. Stoughton
5th Vermont—Colonel Lewis A. Grant
6th Vermont—Major Oscar L. Tuttle
Third Brigade—Col. William H. Irwin
7th Maine—Major Thomas W. Hyde
20th New York—Colonel Ernest von Vegesack
33rd New York—Lieutenant Colonel Joseph W. Corning
49th New York—Lieutenant Colonel William C. Alberger
—Major George W. Johnson
77th New York—Captain Nathan S. Babcock
Artillery—Captain Romeyn B. Ayres
Maryland Light, Battery B—Lieutenant Theodore J. Vanneman
New York Light, 1st Battery—Captain Andrew Cowan
5th US Artillery, Battery F—Lieutenant Leonard Martin

XII Corps—Major General Joseph K. F. Mansfield (mw)
—Brigadier General Alpheus S. Williams
First Division—Brigadier General Alpheus S. Williams
—Brigadier General Samuel W. Crawford (w)
—Brigadier General George H. Gordon

First Brigade—Brigadier General Samuel W. Crawford (w)
  —Colonel Joseph F. Knipe
  10th Maine—Colonel George W. Beal (w)
  28th New York—Captain William H. H. Mapes
  46th Pennsylvania—Colonel Joseph F. Knipe
      —Lieutenant Colonel James L. Selfridge
  124th Pennsylvania—Colonel Joseph W. Hawley (w)
      —Major Isaac L. Haldeman
  125th Pennsylvania—Colonel Jacob Higgins
  128th Pennsylvania—Colonel Samuel Croasdale (k)
      —Lieutenant Colonel William
      Hammersly (w)
      —Major Joel B. Wanner
Third Brigade—Brigadier General George H. Gordon
  —Colonel Thomas H. Ruger
  27th Indiana—Colonel Silas Colgrove
  2nd Massachusetts (Zouaves d'Afrique, attached)
  —Colonel George L. Andrews
  13th New Jersey—Colonel Ezra A. Carman
  107th New York—Colonel R. B. Van Valkenburgh
  3rd Wisconsin—Colonel Thomas H. Ruger
Second Division—Brigadier General George S. Greene
  First Brigade—Lieutenant Colonel Hector Tyndale (w)
      —Major Orrin J. Crane
  5th Ohio—Major John Collins
  7th Ohio—Major Orrin J. Crane
      —Captain Frederick A. Seymour
  66th Ohio—Lieutenant Colonel Eugene Powell
  28th Pennsylvania—Major Ario Pardee, Jr.
  Second Brigade—Colonel Henry J. Stainrook
  3rd Maryland—Lieutenant Colonel Joseph M. Sudsbury
  102nd New York—Lieutenant Colonel James C. Lane
  111th Pennsylvania—Major Thomas M. Walker
  Third Brigade—Colonel William B. Goodrich (k)
      —Lieutenant Colonel Jonathan Austin
  3rd Delaware—Major Arthur Maginnis (w)
      —Captain William J. McKaig
  60th New York—Lieutenant Colonel Charles R. Brundage
  78th New York—Lieutenant Colonel Jonathan Austin
      —Captain Henry R. Stagg
  Purnell Legion—Lieutenant Colonel Benjamin L. Simpson

Artillery—Captain Clermont L. Best
  Maine Light, 4th Battery—Captain O'Neil W. Robinson
  Maine Light, 6th Battery—Captain Freeman McGilvery
  1st New York Light, Battery M—Captain George W. Cothron
  New York Light, 10th Battery—Captain John T. Bruen
  Pennsylvania Light, Battery E—Captain Joseph M. Knap
  Pennsylvania Light, Battery F—Captain R. B. Hampton
  4th US Artillery, Battery F—Lieutenant E. D. Muhlenberg

Cavalry Division—Brigadier General Alfred Pleasonton
  First Brigade—Major Charles J. Whiting
    5th US Cavalry—Captain Joseph H. McArthur
    6th US Cavalry—Captain William P. Sanders
  Second Brigade—Colonel John F. Farnsworth
    8th Illinois Cavalry—Major William H. Medill
    3rd Indiana Cavalry—Major George H. Chapman
    1st Massachusetts Cavalry—Colonel Robert Williams
                —Captain Casper Crowninshield
    8th Pennsylvania Cavalry—Lieutenant Colonel A. E. Griffiths
                —Captain Peter Keenan
  Third Brigade—Colonel Richard H. Rush
    4th Pennsylvania Cavalry—Colonel James H. Childs (k)
                —Lieutenant Colonel James K. Kerr
    6th Pennsylvania Cavalry—Lieutenant Colonel C. Ross Smith
  Fourth Brigade—Colonel Andrew T. McReynolds
    1st New York Cavalry—Major Alonzo W. Adams
    12th Pennsylvania Cavalry—Major James A. Congdon
  Fifth Brigade—Colonel Benjamin F. Davis
    8th New York Cavalry—Colonel Benjamin F. Davis
    3rd Pennsylvania Cavalry—Lieutenant Colonel Samuel W. Owen
  Artillery
    2nd US Artillery, Battery A—Captain John C. Tidball
    2nd US Artillery, Batteries B and L—Captain James M. Robertson
    2nd US Artillery, Battery M—Lieutenant Alexander C. M.
                Pennington, Jr.
    3rd US Artillery, Batteries C and G—Captain Horatio G. Gibson
  Unattached
    15th Pennsylvania Cavalry (detachment)—Colonel William J.
                Palmer

The Army of Northern Virginia

General Robert E. Lee

Longstreet's Corps—Major General James Longstreet
McLaws's Division—Major General Lafayette McLaws
Kershaw's Brigade—Brigadier General Joseph B. Kershaw
2nd South Carolina—Colonel John D. Kennedy (w)
—Major Franklin Gaillard
3rd South Carolina—Colonel James D. Nance
7th South Carolina—Colonel D. Wyatt Aiken (w)
—Captain John S. Hard
8th South Carolina—Lieut. Col. A. J. Hoole
Barksdale's Brigade—Brigadier General William Barksdale
13th Mississippi—Lieutenant Colonel Kennon McElroy
17th Mississippi—Lieutenant Colonel John C. Fiser
18th Mississippi—Major J. C. Campbell
—Lieutenant Colonel William H. Luse
21st Mississippi—Captain John Sims
—Colonel Benjamin G. Humphreys
Cobb's Brigade—Brigadier General Howell Cobb (absent on 9/17)
—Lieutenant Colonel C. C. Sanders
—Lieutenant Colonel William McCrae
16th Georgia—Lieutenant Colonel Henry P. Thomas
24th Georgia—Lieutenant Colonel C. C. Sanders
—Colonel Robert McMillan
15th North Carolina—Lieutenant Colonel William
McCrae
Cobb's Legion (Georgia)—Lieutenant Colonel L. J. Glenn
Semmes's Brigade—Brigadier General Paul J. Semmes
10th Georgia—Major Willis C. Holt (w)
—Captain P. H. Loud
53rd Georgia—Lieutenant Colonel Thomas Sloan (w)
—Captain S. W. Marshborne
15th Virginia—Captain E. W. Morrison (w)
—Captain Edward J. Willis
32nd Virginia—Colonel E. B. Montague
Artillery—Colonel Henry C. Cabell
—Major S. P. Hamilton
Manly's Battery (North Carolina)—Captain Basil C. Manly
Richmond Howitzers (First Company)—Captain E. S.
McCarthy

Troup Artillery (Georgia)—Captain H. H. Carlton
Pulaski Artillery (Georgia)—Captain John P. W. Read
Richmond (Fayette) Artillery—Captain M. C. Macon
Anderson's Division—Major General Richard H. Anderson (w)
—Brigadier General Roger A. Pryor
Armistead's Brigade—Brigadier General Lewis A. Armistead (w)
—Colonel James G. Hodges
9th Virginia—Captain W. J. Richardson
—Captain Joseph J. Phillips
14th Virginia—Colonel James G. Hodges
38th Virginia—Colonel Edward C. Edmonds
53rd Virginia—Captain W. G. Pollard (k)
—Captain Harwood
57th Virginia—Colonel David Dyer
Walker's Division—Brigadier General John G. Walker
Walker's Brigade—Colonel Van H. Manning (w)
—Colonel E. D. Hall
3rd Arkansas—Captain John W. Reedy
27th North Carolina—Colonel John R. Cooke
46th North Carolina—Colonel E. D. Hall
—Lieutenant Colonel William A. Jenkins
48th North Carolina—Colonel R. C. Hill
30th Virginia—Lieutenant Colonel Robert S. Chew (w)
French's Battery (Virginia)—Captain Thomas B. French
Ransom's Brigade—Brigadier General Robert Ransom, Jr.
24th North Carolina—Lieutenant Colonel John L. Harris
25th North Carolina—Colonel H. M. Rutledge
35th North Carolina—Colonel Matthew W. Ransom
49th North Carolina—Lieutenant Colonel Lee M. McAfee
Branch's Field Artillery (Virginia)—Captain James R.
Branch
Hood's Division—Major General John B. Hood
Hood's Brigade—Colonel William T. Wofford
18th Georgia—Lieutenant Colonel Solon Z. Ruff
1st Texas—Lieutenant Colonel P. A. Work
4th Texas—Lieutenant Colonel B. F. Carter
5th Texas—Captain Ike N. M. Turner
Hampton Legion (South Carolina)
—Lieutenant Colonel M. W. Ganz

Law's Brigade—Colonel Evander M. Law
    4th Alabama—Lieutenant Colonel O. K. McLemore (mw)
    —Captain L. H. Scruggs (w)
    —Captain W. M. Robbins
    2nd Mississippi—Colonel J. M. Stone (w)
    —Lieutenant Moody
    11th Mississippi—Colonel P. F. Liddell (k on 9/16)
    —Lieutenant Colonel S. F. Butler (k)
    —Major T. S. Evans (k)
    6th North Carolina—Major Robert F. Webb (w)
Artillery—Major B. W. Frobel
    German Artillery (South Carolina)—Captain W. K. Bachman
    Palmetto Light Artillery (South Carolina)—Captain H. R. Garden
    Rowan Artillery (North Carolina)—Captain James Reilly
Evans's (Independent) Brigade—Brigadier General Nathan G. Evans
    —Colonel P. F. Stevens
    17th South Carolina—Colonel F. W. McMaster
    18th South Carolina—Colonel W. H. Wallace
    22nd South Carolina—Major M. Hilton
    23rd South Carolina—Captain S. A. Durham
    —Lieutenant E. R. White
    Holcombe Legion (South Carolina)—Colonel P. F. Stevens
    Macbeth Artillery (South Carolina)—Captain Robert P. Boyce
Reserve Artillery
    Washington (Louisiana) Artillery—Colonel J. B. Walton
    1st Company—Captain C. W. Squires
    2nd Company—Captain J. B. Richardson
    3rd Company—Captain M. B. Miller
    4th Company—Captain B. F. Eshleman
    Lee's Battalion—Colonel Stephen D. Lee
    Ashland Artillery (Virginia)—Captain Pichegru Woolfolk, Jr.
    Bedford Artillery (Virginia)—Captain Tyler C. Jordan
    Brooks Artillery (South Carolina)—Lieutenant William Elliott
    Eubank's Battery (Virginia)—Captain J. L. Eubank
    Madison Light Artillery (Louisiana)—Captain George V. Moody
    Parker's Battery (Virginia)—Captain William W. Parker

Jackson's Corps—Major General Thomas J. Jackson
>Ewell's Division—Brigadier General Alexander R. Lawton (w)
>>—Brigadier General Jubal A. Early
>>Lawton's Brigade—Colonel Marcellus Douglass (k)
>>>—Major J. H. Lowe
>>>—Colonel John H. Lamar
>>>13th Georgia—Captain D. A. Kidd
>>>26th Georgia—Colonel Edmund N. Atkinson
>>>31st Georgia—Lieutenant Colonel John T. Crowder (k)
>>>>—Major J. H. Lowe
>>>38th Georgia—Captain W. H. Battey (k)
>>>>—Captain Peter Brennan
>>>>—Captain John W. McCurdy
>>>60th Georgia—Major W. B. Jones
>>>61st Georgia—Colonel John H. Lamar
>>>>—Major A. P. McRae (k)
>>>>—Captain Van Valkenberg
>>Early's Brigade—Brigadier General Jubal A. Early
>>>—Colonel William Smith (w)
>>>13th Virginia—Captain F. V. Winston
>>>25th Virginia—Captain R. D. Lilley
>>>31st Virginia—Colonel John S. Hoffman
>>>44th Virginia—Captain D. W. Anderson
>>>49th Virginia—Colonel William Smith (w)
>>>>—Lieutenant Colonel J. C. Gibson
>>>52nd Virginia—Colonel M. G. Harman
>>>58th Virginia—Colonel Edmund Goode
>>Trimble's Brigade—Colonel James A. Walker (w)
>>>15th Alabama—Captain I. B. Feagin
>>>12th Georgia—Captain James G. Rogers (w)
>>>>—Captain Carson
>>>21st Georgia—Major Thomas C. Glover (w)
>>>>—Captain J. C. Nisbit
>>>21st North Carolina—Captain F. P. Miller (k)
>>>1st North Carolina Battalion (attached to 21st North Carolina)
>>Hays's Brigade—Brigadier General Harry T. Hays
>>>5th Louisiana—Colonel Henry Forno
>>>6th Louisiana—Colonel H. B. Strong
>>>7th Louisiana
>>>8th Louisiana—Lieutenant Colonel Trevanion D. Lewis

14th Louisiana—Colonel R. W. Jones
Artillery—Major A. R. Courtney
    Johnson's Battery (Virginia)—Captain John R. Johnson
    Louisiana Guard Artillery (D'Aquin's Battery)—Capt.
        Louis E. D'Aquin
    Chesapeake Artillery (Maryland)—Captain William D.
        Brown (detached)
    Courtney Artillery (Virginia)—Captain J. W. Latimer
        (detached)
    Staunton Artillery (Balthis Battery)—Lieut. Asher W.
        Garber (detached)
    1st Maryland Battery—Captain William F. Dement
        (detached)
Jackson's Division—Brigadier General John R. Jones (i)
    —Brigadier General William E. Starke (k)
    —Colonel Arnold J. Grigsby
Winder's Brigade—Colonel Arnold J. Grigsby
    —Lieutenant Colonel R. D. Gardner (w)
    —Major H. J. Williams
    2nd Virginia—Captain R. T. Colston (detached)
    4th Virginia—Lieutenant Colonel R. D. Gardner
    5th Virginia—Major H. J. Williams
        —Captain E. L. Custis (w)
    27th Virginia—Captain Frank C. Wilson
    33rd Virginia—Captain Jacob B. Golladay (w)
        —Lieutenant David H. Walton
Taliaferro's Brigade—Colonel E. T. H. Warren
    —Colonel James W. Jackson (w)
    —Colonel James L. Sheffield
    47th Alabama—Colonel James W. Jackson (w)
    48th Alabama—Colonel James L. Sheffield
    10th Virginia—Colonel Edward T. H. Warren
    23rd Virginia—Colonel Alexander G. Taliaferro
    37th Virginia—Lieutenant Colonel John F. Terry
Jones's Brigade—Colonel Bradley T. Johnson
    —Captain John E. Penn (w)
    —Captain A. C. Page (w)
    —Captain R. W. Withers
    21st Virginia—Captain A. C. Page (w)
    42nd Virginia—Captain R. W. Withers
    —Captain D. W. Garrett

48th Virginia—Captain John H. Candler
1st Virginia Battalion—Lieutenant C. A. Davidson
Starke's Brigade—Brigadier General William E. Starke (k)
—Colonel Jesse M. Williams (w)
—Colonel Leroy A. Stafford (w)
—Colonel Edmund Pendleton
1st Louisiana—Lieutenant Colonel M. Nolan (w)
—Captain W. E. Moore
2nd Louisiana—Colonel Jesse M. Williams (w)
9th Louisiana—Colonel Leroy A. Stafford (w)
—Lieutenant Col. W. R. Peck
10th Louisiana—Captain H. D. Monier
15th Louisiana—Colonel Edmund Pendleton
1st Louisiana (Zouaves) Battalion—Lieut. Colonel G.
Coppens
Artillery—Major L. M. Shumaker
Alleghany Artillery (Virginia)—Captain Joseph Carpenter
Danville Artillery (Virginia)—Captain George W. Wooding
Lee Artillery (Virginia)—Captain Charles I. Raine
Rockbridge Artillery (Virginia)—Captain W. T. Poague
Baltimore Artillery (Maryland)—Captain J. B.
Brockenbrough
Hampden Artillery (Virginia)—Captain William H. Caskie
D. H. Hill's Division—Major General Daniel H. Hill
Ripley's Brigade—Brigadier General Roswell S. Ripley (w)
—Colonel George Doles
4th Georgia—Colonel George Doles
—Major Robert Smith (k)
—Captain W. H. Willis
44th Georgia—Captain John C. Key
1st North Carolina—Lieutenant Colonel Hamilton A.
Brown
3rd North Carolina—Colonel William L. De Rosset (w)
—Major S. D. Thruston (w)
Rodes's Brigade—Brigadier General Robert E. Rodes
3rd Alabama—Colonel Cullum A. Battle
5th Alabama—Major E. L. Hobson
6th Alabama—Colonel John B. Gordon (w)
—Lieutenant Colonel James N. Lightfoot (w)
12th Alabama—Lieutenant Colonel S. B. Pickens
—Captain Tucker (k)
—Captain Maroney (w)

—Captain A. Proskauer (w)
26th Alabama—Colonel E. A. O'Neal (w)
Garland's Brigade—Colonel D. K. McRae (w)
5th North Carolina—Captain Thomas N. Garrett
12th North Carolina—Captain S. Snow
13th North Carolina—Captain J. M. Hyman
20th North Carolina—Colonel Alfred Iverson
23rd North Carolina—Colonel Daniel H. Christie
Anderson's Brigade—Brigadier General George B. Anderson (mw)
—Colonel C. C. Tew (k)
—Colonel R. T. Bennett
2nd North Carolina—Colonel C. C. Tew (k)
—Major John Howard (w)
—Captain George M. Roberts
4th North Carolina—Colonel Bryan Grimes
—Captain W. T. Marsh (k)
—Captain E. A. Osborne (w)
—Captain D. B. Latham (k)
14th North Carolina—Colonel R. T. Bennett
—Lieutenant Colonel William A. Johnston (w)
—Major A. J. Griffith
30th North Carolina—Colonel F. M. Parker (w)
—Major William W. Sillers
Colquitt's Brigade—Colonel Alfred H. Colquitt
13th Alabama—Colonel Birkett D. Fry (w)
—Lieutenant Colonel W. H. Betts (w)
—Major A. S. Reaves
6th Georgia—Lieutenant Colonel J. M. Newton (k)
—Major P. Tracy (k)
—Lieutenant E. P. Burnett
23rd Georgia—Colonel W. P. Barclay (k)
—Lieutenant Colonel E. F. Best (w)
—Major J. H. Huggins (w)
27th Georgia—Colonel Levi B. Smith (k)
—Lieutenant Colonel C. T. Zachry (w)
—Captain W. H. Rentfro
28th Georgia—Major Tully Graybill (w)
—Captain N. J. Garrison (w)
—Captain R. A. Warthen
—Lieutenant John W. Fuller

Artillery—Major S. F. Pierson
Jones's Battery (Virginia)—Captain William B. Jones
King William Artillery (Virginia)—Captain Thomas H. Carter
Hardaway's Battery (Alabama)—Captain R. A. Hardaway
—Lieutenant John W. Tullis
Jeff Davis Artillery (Alabama)—Captain J. W. Bondurant

Reserve Artillery—Brigadier General William N. Pendleton
Brown's Battalion (1st Virginia Artillery)—Colonel J. Thompson Brown
Powhatan Artillery—Captain Willis J. Dance
Richmond Howitzers, 2nd Company—Captain D. Watson
Richmond Howitzers, 3rd Company—Captain Benjamin H. Smith, Jr.
Salem Artillery—Captain A. Hupp
Williamsburg Artillery—Captain John A. Coke
Cutts' Battalion—Lieutenant Colonel A. S. Cutts
Blackshear's Battery (Georgia)—Captain James A. Blackshear
Irwin Artillery (Georgia)—Captain John Lane
Patterson's Battery (Georgia)—Captain G. M. Patterson
Ross's Battery (Georgia)—Captain H. M. Ross
Lloyd's Battery (North Carolina)—Captain W. P. Lloyd
Jones's Battalion—Major Hilary P. Jones
Turner's Battery (Virginia)—Captain W. H. Turner
Orange Artillery (Virginia)—Captain Jefferson Peyton
Morris Artillery (Virginia)—Captain R. C. M. Page
Wimbish's Battery (Virginia)—Captain Abram Wimbish
Nelson's Battalion—Major William Nelson
Amherst Artillery—Captain T. J. Kirkpatrick
Fluvanna Artillery—Captain John J. Ancell
Virginia Battery—Captain Charles T. Huckstep
Virginia Battery—Captain Marmaduke Johnson
Milledge's Battery (Georgia)—Captain John Milledge
Unattached
Magruder Artillery (Virginia)—Captain T. H. Page, Jr.
Cutshaw's Battery (Virginia)—Captain W. E. Cutshaw
Dixie Artillery (Virginia)—Captain G. B. Chapman
Virginia Battery—Captain W. H. Rice

Cavalry Division—Major General James E. B. Stuart
       Hampton's Brigade—Brigadier General Wade Hampton
              10th Virginia Cavalry—Colonel J. Lucius Davis
              1st North Carolina Cavalry—Colonel L. S. Baker
              2nd South Carolina Cavalry—Colonel M. C. Butler
              Cobb's Legion (Georgia)—Lieutenant Colonel P. M. B. Young
                      —Major William G. Delony
              Jeff Davis (Mississippi) Legion—Lieutenant Colonel W. T. Martin
       Lee's Brigade—Brigadier General Fitzhugh Lee
              1st Virginia Cavalry—Lieutenant Colonel L. T. O'Brien
              3rd Virginia Cavalry—Lieutenant Colonel John T. Thornton (k)
                      —Captain Thomas H. Owen
              4th Virginia Cavalry—Colonel Williams C. Wickham
              5th Virginia Cavalry—Colonel Thomas L. Rosser
              9th Virginia Cavalry—Colonel W. H. F. Lee
       Robertson's Brigade—Colonel Thomas H. Munford
              2nd Virginia Cavalry—Colonel Richard A. Burke
              6th Virginia Cavalry—Colonel Thomas S. Flournoy
              7th Virginia Cavalry—Captain S. B. Myers
              12th Virginia Cavalry—Colonel A. W. Harman
              17th Virginia Battalion
       Horse Artillery—Captain John Pelham
              Pelham's Battery (Virginia)—Captain John Pelham
              Chew's Battery (Virginia)—Captain R. P. Chew
              Hart's Battery (South Carolina)—Captain J. F. Hart

(i)—Incapacitated
(w)—Wounded on 9/17
(mw)—Mortally wounded on 9/17
(k)—Killed on 9/17

Union and Confederate Casualties at Antietam[1]

Union Regiments at Antietam with Casualties Exceeding 50 Percent

	Engaged	Killed	Wounded	Percent Lost
12th Massachusetts*	334	49	165	64.07
69th New York	317	44	152	61.83
9th New York	373	45	176	59.25
3rd Wisconsin*	340	27	173	58.82
63rd New York	341	35	165	58.65
14th Indiana*	320	30	150	56.25
15th Massachusetts*	606	65	255	52.81
59th New York*	381	48	153	52.76

*Unit engaged in the Cornfield or related actions on the Union right/Confederate left flank.

Confederate Regiments at Antietam with Casualties Exceeding 50 Percent

	Engaged	Killed	Wounded	Percent Lost
1st Texas*	226	45	141	82.30
2nd Mississippi*	210	27	127	73.33
13th Georgia*	312	59	166	73.33
Hampton Legion*	77	6	49	71.43

30th Virginia*	236	39	121	67.80
6th Georgia*	261	52	113	63.21
16th Mississippi	228	27	117	63.21
12th Georgia*	100	13	49	62.00
27th North Carolina*	325	31	168	61.23
15th Virginia*	128	11	64	58.59
38th Georgia*	123	18	52	56.91
10th Georgia*	148	15	69	56.76
17th Virginia	55	7	24	56.36
4th Texas*	200	10	97	53.50
7th South Carolina*	268	23	117	52.24
3rd Arkansas*	350	27	155	52.00
61st Georgia*	191	16	81	50.79
44th Georgia*	162	17	65	50.62
27th Georgia	206	15	65	50.49
18th Georgia*	170	13	72	50.00

*Unit engaged in the Cornfield or related actions on the Union right/Confederate left flank.

Greatest Union Regimental Losses—Killed in Battle on September 17, 1862[2]

	Engaged	Killed	Percent Lost
12th Massachusetts*	334	74	22+
69th New York	317	71	17+
15th Massachusetts*	606	108	7+
63rd New York	341	59	17+
42nd New York*	345	58	16+
14th Indiana	320	49	15+
9th New York	373	54	14+
107th Pennsylvania*	190	27	14+
34th New York*	311	41	13+

111 Pennsylvania*	243	33	13+
19th Indiana*	202	28	13+
7th Maine*	181	25	13+
8th Ohio	341	43	12+
82nd New York	339	41	12+
3rd Wisconsin*	340	41	12+
88th New York	302	38	12+
4th New York	540	64	11+
57th New York	309	53	10+
27th Indiana*	409	41	10+

*Unit engaged in the Cornfield or related actions on the Union right/Confederate left flank.

Greatest Confederate Regimental Losses—Killed in Battle on September 17, 1862

	Engaged	Killed	Percent Lost
6th Georgia*	250	81	32+
2nd Mississippi*	210	27	26+
1st Texas*	226	45	19+
13th Georgia*	312	59	18+
30th Virginia*	236	39	16+
38th Georgia*	123	18	14+
17th Virginia	55	7	13+
12th Georgia*	100	13	13
16th Mississippi	228	27	11+
44th Georgia*	162	17	10+
10th Georgia*	148	15	10+
27th North Carolina*	325	31	9+
7th South Carolina*	268	23	8+
61st Georgia*	191	16	8+
15th Virginia*	128	11	8+

3rd Arkansas*	350	27	7+
27th Georgia	206	15	7+
18th Georgia*	170	13	7+
Hampton Legion*	77	6	7+
4th Texas*	200	10	5

*Unit engaged in the Cornfield or related actions on the Union right/Confederate left flank.

Bibliography

Published Works

Adams, Captain John G. B. *Reminiscences of the Nineteenth Massachusetts Regiment* (Boston: Wright, Potter Printing Company, 1899)

Adams, Rev. John R. *Memorial and Letters of Rev. John R. Adams, Chaplain of the 5th Maine and the Twenty-first New York Regiments During the War of the Rebellion* (Privately Printed, 1890)

Allan, William. *Stonewall Jackson, Robert E. Lee, and the Army of Northern Virginia, 1862* (New York: Da Capo Press, 1995)

Anderson, Thomas M. "The Reserve at Antietam," *Century Magazine*, Vol. 32, No. 5. (September 1886)

Andrews, W. H. *Footprints of a Regiment: A Recollection of the 1st Georgia Regulars, 1861–1865* (Atlanta: Longstreet Press, 1992)

Ankrum, Freeman. *Sidelights of Brethren History* (Elgin, OH: The Brethren Press, 1962)

Board of Trustees of the Antietam National Cemetery. *A Descriptive List of the Burial Places of the Remains of Confederate Soldiers, Who Fell in the Battles of Antietam, South Mountain, Monocacy, and Other Points in Washington and Frederick Counties, in the State of Maryland* (Hagerstown, Maryland: The Free Press Print, 1869)

Antietam Battlefield Memorial Commission, *Second Brigade of the Pennsylvania Reserves at Antietam* (Harrisburg: Harrisburg Publishing Co., 1908)

Armstrong, Marion V. *Unfurl Those Colors!: McClellan, Sumner, & the Second Army Corps in the Antietam Campaign* (Tuscaloosa: The University of Alabama Press, 2008)

Bank, John. "The General," *Civil War Times*, August 2018, Vol. 57, No. 4

Baquet, Camille. *History of the First New Jersey Brigade* (Trenton, NJ: MacCrellish and Quigley, 1910)

Barber, Charles, Raymond G. Barber, and Gary E. Swinson. *The Civil War Letters of Charles Barber, Private, 104th New York Volunteer Infantry* (Torrance, California: G. E. Swinson, 1991)

Basler, Roy P. Ed. et. al. *The Collected Works of Lincoln* (The Abraham Lincoln Society, 1953)

Bates, Samuel. *The History of Pennsylvania Volunteers, 1861–1865* (Harrisburg: B. Singerly, State Printer, 1869)

Battles and Leaders of the Civil War (New York: Castle Books, 1956)

Benson, Susan Williams, Ed. *Berry Benson's Civil War Book* (Athens, Georgia, 1962)

Beyer, W. F. and O. F. Keydel, Eds. *Deeds of Valor* (Detroit: Platinum Press, 1903)

Bicknell, George W. *History of the Fifth Regiment Maine Volunteers* (Portland: Hall L. Davis, 1871)

Bidwell, Frederick D. *History of the 49th New York Volunteers* (Albany: J. B. Lyon Co., 1916)

Blackford, William W. *War Years with Jeb Stuart* (New York: Charles Scribner's Sons, 1945)

Boyce, Charles W. *Twenty-eighth Regiment New York State Volunteers* (Buffalo: Matthews and Northrup Co., 1896)

Boyle, John Richards. *Soldiers True; The Story of the One Hundred and Eleventh Regiment Pennsylvania Veteran Volunteers, and of its Campaigns in the War for the Union 1861–1865* (New York: Eaton & Mains, 1903)

Brady, James P. *Hurrah for the Artillery!: Knap's Independent Battery "E," Pennsylvania Light Artillery* (Gettysburg: Thomas Publications, 1992)

Brown, Edmund R. *The Twenty-seventh Indiana Volunteer Infantry in the War of the Rebellion, 1861 to 1865, First Division, 12th and 20th Corps … by a member of Company C* (Monticello, 1899)

Bruce, George A. *The Twentieth Regiment of Massachusetts Volunteer Infantry, 1861–1865* (Boston: Mifflin and Co, 1906)

Burton, Joseph Q. and Theophilius Botsford. *Historical Sketches of the Forty-Seventh Alabama Infantry Regiment, C. S. A.* (Montgomery, AL: 1909)

Campbell, James Havelock. *McClellan: A Vindication of the Military Career of General George McClellan: A Lawyer's Brief* (New York: The Neale Co., 1916)

Carman, Ezra A. and Joseph Pierro, Ed. *The Maryland Campaign of 1862; Ezra A. Carman's Definitive Study of the Union and Confederates at Antietam* (New York: Routledge Books, 2008)

Carman, Ezra A. and Thomas G. Clemens, Ed. *The Maryland Campaign of 1862, Volume II: Antietam.* El Dorado Hills (CA: Savas Beatie, 2012)

Case, Lynn M. and Warren F. Spencer. *The United States and France: Civil War Diplomacy* (Philadelphia: The University of Pennsylvania Press, 1970 and 2016)

Chance, Joseph E., Ed. *My Life in the Old Army: The Reminiscences of Abner Doubleday* (Forth Worth: Texas Christian University Press, 1998)

Chapin, Lewis N. *A Brief History of the 34th Regiment N.Y.S.V* (New York, 1903)

Chase, Salmon P. *Diary and Correspondence, In American Historical Association, Annual Report for 1902, Vol. 2.* (Washington, 1903)

Child, William. *A History of the Fifth New Hampshire Volunteers in the American Civil War, 1861–1865.* (Bristol, NH: R. W. Musgrove, 1893)

Clark, Walter. *Histories of the Several Regiments and Battalions from North Carolina in the Great War, 1861–1865* (Goldsboro, NC: Nash Brothers, 1901)

Coco, Gregory A. *Through Blood and Fire: The Civil War Letters of Major Charles J. Mills, 1862–1865* (Gettysburg: Self-published, 1982)

Collier, Ellen C., Ed. *Letters of a Civil War Soldier: Chandler B. Gillam, 28th New York Volunteers, with Diary of W. L. Hicks* (Xlibris Corp., 2005)

Commager, Henry Steele. *The Blue and the Grey* (Indianapolis, Indiana: Bobs-Merrill Co., 1950)

Conline, John. "Recollections of the Battle of Antietam and the Maryland Campaign," *War Papers Read Before the Michigan Commandery of the Military Order of the Loyal Legion of the United States,* Vol. II (Detroit: James H. Stone Printers, 1898).

Contant, George. *Path of Blood: The True Story of the 33rd New York Volunteers* (Savannah, New York: Seeco Printing, 1997)

Cox, Jacob Dolson. *Reminisces of the Civil War* (New York: Charles Scribner's' Sons, 1900)

Croffut, W. A. and John Morris. *The Military and Civil History of Connecticut During the War of 1861–65* (New York: Ledyard Bill, 1869)

Crowell, Joseph E. *The Young Volunteer: The Civil War Memoirs of Joseph E. Crowell, 13th New Jersey Volunteers* (Falls Church, VA: NOVA Publications, 1997)

Curliss, Newton M. *From Bull Run to Chancellorsville: The Story of the 16th New York Infantry Together with Personal Reminiscences* (New York: G.P. Putman's Sons, 1906)

Davis, Jr. Charles E. *Three Years in the Army: The Story of the 13th Massachusetts Volunteers from July 16, 1861 to August 1, 1864* (Boston: Estes Publishers, 1894)

Dawes, Rufus R. *A Full Blown Yankee of the Iron Brigade: Service with the Sixth Wisconsin Volunteers* (Lincoln, NE: University of Nebraska Press, 1962)

Denney, Robert E. *Civil War Medicine: Care & Comfort of the Wounded* (New York: Sterling Publishing Co., 1995)

Dickert, D. Augustus. *History of Kershaw's Brigade, with Complete Roll of Companies, Biographical Sketches, Incidents, Anecdotes, Etc.* (Newbury, SC: E. H. Hull Co., 1899)

Dinkins, James. *1861–1865 By An Old Johnnie, Personal Recollections and Experiences in the Confederate Army* (Dayton, Ohio: Morningside Books, 1975)

Douglas, Henry Kyd. *I Rode with Stonewall* (Chapel Hill: University of North Carolina Press, 1968)

Dowdey, Clifford and Loius H. Manarin, Eds. *The Wartime Papers of Robert E. Lee* (New York: Da Capo Press, 1961)

Duncan, Louis C. *The Medical Department of the United States Army in the Civil War* (Washington, DC, 1901)

Durkin, James. *The Last Man and the Last Life* (Glenside, PA: Santarelli, 2000)

Dwight, Wilder and Elizabeth Amelia Dwight *Life and Letters of Wilder Dwight, Lieut.-col., Second Mass. Inf. Vols* (Boston: Ticknor and Fields, 1868)

Earle, David M. *History of the Excursion of the 15th Massachusetts Regiment* (Worcester: Press of Charles Hamilton, 1886)

Eby, Cecil D. *A Virginia Yankee in the Civil War: The Diaries of David Hunter Strother* (Chapel Hill: The University of North Carolina Press, 1961)

Eisenhower, John S. D. *Agent of Destiny: The Life and Times of General Winfield Scott* (New York: The Free Press, 1997)

Ernsberer, Don. *Paddy Owen's Regulars: A History of the 69th Pennsylvania "Irish Volunteers" Vol. I* (Xlibris Corp., 2004)

Ernst, Kathleen A. *Too Afraid to Cry: Maryland Civilians in the Antietam Campaign* (Mechanicsburg, (Pennsylvania: Stackpole Books, 1999)

Everson, Guy R. and Edward H. Simpson, Jr., Eds. *"Far, Far From Home:" The Wartime Letters of Dick and Tally Simpson, third South Carolina Volunteers* (New York: Oxford University Press, 1993)

Fairchild, Charles B. *History of the 27th New York Volunteers* (Binghamton, NY: Carl & Matthews, 1888)

Fishel, Edwin C. *The Secret War for the Union: The Untold Story of Military Intelligence in the Civil War* (Boston: Houghton Mifflin Company, 1996)

Folsom, James M. *Heroes and Martyrs of Georgia: Georgia's Record in the Revolution of 1861* (Macon, GA: Burke, Boykin & Company, 1864)

Foreman, Amanda. *A World On Fire: Britain's Crucial role in the American Civil War* (New York: Random House, 2012)

Frassanito, William A. *Antietam: The Photographic Legacy of America's Bloodiest Day* (New York: Charles Scribner's Sons, 1978).

Frye, Dennis E. *2nd Virginia Infantry* (Lynchburg: H. E. Howard, Inc., 1984)

Gaff, Alan D. *On Many a Bloody Field: Four Years in the Iron Brigade* (Bloomington: Indiana University Press, 1996)

Gannon, James P. *Irish Rebels, Confederate Tigers: the 6th Louisiana Volunteers, 1861–1865* (Campbell, CA: Savas Publishing Co., 1998)

Gates, Theodore B. *The Ulster Guard (20th N. Y. State Militia) and the War of the Rebellion* (New York: B. H. Tyrrel, printer, 1879)

Gibbon, John. *Personal Recollections of the Civil War* (New York, 1928)

Gibbs, Joseph. *Three Years in the Bloody Eleventh: The Campaigns of a Pennsylvania Reserve Regiment* (Keystone University Press, 2002)

Gould, John M. *History of the 1st, 10th, 29th Maine Regiment* (Portland: Stephen Barry, Pub., 1871)

Gould, John E. *Joseph K. F. Mansfield, Brigadier General of the US Army, A Narrative of Events connected with his Mortal Wounding at Antietam* (Portland, Maine: Stephen Barry, Pub., 1895)

Government Printing Office. *The War of the Rebellion: A Compilation of the Official Records of the Union and Confederate Armies,* Series I, Volume XIX, Parts 1 and 2 (Washington: Government Printing Office, 1887)

Grandchamp, Robert. *The Boys of Adams' Battery G* (Jefferson, NC: McFarland & Co., 2009)

Green, Robert M. *History of the One Hundred and Twenty-Fourth Regiment Pennsylvania Volunteers in the War of the Rebellion—1862–1863* (Philadelphia: Ware Brothers Company, 1907)

Hale, Laura V. and Stanley S. Phillips. *History of the Forty-Ninth Virginia Infantry C.S.A "Extra Billy Smith's Boys."* (Lynchburg: H. E. Howard, Inc., 1981)

Hamilton, D. H. *History of Company M, First Texas Volunteer Infantry* (Waco, Texas: W. M. Morrison, 1962)

Harsh, Joseph L. *Sounding the Shallows: A Confederate Companion for the Maryland Campaign of 1862* (Kent, OH: Kent State University Press, 2000)

Harsh, Joseph L. *Taken at the Flood; Robert E. Lee and Confederate Strategy in the Maryland Campaign of 1862* (Kent: OH, 1999)

Hartwig, D. Scott. *To Antietam Creek: The Maryland Campaign of 1862* (Baltimore, Maryland: Johns Hopkins University Press, 2012)

Hebert, Walter H. *Fighting Joe Hooker* (Lincoln: University of Nebraska Press, 1999)

Hess, Earl J. *The Rifle Musket in Civil War Combat: Reality and Myth* (Lawrence, KS: University of Kansas Press, 2008)

Hill, Alonzo. *In Memoriam: A Discourse Preached in Worchester, Oct. 5, 1862, on Lieut. Thomas Jefferson Spurr* (Thomson Gale Archival Editions, 1862)

Hinkley, Julian W. *A Narrative of Service with the Third Wisconsin Infantry* (The Wisconsin History Commission, 1912)

History of the Fourth Maine Battery, Light Artillery, in the Civil War, 1861–1865 (Augusta, ME: B. Arliegh and Flynt, 1905)

Holden, Walter, and William Ross, Elizabeth Slomba, Mike Pride. *Stand Firm and Fire Low: The Civil War Writings of Colonel Edward E. Cross* (Hanover, NH: University Press of New England, 2003)

Holt, Daniel M., and James M. Greiner, Janet L. Coryell, and James B. Smither, Eds. *A Surgeon's Civil War: The Letters and Diary of Daniel M. Holt, M.D.* (Kent, OH: Kent State University Press, 1994)

Hood, John Bell. *Advance and Retreat* (New York: Da Capo Press, 1993)

Hotchkiss, Jedediah. *Make Me a Map of the Valley: The Civil War Journal of Stonewall Jackson's Topographer* (Dallas: Southern Methodist University Press, 1973)

Hough, Franklin Benjamin. *History of Duryee's Brigade, During the Campaign in Virginia under Gen. Pope, and in Maryland under Gen. McClellan, and in the Summer and Autumn of 1862* (Albany, 1864)

Hunter, Alexander. *Johnny Reb and Billy Yank* (New York: Neal Publishing Co., 1905)

Hurst, M. B. *History of the Fourteenth Regiment Alabama Volunteers* (Richmond: 1863)

Hyde, Thomas W. *Following the Greek Cross, of Memories of the Sixth Corps* (Boston: Houghton, Mifflin, Co. 1894)

Iobst, Richard W. *The Bloody Sixth: The Sixth North Carolina Regiment Confederate States of America.*

Johnson, Curt and Richard C. Anderson, Jr. *Artillery Hell: The Employment of Artillery at Antietam* (College Station: Texas A&M University Press, 1995)

Johnson, Mark W. *That Body of Brave Men: The U.S. Regular Infantry and the Civil War in the West* (New York: Da Capo Press, 2004)

Johnson, Pharris Deloach. *Under the Southern Cross: Soldier Life with Gordon Bradwell and the Army of Northern Virginia* (Mercer University Press, 1979)

Jones, Howard. *Abraham Lincoln and a New Birth of Freedom* (University of Nebraska Press, 2002)

Jones, Howard. *Union in Peril: The Crisis over British Intervention in the Civil War* (Lincoln: University of Nebraska Press, 1992)

Judd, David W. *The Story of the 33rd New York Volunteers on Two Years Campaign in Virginia and Maryland* (Rochester, NY: Benton and Andrews, 1864)

Kallgren, Beverly Hayes and James L. Crouthamel, Eds. *"Dear Friend Anna" The Civil War letters of a Common Soldier from Maine* (Portland: The University Press of Maine, 1992)

Keegan, John. *Fields of Battle: The Wars for North America* (New York: Vintage Books, 1995)

Kegel, James A. *North with Lee and Jackson: The Lost Story of Gettysburg* (Mechanicsburg, PA: Stackpole Books, 1996)

Krein, David F. *The Last Palmerston Government: Foreign Policy, Domestic Politics, and the Genesis of "Splendid Isolation."* (Ames, Iowa: Iowa State University Press, 1978)

Krick, Robert C. *Lee's Colonels* (Dayton, Ohio: Morningside Bookshop Press, 1979)

Laboda, Lawrence R. *From Selma to Appomattox: The History of the Jeff Davis Artillery* (New York: Oxford University Press, 1994)

Lash, Gary G. *"Duty Well Done" The History of Edward Baker's California Infantry (71st Pennsylvania Infantry)* (Butternut and Blue 2001)

Lee, Susan Pendleton. *Memoirs of William Nelson Pendleton, D.D.: Rector of Latimer Parish* (Philadelphia: J. B. Lippincott Company, 1893)

Letter of the Secretary of War Transmitting report on the Organization of the Army of the Potomac and its Campaigns in Virginia and Maryland (Washington: Government Printing Office, 1887)

Livermore, Thomas L. *Numbers and Losses in the Civil War* (Millwood, NY: Kraus Reprint, 1977)

Longstreet, Helen Dortch. *In the Path of Lee's "Old War Horse"* (Atlanta: 1917)

Longstreet, James. *From Manassas to Appomattox* (New York: Smithmark Books, 1992)

Mainzer, Klaus *Thinking in Complexity: The conceptual Dynamics of Matter, Mind, and Mankind* (Berlin: Springer, 2007)

Marvel, William. *The First New Hampshire Battery, 1861–1865* (Conway, NH: Minuteman Press, 1985)

Mason, Virginia. *The Public Life and Diplomatic Correspondence of James M. Mason* (New York: Neale and Co., 1904)

Matchett, W. B. *Maryland and the Glorious Old 3rd in the War for the Union* (Washington, DC: T. J. Bradshers, 1882)

McClellan, George. *The Armies of Europe: Comprising Descriptions in Detail of the Military Systems of England, France, Russia, Prussia, Austria, and Sardinia* (Philadelphia: J. B. Lippincott & Co., 1861)

McClellan, George. *McClellan's Own Story* (New York: Charles L. Webster and Co., 1887)

McClenthen, Charles S. *Campaign in Virginia and Maryland from Cedar Mountain to Antietam by a Soldier of the 26th New York Volunteers* (Syracuse: Masters & Lee, 1862)

McGrath, Thomas A. *Shepherdstown: Last Clash of the Antietam Campaign September 19–20, 1862* (Lynchburg, VA: Schroeder Publications, 2008)

McPherson, James M. *Battle Cry of Freedom: The Civil War Era* (Oxford: Oxford University Press, 1988)

McPherson, James M. *Crossroads of Freedom: Antietam* (Oxford: Oxford University Press, 2002)

Military Order of the Loyal Legion of the United States, Massachusetts Commandery (University of Michigan Library, 1900)

Miller, C. Eugene and Forrest F. Steinlage. *Der Turner Soldat: A Turner Soldier in the Civil War, Germany to Antietam* (Calmar Publications, 1988)

Moe, Richard. *The Last Full Measure: The Life and Death of the First Minnesota Volunteers* (New York: Avon Books, 1993)

Moore, Frank, Ed. *The Rebellion Record: A Diary of American Events,* Vol. V (New York: G. P. Putnam, 1863)

Morell, Carl A., Ed. *Seymour Dexter, Union army; Journal and Letters; New York Regiment of Elmira, with Illustrations* (Jefferson, North Carolina: McFarland and Co.,1996)

Morse, Charles F. "From Second Bull Run to Antietam," *MOLLUS,* Vol. 1 (Commandery of Missouri. Becktold & Co., 1892)

Moseley, Ronald H., Ed. *The Stillwell Letters: A Georgian in Longstreet's Corps, Army of Northern Virginia* (Mercer University Press, 2002)

Moten, Matthew. *The Delafield Commission and the American Military Profession* (College Station, TX: Texas A&M University Press, 2000)

Mudgett, Timothy B. *Make the Fur Fly: A History of a Union Volunteer Division in the American Civil War* (Smith's Second Division, VI Corps) (Shippensburg, PA: Burd Street Press, 1997)

Murfin, James V. *The Gleam of Bayonets: The Battle of Antietam and Robert E. Lee's Maryland Campaign, September 1862* (Baton Rouge: Louisiana State University Press, 1993)

Murphy, Patricia A. *The Civil War Diary of Ehpriam C. Brown, 1862* (Lakeland Florida: Self-published, 1999)

Murray, R. L. *Madison County Troops in the Civil War* (Wolcott, N.Y.: Benedum Books, 2004)

Murray, R. L., Ed. *New Yorkers in the Civil War: A Historic Journey, Vol. 3* (Wolcott, NY: Benedum Books, 2004)

Murray, R. L., Ed. *New Yorkers in the Civil War: A Historic Journey, Vol. 4* (Wolcott, NY: Benedum Books, 2004)

Murray, R. L. *Ontario County Troops in the Civil War: Volume One: Geneva Soldiers,* from the "Letters From the Front" series (Wolcott, NY: Benedum Books, 2004)

Nagle, Theodore M. *Reminiscences of the Civil War* (Erie, PA: Dispatch Ptg. & Eng. Co., 1923)

National Park Service. *D. R. Miller Farmstead, Antietam National Battlefield: Cultural Landscape Inventory* (Antietam National Battlefield, 2005)

National Park Service. *Miller Farmstead: Antietam National Battlefield: Historic Structures Report* (Oehrlin & Assoc. Architects, National Park Service, 1993)

New York Tribune, 11 February 1862

The Niagara County Historical Society. *100 Years Ago Today: Niagara County in the Civil War as Reported in the Pages of "The Niagara Falls Gazette"* (Lockport, New York: The Niagara County Historical Society, Inc., 1966)

Nichols, G. W. *A Soldier's Story of His Regiment (61st Georgia) and incidentally of the Lawton-Gordon-Evans Brigade* (Continental Book Company, 1961)

Nicolay, John G. and John Hay, *Abraham Lincoln: A History,* Vol. VI (New York: The Century Co., 1890)

Nisbet, James Cooper. *Four Years on the Firing Line* (Jackson, TN: McCowat-Mercer Press, 1914)

Noyes, George F. *The Bivouac; or, Campaign Sketches in Virginia and Maryland* (New York: Harper and Brothers Publishers, 1864)

Owen, William M. *In Camp and Battle with the Washington Artillery of New Orleans. A narrative of Events during the Late Civil War from Bull Run to Appomattox and Spanish Fort* (Boston, Ticknor & Co., 1885)

Palfrey, Francis W. *The Antietam and Fredericksburg* (Wilmington, NC: Broadfoot Publishing Company, 1989)

Palmer, David W. *The Forgotten Hero of Gettysburg: A Biography of General George Sears Greene* (Xlibris, 2005)

Parsons, George W. *Put the Vermonteers Ahead: The First Vermont Brigade in the Civil War* (Shippensburg, PA: White Mane Publishing Co., 1996)

Porter, Alexander Edward. *Fighting for the Confederacy* (Chapel Hill: University of North Carolina Press) 1998

Priest, John Michael. *Antietam: The Soldier's Battle* (Shippensburg, PA: White Mane Publishing, 1989)

Priest, John M. *Turn Then Out to Die Like a Mule: The Civil War letters of John N. Henry, 49th New York, 1861–1865* (Leesburg, VA: Gawley Mount Press, 1995)

Rafuse Ethan S. *Antietam, South Mountain & Harpers Ferry: A Battlefield Guide* (Lincoln: University of Nebraska Press, 2008)

Rafuse, Ethan S. *McClellan's War: The Failure of Moderation in the Struggle for the Union* (Bloomington: Indiana University Press, 2005)

Reese, Timothy J. *High-Water Mark: The 1862 Maryland Campaign in Strategic Perspective* (Baltimore: Butternut and Blue)

Regimental History Committee. *History of the One Hundred and Twenty-fifth Regiment Pennsylvania Volunteers, 1862–1863* (J. B. Lippincott Co., 1906)

Regimental History Committee. *History of the Third Pennsylvania Cavalry, Sixteenth Regiment Pennsylvania Volunteers in the American Civil War* (Philadelphia: Franklin Publishing Co., 1905)

Reidenbaugh, Lowell. *27th Virginia Infantry* (Lynchburg: H. E. Howard, Inc., 1993)

Reidenbaugh, Lowell. *33rd Virginia Infantry* (Lynchburg: H. E. Howard, Inc., 1993)

Report of the Joint Committee on the Conduct of the War (Washington DC: Government Printing Office, 1863)

Richardson, Albert D. *The Secret Service, the Field, the Dungeon, and the Escape* (Hartford, CT: American Publishing Co., 1865)

Robertson, James I. *The Stonewall Brigade* (Baton Rouge: Louisiana State University Press, 1991)

Robertson, James I. *4th Virginia Infantry* (Lynchburg: H. E. Howard, Inc., 1982)

Rosenberg, Shawn W. *The Not So Common Sense: Differences in How People Judge Social and Political Life* (New Haven: Yale University Press, 2002)

Sauers, Richard A. and Tomasak, Peter. *Ricketts' Battery: A History of Battery F, 1st Pennsylvania Light Artillery* (Luzerne National Bank, PA, 2001)

Sears, Stephen W., Ed. *The Civil War Papers of George B. McClellan: Selected Correspondence. 1860–1865* (New York: Da Capo Press, 1992)

Sears, Stephen W. *George B. McClellan; The Young Napoleon* (New York: Ticknor & Fields, 1988)

Sears, Stephen W. *Landscape Turned Red: The Battle of Antietam* (New York: Warner Books, 1983)

Sedgwick, John. *Correspondence of John Sedgwick*, Vols I and II. (Carl and Ellen Battelle Stoeckel, 1902)

Sessarego, Alan. *Letters Home: A Collection of Original Civil War Soldiers' Letters (Antietam, Chancellorsville, Gettysburg).* (Gettysburg: Americana Souvenirs & Gifts, 1996)

Shaw, Robert Gould. *Blue-Eyed Child of Fortune: The Civil War Letters of Robert Gould Shaw* (Marietta: University of Georgia Press, 2004)

Sifakis, Stewart. *Who Was Who in the Confederacy* (New York: Facts on File Press, 1988)

Sifakis, Stewart. *Who Was Who in the Union, Vol. 1* (New York: Facts on File Press, 1988)

Simpson, Col. Harold B. *Hood's Texas Brigade: Lee's Grenadier Guard* (Waco, TX: Texian Press, 1970)

Slocum and His Men (Albany, NY: J. B. Lyon Company, 1904)

Smith, Abram P. *History of the 76th New York Volunteers* (Courtland, New York: 1876)

Smith, J. O. *My First Campaign and Battle: A Jersey Boy at Antietam – Seventeen Days from Home.* (Philadelphia: Patriotic Publishing Co., 1893)

Smith, John L. *Antietam to Appomattox with the 118th Pennsylvania Volunteers, Corn Exchange Regiment.* (Philadelphia: J. L. Smith, 1892)

Snell, Mark A. *From First to Last: The Life of Major General William B. Franklin* (New York: Fordham University Press, 2002)

South Carolina Division, United Daughters of the Confederacy, *Recollections and Reminiscences 1861–1865*, Vol. 12 (2002)

Starr, Louis M. *Bohemian Brigade: Civil War Newsmen in Action* (Madison, WI: University of Wisconsin Press, 1987)

Sterns, Austin C. and Arthur A. Kent, Ed. *Three Years with Company K* (London: Associated University Press, 1976)

Stevens, C. A. *Berdan's United States Sharpshooters in the Army of the Potomac, 1861–1865* (Dayton, OH: Morningside Books, 1984)

Stickley, E. E. *The Confederate Veteran*, Vol. 22 (December 1914)

Stocker, Jeffrey D., Ed. *From Huntsville to Appomattox, R. T. Coles' History of the 4th Regiment, Alabama Volunteer Infantry, C.S.A., Army of Northern Virginia* (Knoxville: University of Tennessee Press, 2005)

Strother, David H. "Personal Recollections of the War," *Harper's New Monthly Magazine*, No. CCXIII, Vol. XXXVI (February 1868)

Styple, William B. *Generals in Bronze: Interviewing the Commanders of the Civil War.* (Kearny, NJ: Belle Grove Publishing Co., 2005)

Styple, William B., Ed. *Letters from the Peninsula: The Civil War Letters of General Philip Kearny.* (Kearny, NJ: Belle Grove Publishing Co., 1988)

Sumner, Samuel S. "The Antietam Campaign," *Civil War and Miscellaneous Papers: Papers of the Military Historical Society of Massachusetts*, Vol. XIV (Boston: The Military Historical Society of Massachusetts, 1918)

Taylor, Walter H. *General Lee: His Campaigns in Virginia, 1861–1865* (Lincoln, NE: University of Nebraska Press, 1994)

Thomas, Henry W. *History of the Doles-Cook Brigade, Army of Northern Virginia, C.S.A.* (Dayton, OH: Morningside Books, 1988)

Thomas, Howard. *Boys in Blue from the Adirondack Foothills* (Prospect, NY: Prospect Books, 1960)

Thomas, Mary Warner. *The Civil War Letters of First Lieutenant James B. Thomas; Adjutant, 107th Pennsylvania Volunteers* (Butternut and Blue, 1995)

Thompson, O. R. Howard and Rausch, Wm. H. *History of the "Bucktails," Kane Rifle Regiment of the Pennsylvania Reserve Corps* (Dayton, OH: Morningside Books, 1988)

Thompson, Orville. *Narrative of the Service of the Seventh Indiana Infantry in the War for the Union: From Philippi to Appomattox* (Self-published, 1920)

21st Regiment Veteran's Association of Buffalo. *Chronicles of the 21st New York: Buffalo's First Regiment.* (Buffalo, New York: 1887)

Vanderslice, Catherine H. *The Civil War Letters of George Washington Beidelman* (New York: Vantage Press, 1918)

Vautier, John D. *History of the 88th Pennsylvania Volunteers in the War for the Union, 1861–1865.* (Philadelphia: J. B. Lippincott Co., 1894)

Von Borcke, Heros. *Memoirs of the Confederate War for Independence, Vol. 1* (Berlin: E. M. Mittler, 1898)

Waitt, Ernest Linden. *History of the Nineteenth Regiment Massachusetts Volunteer Infantry, 1861–1865.* (Salem, MA: Salem Press. 1906)

Walcott, Charles F. *History of the Twenty-First Regiment Massachusetts Volunteers in the War for the Preservation of the Union, 1861–1865.* (Boston, 1901)

Walker, Keven M. *A Guide to the Battlefield Landscapes: Antietam Farmsteads* (Sharpsburg, MD: Western Maryland Interpretive Association, 2010)

Wallace, Jr. Lee A. *5th Virginia Infantry* (Lynchburg, Virginia: H. E. Howard, Inc., 1988)

Walpole, Spenser. *The Life of Lord John Russell, Vol. 2* (University of Michigan, 1889, 1968)

War Talks In Kansas: A Series Of Papers Read Before The Kansas Commandery Of The Military Order Of The Loyal Legion Of The United States (Kansas City, MO: Franklin Hudson Publishing Co., 1906)

War Sketches and Incidents. as Related by Companions of the Iowa Commandery, Military Order of the Loyal Legion of the United States, Vol. I (Des Moines: Press of P. C. Kenyon, 1898)

Warner, Ezra. *Generals in Blue: Lives of the Union Commanders* (Baton Rouge: Louisiana State University Press, 2006)

Washburn, George. *A Complete History and Record of the 108th Regiment New York Vols. from 1862 to 1894* (Rochester: Press of E. R. Andrews, 1894)

Welles, Gideon. "The History of Emancipation," *The Galaxy*, Vol. 14, 1872

Welles, Gideon. *Diary of Gideon Welles, Vol. 1* (Boston, 1911)

Weymouth, A. B. *A Memorial Sketch of Lt. Edgar M. Newcomb of the Nineteenth Massachusetts Volunteers* (Malden, MA: Private Publisher, 1883)

White, Gregory C. *"This Most Bloody & Cruel Drama:" A History of the 31st Georgia Volunteer Infantry* (Baltimore: Butternut and Blue, 1997)

Williams, Alpheus S. *From the Cannon's Mouth: The Civil War Letters of General Alpheus Williams* (Lincoln, NE: University of Nebraska Press, 1995)

Wilshin, Francis F. *Historic Antietam Structures* (National Park Service, 1969)

Wilson, James Harrison. *Under the Old Flag*, Vol. 1 (London: D. Appleton and Co., 1912)

Wilson, Lawrence. *Itinerary of the Seventh Ohio Volunteer Infantry 1861–1864* (New York: The Neale Publishing Company, 1907)

Woodward, E. M. *Our Campaigns; or, the Marches, Bivouacs, Battles, Incidents of Camp Life and History of Our Regiment During Its Three Years Term of Service* (2nd PA Reserves) (New York: International Book Company)

Wyckoff, Mac. *A History of the 2nd South Carolina Infantry: 1861–65* (Sergeant Kirkland's Museum and Historical Society, 1994)

Manuscripts and Unpublished Works

William S. Albert correspondence with Randolph B. Marcy, September 17, 1862, George B. McClellan Papers, Library of Congress, Series I, Vol. 80, Item 16261

William Allan, *Conversations with Lee*, February 16, 1868

William H. Ash letter, September 27, 1862, Author's collection

John C. Babcock, Record of Service, National Archives, Record 2096, Roll 45

Delevan Bates Civil War Letters, Letter of September 22, 1862 http://www.rootsweb.com/~necivwar/CW/bates/genbate1.htr

Edward M. Burruss letter to John C. Burruss, John C. Burruss Papers, Louisiana State University

Rush P. Cady letter to Gustavus Cady, September 27, 1862. Rush P. Cady Collection, Hamilton College Archives, Clinton, NY

Ezra Ayres Carman. "The Maryland Campaign of 1862," Carman Papers, Library of Congress

Carman Memorandum, March 9, 1897, Carman-Cope Letters, Antietam National Battlefield

"The Citizen Soldier" article (12th Massachusetts), 1869, Antietam National Battlefield

Albert V. Colburn message to Edwin V. Sumner September 17, 1862, Records of US Army Continental Commands, Entry 45, Part 2, RG 393. National Archives

John Conline papers, January 7, 1897. http://suvcw.org/mollus/warppaers/MIv2p110.htm

Frederick Crouse, Manuscript, "The Antietam Experience of Frederick Crouse, 128th Pennsylvania," Antietam National Battlefield

Rufus R. Dawes letter to Carman and map, January 14, 1899, Antietam National Battlefield

Rufus R. Dawes letter to E. A. Carman, July 7, 1896, Antietam National Battlefield

John C. Delaney letter to E. A. Carman, March 27, 1891, Antietam National Battlefield

Nelson Henry Davis letter to George McClellan, January 31, 1876, Antietam National Battlefield, Carman Collection

W. W. Dudley sketch map (19th Indiana), Antietam National Battlefield

"Explanation of Hoyt's map" (7th Wisconsin), January 22, 1895, Antietam National Battlefield

The First Light Battery (1st New Hampshire) pamphlet, Manchester, NH, 1891

Edwin Forbes drawing "The Battle of Antietam or Sharpsburg," September 17, 1862, Library of Congress Print and Photograph Collection, Forbes no. 37 and related number key

John V. Ferguson letter, October 16, 1862. John V. Ferguson Letters. New York Military Museum

George Sears Greene, "The Battle of Antietam" manuscript, The Rhode Island Historical Society

Louis Greenleaf letter and map to E. A. Carman, December 13, 1894, Antietam National Battlefield, Carman Collection

Charles H. Hayden letter to Laura Hayden, October 10, 1862. "The Civil War Letters of Charles Harvey Hayden, Patriot & Hero, 97th New York Volunteer Infantry" complied by A. L. Greening, New York State Military Museum

O. T. (Orlando T.) Hanks 1861–1865, 1918, Dolph Briscoe Center for American History, University of Texas at Austin, Box 2R31

W. H. Holstead letter to John Gould, March 9, 1893, Antietam National Battlefield

George B. McClellan Papers, Library of Congress

Dennis McGee letter of September 21, 1862, Mauch Chunk Gazette, October 9, 1862

Herbert von Hammerstein correspondence with Albert V. Colburn, 17 September 1862, George B. McClellan Papers, Library of Congress, Series I, Vol. 80, Item 16261

John D. Hill letter (107th New York), US Army Military History Institute CWTI Collection

History of Lost and Found: Diary of CDM Broomhall, 124th Pennsylvania, http://aotw.org/exhibit.php

"History of the Ninth New York (83rd Volunteers)," Antietam National Battlefield

http.//www.arlingtoncemetary.net/jgibbon.htm

"Living in a Linear World," http://www.case-studies.com

"Linear Thinking and System Thinking," http://www.ftlcomm.com

http://freepages.genealogy.rootsweb.com/~crackerbarrel/Hartsuff.html

http://home.earthlink.net/~tjreesecg/regulars/id 10.html. http://www.civilwarhome.com/Bio/sykesbio.htm

Joseph Hooker military papers, 1861–1864, Box 9, Huntington Library, San Marino, California

Enoch Jones, 26th New York map, March 15, 1893, Antietam National Battlefield

S. D. Lee manuscript "Three Personal Incidents in the Battle of Sharpsburg or Antietam, Fought September 17, 1862," W. F. Smith Papers, Vermont Historical Society

John A. Lehman letter to Mr. Short, April 30, 1866. William Oland Bourne Papers, New York Historical Society

Lafayette McLaws letter to Henry Heth, December 13, 1894, Antietam National Battlefiel, Carman Collection

John Albert Monroe, "Battery D, First Rhode Island Light Artillery, at the Battle of Antietam, September 17, 1862," Personal Narrative of Events in the War of the Rebellion, Being Papers Read Before the Rhode Island Soldiers and Sailors Historical Society, Series 3, No. 16 (Providence: The Rhode Island Soldiers and Sailors Historical Society)

Henry R. Myer, "88th Pennsylvania," Antietam National Battlefield

National Archives, Antietam Battlefield Studies

NAT Letter, 6 Oct. 1862. Private collection of Al Feidler, Jr.

90th Pennsylvania Association letter to E. A. Carman, March 23, 1895, Antietam National Battlefield

90th Pennsylvania map, 5 January 1895, Antietam National Battlefield

Edwin W. Pearce letter (107th Pennsylvania), October 16, 1862. Author's collection

Dudley T. Peebles (18th Mississippi) letter, Antietam National Battlefield

Eugene Powell letter, Antietam Collection, Dartmouth University

John Ransom map of 21st New York movements, May 16, 1895, Antietam National Battlefield

Lieutenant Henry Ropes letters, 20th Massachusetts, September 20, 1862

http://harvardregiment.org/ropesltr1.htr

William F. Rogers letter and map to E. A. Carman, undated, Antietam National Battlefield

George Ruggles telegram to General Sumner, Records of U.S. Army Continental Commands, Telegrams Received, 1862–1865, Entry 45, Part 2, RG 393, National Archives

Alfred Sellers letter to E. A. Carman, January 5, 1895, National Archives, Record Group 94, Antietam Battlefield Board, Antietam National Battlefield

Alfred Sellers letter to Gould, December 31, 1894, National Archives, Record Group 94, Antietam Battlefield Board, Antietam National Battlefield

Lieutenant Colonel L. C. Skinner (104th New York) map to E. A. Carman, March 24, 1895, Antietam National Battlefield

Captain Michael Shuler letter (33rd Virginia Infantry). Author's collection

George W. Smalley, "New York Tribune Narrative"

J. M. Smither letter, 5th Texas, Antietam Collection, Dartmouth College Library

Southern Historical Society Papers, Richmond, Vol. X

John D. Stevens letter, October 9, 1862. Author's collection

Samuel S. Sumner letter to George B. Davies, April 4, 1897, John C. Ropes Files, Military Historical
    Society Collection, Boston: Boston University

The Times, August 15, 1862

"13th Massachusetts," Carman Papers, Antietam National Battlefield

13th Mississippi annotated map, Antietam National Battlefield

United State Geologic Survey (USGS) Digital elevation model (DEM), https://viewer.nationalmap.gov

United States Department of Agriculture—Forest Service (USDA-FS) orthoimagery,
    https://earthexplorer.usgs.gov

Records of US Army Continental Commands, Entry 45, Part 2, RG 393, National Archives

John A. Vautier "88 Penn. Sketch", January 19, 1895, Antietam National Battlefield

John A. Vautier letter, June 1, 1896, Antietam National Battlefield

William B. Westervelt Diary and Memoirs (27th New York), Entries for 15th, 16th, 17th, and 18th
    September 1862, US Army Military History Institute, Manuscript Collection

George Watson letter to John Gould, April 22, 1893, Antietam National Battlefield

B. H. Witcher letter to John Gould, Antietam Collection, Dartmouth University

Captain John H. Woodward memoirs (23rd NY), US Army Military History Institute CWTI Collection

Endnotes

Chapter 1

1   *D. R. Miller Farmstead, Antietam National Battlefield: Cultural Landscape Inventory,* Antietam National Battlefield; National Park Service, 2005; *Miller Farmstead: Antietam National Battlefield: Historic Structures Report* (Oehrlin & Assoc. Architects; National Park Service, 1993); Kathleen A. Ernst, *Too Afraid to Cry: Maryland Civilians in the Antietam Campaign* (Mechanicsburg, Pennsylvania: Stackpole Books, 1999), pp. 132–34; Keven M. Walker, *A Guide to the Battlefield Landscapes: Antietam Farmsteads* (Sharpsburg, MD: Western Maryland Interpretive Association, 2010), pp. 34–38.

2   Walker, *A Guide to the Battlefield Landscapes,* pp. 34–38.

3   Walter H. Taylor, *General Lee: His Campaigns in Virginia, 1861–1865* (Lincoln: University of Nebraska Press, 1994), pp. 116–17; William Allan, *Stonewall Jackson, Robert E. Lee, and the Army of Northern Virginia, 1862* (New York: Da Capo Press, 1995), p. 322

4   Jedediah Hotchkiss, *Make Me a Map of the Valley: The Civil War Journal of Stonewall Jackson's Topographer* (Dallas: Southern Methodist University Press, 1973), p. 78; James A. Kegel, *North with Lee and Jackson: The Lost Story of Gettysburg* (Mechanicsburg, PA: Stackpole Books, 1996), pp. 99–116, p. 151; William Allan, *"Conversations with Lee",* February 16, 1868.

5   *The War of the Rebellion: A Compilation of the Official Records of the Union and Confederate Armies, Series I, Volume XIX, Parts I and II* (Washington, DC, Government Printing Office, 1887), hereafter cited as "OR" listing the specific series, volume, and part used, Vol. XII, Part 2, p. 557.

6   Virginia Mason, *The Public Life and Diplomatic Correspondence of James M. Mason,* Judah Benjamin to James Mason, April 12, 1862 (New York, 1904), p. 294; James M. McPherson, *Crossroads of Freedom: Antietam* (Oxford: Oxford University Press, 2002), p. 37.

7   McPherson, *Crossroads of Freedom: Antietam,* p. 38, p. 58. *The Times,* August 15, 1862.

8   *New York Tribune,* 11 February 1862; McPherson, *Crossroads of Freedom: Antietam,* p. 39; Mason, *Correspondence of James M. Mason,* April 12, 1862, p. 294.

9   Lynn M. Case and Warren F. Spencer, *The United States and France: Civil War Diplomacy* (Philadelphia: The University of Pennsylvania Press, 1970 and 2016), pp. 300–8; McPherson, *Crossroads of Freedom: Antietam,* pp. 58–61; Amanda Foreman, *A World on Fire: Britain's Crucial Role in the American Civil War* (New York: Random House, 2012), pp. 278–81.

10 Spenser Walpole, *The Life of Lord John Russell, Vol. 2* (University of Michigan, 1889 and 1968), p. 349; David F. Krein, *The Last Palmerston Government: Foreign Policy, Domestic Politics, and the Genesis of "Splendid Isolation"* (Ames, Iowa: Iowa State University Press, 1978), p. 66; Foreman *A World on Fire,* pp. 48–51, pp. 173–74, pp. 223–25, pp. 277–1, pp. 292–95; McPherson, *Crossroads of Freedom: Antietam,* pp. 58–61.

11 Foreman, *A World on Fire,* pp.292–95; McPherson, *Crossroads of Freedom: Antietam,* pp. 39–40.

12 Howard Jones, *Abraham Lincoln and a New Birth of Freedom* (University of Nebraska Press, 2002), p. 63; James McPherson, *Battle Cry of Freedom: The Civil War Era* (Oxford; Oxford University Press, 1988), pp. 557–66.

13 John J. Nicolay and John Hay, *Abraham Lincoln: A History,* Vol. VI (New York: The Century Company, 1890, 2009), pp. 158–63; McPherson, *Battle Cry of Freedom,* pp. 357–58, 363–66.

March 10, 1842, Cadet Application Paper, 1803–1866 Record M-688) reel 135, no. 127, LOC; Rafuse, *McClellan's War*, pp. 16–26, p. 29; George B. McClellan to Arthur McClellan, McClellan Papers, Vol. A7/reel 3, LOC.

32 McClellan to Mary Ellen, May 10, 1862, May 22, 1862, September 2, 1862, Sears, *The Civil War Papers of George B. McClellan*, pp. 262–63, p. 273, p. 275, p. 428; McClellan to Burnside, May 21, 1862, Sears, *The Civil War Papers of George B. McClellan*, pp. 269–70; OR, Vol. IX, p. 392.

33 James Havelock Campbell *McClellan: A Vindication of the Military Career of General George McClellan: A Lawyer's Brief* (New York: The Neale Co., 1916), p. 10; Rafuse, *McClellan's War*, p. 36, pp. 62–65.

34 George B. McClellan, *The Armies of Europe: Comprising in Detail of the Military Systems of England, France, Russia, Prussia, Austria, and Sardinia* (Philadelphia: 1861); Matthew Moten, *The Delafield Commission*, pp. 184–91. There is a great deal of myth surrounding the origin of the McClellan saddle but one issue generally not in dispute is that George McClellan was the one who introduced it to the US Army (probably aided by his personal ties to Secretary of War Davis, who was the driver behind adopting a new saddle) and that he copied an existing foreign model, rather creating a unique, original saddle design.

35 McClellan to Mary Ellen McClellan, July 10, 1861, Sears, *The Civil War Papers of George McClellan*, p. 50; John Keegan, *Fields of Battle: The Wars for North America* (New York: Vintage Books, 1995), p. 232; John S. D. Eisenhower *Agent of Destiny: The Life and Times of General Winfield Scott* (New York: The Free Press, 1997), pp. 238–42.

36 Shawn W. Rosenberg *The Not So Common Sense: Differences in How People Judge Social and Political Life* (New Haven: Yale University Press, 2002), pp. 71–78, pp. 79–92; Klaus Mainzer *Thinking in Complexity: The Conceptual Dynamics of Matter, Mind, and Mankind* (Berlin: Springer, 2007), pp. 1–16; http://www.ftlcomm.com, "Linear Thinking and System Thinking;" http://www.case-studies.com, "Living in a Linear World;" Rafuse, *McClellan's War*, pp. 8–9, pp. 27–29, pp. 51–52, pp. 80–81.

37 OR, Vol. XI, Part 1, pp. 5–10.

Chapter 2

1 Clifford Dowdey and Loius H. Manarin, Eds., *The Wartime Papers of Robert E. Lee* (New York: Da Capo Press, 1961), pp. 292–94.

2 Joseph Harsh, *Taken at the Flood; Robert E. Lee and Confederate Strategy in the Maryland Campaign of 1862.* (Kent, Ohio: The Kent State University Press, 1999), pp. 55–57.

3 John Bell Hood *Advance and Retreat* (New York: Da Capo Press, 1993), p. 38.; Southern Historical Society Papers, (Richmond), Vol. X, p. 507; James V. Murfin, *The Gleam of Bayonets: The Battle of Antietam and Robert E. Lee's Maryland Campaign*, September 1862. Baton Rouge: Louisiana State University Press, 1993, pp. 93–94.

4 Murfin, *Gleam of Bayonets*, pp. 110–11.

5 Lee circular "To the People of Maryland," September 8, 1862; Lee to Davis, September 8, 1862, Dowdey. *The Wartime Papers of Robert E. Lee*, pp. 299–300, 301; OR, XIX, Vol. 1, pp. 600–2.

6 Lee to Davis, September 3, 1862; Lee to Davis, September 8, 1862, Dowdey, *The Wartime Papers of Robert E. Lee*, pp. 292–94, p. 299.

7 Lee to Davis, September 3, 1862; Lee to Davis, September 9, 1862, Dowdey, *The Wartime Papers of Robert E. Lee*, pp. 292–94, p. 303.

8 Lee to Davis, September 5, 1862, Dowdey, *The Wartime Papers of Robert E. Lee*, pp. 295–96; "North to Antietam", *Battles and Leaders of the Civil War* (New York: Castle Books, 1956), pp. 605–6.

9 Lee to Davis, September 8, 1862, Dowdey, *The Wartime Papers of Robert E. Lee*, p. 303; *Battles and Leaders*, p. 606.

10 Lee to Davis, September 8, 1862, Dowdey, *The Wartime Papers of Robert E. Lee*, p. 300; *Battles and Leaders*, pp. 605–606.; OR, Vol. XIX, Part 1, pp. 600–1.

11 OR, Vol. XIX, Part 1, pp. 197–98, p. 214.; OR, Vol. IX, Part 1, p. 279. Even so, no sooner did the IX Corps form than one of one of its most capable division commanders was ordered away.

Special Orders Number 224 assigned Major General Jesse Reno to command of the Army of Virginia's III Corps, replacing Irvin McDowell who had asked to be relieved.

12 McClellan to Lincoln, September 6, 1862, Sears, *The Civil War Papers of George B. McClellan*, pp. 436–37.

13 OR, Vol. XIX, Pt. 1, p. 290; McClellan for the first time since resuming command of the Army of the Potomac, in two separate dispatches on September 10, refers indirectly to the existence of the wings and would do so on several occasions before the battle of Antietam. Adding to evidence that McClellan had instituted the wing structure by September 10 are dispatches written that same day by General Reno—referring to himself as "Commanding, Ninth Army Corps"—and a message from Burnside to Hooker, directing the I Corps commander both where and in what formation to move his corps in the next day's advance.

14 McClellan to Halleck, September 8, 1862, Sears, *The Civil War Papers of George B. McClellan*, pp. 438–39; OR, Vol. XIX, Part 1, p. 209.

15 McClellan to Halleck, September 8, 1862, September 9, 1862, September 10, 1862, Sears, *The Civil War Papers of George B. McClellan*, pp. 438–39, pp. 440–41, p. 447; OR, Vol. XIX, Part. 1, p. 234.

16 OR, Vol. IX, Part 1, p. 255. Determining the number of available troops or combatants is a difficult and inexact process and the lack of reliable, official troop strengths for the Army of the Potomac in early September 1862 makes this task even more challenging. These numbers are drawn from Ezra Carman's appendix in his Antietam manuscript (Pierro, *The Maryland Campaign*, Appendix J, pp. 453–65; Clemens, *The Maryland Campaign*, Appendix Two, pp. 569–600.), Murfin's *Gleam of Bayonets* (pp. 85–86 and pp. 125–29), as well as Stephen W. Sears' *Landscape Turned Red: The Battle of Antietam*. New York: Warner Books, 1983, pp. 190–92). Scott Hartwig's book *To Antietam Creek* lists an even lower number, "60,000–62,000 effectives" (p. 593). Troop totals used in each of these works draws from collections of primary sources, including McClellan's papers and "Memorandum Showing the Strength of the Army of the Potomac at the Battle of Antietam."

17 OR, Vol. XIX, Part 1, pp. 219, p. 254, p. 255, p. 271, pp. 281–82.

18 Timothy J. Reese, *High-Water Mark: The 1862 Maryland Campaign in Strategic Perspective* (Baltimore: Butternut and Blue), p. 23.

19 Allan, *Stonewall Jackson, Robert E. Lee, and the Army of Northern Virginia*, pp. 332–33.

20 John Gibbon, *Personal Recollections of the Civil War.* (New York: 1928), p. 73; Murfin, *Gleam of Bayonets*, p. 133.

21 OR, Vol. LI, Part 1, p. 829; Reese, *High-Water Mark*, pp. 22–31.

22 OR, Vol. XIX, Part 1, pp. 45–46.; OR, Vol. LI, Part 1, p. 829; McClellan to William Franklin, September 13, 1862, Sears, *Civil War Papers of George McClellan*, pp. 454–55.

23 McClellan expected to march through, rather than have to fight for, the South Mountain passes as reflected by General Hooker's later comment that "I was requested by the major-General Commanding the Army of the Potomac to ride to the front and examine the country in the neighborhood of where it had been proposed to pass the army over South Mountain." OR, Vol. I, Part 1, p. 214.

24 OR, Vol. XIX, Part 1, p. 417.

25 Sears, *Landscape Turned Red*, pp. 151–54, p. 156. I recognize that there remains disagreement about the origin and use of the nickname "Iron Brigade" for Gibbon's Brigade. Almost certainly no one referred to Gibbon's command as such during the battle, even if it had been coined during the fighting at South Mountain as is the conventional wisdom (and as General McClellan claimed to General John Callis). Regardless if it was earned because of fighting at Second Manassas, South Mountain, Antietam, Gettysburg, or elsewhere, this name makes the brigade familiar with modern readers and so I have chosen to use it in the next.

26 OR, Vol. I, Part 1, p. 417; Sears, *Landscape Turned Red*, pp. 148; 154-155.

27 Franklin to McClellan, September 15, 1862, McClellan Papers, Reel 32, LOC; OR, Vol. I, Part 1, pp. 374–76; Sears, *Landscape Turned Red*, pp. 162–63.

28 OR, Vol. I, Part 1, pp. 380–81, pp. 382–83, p. 401.

29 McClellan to Franklin, September 13, 1862, OR, Vol. I, Part 1, pp. 45–46.

30 OR, Vol. I, Part 1, p. 45; E. A. Carman and Joseph Pierro, Ed., *The Maryland Campaign of 1862; Ezra A. Carman's Definitive Study of the Union and Confederates at Antietam.* (New York: Routledge Books, 2008), pp. 337–343; E. A. Carman and Thomas G. Clemens, Ed., *The Maryland Campaign of 1862, Vol. II: Antietam* (California: Savas Beatie, 2012), pp. 422–47; The Ezra Ayres Carman Papers, LOC. Carman's monumental study of Antietam—and, indeed, of much of the war—is an indispensable source for any student of the battle of Antietam. Although it is not without flaws and errors, Carman's manuscript includes details unavailable anywhere else, most of which he obtained from conversations and correspondence with first-hand sources. I have chosen to source my references to Carman's papers to both Joseph Pierro's book—the first to make Carman's manuscript available in published form—and to Thomas Clemens' more recent and more fulsomely annotated version. In addition to being widely available (as opposed to Carman's original manuscript in the National Archives, which moreover lacks page numbers or other references), both volumes provide sources for many of the unattributed portions of Carman's original manuscript, citing Carman's papers and other sources only available in the holdings of the Library of Congress, Antietam National Battlefield, and in other collections.

31 Lee to Davis, September 12, 1862 and Chilton to McLaws, September 14, 1862, Dowdey, *The Wartime Papers of Robert E. Lee*, pp. 304–5, pp. 307–8; OR, Vol. XIX, Part 1, p. 145; Harsh, *Taken at the Flood*, p. 289, p. 297; OR, Vol. LI, Part 2, pp. 618–19.

32 OR, Vol. XIX, Part 1, p. 148; Harsh, *Taken at the Flood*, pp. 300–3.

33 Lee to Davis, September 16, 1862, Dowdey, *The Wartime Papers of Robert E. Lee*, pp. 309–10; Harsh, *Taken at the Flood*, pp. 303–7; OR, Vol. XIX, Part 1, p. 844.

34 D. Scott Hartwig, *To Antietam Creek: The Maryland Campaign of September 1862* (Baltimore, Maryland: Johns Hopkins University Press, 2012), p. 598; Harsh, *Taken at the Flood*, pp. 372–272. Harsh argues Jackson rejected entrenching because he wished to preserve maneuver during counterattacks. While probably true, Harsh might have taken this thinking further to consider what strategic objectives Lee and Jackson wanted and needed this fight to accomplish.

35 Lee to Davis, September 16, 1862, Dowdey, *The Wartime Papers of Robert E. Lee*, pp. 309–10; Harsh, *Taken at the Flood*, p. 308; OR, Vol. XIX, Part 1, p. 148.

36 McClellan to Halleck, September 15, 1862, Sears, *Civil War Papers of George McClellan*, pp. 461–62.

37 McClellan to Halleck, 8:30a.m. September 15, 1862, Sears, *Civil War Papers of George McClellan*, p. 462; OR, Vol. XIX, Part 1, pp. 28–29, p. 153. Rafuse, *McClellan's War*, pp. 302–4. Reflecting McClellan's "measured aggressiveness," he responded to Franklin's message that he should "drive the enemy in your front," but "be cautious in doing it," essentially duplicating his approach in gradually pushing west from Boonsboro. Later in the day, after receiving Franklin's message that the enemy in Pleasant Valley was retreating, McClellan directed the VI Corps' commander to hold the enemy in check without bringing on battle; the bulk of the army would gather at Sharpsburg for an "affair" before joining Franklin's command. Such shifting intentions reflect the uncertain intelligence available to McClellan and his uncertain, halting efforts to form a plan of action.

38 OR, Vol. XIX, Part 1, pp. 216–7.

39 OR, Vol. I, Part 1, p. 217; Harsh, *Taken at the Flood*, pp. 312–13.

40 Harsh, *Taken at the Flood*, pp. 312–13; OR, Vol. XIX, Part 1, p. 217.

41 OR, Vol. XIX, Part 1, p. 217.

42 Jacob D. Cox *Reminisces of the Civil War* (New York: Charles Scribner's Sons, 1900), p. 300. Rafuse, *McClellan's War*, pp. 304–5. Rafuse argues that McClellan determined at that hilltop

meeting to attack but lacking sufficient remaining daylight, he rejected striking that evening. This is possible—although Rafuse offers no source for this claim—but ignores McClellan's September 15 message to Franklin, which that general took as an indication McClellan intended to attack at Sharpsburg (Marcy to Franklin, September 15, 1862).

43 OR, Vol. I, Part 1, pp. 53–54; Harsh, *Taken at the Flood*, pp. 314–15.

44 Freeman Ankrum, *Sidelights of Brethren History* (Elgin, Ohio: The Brethren Press, 1962), p. 105; Francis F. Wilshin, *Historic Antietam Structures*, (National Park Service, 1969), p. 6; William A. Frassanito, *Antietam: The Photographic Legacy of America's Bloodiest Day* (New York: Charles Scribner's Sons, 1978), p. 109.

45 Catherine H. Vanderslice, *The Civil War Letters of George Washington Beidelman* (New York: Vantage Press, 1918, p. 102.

Chapter 3

1 Joseph Harsh, *Sounding the Shallows: A Confederate Companion for the Maryland Campaign of 1862* (Kent, Ohio: The Kent State University Press, 2000), pp. 18–19.

2 Patricia A. Murphy, *The Civil War Diary of Ephraim C. Brown, 1862* (Lakeland Florida: self-published, 1999), p. 22; OR, Vol. XIX, Part 1, p. 291; Carman and Pierro, Ed., *The Maryland Campaign of 1862*, p. 202; Carman and Clemens, Ed., *The Maryland Campaign of 1862, Volume II*, pp. 18–19; Hartwig, *To Antietam Creek*, pp. 584–85.

3 OR, Vol. XIX, Pt. 1, pp. 844, 922–23, 1022, 1032.

4 Harsh, *Taken at the Flood*, p. 331; William M. Owen, *In Camp and Battle with the Washington Artillery of New Orleans. A narrative of Events during the Late Civil War from Bull Run to Appomattox and Spanish Fort* (Boston, Ticknor & Co., 1885), p. 140; OR, Vol. XIX, Part 1, p. 148; Carman and Pierro, Ed., *The Maryland Campaign*, p. 201; Carman and Clemens, Ed., *The Maryland Campaign, Vol. II*, pp. 17–18.

5 Heros von Borcke, *Memoirs of the Confederate War for Independence, Vol. 1.* (Berlin: E. M. Mittler, 1898), p. 148; Edward Porter Alexander *Fighting for the Confederacy* (Chapel Hill: University of North Carolina Press, 1998), p. 148. Joseph Harsh claims in *Taken at the Flood* that Lee considered moving his army to the left, toward Hagerstown, to get it out of the risky, vulnerable position at Sharpsburg. Lee's objective of this move, Harsh argues, would have been to find maneuvering room for the coming battle and to regain the initiative on his own terms. While all of this makes sense, there is no indication Lee ever did more than consider such an option—if, indeed, he did that much—and his actions on September 15 demonstrate Lee intended to stay and fight.

6 Carman and Pierro, Ed., *The Maryland Campaign*, p. 201; Carman and Clemens, Ed., *The Maryland Campaign, Vol. II*, pp. 17–18.

7 Henry Kyd Douglas, *I Rode With Stonewall* (Chapel Hill: University of North Carolina Press, 1968), p. 166. Harsh *Sounding the Shallows: A Confederate Companion*, Appendix F, pp. 196–97. Harsh notes General Walker's unreliable claims of two different times and days for Jackson's arrival—Carman reports both accounts, uncritically—and I have chosen to side with Harsh and Kyd Douglas. Nonetheless, both Harsh and Rafuse argue that Lee early on the 16th was preparing to move north toward Hagerstown to escape McClellan's army and battle, while also remaining in Maryland (Rafuse, *McClellan's War*, p. 313). While this is certainly possible—his three moves that morning suited multiple purposes—bringing forward artillery ammunition reflects Lee's decision, willingly or not, to fight at Sharpsburg.

8 OR, Vol. XIX, Part 1, pp. 307–8; Sears, *The Civil War Papers of George McClellan*, pp. 465–66.

9 OR, Vol. XIX, Part 1, p. 137, pp. 350–51, p. 353, p. 356, p. 436; Robert E. Denney, *Civil War Medicine: Care & Comfort of the Wounded* (New York: Sterling Publishing Co., 1995), p.

155; Carman and Pierro, Ed., *The Maryland Campaign*, p. 203; Carman and Clemens, Ed., *The Maryland Campaign, Vol. II*, pp. 30–32. Carman says, "Each battery, as soon as it came into position, opened upon such bodies of Confederate infantry as could be seen, and upon the Washington Artillery and Hood's Division batteries, on Cemetery Hill and the batteries on the ridge running north from it…" This statement almost certainly is inaccurate. First, the fog remained until 9:00, according to Carman and other accounts, and it is unlikely the battery commanders could see much beyond the vicinity of the western edge of the creek; they certainly could not have seen all the way to Cemetery Hill or the Sharpsburg ridge. Moreover, none of the OR accounts—Hunt's, Lt. Col. Hays's, Benjamin's, or Weed's—report opening immediately after deploying. Rather, those that mention it, like General Hunt, indicate the enemy opened "soon" on them (similarly suggesting the Confederates opened the artillery duel).

10 OR, Vol. XIX, Part 1, pp. 848–49, p. 1026; Harsh, *Taken at the Flood*, p. 335.

11 Ernst, *Too Afraid to Cry*, pp. 126–129, 140; Walker, *Antietam Farmsteads*, p. 38; Von Borcke, *Memoirs*, Vol. 1, pp. 226–229; Harsh, *Taken at the Flood*, p. 336.

12 OR, Vol. XIX, Part 1, pp. 29–30, p. 54; George McClellan, *McClellan's Own Story* (New York: Charles L. Webster and Co., 1887), p. 588.

13 OR, Vol. XIX, Part 1, pp. 888–89.

14 Lee to Davis, September 16, 1862, Dowdey, *The Wartime Papers of Robert E. Lee*, pp. 309–10; OR, Vol. XIX, Part 1, p. 140.

15 OR, Vol. XIX, Part 1, p. 55, pp. 423–24, pp. 889–90; Carman and Pierro, Ed., *The Maryland Campaign*, p. 205; Carman and Clemens, Ed., *The Maryland Campaign, Vol. II*, pp. 29–30; Sears *Landscape Turned Red*, pp. 180–81; Rafuse, *McClellan's War*, pp. 311–13.

16 The idea that the Union center lies just north of Sharpsburg flies in the face of the traditional understanding of the course of the fighting at Antietam. This traditional interpretation has long portrayed the fighting as moving from the Union right (the Cornfield, East and West Woods), to the center (the Sunken Road), to end at the left (the Burnside Bridge). While this view makes a complex battle more easily understandable, it ignores that there was no fighting in the Union center (held by Porter's V Corps at the Middle Bridge) and that the Sunken Road action should properly be considered part of the action on the Union right. General McClellan himself held this view—as reflected in his first, "preliminary" report of the battle—writing "The condition of things on the right toward the middle of the afternoon … was at this time unpromising. Sumner's, Hooker's, and Mansfield's corps had lost heavily … I was at one time compelled to draw two brigades from Porter's corps (the reserve) to strengthen the right. *Before I left the right to return to the center*, I became satisfied that the line would be held without these two brigades and countermanded the order…" McClellan is referring to his single personal visit to the right sometime after 1:00 that afternoon, during which the countermanded order to Porter to send two brigades was given. The portion of McClellan's report noted in italics (my emphasis) indicates McClellan's view of the field that day. OR, Vol. XIX, Part 1, pp. 30–31.

17 Carman and Pierro, Ed., *The Maryland Campaign*, p. 459, p. 465; Carman and Clemens, Ed., *The Maryland Campaign, Vol. II*, p. 583, pp. 598–99; Hartwig *To Antietam Creek*, pp. 674–86.

18 OR, Vol. XIX, Part 1, p. 118.

19 *Letter of the Secretary of War Transmitting Report on the Organization of the Army of the Potomac and its Campaigns in Virginia and Maryland* (Washington: Government Printing Office, 1887), p. 214; John C. Babcock, Record of Service, National Archives, Record 2096, Roll 45; OR Vol. XIX, Part 2, p. 254; Thomas L. Livermore Numbers and Losses in the Civil War (Millwood, NY: Kraus Reprint, 1977), pp. 92–93; OR, Vol. XIX, Part 1, p. 67; *Report of the Joint Committee on the Conduct of the War* (Washington: Government Printing Office, 1863), p. 441.

20 Albert D. Richardson, *The Secret Service, the Field, the Dungeon, and the Escape* (Hartford, CT: American Publishing Co., 1865), p. 279; Sears, *Landscape Turned Red*, pp. 191.

21   OR, Vol. XIX, Part 1, p. 217, p. 269; *Report of the Joint Committee on the Conduct of the War*, p. 581; Jacob Cox claimed in his *Century Magazine* article that on the afternoon of the 16th "I saw Burnside, and learned from him that McClellan had determined to let Hooker make a movement on our extreme right to turn Lee's position." Some historians have taken this to suggest that McClellan told Burnside about his plans for the coming battle but it is clear that even taking this statement at face value—neither McClellan, Burnside, nor Cox mention it in their OR nor is it raised in their Congressional testimony—all McClellan provided was information about Hooker's movement, not details of his wider battle plan. *Battles and Leaders*, Vol. 2, p. 631. Harsh reports that McClellan ordered Hooker to the right at 1:00p.m., but never provides a source for this claim. Harsh, *Taken at the Flood*, p. 350.

22   McClellan to Mary Ellen McClellan, September 12, 1862, Sears, *The Civil War Papers of George B. McClellan*, pp. 449–50.

23   OR, Vol. XIX, Part 1, p. 217; pp. 258–59, p. 268.

24   OR, Vol. XIX, Part 1, p. 217.

25   Robert Anderson "Official Report" (unpublished in OR) and Owen "Official Report," Joseph Hooker military papers, 1861–64, Box 9, Huntington Library, San Marino, California; John C. Delaney letter to E. A. Carman, March 27, 1891, Antietam National Battlefield. Delaney, of the 104th New York, speculated that "It was possibly 8 p.m. of the 16th when our Regt. was brought to a halt…"

26   Alan D. Gaff, *On Many a Bloody Field: Four Years in the Iron Brigade* (Bloomington: Indiana University Press, 1996), p. 184.

27   OR, Vol. XIX, Part 1, p. 223.

28   OR, Vol. XIX, Part 1, p. 217; Cecil D. Eby, *A Virginia Yankee in the Civil War* (Chapel Hill: University of North Carolina Press, 1961), p. 109; McClellan *McClellan's Own Story*, pp. 590–91. This meeting generated much conflicting comment by the participants, but only Hooker's OR account contains anything of the meeting's substance. David Strother's diary confirms the meeting—as does McClellan's published memoir—but contains little beyond that. Strother added significantly more detail of the meeting in his fanciful postwar *Harper's New Monthly Magazine* article but none of this can be confirmed, particularly his unlikely presentiments of Hooker's wounding the next day. Because so much of what Strother wrote in this post-war article is doubtful when compared with entries in his more reliable wartime diary, I have not included this account. McClellan, too, confirmed the fact of the meeting but similarly added fanciful claims—that he rode "at the head of the column, until the top of the ridge was fairly gained, indicated a new direction to be taken, and then returned to headquarters"—which are doubtful in the extreme, so I also have not included these claims.

29   OR, Vol. LI, Part 1, p. 839; OR, Vol. XIX, Part 1, p. 275. Harsh criticizes McClellan's plan and Hooker's execution here, arguing that advancing so far right missed the "hinge of Lee's line at the Piper farm" and that Hooker risked marching beyond the support of Union artillery and infantry reinforcements. This criticism ignores that no Federal officer—including McClellan—knew the actual right of the Confederate line, so this rightward advance was in keeping with the intelligence then available. Similarly, Hooker carried his own artillery, as would Mansfield and (later) Sumner, providing all the support he needed. Harsh, *Taken at the Flood*, p. 354.

30   OR, Vol. XIX, Part 1, p. 217, p. 269.

31   Carman and Pierro, Ed., *The Maryland Campaign*, p. 206; Carman and Clemens, Ed., *The Maryland Campaign, Vol. II*, pp. 29–37.

32   Carman and Pierro, Ed., *The Maryland Campaign*, p. 206; Carman and Clemens, Ed., *The Maryland Campaign, Vol. II*, pp. 29–37.

33   Samuel W. Owen "Official Report" (unpublished in OR), Joseph Hooker military papers, 1861–64, Box 9, Huntington Library, San Marino, California; *History of the Third Pennsylvania Cavalry,*

Sixteenth Regiment Pennsylvania Volunteers in the American Civil War (Philadelphia: Franklin Publishing Co., 1905), pp. 121–22. Owen's unpublished OR states a squadron—normally two companies—while the 3rd Pennsylvania's regimental history reported three companies.

34   *History of the Third Pennsylvania Cavalry*, pp. 121–22.
35   *History of the Third Pennsylvania Cavalry*, pp. 121–22.
36   Truman Seymour "Official Report" (unpublished in OR), Joseph Hooker military papers, 1861–64, Box 9, Huntington Library, San Marino, California; OR, Vol. XIX, Part 1, p. 217, p. 269. Claims for the Sharps infantry rifle's rate of fire vary widely, with many modern sources claiming up to ten rounds per minute. This figure almost certainly is achieved when firing modern brass cartridges, rather than using the paper cartridge and separate percussion cap used during the Civil War. Regardless, the Sharps' rate of fire was considerably greater than that of conventional muskets.
37   OR, Vol. XIX, Part 1, p. 272.
38   OR, Vol. XIX, Part 1, p. 923, p. 936, p. 955, p. 1009. Although Captain Turner's OR account of the actions of the 5th Texas on the 16th does not clearly indicate that his regiment was pushed back, it does indicate that it entered the East Woods and advanced as far as the western fence line because Turner notes that they were "ordered to the edge of the woods to support our (the 4th Texas') skirmishers, which were then east of the East Woods. Moreover, Carman's account clearly describes the 5th Texas falling back, noting that the Bucktails were "driving in the skirmishers of the 4th Texas and some of the 5th Texas … slowly following them into the woods…" Carman and Pierro, Ed., *The Maryland Campaign,* p. 207; Carman and Clemens, Ed., *The Maryland Campaign, Vol. II*, pp. 33–36.
39   Carman and Pierro, Ed. *The Maryland Campaign,* p. 207; Carman and Clemens, Ed., *The Maryland Campaign, Vol. II*, pp. 33–36; OR, Vol. XIX, Part 1, p. 272.
40   Carman and Pierro, Ed., *The Maryland Campaign,* p. 207; Carman and Clemens, Ed., *The Maryland Campaign, Vol. II*, pp. 33–36; O. R. Howard Thompson, and Wm. H. Rausch, *History of the "Bucktails," Kane Rifle Regiment of the Pennsylvania Reserve Corps* (Dayton, Ohio: Morningside Books, 1988), pp. 209–10.
41   Truman Seymour "Official Report" (unpublished in OR), Joseph Hooker military papers, 1861–64, Box 9, Huntington Library, San Marino, California; Thompson, *History of the "Bucktails,"* pp. 209–10.
42   OR, Vol. XIX, Part 1, p. 272.
43   Seymour "Official Report" and Cooper "Report of the Actions Battery B First Regiment Penn. Artillery in the Battles of Sept. 14, 16, and 17 1862" (unpublished portion of OR), Joseph Hooker military papers, 1861–64, Box 9, Huntington Library, San Marino, California; Carman and Pierro, Ed., *The Maryland Campaign*, p. 207 Carman and Clemens, Ed., *The Maryland Campaign, Vol. II*, pp. 33–36.
44   Seymour "Official Report," Joseph Hooker military papers, 1861–64, Box 9, Huntington Library, San Marino, California; Carman and Pierro, Ed., *The Maryland Campaign,* p. 207; Carman and Clemens, Ed., *The Maryland Campaign, Vol. II*, pp. 33–36.
45   Anderson "Official Report" and Seymour "Official Report," Joseph Hooker military papers, 1861–64, Box 9, Huntington Library, San Marino, California; OR, Vol. XIX, Part 1, p. 268–69.
46   OR, Vol. XIX, Part 1, p. 269; Carman and Clemens, Ed., *The Maryland Campaign, Vol. II*, pp. 33–36; Hartwig, *To Antietam Creek*, p. 615.
47   D. R. Ransom "Official Report" (unpublished in OR) and J. J. Cooper "Report" (unpublished portion of OR), Joseph Hooker military papers, 1861–64, Box 9, Huntington Library, San Marino, California; Carman and Clemens, Ed., *The Maryland Campaign, Vol. II*, p. 39; Carman and Pierro, Ed., *The Maryland Campaign,* p. 207; OR, Vol. XIX, Part 1, pp. 268–69. Although Carman's manuscript reports Ransom's Battery deployed south of the North Woods, Ransom

report only notes it posted "on the edge of a woods several hundred yards to the right [of Cooper's Battery]," leaving it unclear if this is north or south of the North Woods. However, Ransom's OR states the battery was 800 yards from the enemy and Cooper's indicates Ransom's Battery helped drive away the Confederate battery (Lane's), suggesting Carman is probably correct.

48 Seymour "Official Report," Ransom "Official Report," and Cooper "Report," Joseph Hooker military papers, 1861–64, Box 9, Huntington Library, San Marino, California; O.R., Vol. XIX, Part 1, p. 927; Carman and Pierro, Ed., *The Maryland Campaign*, p. 208; Carman and Clemens, Ed., *The Maryland Campaign, Vol. II*, pp. 36–38.

49 Joseph L. Simpson "Official Report of Lieut. Simpson, Batty. A, 1st Penn. Artillery, Engagements of September 16th & 17th, 1862" (unpublished in OR) and Ransom "Official Report," Joseph Hooker military papers, 1861–64, Box 9, Huntington Library, San Marino, California; Carman and Pierro, Ed., *The Maryland Campaign*, p. 208; Carman and Clemens, Ed., *The Maryland Campaign, Vol. II*, pp. 36–38.

50 Jeffrey D. Stocker, Ed., *From Huntsville to Appomattox, R. T. Coles' History of the 4th Regiment, Alabama Volunteer Infantry, C.S.A., Army of Northern Virginia* (Knoxville, The University of Tennessee Press, 2005), pp. 65–66; John A. Lehman letter to Mr. Short, 30 April 1866, William Oland Bourne Papers, New York Historical Society.

51 OR, Vol. XIX, Part 1, p. 967, p. 954. General Jackson's location that night remains a bit of an enigma. Fitz Lee claimed that a lone rider, whom he identified as Jackson, emerged from the darkness on Nicodemus Heights to grab some sleep nearby his own field bivouac. Other sources placed Jackson on a couch in the Grove house in Sharpsburg, while Hood's account has Jackson in yet another spot sleeping in the field. While Jackson's location cannot be determined using only the available sources, it's possible that all of these are true and that Stonewall spent portions of the night sleeping in each of these locations.

52 OR, Vol. XIX, Part 1, p. 922.

53 OR, Vol. XIX, Part 1, pp. 976–77. Harsh suggests Lee's deployment, particularly Stuart's cavalry on the far Confederate left, might have been meant as a trap to lure Hooker's attack into striking far forward and with the river to his flank or rear. Perhaps, but highly unlikely; no sources back this claim and Lee's deployments and actions suggest he'd adopted a more conventional defensive approach here. Harsh, *Taken at the Flood*, p. 364.

54 Seymour "Official Report," Joseph Hooker military papers, 1861–64, Box 9, Huntington Library, San Marino, California; Carman and Pierro, Ed., *The Maryland Campaign*, p. 216; Carman and Clemens, Ed., *The Maryland Campaign, Vol. II*, pp. 57–60.

55 Susan Pendleton Lee, *Memoirs of William Nelson Pendleton, D.D.: Rector of Latimer Parish* (Philadelphia: J. B. Lippincott Company, 1893), pp. 218–19; Harsh, *Taken at the Flood*, pp. 337–38.

56 Owen "Official Report," Joseph Hooker military papers, 1861–64, Box 9, Huntington Library, San Marino, California; Carman and Pierro, Ed., *The Maryland Campaign*, p. 209; Carman and Clemens, Ed., *The Maryland Campaign, Vol. II*, pp. 38–41.

57 OR, Vol. XIX, Part 1, p. 217.

58 OR, Vol. XIX, Part 1, p. 217.

59 OR, Vol. XIX, Part 1, p. 217. McClellan's staffer Major David Strother claimed in 1868 that McClellan rode to the front late on the 16th—apparently taking only Strother and "a citizen"—but there is no other source backing up this claim. Moreover, Strother claimed they met with General Hooker but if this is so, why did Hooker not then ask for reinforcements, rather than by sending a dispatch to headquarters? Perhaps because like other claims made in Strother's 1868 *Harpers* article, this was fabricated or misremembered.

60 Carman and Pierro, Ed., *The Maryland Campaign*, p. 209; Carman and Clemens, Ed., *The Maryland Campaign, Vol. II*, pp. 38–41; Palfrey, *The Antietam and Fredericksburg* (Wilmington,

North Carolina: Broadfoot Publishing Company, 1989), pp. 119–21. Sears, *Landscape Turned Red*, pp. 190–92, 195–96. Carman is unsparing in attacking McClellan, stating "This first step was a blunder, in that the movement was made in the afternoon of the sixteenth at an hour too late to accomplish anything before dark and serving no purpose, save to inform Lee where he was to be attacked." Palfrey echoes this view in his own work.

61   Perhaps reflecting McClellan's concern about how Lee might react to this development, at 7:30 that evening he had Ruggles craft a message to Sumner directing him to by dawn have two batteries covering the Upper Bridge crossings; Sumner in response had Mansfield move two XII Corps batteries—Robinson's and McGilvery's—back across the Antietam for this purpose (OR, Vol XIX, Part 1, p. 482).

62   OR, Vol. XIX, Part1, p. 217, p. 269; *Report of the Joint Committee on the Conduct of the War*, p. 581.

Chapter 4

1   OR, Vol. XIX, Part 1, p. 218; Austin C. Sterns and Arthur A. Kent, ed., *Three Years with Company K* (London: Associated University Press, 1976), p. 125; Harsh, *Sounding the Shallows: A Confederate Companion*, p. 19; *History of Lost and Found: Diary of CDM Broomhall, 124*th *Pennsylvania*, http://aotw.org/exhibit.php, Entry for September 16th, 1862; R. L. Murray, Ed., *New Yorkers in the Civil War: A Historic Journey, Vol. 4* (Wolcott, N.Y.: Benedum Books, 2004), p. 76; Louis C. Greenleaf letter to E. A. Carman, 13 December 1894, Antietam National Battlefield.

2   OR, Vol. XIX, Part 1, p. 610; Lee A. Wallace, Jr. *5th Virginia Infantry* (Lynchburg: Virginia, H. E. Howard, Inc., 1988), pp. 41–42; E. E. Stickley, *Confederate Veteran*, Vol. 22 (December 1914), p. 555.

3   OR, Vol. XIX, Part 1, p. 218, p. 275, p. 475. General Williams notes in his report of the battle of Antietam that his division and the XII Corp—which he would command upon General Mansfield's death—bivouacked that night near the "farm of J. Poffenberger." This is almost certainly an error because it would place the XII Corps on the same ground then held by much of the I Corps. He most likely means the Samuel Poffenberger farm; Brown, *The Twenty-seventh Indiana*, p. 238.; Beverly Hayes Kallgren and James L. Crouthamel, Eds., *"Dear Friend Anna" The Civil War letters of a Common Soldier from Maine* (Portland: The University Press of Maine, 1992), p. 33; Carman and Pierro, Ed., *The Maryland Campaign*, p. 215; Carman and Clemens, Ed., *The Maryland Campaign, Vol. II*, pp. 51–56; John E. Gould *Joseph K. F. Mansfield, Brigadier General of the US Army, A Narrative of Events Connected with his Mortal Wounding at Antietam* (Portland, Maine: Stephen Barry, Pub., 1895), p. 9.

4   Carman and Pierro, Ed., *The Maryland Campaign*, p. 453, p. 454, p. 459, p. 465; Carman and Clemens, Ed., *The Maryland Campaign, Vol. II*, pp. 569–70, pp. 572–73, pp. 583–84, pp. 598–99.

5   OR, Vol. XIX, Part. 1, p. 217, p. 275; OR, XIX, Pt, 2, p. 297.

6   Carman and Pierro, Ed., *The Maryland Campaign*, p. 215; Carman and Clemens, Ed., *The Maryland Campaign, Vol. II*, pp. 51–56.; OR, Vol. XIX, Part 1, p. 218, p. 222, p. 845. Although Hooker recorded this night-time reconnaissance late on the 16th in his OR (OR, Vol. XIX, Part 1, p. 218), he never mentions Meade making the journey with him. Nor does Meade mention this in his OR. Carman describes the two generals riding together in his manuscript (Carman and Pierro, Ed., The Maryland Campaign, p. 215), and given that Hooker was riding to observe the deployments and state of Meade's Division and skirmishers—then closest to the enemy—it seems at least reasonable that Hooker might have taken Meade with him. Nonetheless, details of this ride remain in dispute.

7   OR, Vol. XIX, Part 1, p. 218, p. 222, p. 845. Hooker recorded this night-time reconnaissance late on the 16th in his OR (OR, Vol. XIX, Part 1, p. 218).

8   Seymour "Official Report," Joseph Hooker military papers, 1861–1864, Box 9, Huntington Library, San Marino, California; OR, Vol. XIX, Part 1, p. 218.

9   Carman and Pierro, Ed., *The Maryland Campaign,* p. 220; Carman and Clemens, Ed., *The Maryland Campaign, Vol. II,* pp. 67–71.

10 R. C. Dawes letter to E. A. Carman, July 7, 1896, Antietam National Battlefield; Simpson "Official Report," Joseph Hooker military papers, 1861–1864, Box 9, Huntington Library, San Marino, California; OR, Vol. XIX, Part 1, p. 223.

11 OR, Vol. XIX, Part 1, p. 1009; Curt Johnson and Richard C. Anderson, Jr, *Artillery Hell: The Employment of Artillery at Antietam* (College Station: Texas A&M University Press, 1995), pp. 85–100.

12 William W. Blackford, *War Years with Jeb Stuart* (New York: Charles Scribner's Sons, 1945), p. 151.

13 John Bank, "The General," *Civil War Times,* August 2018, Vol. 57, No. 4, p. 47.

14 NAT Letter, October 6, 1862, Private collection of Al Feidler, Jr; Ernst, *Too Afraid to Cry.* P. 135.

15 Douglas, *I Rode with Stonewall,* pp. 170–71; Alexander Hunter, *Johnny Reb and Billy Yank* (New York: Neal Publishing Co., 1905), pp. 286–87; Ernst, *Too Afraid to Cry,* pp. 136–40.

16 OR, Vol. XIX, Part 1, p. 1008. Another impact of this shell might also have been that it removed an incompetent general from command of this important division, replacing him with a highly effective officer. Jones's wounding by this shell remains a subject of debate because he was rendered incapable of command by being stunned and wasn't physically wounded. What does not remain in dispute is that Jones was observed hiding behind a tree during the battle of Fredericksburg and abandoned his brigade (bringing on charges of cowardice) or that he again abandoned his command at the battle of Chancellorsville, claiming an ulcerated leg rendered him unfit to lead just then (an act that once again brought on a charge of cowardice).

17 Stewart Sifakis, *Who Was Who in the Confederacy: A Biographical Encyclopedia of more than 1000 Participants* (New York: Facts on File, 1988), p. 266.

18 Carman and Pierro, Ed., *The Maryland Campaign,* pp. 220–21; Carman and Clemens, Ed., *The Maryland Campaign, Vol. II,* pp. 69–73; Johnson and Anderson, *Artillery Hell,* p. 13.

19 http.//www.arlingtoncemetary.net/jgibbon.htm.

20 Ezra Warner, *Generals in Blue: Lives of the Union Commanders* (Baton Rouge: Louisiana State University Press, 2006), pp. 212–13. Sears notes in *Landscape Turned Red* (pp. 205–7) that Duryee's was the "lead brigade" but implies this was Ricketts' plan all along instead of how events actually unfolded. Ricketts intended Hartsuff to lead, supported by Duryee and Christian as noted in his OR (p. 259), which Sears omits any mention of: "the [Third; Hartsuff's] Brigade moved forward supported by Second [Christian's] Brigade on the left and First Brigade [Duryee's] on the right…"

21 Warner, *Generals in Blue,* pp. 133–34.; Stewart Sifakis, *Who Was Who in the Union, Vol. 1* (New York: Facts on File Press, 1988). P. 77, p. 121.

22 Sifakis, *Who Was Who in the Union, Vol. 1,* p. 77, p. 121.

23 Carman and Pierro, Ed., *The Maryland Campaign,* p. 216; Carman and Clemens, Ed., *The Maryland Campaign, Vol. II,* pp. 55–57.

24 Seymour "Official Report," Joseph Hooker military papers, 1861–1864, Box 9, Huntington Library, San Marino, California; Carman and Pierro, Ed., *The Maryland Campaign,* p. 216; Carman and Clemens, Ed., *The Maryland Campaign, Vol. II,* pp. 55–57.

25 Carman and Pierro, Ed., *The Maryland Campaign,* p. 216; Carman and Clemens, Ed., *The Maryland Campaign, Vol. II,* pp. 55–57.

26 Carman and Pierro, Ed., *The Maryland Campaign,* p. 218, p. 220; Carman and Clemens, Ed., *The Maryland Campaign, Vol. II,* pp. 61–63; OR, Vol. XIX, Part 1, p. 978.

27   Carman and Pierro, Ed., *The Maryland Campaign*, p. 218, p. 220; Carman and Clemens, Ed., *The Maryland Campaign, Vol. II*, pp. 61–63, pp. 67–71; OR, Vol. XIX, Part 1, p. 923.

28   Harsh, *Sounding the Shallows*, pp. 19–20.

Chapter 5

1   Charles E. Davis, Jr, *Three Years in the Army: The Story of the 13th Massachusetts Volunteers from July 16, 1861 to August 1, 1864* (Boston: Estes Publishers, 1894), p. 135; Stearns, *Three Years with Company K*, pp. 125–26.

2   John A. Vautier "88 Penn. Sketch", January 19, 1895, Antietam National Battlefield; Carman and Pierro, Ed., *The Maryland Campaign*, p. 217; Carman and Clemens, Ed., *The Maryland Campaign, Vol. II*, pp. 57–61; OR, Vol. XIX, Part 1, p. 218.

3   "History of the Ninth New York (83rd Volunteers)," Antietam National Battlefield; "13th Massachusetts," Carman Papers, Antietam National Battlefield; OR, Vol. XIX, Part 1, p. 259.

4   John C. Delaney letter to E. A. Carman, March 27, 1891, Antietam National Battlefield; "History of the Ninth New York (83rd Volunteers)," Antietam National Battlefield; George Kendall letter to Rollins, December 17, 1891, Antietam National Battlefield; OR, Vol. XIX, Pt. 1, p. 262; Hough, *History of Duryee's Brigade*, p. 167.

5   John C. Delaney letter to E. A. Carman, March 27, 1891, Antietam National Battlefield; Carman and Pierro, Ed., *The Maryland Campaign*, p. 217; Carman and Clemens, Ed., *The Maryland Campaign, Vol. II*, pp. 57–61. Because of army politics and other reasons, Duryee never submitted an official report for his brigade's actions at Antietam (what he did submit was merely a list of officers and men who "behaved with gallantry," found in OR, Vol. XIX, Part 1, pp. 259–60.). However, it is clear from notes and commentary included in Carman's Antietam manuscript that Duryee provided a detailed account of his command's actions to Carman, suggesting Carman's version probably accurately reflects the brigade's movements and actions. Positions for Duryee's advance are derived also from the map provided by Lieutenant Colonel L. C. Skinner (104th New York) to E. A. Carman, March 24, 1895, Antietam National Battlefield.

6   Carman and Pierro, Ed., *The Maryland Campaign*, p. 217; Carman and Clemens, Ed., *The Maryland Campaign, Vol. II*, pp. 57-61; Richard A. Sauers and Peter Tomasak, *Ricketts' Battery: A History of Battery F, 1st Pennsylvania Light Artillery* (Published by Luzerne National Bank, PA, 2001), p. 52; Lieutenant Colonel L. C. Skinner (104th New York) map to E. A. Carman, March 24, 1895, Antietam National Battlefield.

7   John C. Dalaney letter to E. A. Carman, March 27, 1891, Antietam National Battlefield; 90th Pennsylvania Association letter to E. A. Carman, March 23, 1895, Antietam National Battlefield; OR, Vol. XIX, Part 1, p. 262; Franklin Benjamin Hough, *History of Duryee's Brigade, During the Campaign in Virginia under Gen. Pope, and in Maryland Under Gen. McClellan, and in the Summer and Autumn of 1862* (Albany, 1864), p. 118.

8   Hough, *History of Duryee's Brigade*, p. 119; Carman and Clemens, Ed., *The Maryland Campaign, Vol. II*, p. 58. Carman's account is the only record suggesting Union artillery shelled the Cornfield before Duryee's troops entered. Although Carman specifically refers to "canister," more likely he means "case shot," an anti-personnel round with the range to reach the field, which canister rounds lack.

9   Carman and Pierro, Ed., *The Maryland Campaign*, p. 217; Carman and Clemens, Ed., *The Maryland Campaign, Vol. II*, pp. 57–61; Pharris Deloach Johnson, *Under the Southern Cross: Soldier Life with Gordon Bradwell and the Army of Northern Virginia* (Mercer University Press, 1979), p. 89.

10   John C. Delaney letter to E. A. Carman, March 27, 1891, Antietam National Battlefield; Lieutenant Colonel L. C. Skinner (104th New York) map to E. A. Carman, March 24, 1895, Antietam

National Battlefield; Carman and Pierro, Ed., *The Maryland Campaign,* p. 217; Carman and Clemens, Ed., *The Maryland Campaign, Vol. II,* pp. 57–61; John C. Whiteside letter, October 4, 1862, Bentley Historical Library, University of Michigan.

11 John C. Delaney letter to E. A. Carman, March 27, 1891, Antietam National Battlefield; Lieutenant Colonel L. C. Skinner (104th New York) map to E. A. Carman, 24 March 1895, Antietam National Battlefield; Carman and Pierro, Ed., *The Maryland Campaign,* p. 217; Carman and Clemens, Ed. The Maryland Campaign, Vol. II, pp. 57–61.

12 Carman and Pierro, Ed., *The Maryland Campaign,* p. 217; Carman and Clemens, Ed., *The Maryland Campaign, Vol. II,* pp. 57-61; OR, Vol. XIX, Part. 1, pp. 976–77.

13 OR, Vol. XIX, Part 1, pp. 976–77.

14 John C. Delaney letter to E. A. Carman, March 27, 1891, Antietam National Battlefield; Lieutenant Colonel L. C. Skinner (104th New York) map to E. A. Carman, March 24, 1895, Antietam National Battlefield; Carman and Pierro, Ed., *The Maryland Campaign,* p. 217; Carman and Clemens, Ed., *The Maryland Campaign, Vol. II,* pp. 57-61; Charles Barber, Raymond G. Barber, and Gary E. Swinson *The Civil War Letters of Charles Barber, Private, 104th New York Volunteer Infantry* (Torrance, California: G. E. Swinson, 1991), pp. 94–95.

15 OR, Vol. XIX, Part 1, p. 977; Carman and Pierro, Ed., *"The Maryland Campaign,"* p. 218; Carman and Clemens, Ed., *The Maryland Campaign, Vol. II,* pp. 61–63.

16 Carman and Pierro, Ed., *The Maryland Campaign,* p. 217; Carman and Clemens, Ed., *The Maryland Campaign, Vol. II,* pp. 61–63.

17 Enoch Jones, 26th New York map, March 15, 1893, Antietam National Battlefield; Carman and Pierro, Ed., *The Maryland Campaign,* p. 218; Carman and Clemens, Ed., *The Maryland Campaign, Vol. II,* pp. 6163; OR, Vol. XIX, Part 1, p. 923.

18 Carman and Pierro, Ed., *The Maryland Campaign,* p. 218; Carman and Clemens, Ed., *The Maryland Campaign, Vol. II,* pp. 61–63; Johnson, *Under the Southern Cross,* pp. 91–92.; OR, Vol. XIX, Pt. 1, p. 923.

19 Edwin W. Pearce letter (107th Pennsylvania), October 16, 1862, Author's Collection; Charles H. Hayden letter to Laura Hayden, October 10, 1862; "The Civil War Letters of Charles Harvey Hayden, Patriot & Hero, 97th New York Volunteer Infantry" complied by Al Greening, New York State Military Museum; Rush P. Cady letter to Gustavus Cady, September 27, 1862. Rush P. Cady Collection, Hamilton College Archives, Clinton, NY; Hough, *History of Duryee's Brigade,* p. 181; Lieutenant Colonel L. C. Skinner (104th New York) map to E. A. Carman, March 24, 1895, Antietam National Battlefield.

20 John C. Delaney letter to E. A. Carman, March 27, 1891, Antietam National Battlefield; Lieutenant Colonel L. C. Skinner (104th New York) map to E. A. Carman, March 24, 1895, Antietam National Battlefield; Carman and Pierro, Ed., *The Maryland Campaign,* p. 218; Carman and Clemens, Ed., *The Maryland Campaign, Vol. II,* pp. 61–63. In contributing to Carman's history of the battle, Duryee claimed he was told that elements of Seymour's Brigade—the 2nd Pennsylvania Reserves and skirmishers of the 1st and 6th Reserves—were being driven back by Confederate troops, who were then flooding into the East Woods, threatening his flank and forcing him to retreat. Because there's no proof that Walker's attack by Trimble's Brigade ever entered the East Woods, the claim that an "intelligence failure" prompted his retreat seems to be little more than a convenient excuse for ordering retreat. I believe that, more likely, the condition of his brigade after half an hour of intense fighting and significant casualties had taken their toll, forcing retreat as the only option to death; John C. Whiteside letter, October 4, 1862, Bentley Historical Library, University of Michigan.

21 John C. Delaney letter to E. A. Carman, March 27, 1891, Antietam National Battlefield.

22 John C. Delaney letter to E. A. Carman, March 27, 1891, Antietam National Battlefield; Carman and Pierro, Ed., *The Maryland Campaign,* p. 218; Carman and Clemens, Ed., *The Maryland Campaign, Vol. II,* pp. 61–63.

23 "History of the Ninth New York (83rd Volunteers)," Antietam National Battlefield; George Kendall letter to Rollins, December 17, 1891, Antietam National Battlefield; Carman and Pierro, Ed., *The Maryland Campaign,* pp. 218–19; Carman and Clemens, Ed., *The Maryland Campaign, Vol. II*, pp. 63–67. After the war, a story circulated that early in the battle Hooker, seeing his attack stalling, sent word to Doubleday (or sometimes Ricketts) to "Give me your best brigade," in response to which Hartsuff's Brigade was advanced into battle. It is unclear where this story actually originated but Abner Doubleday repeated a version of it in a *National Tribune* article; regardless, given that Hooker later claimed to have no recollection of the incident, it is most likely apocryphal. "History of the Ninth New York (83rd Volunteers), Antietam National Battlefield; Hartsuff's Brigade file, Quotations No. 4, 5, 6, 7, 8, 9, 10, 11, Carman Papers, Antietam National Battlefield.

24 John D. Vautier, *History of the 88th Pennsylvania Volunteers in the War for the Union, 1861–1865.* (Philadelphia: J. B. Lippincott Co. 1894), p. 74; John A. Vautier letter, June 1, 1896, Antietam National Battlefield; W. H. Holstead letter to John Gould, March 9, 1893, Antietam National Battlefield; George Watson letter to John Gould, April 22,1893, Antietam National Battlefield.

25 W.H. Holstead letter to John Gould, March 9, 1893, Antietam National Battlefield; Henry R. Myer manuscript "88th Pennsylvania:" Antietam National Battlefield; George Watson letter to John Gould, April 22, 1893, Antietam National Battlefield. Carman and Pierro, Ed., *The Maryland Campaign,* p. 224; Carman and Clemens, Ed., *The Maryland Campaign, Vol. II*, pp. 79–83.

26 Gregory C. White *"This Most Bloody & Cruel Drama:" A History of the 31st Georgia Volunteer Infantry* (Baltimore: Butternut and Blue, 1997), p. 51.

27 OR, Vol. XIX, Part 1, p. 975.

28 James P. Gannon, *Irish Rebels, Confederate Tigers: the 6th Louisiana Volunteers, 1861–1865.* (Campbell, CA: Savas Publishing Co., 1998), pp. 135–36; OR, Vol. XIX, Part 1, pp. 978–79. Sears's *Landscape Turned Red* refers to Hays's Brigade as the Louisiana Tigers and uses the term throughout his account to describe all of Hays's Brigade's various actions and movements (pp. 208–10). While useful in simplifying often-complex movements and adding color to his account, doing so obscures the actions of Hays's various individual regiments, so I have avoided using the term too generally.

29 Rufus R. Dawes letter to E. A. Carman, July 7, 1896, Antietam National Battlefield.

30 "History of the Ninth New York (83rd Volunteers)," Antietam National Battlefield; Carman and Pierro, Ed. *The Maryland Campaign,* p. 219; Carman and Clemens, Ed., *The Maryland Campaign, Vol. II*, pp. 65–67.

31 George Kendall letter to Rollins, December 17, 1891, Antietam National Battlefield.

32 Stearns, *Three Years with Company K*, pp. 126–27.

33 Stearns, *Three Years with Company K*, pp. 126–27.

34 George Kendall letter to Rollins, December 17, 1891, Antietam National Battlefield.

35 "The Citizen Soldier" article (12th Massachusetts), 1869; "History of the Ninth New York (83rd Volunteers)," Antietam National Battlefield; "13th Massachusetts," Carman Papers, Antietam National Battlefield; Carman and Pierro, Ed., *The Maryland Campaign,* p. 234; Carman and Clemens, Ed., *The Maryland Campaign, Vol. II*, pp. 64–65.

36 George Kendall letter to Rollins, December 17, 1891, Antietam National Battlefield; Carman and Pierro, Ed., *The Maryland Campaign,* p. 234; Carman and Clemens, Ed., *The Maryland Campaign, Vol. II*, pp. 64–65; Stearns, *Three Years with Company K*, p. 127; OR, Vol. XIX, Part 1, pp. 978–79.

37 Stearns, *Three Years with Company K*, pp. 128–29.

38 Carman and Pierro, Ed., *The Maryland Campaign,* p. 219.

39 Henry R. Myer manuscript "88th Pennsylvania:" Antietam National Battlefield; John A. Vautier "88 Penn. Sketch", January 19, 1895, Antietam National Battlefield; Vautier, *History of the 88th Pennsylvania Volunteers.* p. 109; Henry R. Myer manuscript "88th Pennsylvania," Antietam

National Battlefield; George Watson letter to John Gould, April 22, 1893, Antietam National Battlefield.

40   Vautier, *History of the 88th Pennsylvania Volunteers.* p. 109; James Durkin, *The Last Man and the Last Life* (Glenside, PA: J. M. Santarelli, 2000), pp. 84–87; W. H. Holstead letter to John Gould, March 9, 1893, Antietam National Battlefield.

41   Alfred Sellers letter to Gould, December 31, 1894, National Archives, Record Group 94, Antietam Battlefield Board, Antietam National Battlefield; Alfred Sellers letter to E. A. Carman, January 5, 1895; 90th Pennsylvania map, January 5, 1895, Antietam National Battlefield; George Watson letter to John Gould, April 22, 1893, Antietam National Battlefield; "13th Massachusetts," Carman Papers, Antietam National Battlefield; Durkin, *The Last Man and the Last Life*, p. 87. The 90th Pennsylvania's movements and those of Christian's Brigade are complicated and I believe that both Carman's (Carman and Pierro, p. 224, and Carman and Clemens, pp. 81–82) and Sears' (*Landscape Turned Red*, pp. 207–10) accounts are at least partly in error. Carman's account is largely correct but has the Coulter and Lyle interaction occurring after Christian's Brigade had departed the East Woods, which is contradicted by the 90th's Major Sellers' observation of the brigade being "at a standstill in the hollow of the woods..." during the conversation. Sears incorrectly claims Lyle was already in command of Christian's Brigade at the time of Coulter's plea, which is contradicted by many sources, including Major Sellers's; Lyle assumed brigade command only after all of Christian's various regiments had fallen back (Durkin, *The Last Man and the Last Life*, p. 95).

42   Alfred Sellers letter to E. A. Carman, January 5, 1895, Antietam Battlefield Board; John A. Vautier "88 Penn. Sketch", January 19, 1895, Antietam National Battlefield; Seymour "Official Report," Joseph Hooker military papers, 1861–1864, Box 9, Huntington Library, San Marino, California; Carman and Pierro, Ed, *The Maryland Campaign,* p. 224; W. H. Holstead letter to John Gould, March 9, 1893, Antietam National Battlefield; Carman and Clemens, Ed., *The Maryland Campaign, Vol. II*, pp. 79–83.

43   "The Citizen Soldier" article (12th Massachusetts), 1869; Stearns, *Three Years with Company K*, p. 130; George Kendall letter to Rollins, December 17, 1891, Antietam National Battlefield; Carman and Pierro, Ed. *The Maryland Campaign,* p. 224; Carman and Clemens, Ed., *The Maryland Campaign, Vol. II*, pp. 79–83.

44   Gannon, *Irish Rebels*, p. 136.

Chapter 6

1   OR, Vol. XIX, Part 1, pp. 223–24.
2   Carman and Pierro, Ed., *The Maryland Campaign,* pp. 219–20; Carman and Clemens, Ed., *The Maryland Campaign, Vol. II*, pp. 68–70. Although Jones's Brigade was officially commanded by Colonel Bradley Johnson, Johnson was detached from the brigade during the battle, first to serve as provost marshal in Frederick and—when that city was abandoned to Union control—Johnson was sent to Richmond with important dispatches.
3   Rufus R. Dawes *A Full-Blown Yankee of the Iron Brigade: Service with the Sixth Wisconsin Volunteers* (Lincoln, NE: University of Nebraska Press, 1962). p. 87; R. R. Dawes letter to E. A. Carman, July 7, 1896, Antietam National Battlefield; Dawes letter to Carman and map, January 14, 1899, Antietam National Battlefield.
4   OR, Vol. XIX, Part 1, p. 248.
5   R. R. Dawes letter to E. A. Carman, July 7, 1896, Antietam National Battlefield; Dawes letter to Carman and map, January 14, 1899, Antietam National Battlefield; Dawes *A Full-Blown Yankee of the Iron Brigade*, p. 88.

6   R. R. Dawes letter to E. A. Carman, July 7, 1896, Antietam National Battlefield; Dawes letter to Carman and map, January 14, 1899, Antietam National Battlefield; Dawes *A Full-Blown Yankee of the Iron Brigade*, p. 88; OR, Vol. XIX, Part 1, p. 255.

7   R. R. Dawes letter to E. A. Carman, July 7, 1896, Antietam National Battlefield; Dawes letter to Carman and map, January 14, 1899, Antietam National Battlefield; OR, Vol. XIX, Part 1, p. 248.

8   R. R. Dawes letter to E. A. Carman, July 7, 1896, Antietam National Battlefield; Louis C. Greenleaf letter and map to E. A. Carman, December 13, 1894, Antietam National Battlefield; Carman and Pierro, Ed., *The Maryland Campaign*, p. 221; Carman and Clemens, Ed., *The Maryland Campaign, Vol. II*, pp. 70–71; OR, Vol. XIX, Part 1, p. 232.

9   R.R. Dawes letter to E.A. Carman, July 7, 1896, Antietam National Battlefield; Dawes letter to Carman and map, January 14, 1899, Antietam National Battlefield; Carman and Pierro, Ed., *The Maryland Campaign*, pp. 221–22; Carman and Clemens, Ed., *The Maryland Campaign, Vol. II*, pp. 70–76; OR, Vol. XIX, Part 1, p. 255.

10   Dawes letter to Carman and map, January 14, 1899, Antietam National Battlefield; Dawes *A Full-Blown Yankee of the Iron Brigade*, p. 89. Carman and Pierro, Ed., *The Maryland Campaign*, p. 222; Carman and Clemens, Ed., *The Maryland Campaign, Vol. II*, pp. 76–77; OR, Vol. XIX, Part 1, p. 255.

11   R. R. Dawes letter to E. A. Carman, July 7, 1896, Antietam National Battlefield; R. R. Dawes letter to E. A. Carman, July 7, 1896, Antietam National Battlefield; Dawes *A Full-Blown Yankee of the Iron Brigade*, p. 90; OR, Vol. XIX, Part 1, p. 255.

12   "Explanation of Hoyt's map" (7th Wisconsin), January 22, 1895, Antietam National Battlefield; OR, Vol. XIX, Part 1, p. 248; W. W. Dudley sketch map (19th Indiana), Antietam National Battlefield; Carman and Pierro, Ed., *The Maryland Campaign*, p. 222; Carman and Clemens, Ed., *The Maryland Campaign, Vol. II*, pp. 72–76; Gaff, *On Many a Bloody Field*, p. 185.

13   OR, Vol. XIX, Part 1, p. 229.

14   "Explanation of Hoyt's map" (7th Wisconsin), January 22, 1895, Antietam National Battlefield; W. W. Dudley sketch map (19th Indiana), Antietam National Battlefield.

15   W. W. Dudley sketch map (19th Indiana), Antietam National Battlefield; Carman and Pierro, Ed., *The Maryland Campaign*, p. 222; Carman and Clemens, Ed., *The Maryland Campaign, Vol. II*, pp. 72–76; Gaff, *On Many a Bloody Field*, p. 185.

16   R. R. Dawes letter to E. A. Carman, July 7,1896, Antietam National Battlefield; Dawes letter to Carman and map, January 14,1899, Antietam National Battlefield; "Explanation of Hoyt's map" (7th Wisconsin), January 22, 1895, Antietam National Battlefield; W. W. Dudley sketch map (19th Indiana) , Antietam National Battlefield; OR, Vol. XIX, Part 1, p. 251.

17   Joseph E. Chance, Ed., *My Life in the Old Army: The Reminiscences of Abner Doubleday* (Forth Worth: Texas Christian University Press, 1998), p. 248; OR, Vol. XIX, Part 1, p. 224; Carman and Clemens, Ed., *The Maryland Campaign, Vol. II*, pp. 75–76, 80.

18   OR, Vol. XIX, Part 1, p. 1009.

19   Carman and Pierro, Ed., *The Maryland Campaign*, pp. 222–23; Carman and Clemens, Ed., *The Maryland Campaign, Vol. II*, pp. 76–79.

20   Carman and Pierro, Ed., *The Maryland Campaign"* p. 222; Carman and Clemens, Ed., *The Maryland Campaign, Vol. II*, pp. 76–77; OR, Vol. XIX, Pt. 1, p. 1012.

21   R. R. Dawes letter to E. A. Carman, July 7, 1896, Antietam National Battlefield; Dawes letter to Carman and map, January 14, 1899, Antietam National Battlefield.

22   Carman and Pierro, Ed., *The Maryland Campaign*, p. 223; Carman and Clemens, Ed., *The Maryland Campaign, Vol. II*, pp. 78–79; OR, Vol. XIX, Part 1, p. 248.

23   90th Pennsylvania map, January 5, 1895, Antietam National Battlefield; Rufus R. Dawes letter to E. A. Carman, July 7, 1896, Antietam National Battlefield; OR, Vol. XIX, Part 1, p. 978.

24 R. R. Dawes letter to E. A. Carman, July 7, 1896, Antietam National Battlefield; Dawes letter to Carman and map, January 14, 1899, Antietam National Battlefield; Carman and Clemens, Ed., *The Maryland Campaign, Vol. II*, p. 65, p. 77.

25 Carman and Pierro, Ed., *The Maryland Campaign*, p. 223; Carman and Clemens, Ed., *The Maryland Campaign, Vol. II*, pp. 78–79; OR, Vol. XIX, Part 1, p. 248.

26 Dawes *A Full-Blown Yankee of the Iron Brigade*, pp. 90–91.; Carman and Pierro, Ed., *The Maryland Campaign*, p. 223; Carman and Clemens, Ed., *The Maryland Campaign, Vol. II*, pp. 78–79. Dawes's account of the 6th Wisconsin's action here is typical of many post-battle accounts provided by participants because it seems to merge two distinct events. Dawes clearly describes the 6th moving to the southern edge of the Cornfield and opening fire on the enemy; almost certainly the 26th, 38th, and 61st Georgia regiments on the left flank of Lawton's Brigade. However, then he describes moving to the attack across an open field until reaching the Hagerstown Pike and engaging in a deadly firefight across that road. At some point in this action, he must have witnessed the Georgians retiring; if this had not happened, the 6th and 2nd Wisconsin would have been exposing their left flank to the enemy when marching toward the Hagerstown Pike.

27 Dawes, *A Full-Blown Yankee of the Iron Brigade*, pp. 90–91.

28 Dawes, *A Full-Blown Yankee of the Iron Brigade*, p. 94.

29 Dawes, *A Full-Blown Yankee of the Iron Brigade*, pp. 92–93.

30 OR, Vol. XIX, Part 1, p. 229, p. 246; Theodore B. Gates, *The "Ulster Guard" (20th N. Y. State Militia) and the War of the Rebellion* (New York, B. H. Tyrrel, printer, 1879), pp. 317–18.

31 Carman and Pierro, Ed., *The Maryland Campaign*, p. 224; Carman and Clemens, Ed., *The Maryland Campaign, Vol. II*, pp. 80–82; John Michael Priest, *Antietam: The Soldier's Battle* (Shippensburg, PA: White Mane Publishing, 1989), p. 328.

32 R. C. Dawes letter to E. A. Carman, July 7, 1896, Antietam National Battlefield; Dawes letter to Carman and map, January 14, 1899, Antietam National Battlefield; OR, Vol. XIX, Part 1, p. 233; Carman and Pierro, Ed., *The Maryland Campaign*, p. 224; Carman and Clemens, Ed., *The Maryland Campaign, Vol. II*, pp. 80–82.

33 Carman and Pierro, Ed., *The Maryland Campaign*, p. 224; Carman and Clemens, Ed., *The Maryland Campaign, Vol. II*, pp. 80–82; Priest, *Antietam: The Soldier's Battle*, p. 328.

Chapter 7

1 OR, Vol. XIX, Part 1, p. 218, pp. 269–70.

2 Col. Harold B. Simpson *Hood's Texas Brigade: Lee's Grenadier Guard* (Waco, Texas: Texian Press, 1970), p. 171, footnote 68; *Confederate Veteran*, Vol. 22 (December 1914), p. 555.

3 *Battles and Leaders*, Vol. 2, p. 555.

4 Carman and Pierro, Ed., *The Maryland Campaign*, p. 226; Carman and Clemens, Ed., *The Maryland Campaign, Vol. II*, pp. 86–88.

5 *Confederate Veteran*, Vol. 22, (December 1914), p. 555.

6 Simpson, *"Hood's Texas Brigade"* p. 172; Determining exactly when any particular event occurred during the fighting at Antietam is often impossible because of the conflicting times cited in reports and by those who published accounts of the battle. As Ezra Carman wrote in explaining the problem encountered in compiling his own massive study of the battle, "No two or more men will agree upon such points." There are, however, a few events where nearly everyone who wrote of the event agrees; one of these is that Hood's Division crossed the Hagerstown Pike at 7:00.

7 Carman and Pierro, Ed., *The Maryland Campaign*, p. 227; Carman and Clemens, Ed., *The Maryland Campaign, Vol. II*, pp. 88–89; OR, Vol. XIX, Pt. 1, p. 923, p. 928, p. 932, pp. 937–38.

8 OR, Vol. XIX, Part 1, p. 937.

9   Dawes, *A Full-Blown Yankee of the Iron Brigade*, p. 91.
10 Dawes, *A Full-Blown Yankee of the Iron Brigade*, p. 91; C. A. Stevens *Berdan's United States Sharpshooters in the Army of the Potomac, 1861–1865*. (Dayton, Ohio: Morningside Books, 1984), p. 203.
11 OR, Vol. XIX, Part 1, p. 246, p. 928, p. 930; Gates, *The Ulster Guard (20th MYSM)*, pp. 318–19.
12 OR, Vol. XIX, Part 1, p. 930.
13 "Explanation of Hoyt's map" (7th Wisconsin), January 22, 1895, Antietam National Battlefield; W. W. Dudley sketch map (19th Indiana), Antietam National Battlefield; OR, Vol. XIX, Part 1, p. 928; Gates, *The Ulster Guard (20th MYSM)*, pp. 318–19.
14 Carman and Pierro, Ed., *The Maryland Campaign*, p. 229; Carman and Clemens, Ed., *The Maryland Campaign, Vol. II*, pp. 91–93; OR, Vol. XIX, Part 1, p. 935.
15 John A. Vautier "88 Penn. Sketch", January 19, 1895, Antietam National Battlefield; Enoch Jones, 26th New York map, March 15, 1893, Antietam National Battlefield; 90th Pennsylvania map, January 5, 1895, Antietam National Battlefield; W. H. Holstead letter to John Gould, March 9, 1893, Antietam National Battlefield; Carman and Pierro, Ed., *The Maryland Campaign*, pp. 224–25; Carman and Clemens, Ed., *The Maryland Campaign, Vol. II*, pp. 80–84.
16 OR, Vol. XIX, Part 1, p. 937.
17 OR, Vol. XIX, Part 1, p. 937.
18 W. F. Beyer and O. F. Keydel, Eds., *Deeds of Valor* (Platinum Press, Detroit, 1903), p. 90.
19 Beyer, *Deeds of Valor*, p. 90.
20 90th Pennsylvania map, January 5, 1895, Antietam National Battlefield; Durkin, *The Last Man and the Last Life*, pp. 90–92; Carman and Pierro, Ed., *The Maryland Campaign*, p. 227; Carman and Clemens, Ed., *The Maryland Campaign, Vol. II*, pp. 88–89.
21 Carman and Pierro, Ed., *The Maryland Campaign*, pp. 227–28; Carman and Clemens, Ed., *The Maryland Campaign, Vol. II*, pp. 88–91.
22 James Cooper Nisbet, *Four Years on the Firing Line*, Bell Wiley, Ed. (Jackson, TN: McCowat-Mercer Press, 1914), p. 102; Priest, *Antietam: The Soldier's Battle*, p. 57.
23 OR, Vol. XIX, Part 1, pp. 937–38.
24 Charles S. McClenthen *Campaigns in Virginia and Maryland from Cedar Mountain to Antietam; by a Soldier of the 26th New York Volunteers* (Syracuse, Maters & Lee, 1862), pp. 40–41; W. H. Holstead letter to John Gould, 9 March 1893, Antietam National Battlefield; Vautier, *History of the 88th Pennsylvania Volunteers*, p. 109; John A. Vautier letter, June 1, 1896, Antietam National Battlefield.
25 OR, Vol. XIX, Part 1, p. 229.
26 OR, Vol. XIX, Part 1, p. 229.
27 Beyer, *Deeds of Valor*, pp. 75–76.
28 OR, Vol. XIX, Part 1, pp. 248–49.
29 Dawes letter to Carman and map, January 14, 1899, Antietam National Battlefield; Dawes, *A Full-Blown Yankee of the Iron Brigade*, p. 91; OR, Vol. XIX, I, p. 249.
30 OR, Vol. XIX, Part 1, p. 928.
31 OR, Vol. XIX, Part 1, p. 935.
32 "Explanation of Hoyt's map" (7th Wisconsin), January 22, 1895, Antietam National Battlefield; W. W. Dudley sketch map (19th Indiana), Antietam National Battlefield; OR, Vol. XIX, Part 1, p. 251.
33 "Explanation of Hoyt's map" (7th Wisconsin), January 22, 1895, Antietam National Battlefield; OR, Vol. XIX, Part 1, p. 935; Gates, *The Ulster Guard (20th MYSM)*, pp. 318–19.
34 Gaff, *On Many a Bloody Field*, pp. 186–87.
35 Gaff, *On Many a Bloody Field*, pp. 186–87.

36 William F. Rogers letter and map to E. A. Carman, undated, Antietam National Battlefield; 21st Regiment Veteran's Association of Buffalo, *Chronicles of the 21st New York: Buffalo's First Regiment* (Buffalo, New York: 1887), p. 291; "Explanation of Hoyt's map" (7th Wisconsin), January 22, 1895, Antietam National Battlefield; W. W. Dudley sketch map (19th Indiana), Antietam National Battlefield; Louis C. Greenleaf letter and map to E. A. Carman, December 13, 1894, Antietam National Battlefield.

37 William F. Rogers letter to E. A. Carman, undated, Antietam National Battlefield; *Chronicles of the 21st New York*, p. 291.

38 W. W. Dudley sketch map (19th Indiana), Antietam National Battlefield; OR, Vol. XIX, Part 1, p. 244.

39 Ransom "Official Report," Joseph Hooker military papers, 1861–1864, Box 9, Huntington Library, San Marino, California; Carman and Pierro, Ed., *The Maryland Campaign*, p. 231; Carman and Clemens, Ed., *The Maryland Campaign, Vol. II*, pp. 99–103; OR, Vol. XIX, Part 1, p. 932. Clemens indicates that the source for this quote from Hood is a May 28, 1984 letter from William B. Wall of the 1st Texas (in the Gould Papers), listed in his book on p. 102, footnote 91.

40 OR, Vol. XIX, Part 1, p. 932; Carman and Pierro, Ed., *The Maryland Campaign*, p. 231; Carman and Clemens, Ed., *The Maryland Campaign, Vol. II*, p. 99–103.

41 Carman and Pierro, Ed., *The Maryland Campaign*, p. 229; Carman and Clemens, Ed., *The Maryland Campaign, Vol. II*, pp.99–103; Lee, *Memoirs of William N. Pendleton*, p. 216; Alexander Pendleton to his mother, September 21, 1862, Lee, *Memoirs*, p. 216.

42 Carman and Pierro, Ed., *The Maryland Campaign*, p. 229; Richard A. Sauers and Peter Tomasak *Ricketts' Battery: A History of Battery F, 1st Pennsylvania Light Artillery* (Luzerne National Bank, publisher, 2001), p. 53. William H. Thurston claimed in an 1895 letter that Matthews's Battery was overrun during a Confederate infantry attack and was forced to briefly abandon its guns. This event—if it occurred—may have happened while the battery was forward deployed during this time.

43 Anderson "Official Report," Joseph Hooker military papers, 1861–1864, Box 9, Huntington Library, San Marino, California; OR, Vol. XIX, Part 1, p. 269.

44 OR, Vol. XIX, Part 1, p. 269.

45 OR, Vol. XIX, Part 1, pp. 269–70.

46 OR, Vol. XIX, Part 1, p. 270, p. 274; Carman and Clemens, Ed., *The Maryland Campaign, Vol. II*, pp. 95–96.

47 OR, Vol. XIX, Part 1, p. 271.

48 Henry Steele Commager, *The Blue and the Grey* (Indianapolis, Indiana: Bobs-Merrill Co.,1950), pp. 306–7; Priest, *Antietam: The Soldier's Battle*, p. 65; OR, Vol. XIX, Part 1, p. 938.

49 OR, Vol. XIX, I, p. 271, p. 938; Carman and Pierro, Ed., *The Maryland Campaign*, p. 231; Carman and Clemens, Ed., *The Maryland Campaign, Vol. II*, pp. 99–103.

50 Anderson "Official Report," Joseph Hooker military papers, 1861–1864, Box 9, Huntington Library, San Marino, California; OR, Vol. XIX, I, p. 933.

51 Commager, *The Blue and the Grey*, p. 306; Carman and Pierro, Ed., *The Maryland Campaign*, p. 231; Carman and Clemens, Ed., *The Maryland Campaign, Vol. II*, pp.99–103; Priest, *Antietam: The Soldier's Battle*, p. 66; O. T. Hanks Reminiscences, 1861–1865, 1918, Dolph Briscoe Center for American History, The University of Texas at Austin, Box 2R31.

52 Carman and Pierro, Ed., *The Maryland Campaign*, pp. 231–32; Carman and Clemens, Ed., *The Maryland Campaign, Vol. II*, pp. 99–105. A soldier in the 12th Massachusetts' Company G claimed in an 1869 article that "our brigade (Hartsuff) captured the colors of the First Texas", a claim echoed by the 12th's George Kendall in an 1891 letter. If this is so, they almost certainly found—rather than "captured"—the flag because his brigade never fought the 1st Texas that day.

"The Citizen Soldier" article (12th Massachusetts), 1869, Antietam National Battlefield; George Kendall letter to Rollins, December 17, 1891, Antietam National Battlefield.

53 OR, Vol. XIX, Part 1, p. 938.

54 William F. Rogers letter and map to E. A. Carman, undated, Antietam National Battlefield; W. W. Dudley sketch map (19th Indiana), Antietam National Battlefield; OR, Vol. XIX, Part 1, p. 928, p. 938.

55 Harsh chiefly blames Hood's failure on unfortunate timing (*Taken at the Flood*, pp. 374–75), claiming that Early's recall to a new position near the Dunker Church failed to push Doubleday's troops far enough back, which in turn allowed them to threaten Hood's left flank. Although this played a role in Hood's failure, it hardly is the key event driving that result and Harsh ignores other Hood mistakes, such as allowing the gap to grow between Wofford's and Law's Brigades.

56 Hood, *Advance and Retreat*, p. 43.

57 OR, Vol. XIX, Part 1, p. 223, p. 259; Earl J. Hess *The Rifle Musket in Civil War Combat: Reality and Myth* (Lawrence, Kansas: University of Kansas Press, 2008), pp. 2–8.

Chapter 8

1 John M. Gould, *History of the 1st, 10th, 29th Maine Regiment* (Portland: Stephen Barry, Pub., 1871), p. 232; Brown, *The Twenty-seventh Indiana*, p. 239.

2 Alpheus S. Williams, *From the Cannon's Mouth: The Civil War Letters of General Alpheus Williams* (Lincoln: University of Nebraska Press, 1995), p. 125; Carman and Pierro, Ed., *The Maryland Campaign*, p. 235; Carman and Clemens, Ed., *The Maryland Campaign*, Vol. II, pp. 111–13.

3 Alpheus S. Williams, *From the Cannon's Mouth*, p. 125; Carman and Pierro, Ed., *The Maryland Campaign*, p. 235; Carman and Clemens, Ed., *The Maryland Campaign*, Vol. II, pp. 111–13.

4 Gould, *History of the 1st, 10th, 29th Maine*, p. 234.

5 OR, Vol. XIX, Part 1, pp. 484–87, p. 938; Carman and Pierro, Ed., *The Maryland Campaign*, p. 236.

6 Carman and Pierro, Ed., *The Maryland Campaign*, p. 236; Carman and Clemens, Ed., *The Maryland Campaign, Vol. II*, pp. 113–17; OR, Vol. XIX, Part 1, p. 484, p. 494, p. 505. Sears's *Landscape Turned Red* account of the XII Corps (pp. 224–28) very much glosses over important details of the corps' movements and role, perhaps explaining why it has been so overlooked and confused. For example, Sears says "Whatever role Hooker and McClellan originally had originally intended for the XII Corps … its mission now was to shore up Hooker's wrecked formations." While this is partly true, Sears ignores Hooker's original "new/old regiments plan" and other indications Hooker was using the corps to reignite his attack and launches straight into its often-confusing movements—and even then Sears never offers any idea what role and purpose Hooker, Mansfield, or Williams had for the movements he relates.

7 Carman and Pierro, Ed., *The Maryland Campaign*, p. 236; Carman and Clemens, Ed., *The Maryland Campaign*, Vol. II, pp. 113–15; OR, Vol. XIX, Part 1, p. 484, p. 494.

8 OR, Vol. XIX, Part 1, p. 1033. For a thorough discussion of D. H. Hill's meeting with Lee and the wounding of his horse, see Harsh, *Sounding the Shallows*, Research Appendixes on the battle of Antietam, September 17–18, Appendix L, pp. 203–4.

9 OR, Vol. XIX, Part 1, p. 1033; Henry W. Thomas, *History of the Doles-Cook Brigade, Army of Northern Virginia, C.S.A.* (Dayton: Morningside Books, 1988), pp. 469–71. Sergeant Shinn of the 3rd North Carolina wrote Samuel Mumma, Jr., claiming that he was the one who torched his family's home and that it was done to deny the building to Union troops as cover.

10 Thomas, *History of the Doles-Cook Brigade*, p. 69.

11 W. H. Holstead letter to John Gould, March 9, 1893, Antietam National Battlefield; OR, Vol. XIX, Part 1, p. 1033; Carman and Pierro, Ed., *The Maryland Campaign*, p. 237; Carman and Clemens, Ed., *The Maryland Campaign*, Vol. II, pp. 113–20.

12 Anderson "Official Report," Joseph Hooker military papers, 1861–1864, Box 9, Huntington Library, San Marino, California.

13 Carman and Pierro, Ed., *The Maryland Campaign*, pp. 233–34; Carman and Clemens, Ed., *The Maryland Campaign, Vol. II*, pp. 106–10; OR, Vol. XIX, Part 1, p. 269.

14 OR, Vol. XIX, Part 1, p. 270.

15 "Explanation of Hoyt's map" (7th Wisconsin), January 22, 1895, Antietam National Battlefield; Anderson "Official Report," Joseph Hooker military papers, 1861–1864, Box 9, Huntington Library, San Marino, California; OR, Vol. XIX, Part 1, p. 249.

16 Anderson "Official Report", Joseph Hooker military papers, 1861–1864, Box 9, Huntington Library, San Marino, California; W. W. Dudley sketch map (19th Indiana), Antietam National Battlefield; OR, Vol. XIX, Part 1, p. 270. Meade's OR, cited here, implies that Anderson was withdrawn upon the arrival of the XII Corps, rather than being pushed back by Ripley's Brigade. However, Anderson never mentions such an order in his unpublished OR and even if Meade did order Anderson back, the fact remains that the Union relinquished control of the Cornfield to Doles's men.

17 Ransom "Official Report," Joseph Hooker military papers, 1861–1864, Box 9, Huntington Library, San Marino, California; Carman and Pierro, Ed., *The Maryland Campaign*, p. 240; Carman and Clemens, Ed., *The Maryland Campaign, Vol. II*, pp. 118–21.

18 Carman and Pierro, Ed., *The Maryland Campaign*, p. 236; Carman and Clemens, Ed., *The Maryland Campaign, Vol. II*, pp. 113–17.

19 OR, Vol. XIX, Part 1, p. 475, pp. 504–5; Carman and Pierro, Ed., *The Maryland Campaign*, p. 242; Carman and Clemens, Ed., *The Maryland Campaign, Vol. II*, pp. 133–36. It remains unclear exactly who ordered the flanking attack of Greene's Division. General Williams claimed in his OR account that after learning of Mansfield's wounding (and his rise to XII Corps command) that Greene "was directed to the ridge on the left…" General Greene, however, in his OR account claimed, "The division was carried into action about 6:30 am, under the orders of Brigadier General Mansfield." Almost certainly, it was General Hooker's plan and that Mansfield first issued the order starting Greene's Division into battle. Perhaps Williams was unaware when he assumed command that Greene was already moving into place and assumed that it was he, not Mansfield, who ordered this move.

20 The Niagara County Historical Society, *100 Years Ago Today: Niagara County in the Civil War as Reported in the Pages of "The Niagara Falls Gazette"* (Lockport, New York: The Niagara County Historical Society, Inc., 1966), No. 17, p. 124; OR, Vol. XIX, Part 1, p. 487, p. 489.

21 OR, Vol. XIX, Part. 1, p. 493.

22 Gould, *History of the 1st, 10th, 29th Maine Regiment*, pp. 237–40.

23 Gould, *History of the 1st, 10th, 29th Maine Regiment*, pp. 237–40; Gould, *Joseph K. F. Mansfield*, pp. 12–13.; OR, Vol. XIX, Part 1, p. 489.

24 Gould, *Joseph K. F. Mansfield*, pp. 15–18. There are many versions of the mortal wounding of General Mansfield, nearly all written by men at Antietam that day who might have seen the general fall. However, many accounts may be dismissed because the individual making the claim was nowhere near the East Woods or the location of Crawford's Brigade that morning. The reports cited by some members of Crawford's Brigade—particularly Captain Gardiner, Lieutenant Dunegan, and Sergeant Keatley of the 125th Pennsylvania—cannot be so easily dismissed because they almost certainly saw the general that morning and all reported he was wounded in or near the East Woods. None of them, however, contain the level of detail that Gould—who wrote

an entire book devoted to Mansfield's wounding, based on his own and other eyewitnesses' accounts—provides and which could have been corroborated or refuted by other members of the regiment who were then still living. This suggests that Gould's account is the most likely to be accurate.

Chapter 9

1   Williams, *From the Cannon's Mouth*, pp. 125–26.
2   Williams, *From the Cannon's Mouth*, p. 126. Williams's timeline for meeting Hooker and deploying the 124th Pennsylvania, reported in his letter of September 22, is at odds with his account in the Official Records and, by extension, Carman's account in *The Maryland Campaign*. Williams writes in his Sletter—the source for the account in *From the Cannon's Mouth*—that he met with Hooker in the plowed field before learning that he commanded the XII Corps in Mansfield's place, and after that he led the 124th Pennsylvania into place near the Hagerstown Pike. Williams's September 29 account in the OR claims he reported to Hooker after learning of Mansfield's wounding and that after this he directed the deployment of the corps (even though the XII Corps was already engaged in battle—the cause of Mansfield's wounding). Carman further claims Williams led the 124th westward to the Pike on Hooker's much earlier orders first; only when on his way back and looking for the 125th Pennsylvania did he learn of Mansfield's wounding and subsequently reported to Hooker. Sadly, Hooker never wrote of the meeting in his official report of the battle. I have chosen General Williams's September 22 account over Carman's because this firsthand account was written closest to September 17, 1862 and so is more likely to accurately record the details of the meeting.
3   Diary of CDM Broomhall, September 17 entry.
4   Ellen C. Collier, Ed., *Letters of a Civil War Soldier: Chandler B. Gillam, 28th New York Volunteers, with Diary of W. L. Hicks* (Xlibris Corp., 2005), p. 249.OR, Vol. XIX, Part 1, p. 487.
5   OR, Vol. XIX, Part 1, p. 487.
6   Carman and Pierro, Ed., *The Maryland Campaign*, pp. 237–38; Carman and Clemens, Ed., *The Maryland Campaign, Vol. II*, pp. 113–25.
7   OR, Vol. XIX, Part 1, pp. 494–96; Frederick Crouse, Manuscript, *The Antietam Experience of Frederick Crouse, 128th Pennsylvania*, Antietam National Battlefield; Carman and Pierro, Ed., *The Maryland Campaign*, pp. 237–38; Carman and Clemens, Ed., *The Maryland Campaign, Vol. II*, pp. 120–23.Carman claims the 3rd North Carolina moved in response to Greene's Division, but this unlikely and probably due instead to the presence of Crawford's veteran regiments.
8   Brown, *The Twenty-seventh Indiana*, p. 243.
9   90th Pennsylvania Association letter to E. A. Carman, March 23, 1895, Antietam National Battlefield; OR, Vol. XIX, Part 1, pp. 494–95.
10   OR, Vol. XIX, Part 1, pp. 494–95.
11   OR, Vol. XIX, Part 1, pp. 494–95.
12   OR, Vol. XIX, Part 1, p. 487.
13   Brown, *The Twenty-seventh Indiana*, p. 246.
14   Carman and Pierro, Ed., *The Maryland Campaign*, p. 240; Carman and Clemens, Ed., *The Maryland Campaign, Vol. II*, pp.126–30; OR, Vol. XIX, Part 1, p. 1022, pp. 1053–54. Sears claims Colquitt's Brigade came "from the center" (*Landscape Turned Red*, p. 230) because he accepts the—in my analysis, mistaken—view that the Sunken Road position was the center of Lee's overall line. The brigade originated there but it was not "the center."
15   OR, Vol. XIX, Part 1, p. 845; Carman and Pierro, Ed., *The Maryland Campaign*, p. 240; Carman and Clemens, Ed., *The Maryland Campaign, Vol. II*, pp. 126–30.

16 Julian W. Hinkley *A Narrative of Service with the Third Wisconsin Infantry* (The Wisconsin History Commission, 1912), pp.54–55; Ransom "Official Report," Joseph Hooker military papers, 1861–1864, Box 9, Huntington Library, San Marino, California; Carman and Pierro, Ed., *The Maryland Campaign*, p. 240; Carman and Clemens, Ed., *The Maryland Campaign, Vol. II*, pp.126–30.

17 Hinkley, *A Narrative of Service*, p. 55; B. H. Witcher letter to John Gould, 6th Georgia, Antietam Collection, Dartmouth College Library.

18 OR, Vol. XIX, Part 1, p. 495, pp. 498–99.

19 OR, Vol. XIX, Part 1, p. 1054.

20 OR, Vol. XIX, Part 1, p. 1040.

21 OR, Vol. XIX, Part 1, p. 1044.

22 OR, Vol. XIX, Part 1, p. 1043.

23 OR, Vol. XIX, Part 1, p. 475.

24 OR, Vol. XIX, Part 1, p. 475.

25. Carman and Pierro, Ed., *The Maryland Campaign*, pp. 242–43; Carman and Clemens, Ed., *The Maryland Campaign, Vol. II*, pp. 133–42.

26 OR, Vol. XIX, Part 1, pp. 504–10; Carman and Pierro, Ed., *The Maryland Campaign*, pp. 242–43; Carman and Clemens, Ed., *The Maryland Campaign, Vol. II*, pp.133–39; Eugene Powell letter, Antietam Collection, Dartmouth University.

27 OR, Vol. XIX, Part 1, p. 1044; J. M. Smither, letter, 5th Texas, Antietam Collection, Dartmouth College Library; Sears, *Landscape Turned Red*, p. 232.

28 Carman and Pierro, Ed., *The Maryland Campaign*, p. 244; Carman and Clemens, Ed., *The Maryland Campaign, Vol. II*, pp. 143–45.

29 W. B. Matchett *Maryland and the Glorious Old 3rd in the War for the Union* (Washington, D.C.: T. J. Bradsher, 1882), p. 22; OR, Vol. XIX, I, p. 512.

30 Brown, *The Twenty-seventh Indiana*, p. 251.

31 Robert Shaw to Francis Shaw, September 21, 1862, Robert Gould Shaw, *Blue-Eyed Child of Fortune: The Civil War Letters of Robert Gould Shaw* (Marietta: The University of Georgia Press, 2004), p. 240. Charles F. Morse, "From Second Bull Run to Antietam" *MOLLUS*, Vol. 1 (Commandery of Missouri. Becktold & Co., 1892), p. 275.

32 John Richards Boyle, *Soldiers True; The Story of the One Hundred and Eleventh Regiment Pennsylvania Veteran Volunteers, and of its Campaigns in the War for the Union 1861–1865* (New York: Eaton & Mains, 1903), p. 58; Lawrence Wilson, *Itinerary of the Seventh Ohio Volunteer Infantry 1861–1864* (New York: The Neale Publishing Company, 1907), p. 208; OR, Vol. XIX, Pt. 1, pp. 506–14. Sears claims the "the Pennsylvanians and Ohioans followed up their fire with a charge into the corn…" (*Landscape Turned Red*, p. 233), but no first-hand accounts suggest such a charge occurred. Rather, they note the steady, organized general advance that I believe was key to Greene's success.

33 OR, Vol. XIX, Part 1, p. 845, pp. 1053–54; Brown, *The Twenty-seventh Indiana*, p. 250.

34 B. H. Witcher letter to Gould, Antietam Collection, Dartmouth University; Sears, *Landscape Turned Red*, p. 233.

35 Ethan S. Rafuse, *Antietam, South Mountain & Harpers Ferry: A Battlefield Guide* (Lincoln: University of Nebraska Press, 2008), pp. 55–56.

36 OR, Vol. XIX, I, p. 1023, pp. 1053–54; Carman and Pierro, Ed., *The Maryland Campaign*, p. 243; Carman and Clemens, Ed., *The Maryland Campaign, Vol. II*, pp.136–39; Sears, *Landscape Turned Red*, p. 233.

37 OR, Vol. XIX, Part 1, p. 1053.

38 Harsh, *Sounding the Shallows: A Confederate Companion*, p. 19.

Chapter 10

1   Samuel S. Sumner letter to George B. Davies, April 4, 1897, John C. Ropes Files, Military Historical Society Collection, Boston University, Boston; Marion V. Armstrong, *Unfurl Those Colors!: McClellan, Sumner, & the Second Army Corps in the Antietam Campaign* (Tuscaloosa: The University of Alabama Press, 2008), p. 166.

2   Randolph B. Marcy to Edwin V. Sumner, September 17, 1862, Telegrams Received, 1862–1865, Records of the US Army Continental Commands, Entry 45, Part 2 RG 393, National Archives; OR, Vol. XIX, Part 1, p. 275; Armstrong, *Unfurl Those Colors!*, p. 167. Rafuse argues McClellan ordered Sumner to the Union right prematurely and was deviating from his plan (Rafuse, *McClellan's War*, p. 314), although unable to recall the corps. This argument ignores the previous night's order sending the II Corps artillery across the upper bridge and McClellan's dual messages to Hooker and Sumner, referring the II Corps to guide toward Sharpsburg if all was well with Hooker's attack.

3   George Ruggles to General Sumner, *Records of U.S. Army Continental Commands*, Telegrams Received, 1862–1865, Entry 45, Part 2, RG 393, National Archives; OR, Vol. XIX, Part 1, p. 51, p. 55, p. 217; Armstrong, *Unfurl Those Colors!*, pp. 154–59; Samuel S. Sumner, "The Antietam Campaign," *Civil War and Miscellaneous Papers: Papers of the Military Historical Society of Massachusetts*, Vol. XIV (Boston: The Military Historical Society of Massachusetts, 1918), Chapter II, p. 10.

4   OR, Vol. XIX, Part 1, p. 275; Randolph B. Marcy to Edwin V. Sumner, September 17, 1862, Telegrams Received, 1862–1865, Records of the US Army Continental Commands, Entry 45, Part 2 RG 393, National Archives; Armstrong, *Unfurl Those Colors!*, p. 167. Sears argues McClellan remained uncertain about the II Corps's role—thinking it "too risky to commit the II Corps…," until finally sending Sumner to the right (*Landscape Turned Red*, p. 241)—and fails to explain what settled his mind. I believe Sears was unable to find a driver for this decision because McClellan had earlier decided to use Sumner's troops on the right for either of the two roles noted in his dispatch to Sumner.

5   OR, Vol. XIX, Part 1, pp. 30–31, p. 61, p. 419, p. 424. There remains a good deal of confusion about just when McClellan ordered Burnside to begin the attack to take the Lower Bridge. Generals McClellan, Burnside, and Jacob Cox—commanding the IX Corps alongside Burnside—all agree that an early morning message was sent warning the IX Corps to prepare, but not launch, its assault. However, the timing of the actual attack message remains in dispute. McClellan claims he sent the message at 8:00 ordering an attack on the bridge, while Cox reported the order was received "around 9 o'clock," and Burnside claimed the message arrived at 10:00. McClellan's order might well have been issued at 8:00 because it would roughly coincide with his decision to begin setting other parts of his battle plan into motion. Cox's recollection that it arrived at 9:00 also is likely accurate; the hour it took to reach him can be explained by both the nearly one mile the order had to travel from McClellan's headquarters to the front, as well as the additional delay of having to go through General Burnside's headquarters—as the wing commander—before reaching the IX Corps. Burnside's recollection could be true, but in any case, both Burnside and Cox cannot be correct. In choosing which general to believe, it is clear that Burnside has much more reason than Cox to skew his report in the wake of his performance at Antietam. For this reason, I have chosen to accept Cox's account.

6   Vanderslice, *The Civil War Letters of George Washington Beidelman*, p. 102; Don Ernsberer, *Paddy Owen's Regulars: A History of the 69th Pennsylvania "Irish Volunteers" Vol. I* (Xlibris Corp., 2004), p. 305; George Washburn, *A Complete History and Record of the 108th Regiment New York Vols. from 1862 to 1894.* (Rochester: Press of E. R. Andrews, 1894), p. 24.

7   Boyle, *Soldiers True*, p. 58; Wilson, *Itinerary of the Seventh Ohio*, p. 208; OR, Vol. XIX, Part 1, pp. 506–14. Rafuse mistakenly says the XII Corps "was able by 8:45 to secure the Dunkard Church plateau…" and so McClellan had no need to send the II Corps right (Rafuse, *McClellan's War*, p. 315). By that time, however, Greene and Gordon's XII Corps command remained on the eastern side of the Pike, not on the ridge or within Confederate lines.

8   OR, Vol. XIX, Part 1, p. 476, p. 485, p. 915.

9   OR, Vol. XIX, Part 1, p. 476, p. 485, p. 915.

10 OR, Vol. XIX, Part 1, p. 820, pp. 968–69.

11 OR, Vol. XIX, Part 1, p. 969.

12 OR, Vol. XIX, Part 1, p. 969.

13 OR, Vol. XIX, Part 1, pp. 969–70.

14 OR, Vol. XIX, Part 1, p. 970.

15 Hooker never directly stated that he was aware that Sumner's II Corps was on its way. However, he points out in his official report that while surgeons were examining his wound "Sumner's corps appeared upon the field on my immediate right, and I have a indistinct recollection of having seen Sedgwick's division pass to the front." It is likely that Hooker—despite his wounded state—knew the II Corps was on its way and that these fresh men must be them. It cannot be completely discounted, however, that Hooker might be filling in gaps with knowledge gained after the battle. OR, Vol. XIX, Part 1, p. 219; Williams, *From the Cannon's Mouth*, p. 127.

16 OR, Vol. XIX, Part 1, pp. 1022–23, pp. 1036–37.

17 OR, Vol. XIX, Part 1, p. 476.

18 OR, Vol. XIX, Part 1, p. 495; Carman and Clemens, Ed., *The Maryland Campaign, Vol. II*, p. 157, p. 160, p. 165.

19 OR, Vol. XIX, Part 1, p. 495.

20 John Albert Monroe "Battery D, First Rhode Island Light Artillery, at the Battle of Antietam, September 17, 1862," Personal Narrative of Events in the War of the Rebellion, Being Papers Read Before the Rhode Island Soldiers and Sailors Historical Society, Series 3, No. 16 (Providence: The Rhode Island Soldiers and Sailors Historical Society), pp. 21–22.

21 Harsh claims Hooker was wounded between 8:30 and 9:00 (*Taken at the Flood*, p. 377) but offers no source for this claim.

22 *History of the One Hundred and Twenty-fifth Pennsylvania Volunteers,* p. 69; Williams, *From the Cannon's Mouth,* p. 127.

23 Eby, *A Virginia Yankee in the Civil War*, p. 110. When considering these events, I used Strother's diaries rather than his "Personal Recollections of the War," published in *Harper's New Monthly Magazine* in 1868. Although there is useful information contained in the latter source—and I have used it very sparingly—the disparity between what he recorded in his wartime diaries and the additional detail and claims made only in the postwar *Harper's* article suggest the latter source contains highly doubtful information, added presumably to make a better story for his publisher and readers. Cecil Eby, Jr. provides a detailed explanation of this problem in the introduction of his 1989 published version of the dairies, noting "few would quarrel with the assertion that Strother's notebooks [the diaries] are superior to his Recollections at almost all points." Similarly, questions remain about what General McClellan was doing in the Pry House until he emerged on the lawn. Captain Sumner and the Pry family both claimed McClellan was asleep—the latter source until nearly 8:00—but the 7:20 order suggests McClellan was stirring well before that (S. Sumner, "The Antietam Campaign," *MOLLUS*, Vol. 14, Chapter II, p. 10; Walker, *Antietam Farmsteads*, p. 134). Regardless, McClellan was isolated from all, perhaps except his staff, until the battle was well underway.

24 Rafuse points out that McClellan has long been criticized for not issuing written orders, which Rafuse attributes to McClellan wishing to maintain maximum flexibility (Rafuse, *McClellan's War*,

p. 310). This is probably the case, although Rafuse then argues McClellan did so while waiting to see if Hooker would succeed before deciding what to do next. No evidence exists to suggest McClellan was being this flexible; rather, unit movements and McClellan's actions suggest he quite rigidly adhered to his plan's terms and that the flexibility McClellan sought was a post-battle ability to control debate about how the plan succeeded and who drove the unfolding fight.

Chapter 11

1   *Report of the Joint Committee on the Conduct of the War*, pp. 368–69; "North to Antietam", *Battles and Leaders of the Civil War*, p. 643. This *Battles and Leaders* article is the only account claiming that Hooker and Sumner talked briefly. It is highly doubtful that the author of this article, General Jacob D. Cox, could have witnessed this event because, as acting commander of the IX Corps, Cox was at that moment well south of Hooker and Sumner, across the Boonsboro Pike. Hooker mentions in his testimony before Congress that he talked with Sumner, but this statement is rife with errors—including that he, not McClellan, asked for reinforcements and that this request came after Hooker sustained his foot wound—which calls into question the detail and accuracy of this story.

2   Johnston to McClellan April 13, 1856, McClellan Papers, LOC; Rafuse, *McClellan's War*, p. 192; Sears, *The Civil War Papers of George B. McClellan*, p. 257, p. 286, p. 296.

3   Records of US Army Continental Commands, Entry 45, Part 2, RG 393, National Archives; Albert V. Colburn message to Edwin V. Sumner 17 September, 1862; Armstrong *Unfurl Those Colors!*, pp. 171–72.

4   There has been considerable confusion over the years about the formation in which Sedgwick's Division arrived at the Cornfield. Did they march to the East Woods in three parallel columns, as Sumner's OR clearly states, or did they advance in a battle front, as General Howard and other officers noted in their reports? After reading through all the Official Reports submitted by Sumner and the commanders in Sedgwick's Division, I believe that they advanced in both formations at different points in the march. Some of this confusion probably is a result of General Sumner personally observing only the column formation, which was abandoned shortly after he rode forward to scout the ground for his attack, so he missed the deployment to a battle front. Sadly, General Sedgwick—who probably issued the orders for his division's formations and movements—never submitted a report for Antietam and his death during the 1864 battle of Spotsylvania prevented any opportunity for later comment. But the number of other officers who clearly reported moving from a column to a battle front, back into a column, and finally back to a battle front before crossing the Cornfield, were themselves there—unlike General Sumner—suggesting their reports reflect the actual moves of Sedgwick's Division on the march. For details see OR, Vol. XIX, Part 1, p. 305, pp. 310–11, p. 313, p. 314, p. 315, pp. 319–20.

5   Adams *Reminiscences of the Nineteenth Massachusetts*, Chapter VI; Gary G. Lash, *"Duty Well Done" The History of Edward Baker's California Infantry (71st Pennsylvania Infantry)*, (Butternut and Blue, 2001), pp. 262–64.

6   *Chronicles of the 21st New York*, p. 292.

7   *Chronicles of the 21st New York*, p. 292; Murray, Ed., *New Yorkers in the Civil War, Vol. 4*, p. 78; William F. Rogers letter to E. A. Carman, undated, Antietam National Battlefield; Louis C. Greenleaf map to E. A. Carman, December 13, 1894, Antietam National Battlefield; OR, Vol. XIX, Part 1, p. 244.

8   *Chronicles of the 21st New York*, p. 292; Murray, Ed., *New Yorkers in the Civil War, Vol. 4*, p. 78; OR, Vol. XIX, Part 1, p. 244; Theodore M. Nagle *Reminiscences of the Civil War* (Erie, Pennsylvania: Dispatch Ptg. & Eng. Co., 1923), pp. 41–42; William F. Rogers letter to E. A. Carman, undated,

Antietam National Battlefield, p. 4; Louis C. Greenleaf letter, map to E. A. Carman, December 13, 1894, Antietam National Battlefield.

9   Robert M. Green *History of the One Hundred and Twenty-Fourth Regiment Pennsylvania Volunteers in the War of the Rebellion—1862–1863* (Philadelphia, Ware Brothers Company, 1907), pp. 31–32; Diary of CDM Broomhall, September 17 entry.

10 Regimental History Committee, *History of the One Hundred and Twenty-fifth Regiment Pennsylvania Volunteers*, (J. B. Lippincott Co., 1906). pp. 69–71.

11 *History of the One Hundred and Twenty-fifth Regiment Pennsylvania Volunteers*, pp. 69–71.

12 OR, Vol. XIX, Part 1, p. 970.

13 OR, Vol. XIX, Part 1, p. 970.

14 Carman and Pierro, Ed., *The Maryland Campaign*, pp. 256–57; Carman and Clemens, Ed., *The Maryland Campaign, Vol. II*, pp. 179–83; OR, Vol. XIX, Part 1, p. 909.

15 OR, Vol. XIX, I, pp. 857–58; Lafayette McLaws letter to Henry Heth, December 13, 1894. "Report of Gen. Lafayette McLaws, Comdg. Division—Division Artillery—Report of Gen. J. B. Kershaw," National Archives, Record Group 94, Box 2. This latter source contains a detailed conversation that McLaws claims to have had with Lee at this moment in the battle. This meeting and Lee's orders to McLaws—to hold his troops ¼ mile from town in reserve until called upon—are almost certainly accurate and reinforced by subsequent events reported in the OR and in soldier accounts. McLaws's conversation with Lee may have occurred as he reported to Heth, but as likely, McLaws was at least in part embellishing the story. For this reason, I have chosen to avoid including this account, found in Carman's *The Maryland Campaign* and other sources.

16 Harsh, *Taken at the Flood*, pp. 380–81.

17 OR, Vol. XIX, Part 1, pp. 857–58; Carman and Pierro, Ed., *The Maryland Campaign*, pp. 257–59; Carman and Clemens, Ed., *The Maryland Campaign, Vol. II*, pp. 183–89.

18 Lafayette McLaws letter to Henry Heth, December 13, 1894, Antietam National Battlefield, Carman Collection.

19 OR, Vol. XIX, Part 1, p. 858.

20 OR, Vol. XIX, Part 1, p. 914.

21 South Carolina Division, United Daughters of the Confederacy, *Recollections and Reminiscences 1861–1865*, Vol. 12 (2002), pp. 349–51; Carman and Pierro, Ed., *The Maryland Campaign*, p. 259; Carman and Clemens, Ed., *The Maryland Campaign, Vol. II*, pp.186–89; Andrews, *Footprints of a Regiment*, pp. 78–79. Andrews's mention of "General Anderson" reflects the post-war nature of his volume because Anderson was not promoted to that rank until November 1862.

22 Robert Wallace Shand, "Incidents in the Life of a Private Soldier in the War Waged by the United States Against the Confederate States 1861–1865," Antietam National Battlefield, pp. 36–37; Carman and Pierro, Ed., *The Maryland Campaign*, p. 259; Carman and Clemens, Ed., *The Maryland Campaign, Vol. II*, pp. 186–89; OR, Vol. XIX, Part 1, p. 859, p. 865, p. 871.

23 OR, Vol. XIX, Part 1, p. 970; W. H. Andrews, *Footprints of a Regiment: A Recollection of the 1st Georgia Regulars, 1861–1865* (Atlanta: Longstreet Press, 1992), pp. 78–79.; *History of the One Hundred and Twenty-fifth Regiment Pennsylvania Volunteers*, pp. 71–73.

24 Samuel S. Sumner, "The Antietam Campaign," *Civil War and Miscellaneous Papers: Papers of the Military Historical Society of Massachusetts*, Vol. XIV (Boston: The Military Historical Society of Massachusetts, 1918), Chapter II, p. 10.

25 Sumner, "The Antietam Campaign," p. 10.

26 Rafuse curiously claims Sumner intended to drive the II Corps onto the Dunker Church ridge and then "wheel left to envelope the rebel line" (Rafuse, *McClellan's War*, pp. 316–17). This assumes that Sumner believed his attack would be a turning, maneuver assault, rather than the

frontal assault Sumner's "column of brigades" formation suggests he intended, and that Sumner had any idea where the actual end of Lee's line was. There is no proof for either assumption.

27 Sumner, "The Antietam Campaign," p. 11.

28 OR, Vol. XIX, Part 1, p. 315.

29 Lash, "Duty Well Done," p. 264; Vanderslice, *The Civil War Letters of George Washington Beidelman*, p. 102.

30 OR, Vol. XIX, Part 1, p. 320.

31 OR, Vol. XIX, Part. 1, p. 305; Carman and Pierro, Ed., *The Maryland Campaign*, p. 259; Carman and Clemens, Ed., *The Maryland Campaign, Vol. II*, pp.186–89. Sumner's demand for a regiment to support Mansfield and the detaching of the 71st Pennsylvania remains in doubt. Howard, in his OR, states that this was the case, though Sumner never mentions it in his report. Carman's manuscript states that the 71st's Colonel Wistar doesn't recall any such order or move that would delay the brigade, although Carman never provided a source for this claim and Pierro cannot find its source, either. Possibly it happened, or possibly Howard concocted it to explain his delay. I am skeptical it happened—though I have included it—but emphasize that the important fact is that Howard's Brigade hesitated to advance, whatever the reason.

32 OR, Vol. XIX, Part 1, p. 313.

33 Richard Moe, *The Last Full Measure: The Life and Death of the First Minnesota Volunteers* (New York: Avon Books, 1993), p. 181.

34 *History of the One Hundred and Twenty-fifth Regiment Pennsylvania Volunteers*, pp.72–73; Lewis N. Chapin, *A Brief History of the 34th Regiment N.Y.S.V.* (New York, 1903), pp. 62–64; OR, Vol. XIX, Part 1, pp. 315–16.

35 OR, Vol. XIX, Part 1, p. 311.

36 Moe, *Last Full Measure*, p. 182; OR, Vol. XIX, Part 1, p. 311.

37 OR, Vol. XIX, Part 1, p. 311, pp. 319–20

38 Lieutenant Henry Ropes letters, 20th Massachusetts, September 20, 1862. http://harvardregiment.org/ropesltr1.htr

39 Lieutenant Henry Ropes letters, 20th Massachusetts, September 20, 1862. http://harvardregiment.org/ropesltr1.htr

40 OR, Vol. XIX, Part 1, p. 1010.

41 John T. Parham, "Thirty-Second at Sharpsburg," Southern Historical Society Papers, pp. 255–52; Carman and Pierro, Ed., *The Maryland Campaign*, p. 263; Carman and Clemens, Ed., *The Maryland Campaign, Vol. II*, pp. 198–200; OR, Vol. XIX, Part 1, p. 874; Ronald H. Moseley, Ed., *The Stillwell Letters: A Georgian in Longstreet's Corps, Army of Northern Virginia* (Mercer University Press, 2002), p. 46; Robert C. Krick, *Lee's Colonels* (Dayton, Ohio: Morningside Bookshop Press, 1979).

42 Edward M. Burruss letter to John C. Burruss; John C. Burruss Papers, Louisiana State University; South Carolina Division UDC, *Recollections and Reminiscences*, p. 350; Shand, "Incidents," pp. 36–37; 13th Mississippi Infantry annotated map, Antietam National Battlefield; OR, Vol. XIX, Part 1, pp. 970–71.

43 Shand, "Incidents," pp. 36–37; Edward M. Burruss letter to John C. Burruss; John C. Burruss Papers, Louisiana State University; Carman and Pierro, Ed., *The Maryland Campaign*, p. 255; Carman and Clemens, Ed., *The Maryland Campaign, Vol. II*, pp. 175–78; *History of the One Hundred and Twenty-fifth Regiment Pennsylvania Volunteers*, p. 74.

44 Shand, "Incidents," pp. 36–37.

45 Chapin, *A Brief History of the 34th Regiment*, p. 64; OR, Vol. XIX, Part 1, pp. 315–16, pp. 320–21, pp. 883–84; Carman and Pierro, Ed., *The Maryland Campaign*, pp. 264–65; Carman and Clemens, Ed., *The Maryland Campaign, Vol. II*, pp. 201–7.

46   Ernest Linden Waitt, *History of the Nineteenth Regiment Massachusetts Volunteer Infantry, 1861–1865* (Salem, MA: Salem Press, 1906), p. 137; Carman and Pierro, Ed., *The Maryland Campaign*, p. 266; Carman and Clemens, Ed., *The Maryland Campaign, Vol. II*, pp. 207–10.

47   Carman and Pierro, Ed., *The Maryland Campaign*, p. 266; Carman and Clemens, Ed., *The Maryland Campaign, Vol. II*, pp. 207–10.

48   *Correspondence of John Sedgwick, Vol. II.* (Carl and Ellen Battelle Stoeckel, 1902), pp. 158–59; Denney, *Civil War Medicine*, p. 156.

49   Carman and Pierro, Ed., *The Maryland Campaign*, p. 267; Carman and Clemens, Ed., *The Maryland Campaign, Vol. II*, pp. 210–12; OR, Vol. XIX, Part 1, pp. 320–21; Francis W. Palfrey, *The Antietam and Fredericksburg*, p. 87.

50   OR, Vol. XIX, Part 1, p. 311.

51   William F. Rogers letter and map to E. A. Carman, undated, Antietam National Battlefield; Carman and Pierro, Ed., *The Maryland Campaign*, p. 269; Carman and Clemens, Ed., *The Maryland Campaign, Vol. II*, pp. 215–18; OR, Vol. XIX, Part 1, p. 311; Louis Greenleaf letter and map to E. A. Carman December 13, 1894, Antietam National Battlefield.

52   S. Sumner, "The Antietam Campaign," pp. 11–12; OR, Vol. XIX, Part 1, pp. 275–76. It is important to note that while General Sumner probably knew that French's Division wasn't coming as ordered, he nonetheless apparently still didn't know exactly where French was. The message sent sometime around 11:00 to headquarters—noted in OR, Vol. XIX, Part 1, p. 134—clearly shows that even as the first of Smith's VI Corps units were arriving on the field, Sumner still had not located French's position. Armstrong nonetheless argues that Sumner both knew all along where French's Division was and that Sumner ordered the attack on the Sunken Road (Armstrong, *Unfurl Those Colors!*, p. 247). Although he sources this claim to Carman's text (Chapter 9, note 5, which cites Carman's Chapter 18, p. 7) this material never suggests that Sumner specifically ordered the attack there and instead claims that French of his own accord chose to "engage the Confederates in the Sunken Road, whose presence there threatened the left and rear of the Union line. To have done otherwise, under the circumstances, unless under specific orders, would have been highly reprehensible" (Carman and Clemens, Ed., *The Maryland Campaign, Vol. II*, p. 246). Armstrong also suggests that Sumner sent two messengers to General French (Armstrong, *Unfurl Those Colors!*, pp. 203–5, p. 208, p. 215) but he may be confusing Captain Sumner's apparently single visit as having occurred twice.

53   S. Sumner, "The Antietam Campaign," pp. 11–12; OR, Vol. XIX, Part 1, p. 324. Sumner's actions show he did not intend for French or Richardson to attack the Sunken Road position. Captain Sumner's July 1917 Massachusetts Historical Society paper notes that French was "to connect with Sedgwick ... to make a vigorous attack in order to aid the advance of the leading division." Captain Sumner mentions no plan to attack the Sunken Road and makes clear that in ordering French to support Sedgwick, the general was unaware French's Division was already fighting at the Sunken Road. In fact, there simply is no evidence that Sumner ever even knew about the Confederate salient in the Sunken Road before opening his attack on the West Woods—none—let alone that he planned for an attack there. Moreover, Sumner's official report describes Sedgwick's fight in detail but mentions French and Richardson's engagement only in passing.

       Sumner probably intentionally abandoned his initial battle plan to use both II Corps divisions in unison upon learning from his son that French was already fighting and wouldn't be coming as ordered. General Sumner's actions suggest he knew at some point early in Sedgwick's attack that French wasn't coming and why, according to the timeline related in the captain's 1917 paper. The sudden change in plans probably explains why General Sumner spent the attack acting not as a corps commander, but rather as General Sedgwick's duplicate in commanding the actions of a single division. Perhaps most significantly, that Sumner called for reinforcements from Alpheus Williams's used-up XII Corps and newly arriving batteries—rather than from French's or Richardson's Divisions—further suggests Sumner knew he couldn't expect help from French or Richardson. Sumner's decision to let the situation play itself out meant that from that moment forward Sedgwick's and French's Divisions would each fight a completely distinct, disconnected action. Gone was the single, direct point of attack for which Sedgwick's formation and pace of assault on the West Woods had been crafted. Having each division fight its own action also meant that both divisions lost any advantage they may have possessed over the enemy in mass and manpower had they been fighting together. At the same time, this course ensured that any success either division might have secured couldn't be taken advantage of because there were no longer any reinforcements available at Sumner's immediate beck and call.

54 Carman and Pierro, Ed., *The Maryland Campaign*, p. 268, p. 273; Carman and Clemens, Ed., *The Maryland Campaign, Vol. II*, pp. 212–15; OR, Vol. XIX, Part 1, p. 322.

55 OR, Vol. XIX, Pt. 1, pp. 308–9, pp. 482–83; Dudley T. Peebles (18th Mississippi) letter, Antietam National Battlefield; 13th Mississippi Infantry annotated map, Antietam National Battlefield.

56 Edward M. Burruss letter to John C. Burruss; John C. Burruss Papers, Louisiana State University; D. Augustus Dickert, *History of Kershaw's Brigade, with Complete Roll of Companies, Biographical Sketches, Incidents, Anecdotes, Etc.* (Newbury: S. C., E. H. Hull Co., 1899), p. 156. Barksdale claimed in his OR that he stopped because, "I did not deem it prudent, however, without more support, to advance farther, and I therefore ordered these regiments to fall back to the woods in front of my first position." While he might have feared moving too far, the artillery on his right would have magnified these concerns and better explain his sudden halt in the face of victory. OR, Vol. XIX, Part 1, p. 883, p. 868; Dudley T. Peebles (18th Mississippi) letter, Antietam National Battlefield.

57 John T. Parham, "Thirty-Second at Sharpsburg," Southern Historical Society Papers, pp. 252–53; OR, Vol. XIX, Part 1, pp. 874–75.

58 Almost certainly it was not Patrick's entire brigade that took part in this defense. Colonel William F. Rogers noted to Carman in his letter that the 21st and 35th New York became detached from the rest of Patrick's Brigade at some point after the fight across the Hagerstown Pike, commenting that "All the morning after I had passed Gen. Hooker in the woods, I was acting and fighting as an independent command with the exception of the Thirty-fifth. Where the other regiments of the brigade were operating I know not, nor did I receive any orders directing my movements." This suggests that Patrick had only the 23rd and 80th New York regiments with him at this moment. William F. Rogers letter to E. A. Carman. Antietam National Battlefield, Carman Collection.

59 OR, Vol. XIX, Part 1, p. 230, p. 314, pp. 316–17, p. 874; Moe, *The Last Full Measure*, pp. 184–87; Carman and Pierro, Ed., *The Maryland Campaign*, pp. 270–72; Carman and Clemens, Ed., *The Maryland Campaign, Vol. II*, pp. 219–23.

60 OR, Vol. XIX, Part 1, p. 230, p. 314, p. 874; Lafayette McLaws letter to Henry Heth, December 13, 1894. Antietam National Battlefield, Carman Collection.

61 OR, Vol. XIX, Part 1, p. 971; Carman and Pierro, Ed., *The Maryland Campaign*, p. 273; Carman and Clemens, Ed., *The Maryland Campaign, Vol. II*, pp. 228–30. Carman claims that the 13th New Jersey and the 2nd Massachusetts faced Ransom's Brigade, of Walker's Division, in their fight across the Hagerstown Pike, but he very likely is mistaken. Ransom's Brigade was on the field but deployed farther south than Gordon's two regiments, nearer the Dunker Church, and most of Ransom's regiments were later involved in the repulse of Greene's Division from the West Woods. Ransom's OR account mentions several attacks—which probably is the source of Carman's belief that he faced Ransom. More likely, though, the two regiments probably faced

one of two brigades commanded at that moment by Jubal Early. Early's Brigade might have been in that position when it stopped to reform along the Hagerstown Pike after falling back from chasing Sedgwick's Division from the West Woods; as Early noted in his OR, "I caused the regiments of the brigade to be reformed and placed in position as before" (roughly the same spot in the West Woods they'd held at 8:30, when the Union XII Corps first came onto the field). It is also possible, though less likely, that the 13th New Jersey and 2nd Massachusetts faced Armistead's Brigade. This brigade, under the command of Colonel Hodges, reported to Early, as he explained, "[s]hortly after the repulse of the enemy ... and I placed it in line in the position occupied by my brigade, and placed the latter in line on the edge of the plateau which has been mentioned and parallel to the Hagerstown road, but under cover." Early's comment that he placed Armistead's Brigade "under cover" strongly suggests they might have been the unit that Private Crowell reported as rising unexpectedly from the ground. Sadly, Colonel Hodges never left an official report of the battle.

62 Joseph E. Crowell, *The Young Volunteer: The Civil War Memoirs of Joseph E. Crowell, 13th New Jersey Volunteers* (Falls Church, VA: NOVA Publications, 1997), pp. 120–21.

63 Crowell, *The Young Volunteer*, p. 120.

64 OR, Vol. XIX, Part 1, p. 309, p. 483, p. 859.

65 OR, Vol. XIX, Part 1, p. 858, p. 883, p. 956.

66 Eby, *A Virginia Yankee in the Civil War*, pp. 110–11; James Harrison Wilson, *Under the Old Flag*, Vol. 1 (London: D. Appleton and Co., 1912), p. 109.

67 Wilson, *Under the Old Flag*, p. 109. Most historians have ignored McClellan's inability to see important portions of the battlefield or have used Strother's and Wilson's accounts broadly to suggest McClellan was observing the battle throughout its entirety. Sears, for example, claims Strother's "redan of fencerails" scene occurred at 7:30—claiming it happened as A. P. Hill's men were leaving Harpers Ferry at 7:30—to suggest McClellan was watching Hood's counterattack in the Cornfield (*Landscape Turned Red*, pp. 15–16). Rafuse accepts Strother's *Harper's* account that McClellan could see through the West Woods to observe McLaws striking Sedgwick "like a fiery avalanche" (Rafuse, *McClellan's War*, p. 317). In fact, McClellan could see almost nothing of the Cornfield fight from the Pry House. Armstrong (Armstrong, *Unfurl Those Colors!*, p. 247), curiously, argues McClellan "could not see most of the fighting in the vicinity of the sunken road," which stands in contrast to Wilson's account and the view indicated by USGS and US Forest Service data (see Note 34).

68 George F. Noyes *The Bivouac; or, Campaign Sketches in Virginia and Maryland* (New York: Harper and Brothers Publishers, 1864), p, 196; Edwin Forbes drawing "The Battle of Antietam or Sharpsburg," September 17, 1862, LOC Print and Photograph Collection, Forbes no. 37 and related number key; United State Geologic Survey (USGS) Digital elevation model (DEM), https://viewer.nationalmap.gov; United States Department of Agriculture – Forest Service (USDA-FS) orthoimagery, https://earthexplorer.usgs.gov. Rafuse accepts Strother's claim in his probably fanciful 1868 *Harper's* article that mid-morning McClellan moved his headquarters from the Pry House to a still-unlocated "commanding knoll" south of the Boonsboro Pike and so could see much of the entire battlefield by mid-morning (Rafuse, *McClellan's War*, p. 316 and Note 49). No other source exists to verify Strother's post-war claim, although Strother may be confusing this with McClellan's ride to the Union center later in the day—when he and Porter and other staffers met with General George Sykes—which in any case does not indicate McClellan moved his headquarters so. McClellan used the Pry House as his forward headquarters until moving it into Sharpsburg on the 19th (Walker, *Antietam Farmsteads*, p. 129).

69 Eby, *A Virginia Yankee in the Civil War*, pp. 110–11.

Chapter 12

1   Herbert von Hammerstein correspondence with Albert V. Colburn, September 17, 1862, George B. McClellan Papers, LOC, Series I, Vol. 80, Item 16261; William S. Albert correspondence with Randolph B. Marcy, September 17, 1862, George B. McClellan Papers, LOC, Series I, Vol. 80, Item 16261; OR, Vol. XIX, Part 1, p. 376; Armstrong, *Unfurl Those Colors*, p. 199; OR, LI, Part 2, p. 842. General Williams sent a message by signal flag at 9:00 to McClellan that "Genl Mansfield is dangerously wounded. Genl Hooker wounded severally in the foot. Genl Sumner I hear is advancing. We hold the field at present. Please give us all the aid you can." (LOC, McClellan Papers, reel 32). Although reinforcing the news related in von Hammerstein's and Albert's messages—it bears little indication of the battle's state, as do the aides' intelligence, and probably had less impact on McClellan's understanding at that time. Sears claims Albert's message was delivered via signal flag (*Landscape Turned Red*, p. 254), but offers no evidence for this claim.

2   OR, Vol. XIX, Part 1, p. 227; David W. Palmer, *The Forgotten Hero of Gettysburg: A Biography of General George Sears Greene* (Xlibris, 2005), p. 87. Harsh curiously claims that Greene's Division "had advanced westward from the Mumma farm to support the guns" (Harsh, *Taken at the Flood*, pp. 392–93). This ignores that the guns arrived to support Greene's ammunition-short infantry, not the other way around, and that Greene's men had taken this ground from the Confederates.

3   South Carolina Division UDC, *Recollections and Reminiscences*, pp. 350–51; Shand, "Incidents," pp. 36–37.

4   South Carolina Division UDC, *Recollections and Reminiscences*, pp. 350–51; OR, Vol. XIX, Part 1, pp. 864–66. Kershaw later claimed his men "made constant progress for some time along the whole line, driving in column after column of the enemy." This is sheer fantasy, however, because until Greene's Division was resupplied there simply were no such infantry attacks on Kershaw's men.

5   South Carolina Division UDC, *Recollections and Reminiscences*, pp. 350–51; OR, Vol. XIX, Part 1, pp. 864–69.

6   OR, Vol. XIX, Part 1, p. 918.

7   Boyle, *Soldiers True*. pp. 60–61.

8   OR, Vol. XIX, Part 1, p. 865, p. 918; Boyle, *Soldiers True*, p. 59.

9   OR, Vol. XIX, Part 1, pp. 506–10.

10   OR, Vol. XIX, Part 1, pp. 864–65.

11   George Sears Greene, "The Battle of Antietam" manuscript, p. 2, The Rhode Island Historical Society. Box 1, Folder 8.

12   OR, Vol. XIX, Part 1, p. 508.

13   Carman and Pierro, Ed., *The Maryland Campaign*, p. 301; Carman and Clemens, Ed., *The Maryland Campaign, Vol. II*, pp.303–9.

14   Carman and Pierro, Ed., *The Maryland Campaign*, pp. 301–2; Carman and Clemens, Ed., *The Maryland Campaign, Vol. II*, pp. 303–11.

15   Carman and Pierro, Ed., *The Maryland Campaign*, p. 302; Carman and Clemens, Ed., *The Maryland Campaign, Vol. II*, pp. 309–11.

16   OR, Vol. XIX, Part 1, p. 211; Eby, *A Virginia Yankee in the Civil War*, pp. 110–11. James Harrison Wilson, *Under the Old Flag*, p. 109.

17   OR, Vol. XIX, Part 1, p. 63; Carman and Clemens, Ed., *The Maryland Campaign, Vol. II*, pp. 395–405, 408–17, p. 418, pp. 421–30.

18   OR, Vol. XIX, Part 1, p. 211; Carman and Pierro, Ed., *The Maryland Campaign*, p. 320; Carman and Clemens, Ed., *The Maryland Campaign, Vol. II*, pp. 366–69.

19 Carman and Pierro, Ed., *The Maryland Campaign*, p. 319; Carman and Clemens, Ed., *The Maryland Campaign, Vol. II*, pp. 363–66.

20 Carman and Pierro, Ed., *The Maryland Campaign*, p. 319; Carman and Clemens, Ed., *The Maryland Campaign, Vol. II*, pp. 363–66; Sears, *The Civil War Papers of George B. McClellan*, p. 467.

21 OR, Vol. XIX, Part 1, p. 134. Nelson Henry Davis letter to George McClellan, January 31, 1876, Antietam National Battlefield, Carman Collection. The exact time that Sumner sent this message—relayed by signal flag and reported by Lieutenant Peter Taylor of the 49th New York as having been received by the Army of the Potomac's headquarters' signal station—remains uncertain. However, its contents suggest the message was sent sometime in the late morning but before noon because it requests information on the location of Slocum's Division, suggesting Sumner already knew the location of Smith's Division of the VI Corps, which arrived first (Franklin notes in his OR that Slocum arrived around 11:00, although Slocum recorded his arrival time as noon). Major Davis also suggests in his 1876 letter to McClellan that he arrived on his first visit to Sumner at the same time that the "head of Franklin's Corps arrived." In any case, the signal indicates that at around 11:00 Sumner still was unaware of the location of French's Division. Another interesting point suggested by the contents of Davis's letter and Sumner's signal message is that Major Davis might have been the person who finally told Sumner just where French's Division was fighting. Davis recorded that "en route to him [Sumner] I passed through the commands of Richardson and French, The latter at the time was hotly engaged…" indicating he knew French's location and might have shared this information with Sumner. Although we cannot be certain that it was Davis who provided Sumner this intelligence, Sumner never again that afternoon asked for news of French's position. If this is so, it reinforces the idea that Sumner had lost track of French and certainly hadn't ordered his attack on the Sunken Road.

22 John L. Smith, *Antietam to Appomattox with the 118th Pennsylvania Volunteers*, Corn Exchange Regiment. (Philadelphia: J. L. Smith, 1892), pp. 42–43; OR, Vol. XIX, Part 1, pp. 338–39, p. 351; Carman and Pierro, Ed., *The Maryland Campaign*, p. 320; Carman and Clemens, Ed., *The Maryland Campaign, Vol. II*, pp. 366–69. Reflecting McClellan's commitment to the center attack at noon, he began the ride by directing staffer Colonel Alexander S. Webb to have Sykes move more Regulars across the Middle Bridge. Carman suggests that Webb's mission—"riding into the very jaws of death," as Smith wrote—was to send the 2nd/10th Regulars forward. Porter confirms it in his OR account when he explains that McClellan himself was the authority that ordered a portion of Sykes's command forward to aid Pleasanton.

23 Robert Grandchamp, *The Boys of Adams' Battery G* (Jefferson, NC: McFarland & Co., 2009), pp. 80–81; Rhodes letter to Carman, March 21, 1896, Antietam National Battlefield Collection.

24 OR, Vol. XIX, Part 1, p. 326, p. 482, p. 505; Carman and Pierro, Ed., *The Maryland Campaign*, p. 302; Carman and Clemens, Ed., *The Maryland Campaign, Vol. II*, pp. 309–11.

25 OR, Vol. XIX, Part 1, p. 923.

26 Boyle, *Soldiers True.* pp. 60–61.

27 Carman and Pierro, Ed., *The Maryland Campaign*, p. 302; Carman and Clemens, Ed., *The Maryland Campaign, Vol. II*, pp. 309–11; OR, Vol. XIX, Part 1, p. 482.

28 OR, Vol. XIX, Part 1, p. 920.

29 Carman and Pierro, Ed., *The Maryland Campaign*, p. 302; Carman and Clemens, Ed., *The Maryland Campaign, Vol. II*, pp. 309–11.

30 Carman and Pierro, Ed., *The Maryland Campaign*, p. 302 (note 9), p. 304 (note 18), Carman and Clemens, Ed., *The Maryland Campaign, Vol. II*, pp. 309–11.

31 Carman and Pierro, Ed., *The Maryland Campaign*, p. 302 (note 9), p. 304 (note 18), Carman and Clemens, Ed., *The Maryland Campaign, Vol. II*, pp. 309–11.

32   Carman and Pierro, Ed., *The Maryland Campaign*, p. 304; Carman and Clemens, Ed., *The Maryland Campaign, Vol. II*, pp. 315–17.

33   Carman and Pierro, Ed., *The Maryland Campaign*, p. 304; Carman and Clemens, Ed., *The Maryland Campaign, Vol. II*, pp. 315–17.

34   J. O. Smith, *My First Campaign and Battle: A Jersey Boy at Antietam – Seventeen Days from Home*, (Philadelphia: Patriotic Publishing Co., 1893), p. 287.

35   OR, Vol. XIX, Part 1, p. 326; James P. Brady, *"Hurrah for the Artillery!: Knap's Independent Battery "E," Pennsylvania Light Artillery* (Gettysburg: Thomas Publications, 1992), pp. 152–62.

36   OR, Vol. XIX, Part 1, p. 326; Brady "Hurrah for the Artillery!" pp. 152–62.

37   Greene, "The Battle of Antietam," pp. 2–3.

38   Carman and Pierro, Ed., *The Maryland Campaign*, p. 305; Carman and Clemens, Ed., *The Maryland Campaign, Vol. II*, pp. 318–20; James Longstreet, *From Manassas to Appomattox* (New York: Smithmark Books, 1992), p. 250.

39   Walter Clark, *Histories of the Several Regiments and Battalions from North Carolina in the Great War*, (Goldsboro, NC: Nash Brothers, 1901), p. 436; OR, Vol. XIX, Part 1, p. 327, p. 840, p. 872; Carman and Clemens, Ed., *The Maryland Campaign, Vol. II*, pp. 318–23.

Chapter 13

1   OR, Vol. XIX, I, p. 376.

2   Carman and Pierro, Ed., *The Maryland Campaign*, pp. 406–8; Carman and Clemens, Ed., *The Maryland Campaign, Vol. II*, pp. 534–35.

3   Miller, C. Eugene and Forrest F. Steinlage, *Der Turner Soldat: A Turner Soldier in the Civil War, Germany to Antietam* (Calmar Publications, 1988), p. 48.

4   Thomas W. Hyde, *Following the Greek Cross, of Memories of the Sixth Corps* (Boston: Houghton, Mifflin, Co., 1894), p. 94; John Conline papers, January 7, 1897. http://suvcw.org/mollus/warppaers/MIv2p110.htm; Timothy B. Mudgett, *Make the Fur Fly: A History of a Union Volunteer Division in the American Civil War* (Shippensburg, PA: Burd Street Press, 1997), p. 32; William B. Westervelt Diary and Memoirs, (27th New York), Entries for 15, 16, 17, and 18 September 1862, USAHEC (USMHI) Manuscript Collection.

5   OR, Vol. XIX, I, p. 376, p. 402.

6   OR, Vol. XIX, I, p. 134. Sumner's 11:00 note asking about the location of Slocum's Division also suggests that Smith's Division was on the field and at Sumner's disposal by that time, reinforcing the idea that the VI Corps was first on the field at 11:00.

7   OR, Vol. XIX, I, p. 402.

8   OR, Vol. XIX, I, pp. 404–5. Vanneman reported that Franklin had ordered him forward, but he is almost certainly mistaken. Smith's OR mentions his specifically sending forward two batteries—though he does not name them—while Franklin's does not. Moreover, Franklin almost certainly wasn't yet on the field when the batteries were ordered into the Cornfield.

9   Hyde, *Following the Greek Cross*, pp. 95–96; Mudgett, *Make the Fur Fly*, pp. 34–35; George Contant, *Path of Blood: the True Story of the 33rd New York Volunteers* (Savannah, New York: Seeco Printing, 1997), pp. 235–37; Miller, *Der Turner Soldat*, pp. 48–49; OR, Vol. XIX, Part 1, pp. 402–3, pp. 409–12.

10   Hyde, *Following the Greek Cross*, pp. 95–96; Mudgett, *Make the Fur Fly*, pp. 34–35; George Contant *Path of Blood*, pp. 235–37; Miller, *Der Turner Soldat*, pp. 48-49; OR, Vol. XIX, Part 1, pp. 402–3, 409–12.

11   Hyde, *Following the Greek Cross*, pp. 97; OR, Vol. XIX, Part 1, p. 409.

12   Hyde, *Following the Greek Cross*, pp. 97; OR, Vol. XIX, Part 1, p. 409.

13 OR, Vol. XIX, Part 1, pp. 402–3, pp. 408–9. Smith's and Brooks' ORs offer an indication of the first time on September 17th that Sumner finally knew the whereabouts of French's Division. Weighing the contents of Franklin's, Smith's, and Brooks's ORs and Sumner's 11:00 message, it is also clear that no VI Corps unit was moving forward until well after 11:00 and the advances of Irwin and Brooks probably didn't occur until 11:30 at the earliest.

14 OR, Vol. XIX, Part 1, pp. 377–78. Franklin's time of arrival on the field—like so much of the timing of events at Antietam—remains uncertain. Franklin comments in his OR that "just after my arrival on the field General French reported his ammunition exhausted, and General Brooks was ordered to reinforce him," indicates that he is highly unlikely to have been on the field before 11:00, when Sumner was still unaware of French's location. However, he was almost certainly on the field by noon, as reflected in Franklin's OR statement that he waited for Bartlett's Brigade—which arrived at noon—to rejoin Slocum's Division before ordering his planned attack toward the Dunker Church.

15 "Battles and Leaders", North to Antietam, p. 597; OR, Vol. XIX, Part 1, pp. 377–78.

16 Wilson, Under the Old Flag, p. 112.

17 Franklin almost certainly had met with Sumner when first arriving at the front, although he does not specifically say so in his OR. Wilson mentions Franklin's presence when he passes along McClellan's orders (Wilson, Under the Old Flag, pp. 113–14) and a careful reading of Franklin's OR supports this, too. For example, Franklin's statement that "just after my arrival on the field General French reported his ammunition exhausted, and General Brooks was ordered to re-enforce him," suggests Franklin was present at Sumner's II Corps headquarters to hear French's report—which otherwise he would have no reason to know about—and to see one of his own brigades ordered away by some higher authority (almost certainly General Sumner). Franklin's second meeting with Sumner was, however, specifically mentioned in his OR, Vol. XIX, Part 1, p. 377.

18 Wilson, Under the Old Flag, pp. 112.

19 Wilson, Under the Old Flag, pp. 112–14.

20 Charles B. Fairchild, History of the 27th New York Volunteers (Binghamton, NY: Carl & Matthews, 1888), p. 95.

21 Carman and Pierro, Ed., The Maryland Campaign, pp. 307–8; Carman and Clemens, Ed., The Maryland Campaign, Vol. II, pp. 323–27.

22 OR, Vol. XIX, Part 1, p. 923.

23 OR, Vol. XIX, Part 1, p. 377. Franklin makes it clear in his OR that an attack was planned when he wrote "Immediately after its [Slocum's Division's] arrival two of his brigades (Newton's and Torbert's) were formed in column of attack, to carry the wood in the immediate vicinity of the white church." We cannot be certain that this attack wasn't the idea of General Sumner, but there is no evidence that he was behind this plan or that he was even in a frame of mind to attack anymore by midday, reflected by the exchange between Sumner and McClellan reported by James Wilson. Unfortunately, Sumner's own OR ceases its narrative after Sedgwick's repulse, save an extremely brief mention of French's and Richardson's fight.

24 US Congress, Report of the Committee on the Conduct of the War, p. 626; OR, Vol. XIX, Part1, p. 377.

25 A recent author writing about Franklin's behavior at Antietam has suggested the general was laboring under the threat of the charges leveled by Major General Pope in the wake of the Union disaster at Second Manassas. Although this is possible—McClellan knew of the charges and could have told Franklin—and would help explain Franklin's unusual aggressiveness, no known sources support that Franklin knew of Pope's charges. Franklin's biographer Snell notes in his biography—From First to Last, p. 170—that Franklin never mentioned the issue in letters written

during the Maryland Campaign. Steven R. Stotelmyer *Too Useful To Sacrifice* (Savas Beatie, El Dorado Hills, CA, 2019).

26 Franklin, "Notes on Crampton's Gap and Antietam," from *Battles and Leaders, Vol. II*, p. 597; Carman and Pierro, Ed., *The Maryland Campaign*, p. 308; Carman and Clemens, Ed., *The Maryland Campaign, Vol. II*, pp. 324–27.

27 Wilson, *Under the Old Flag*, p. 114.

28 US Congress, Report *of the Committee on the Conduct of the War*, p. 626; OR, Vol. XIX, Part 1, p. 62.

Chapter 14

1 Sears, *The Civil War Papers of George B. McClellan*, pp. 467–68. McClellan also took time—amidst the greatest battle of the war to date—at 1:45 to reassure his wife that he and her father remained safe.

2 Carman and Pierro, Ed., *The Maryland Campaign*, p. 341; Carman and Clemens, Ed., *The Maryland Campaign, Vol. II*, pp. 435–40. Harsh, *Taken at the Flood*, pp. 407–10. Harsh argues Lee wanted to attack and that it was Lee's plan alone, not Jackson's or initiated with Jackson's plan in mind, but he offers no sources for this judgement. Similarly, Harsh claims the planned attack was chiefly to have Jackson open a north-bound escape route to allow his army to remain in Maryland and maneuver ahead of a future battle. This fits Harsh's argument earlier in the book that Lee sought to escape and maneuver rather than fight at Antietam, but it ignores that by this point such an exposed move was unlikely and unwise with a battle-weakened force and that Lee apparently planned to attack on the 18th (as recorded by Colonel Lee).

3 Walker, "Sharpsburg" from *Battles and Leaders, Vol. II*, pp. 679–80; OR, Vol. XIX, Part 1, p. 151, p. 956.

4 Walker, "Sharpsburg" from *Battles and Leaders, Vol. II*, pp. 679–80.; OR, Vol. XIX, Part 1, p. 151, p. 956. Lee makes it clear in his OR that he gave Jackson the order to turn the Union right, but doesn't say if it was he or Jackson who conceived the plan. Given Lee's longstanding penchant for letting his trusted commanders plan their own actions, I believe that Jackson is the one most likely to have directed his and Stuart's moves.

5 Longstreet, *From Manassas to Appomattox*, pp. 256–57. Oddly, Longstreet makes no mention in his OR of any plans to attack (OR, Vol. XIX, Part 1, pp. 840–41). Walker's report, however, makes it clear that Longstreet did order an attack in the late afternoon (OR, Vol. XIX, Part 1, p. 916.).

6 Walker, "Sharpsburg" from *Battles and Leaders, Vol. II*, pp. 679–80. Rafuse repeats Harsh's claim that Lee's attack in the Cornfield and Stuart's attack near the North Woods was intended chiefly to open an escape route to the north rather than an effort to take the offensive to turn the battle in the South's favor (Rafuse, *McClellan's War*, p. 324). If opening an escape route was Stuart's objective then why, having discovered the route to New Industry and Hagerstown beyond lay open and unimpeded by any Union troops, did he attack Union forces near the North Woods? Moreover, this argument ignores that Lee retained two escape routes, making it unnecessary to fight for this one.

7 OR, Vol. XIX, Part 1, p. 226, p. 820, p. 1010. Stuart mistakenly indicates that this movement occurred on the 18th ("On the next day it was determined, the enemy not attacking, to turn the enemy's right."). Such deliberations among the Confederate command staff did take place on the 18th but Stuart must have confused the two considerations of attacking the Union right when writing his report, which is understandable because he wrote that report on February 13, 1864—a year and a half after the battle of Antietam.

8 OR, Vol. XIX, Part 1, p. 820.

9 OR, Vol. XIX, Part 1, p. 820.

10 Simpson "Official Report," Joseph Hooker military papers, 1861–1864, Box 9, Huntington Library, San Marino, California; OR, Vol. XIX, Part 1, p. 226, p. 230. pp. 270–71, p. 820.

11 OR, Vol. XIX, Part 1, pp. 956–57; Clark, *Histories of the Several Regiments and Battalions from North Carolina in the Great War*, p. 78; Harsh, *Taken at the Flood*, pp. 400–1.

12 John Conline, "Recollections of the Battle of Antietam and the Maryland Campaign," *War Papers Read Before the Michigan Commandery of the Military Order of the Loyal Legion of the United States*, Vol. II (Detroit: James H. Stone Printers, 1898).

13 Hyde, *Following the Greek Cross*, pp. 99–105; Carman, *The Maryland Campaign*, p. 315.

14 Hyde, *Following the Greek Cross*, pp. 101–5; Carman, *The Maryland Campaign*, p. 315.

15 Hyde, *Following the Greek Cross*, pp. 104–5; John Conline "Recollections of the Battle of Antietam and the Maryland Campaign;" Carman and Clemens, Ed., *The Maryland Campaign*, p. 345–51; John Conline "Recollections of the Battle of Antietam and the Maryland Campaign."

16 OR, Vol. XIX, Part 1, p. 357.

17 Thomas M. Anderson "The Reserve at Antietam," *Century Magazine*, Vol. 32, No. 5 (September 1886); Carman and Pierro, Ed., *The Maryland Campaign*, pp. 327–28; Carman and Clemens, Ed., *The Maryland Campaign, Vol. II*, pp. 389–92.

18 Murphy, *Diary of Ephraim C. Brown*, p. 24.

Chapter 15

1 Charles F. Morse, *"From Second Bull Run to Antietam,"MOLLUS*, pp. 275–76; Carl A. Morell, Ed., *Seymour Dexter, Union Army; Journal and Letters; New York Regiment of Elmira, with Illustrations* (Jefferson, North Carolina: McFarland and Co., 1996), p. 107.

2 Mac Wyckoff, *A History of the 2nd South Carolina Infantry: 1861–65* (Sergeant Kirkland's Museum and Historical Society, 1994), p. 48; Edward M. Burruss letter to John C. Burruss; John C. Burruss Papers, Louisiana State University; John D. Stevens letter, October 9, 1862. Author's collection.

3 Abram P. Smith, *History of the 76th New York Volunteers* (Courtland, New York: 1876), pp. 167–68.

4 John C. Whiteside letter, October 4, 1862, Bentley Historical Library, University of Michigan.

5 David Judd, *The Story of the 33rd New York Volunteers on Two Years Campaigning in Virginia and Maryland* (Rochester, New York: Benton and Andrews, 1864), pp. 196–99.

6 Daniel M. Holt, James M. Greiner, Janet L. Coryell, and James B. Smither, Eds., *A Surgeon's Civil War: The Letters and Diary of Daniel M. Holt, M.D.* (Kent, Ohio: Kent State University Press, 1994), p. 28; Murphy, *Diary of Ephraim C. Brown*, pp. 24–25.

7 Board of Trustees of the Antietam National Cemetery, *A Descriptive List of the Burial Places of the Remains of Confederate Soldiers, Who Fell in the Battles of Antietam, South Mountain, Monocacy, and Other Points in Washington and Frederick Counties, in the State of Maryland* (Hagerstown, Maryland: The Free Press Print, 1869), p. 26, p. 32, pp. 34–36.

8 Wilder Dwight and Elizabeth Amelia Dwight, *Life and Letters of Wilder Dwight, Lieut.-col., Second Mass. Inf. Vols.* (Boston, Ticknor and Fields, 1868), pp. 293–95, pp. 348–49.

9 White, *A History of the 31st Georgia*, p. 51.

10 Priest, *Antietam: The Soldier's Battle*, pp. 57–58, p. 305; E. E. Stickley, "The Confederate Veteran," Vol. XXII, pp. 66–67.

11 Stearns, *Three Years with Company K*, pp. 128–30.

12 Smith, *My First Campaign and Battle*, p. 288.

13 Gregory A. Coco, *Through Blood and Fire: The Civil War Letters of Major Charles J. Mills, 1862–1865* (Gettysburg: Self-published, 1982), p. 33; Denney, *Civil War Medicine*, p. 155.

14 Denney, *Civil War Medicine*, pp. 157–60; Andrews, *Footprints of a Regiment*, pp. 180–81.

15 Denney, *Civil War Medicine*, pp. 155–67.

16 Crowell, *The Young Volunteer*, pp. 130–31.

17 Shand, *Incidents*, pp. 37–38.

18 OR, Vol. XIX, Part 2, p. 32.

19 *Report of the Joint Committee on the Conduct of the War*, p. 627.

20 OR, Vol. XIX, Part 1, pp. 32, 66; *Report of the Joint Committee*, p. 628; OR, Vol. LI, Part 2, p. 844. McClellan later claimed he rode right to Franklin on the 19th at 9:00 in order to explain why he'd rescinded approval for Franklin's attack the night before and to approve Franklin making the attack once Couch's and Humphrey's reinforcements arrived; the general finishes by noting that the poor condition of these reinforcements, once arrived, persuaded him to again call off Franklin's attack. Although Rafuse reports this as fact (Rafuse, *McClellan's War*, p. 328), I remain highly skeptical that this event occurred. Franklin's statements to Congress makes no mention of an 18th meeting and Franklin indicated McClellan never directly told him why the attack was called off. Also, as Rafuse rightly notes, Couch's and Humphrey's troops arrived prior to McClellan's stated meeting time, undermining McClellan's claim they were the reason for standing down.

21 OR, Vol. XIX, Part 2, p. 322, pp. 330–31; Carman and Clemens, Ed. *The Maryland Campaign, Vol. II*, pp. 508–10. Pleasonton's cavalry had spent the 18th gathering stragglers and only pursued Lee's army on the 19th when it was clear the enemy was long gone. When he reached Shepherdstown's Blackford's Ford, Pleasonton engaged Lee's artillery guarding the crossing with his own guns. Reflecting McClellan's now-passive approach, the general sent a dispatch to his cavalry chief barring him from crossing the Potomac "unless he saw a splendid opportunity to inflict great damage upon the enemy without loss to himself." Given that such a bloodless attack was certainly impossible, this dispatch cannot be called an order—or even an offered opportunity—to attack.

22 OR, Vol. XIX, Part 1, p. 151.

23 S. D. Lee manuscript "Three Personal Incidents in the Battle of Sharpsburg or Antietam, Fought September 17, 1862" W. F. Smith Papers, Vermont Historical Society; Murfin, *Gleam of Bayonets*, pp. 294–95; Rafuse, *McClellan's War*, p. 329; Carman Memorandum, March 9, 1897, Carman-Cope Letters, Antietam National Battlefield. One reason this account by S. D. Lee is not fully accepted by historians is his claim that General Lee convened a Council of War on the evening of the 17th, about which Colonel Lee provides a detailed account. Not only does this clash with historians' belief that Lee only ever convened two such Councils, but no other general reportedly present ever mentioned this event. Longstreet, in *From Manassas to Appomattox*, mentions arriving at Lee's headquarters late on the 17th, but suggests he went to "make report," suggesting he went on his own rather than having been summoned for a Council. Similarly, Charles Marshall—on Lee's staff during the battle—denied that this council occurred as S. D. Lee claimed. Though we lack information supporting that such a meeting occurred, we similarly cannot completely discount that it did happen as Lee claims.

24 OR, Vol. XIX, Part 1, pp. 142–43.

25 For a detailed account of the battle, see Thomas A. McGrath's *Shepherdstown: Last Clash of the Antietam Campaign September 19–20, 1862* (Lynchburg, VA: Schroeder Publications, 2008); Lee, *Memoirs of William N. Pendleton*, pp. 219–23.

26 I derive these numbers from Carman's study, which reflect his own accounting that used both the official numbers and his own research based on contacting original sources. Moreover, Carman's study takes into account at least some of the many soldiers who had died of wounds at Antietam, but who had lived past the point that the government counted them in the battle's total. Although Livermore's numbers differ slightly, they come very close to matching Carman's figures. Regardless which might actually be more accurate, creating a fully complete and highly detailed accounting now is impossible, so both Carman and Livermore can be generally accepted

as being reasonably accurate. Carman and Pierro, Ed., *The Maryland Campaign*, p. 459, p. 469, p. 323; Carman and Clemens, Ed., *The Maryland Campaign, Vol. II*, pp. 377–80, p. 583, pp. 601–2; Livermore, *Numbers and Loses*, pp. 92–93.

27   Joseph Hooker military papers, 1861–1864, Box 9, Huntington Library, San Marino, California.

28   Louis C. Duncan, *The Medical Department of the United States Army in the Civil War* (Washington, DC, 1901), p. 18.

29   OR, Vol. XIX, Part 1, pp. 141–42.

30   Amanda Foreman, *A World On Fire*, p. 354.

31   OR, Vol. XIX, Part 1, pp. 32–33; McClellan, *McClellan's Own Story*, pp. 606–11; John G. Nicolay and John Hay, *Abraham Lincoln: A History*, p. 159.

32   OR, Vol. XIX, Part 1, pp. 63–64, pp. 66–67. Burnside later played into McClellan's finger-pointing when he brazenly lied to Congress, claiming McClellan had held Burnside and the IX Corps from attacking early on the 18th; McClellan's OR account not surprisingly claimed instead that Burnside had asked for more troops early on the 18th not to launch his own attack, but rather so that the IX Corps could be withdrawn and spared before an expected attack by Lee.

33   Howard Jones, *Union in Peril: The Crisis over British Intervention in the Civil War* (Lincoln: University of Nebraska Press, 1992), pp. 165–80, pp. 224–28.

34   OR, Vol. XIX, Part 1, pp. 32–33, pp. 150–52.

35   John V. Ferguson letter, October 16, 1862, John V. Ferguson Letters, New York Military Museum.

36   John V. Ferguson letter, October 16, 1862.

Appendix 2

1   These tables are derived from Carman's Appendix L. Carman himself derived several of these tables from William F. Fox's *Regimental Losses in the American Civil War, 1861–1865: A Treatise on the Extent and Nature of the Mortuary Losses in the Union Regiments with Full and Exhaustive Statistics Compiled from the Official Records on file in the State Military Bureaus and was Washington* (Albany, NY: Albany Publishing Co., 1889), as well as from his own research, drawing on casualty numbers reported to him in various personal letters.

2   This table is derived from William F. Fox's *Regimental Losses in the American Civil War, 1861–1865: A Treatise on the Extent and Nature of the Mortuary Losses in the Union Regiments with Full and Exhaustive Statistics Compiled from the Official Records on file in the State Military Bureaus and was Washington* (Albany, NY: Albany Publishing Co., 1889), although I have revised the order Fox used so that it reflects units by the percentage of men killed. Fox notes that these figures include those mortally wounded, as well as those killed outright. This may help explain the discrepancy between Carman's and Fox's numbers—for example, Carman lists the 12th Massachusetts' killed as 49, while Fox lists 74—in which Fox nearly always lists a higher number.

Index